Pnei Hashem

פני השם

Copyright © 2022 by Visage Books

ISBN 978-1-4958-2212-4 Paperback
ISBN 978-1-4958-2290-2 Hardcover

Printed in the United States of America

CONTENTS

Chapter 4: SOURCE

Chapter 5: INFINITE POTENTIAL

Chapter 6: WRAPPINGS AND TRAPPINGS

Chapter 7: BEING GODLY

PART TWO: PRACTICE

Chapter 8: LIFE-CYCLE

Chapter 9: DAILY PRACTICE

Chapter 10: HOLY DAYS & HOLIDAYS

Chapter 11: END GAME

Preface

There is a wisdom awaiting you that is not supposed to be a secret. It is ancient, and it is available, but it is widely unknown. It has been hidden for too long, and it is time for it to become revealed. This wisdom will change everything, if we allow it. Where there was conflict, there will be peace. Where there was animosity, there will be empathy. Where there was fear, there will be courage. Where there was shame, there will be self-acceptance and esteem. Where there was scarcity, there will be abundance.

Existence is not meaningless. Humanity is not irredeemable. The future is not bleak. The alienation and despair that lurk just beneath the surface of the modern psyche are not the inevitable human condition. They are the result of misguided ideologies that pervade our global culture and invade our every thought. Each of us - each and every one of us - is so much more than we imagine. We are here for a reason, and we are equipped with all of the capabilities that we require.

The ideas contained in the following pages are not new or progressive. They are as old as the world. The path explored here is a Torah path. Torah is the divine will and wisdom that was transmitted through Moses to the fledgling nation of Israel so that its light would be disseminated to illuminate a dark world.

The "Bible" that many have been exposed to is radically different from Torah in its authentic essence. Many westerners have turned to alternate sources for wisdom and spirituality because the "Judeo-Christianity" that they have been reared on has not offered them the inspiration or solace that they seek. Torah is no more western than eastern or northern or southern. It does not have a geographic bearing or bias. God is not the God of some and not others.

The insights herein are gleaned, in large part, from Chasidic philosophy and the Torah's mystic teachings. They are equally applicable to those who observe Torah's laws strictly, those who follow other spiritual practices, and those who engage in no practice at all. The existence of God is not questioned in these pages, nor is it proven or defined. One need not be a "believer" to explore the Torah's wisdom tradition.

Ultimately, this is a book about you. You may not see yourself in it at first, but by the end you will hopefully recognize yourself more clearly. It is a book about life and its meaning and your place in this big, swirling thing we call existence. There are big ideas and questions addressed, but not with big language or overly sophisticated concepts.

This book might be described as spiritual, or even a bit mystical; but don't worry, it isn't aiming to convert you or convince you or control you. Its goal is simply to present you with questions - and even a few answers - that will eventually acquaint you with someone who you deserve to know, someone who you will love, and someone to whom you may have sadly never been properly introduced: you.

You may be wondering, justifiably, how the author of this book can pretend to know you if you have likely never met. Part of you may also be bristling at the presumption that this author knows more about you than you know about yourself. Here's the thing: the you that you will find in the following pages is the same you that the author found in the many pages studied before writing this book. What you, and I, and every one of us will come to recognize and appreciate at some point, is that we are not the many surface things that distinguish us from everyone else, but rather the single thing that every "you" has in common. In chapter three, we will learn the revolutionary mystic insight of what that "you" truly is. The subsequent chapters will then help us to penetrate and incorporate this life-changing revelation.

This is not a book for any particular type of reader. It will resonate, hopefully, with those who seek, but that is true of all of us. Some seek more intentionally and openly than others. But everyone is seeking something, somewhere, somehow. It is the nature of human life. What is most important as you explore the following pages is curiosity, and perhaps even hope that you will find something (or someone) in these pages that you didn't know before.

Part One: Face To Face

Chapter 1: GETTING LOST

The First Question

Where are you?

Right now, as you read this page, where are you?

'In my bedroom,' you might answer. Or 'on the train.' Or 'at the park'. Or 'flying over the Grand Canyon on my way to visit my best friend in Los Angeles.' Or any number of locations you may be at this moment. But none of these will truly answer the question.

Where are you?

Let's begin with a simple exercise. Point to yourself. Where is your finger pointing? Most of us will point to our chest or our face. But is that you? Can you really point to who you are? Perhaps we'll admit that the body is not who I am, because the body changes. We know that most of the cells of our body regenerate within a decade, so most of our body is no longer the same material that it was just ten years past. Our DNA remains the same though, so perhaps we are our DNA. But DNA is not conscious. It replicates, but it does not think or feel. There is something that is lodged within this body, within this flesh and bone that is formed by our DNA. So when we point to our body, we are perhaps indicating that our self is somewhere within this. I can't touch it per se, but this is where it lives.

If so, we have perhaps determined its vicinity, but we have indicated nothing of its nature with the pointing of our finger. We have not identified it or pinpointed it. We have merely located it approximately. But let's not settle for approximates. We were not given the gift of life to treat it haphazardly. We can be lazy with many things, but understanding who, what, and where we are doesn't seem to be one of those things we should cast off with abandon.

Where are you? It is the primary question. Quite literally, it is the very first question that humanity is asked by its Creator:

וַיִּקְרָא יְ-הֹוָה אֱ-לֹהִים אֶל־הָאָדָם וַיֹּאמֶר לוֹ אַיֶּכָּה:

Vayikra A-donai E-lohim el ha'adam vayomer lo ayecha.
And the Lord God called to man and He said to him
'where are you'?
(Genesis 3:9)

The question came on the first day that humanity existed, which was the sixth day of creation. As the story in Genesis details, throughout the first five days, God created the heavens and the earth and all of their components and inhabitants. On day six, He created Adam and Eve and placed them into His garden to work it and perfect it. He provided and allowed them everything, but forbade them only one thing - from the fruit of the tree that grows in the middle of the garden you shall not eat, the tree of the knowledge of good and evil. But Adam and Eve could not resist. Within hours of their creation, they had committed the one act that they had been forbidden. They ate the fruit. They then heard God approaching them, and they hid. God called out to them, "ayecha/where are you?"

The question was not God's question. God, according to Torah, is omniscient - He knew precisely where they were. The question was for them - do *you* know where you are? Adam and Eve had gotten lost, and all of us since then - their children - have been lost as well.

Adam and Eve knew that they were in the garden of Eden. It's not that they had journeyed some great distance from their home and weren't familiar with the way back to where they'd started. Their feet had not carried them far. The issue was not one of geography, and it was not a place that they had lost. It was *themselves*. They were home, but the home was empty. The question was not "what is this place," but rather "are *you* in this place?" The emphasis of the question was not "where" - WHERE are you - but rather "you" - where are YOU? Their surroundings were familiar, but as they wandered through it, they could not identify its inhabitants. Who is this? Who is acting this way?

Prior to eating the fruit, the Midrash[1] tells us, Adam's and Eve's skin was diaphanous. They could see into themselves and each other. Their surface did not conceal their interior. God had created them transparent because there was no separation between their core and their veneer. They were completely unified in body and soul. Their actions matched their intentions. Their essence was manifest in everything they did. They were naked, but they were not ashamed, because there was no split between their most intimate recesses and their outer reality.

But then they ate the fruit. And there was shame. Their skin had become opaque, and they could no longer see where the true 'me' was within them. The translucent skin receded and they were wrapped in the flesh that we, their descendants, are covered in now. We maintain remnants of that primordial skin in our fingernails and toenails. From these we have an idea of what Adam and Eve originally looked like.

After the "sin," Adam and Eve hid, because they were ashamed of what they had done. They suddenly felt their nakedness, because the new flesh was a sign of their failure. Before, they were confident and secure - they knew who and where they were. But now they were unsure. Who am I? Where am I? What have I done? Suddenly they experienced a tremendous gulf between their inner essence and their outward reality. They had ingested the knowledge of good and evil. They had internalized a duality that did not exist in the paradise of the garden. In paradise, there is no conflict, no tension. In this new realm, "east of Eden" where they were exiled, there is perpetual conflict because of the tension that persists between the interior and the exterior, the soul and the body, the godly essence and its animalistic casing.

In this post-Eden existence, it is therefore difficult to point to precisely who and where we are. We show our face, "פנים/PaNiM" in

---

[1] Midrash is a collection of Rabbinic teachings that provides additional details and background to the Torah's narratives. See Breishis Rabba 20:12, Pirkei D'Rabbi Eliezer 14:3.

Hebrew, but we rarely show our inner essence, or "פְּנִימִיּוּת/PNiMyus." The words for 'face' and 'inwardness' share the same root in Hebrew - "פ-נ-ם/PNM" - because the intention for humanity is that our interior will be the same as our exterior. But we have yet to live up to this ideal. And this is our struggle and the source of our existential angst. The pain of life is our dissatisfaction with living on the surface. It is the discomfort of wearing a skin that conceals who we truly are. It is the suffocation of our truth under a mantle of facade.

Where are you?

You can identify your location at this moment - your bedroom, the train, the park, the plane, whatever the case may be - but what is more difficult to identify is the self that is occupying that space. Who are you? What are you? Are you the one who acts this way, thinks this way, feels this way? Is this truly you? Where did this 'you' come from? What made it what it is today? Is it authentic - is it what it has always been? Is it what it was made, or meant, to be? Is it what you would have liked to become?

If I look in the mirror right now, I see a face that I have seen many times before. It has changed over the years, but it is generally the same face I have met in the mirror for decades. I know the name by which that face is called - it's my name. I know that I call it me, but I suddenly realize that it is not me. My name is not who I am, nor is my face or my body. I don't know precisely who I am, but I know what I am not. I am not the skin that dresses my bones, or the bones that support my sinews and flesh. They will eventually be buried in the ground, but I will have already left them lifeless. I am the life behind the face. I am housed here, but I am not visible in the mirror. I am the one looking, but I am not the one seen.

Who am I?! Where am I?! How did I lose myself, and most importantly, how do I find me?!

A Hidden World

It's not your fault that "you" are lost!

This is essential to establish right from the start. You are not lost because you are wicked, or sinful, or deviant. There is no shame in being lost, no guilt to bear or blame to be assessed. It was not Adam and Eve's fault that they lost themselves, and it isn't yours, or mine, or any of us who have gotten lost - and that is to say, all of us. It is no coincidence, no bad luck, and no failure. We were created to be missing. That is the way God designed it.

We can see this in the Hebrew word for "world" - "עולם/olam." The etymology of this word is from the root "ע-ל-ם", which also forms the word "העלם/helam," meaning "hidden." Tracing the word back to its source enables us to trace God's intention for the universe back to its root. He created the world, "עולם/olam," to be a realm of concealment, "העלם/helam." Creation is thus a process of getting lost. Our mission and purpose, our raison d'etre, is the process of getting found and finding what has been concealed.

What is it that was to be concealed in this world of hiddenness? The Creator Himself. He would hide Himself behind the veneer of the material world. And along with Himself, He would hide the source and essence of all things, including your essence, or the ultimate you. It would be a realm where surface would prevail over substance. The spiritual would be encased in the corporeal to the extent that it was virtually imperceptible. The inhabitants of this world would be so enmeshed in their physical and material pursuits that they would not only come to mistake themselves for their appetites - in other words to lose themselves in their own skin - but they would have the ability, and even the propensity, to deny the existence of their Creator.

Why would God possibly create such a world?!

Why would He desire a realm of division and confusion, a place where the truth of things would be buried beneath a veil of distortion? What could be His reason for fabricating beings who could so easily become distracted, misguided, and disoriented? Why would He want His creations to be lost and corrupted? Why would He fashion a universe in which He Himself would be so commonly disregarded or denied?

We could suggest, as many have, that none of this concealment was His intention. It was, rather, a consequence of our failure to fulfill His command. Maybe the world is as dark and confused as it is because of our sin. This is not an uncommon belief, and many are raised with the doctrine of "original sin." According to this perspective, the story of Adam and Eve, which we related above, is pretty straightforward and pretty damning. They were created clear and unified, they transgressed, and as a result, they became lost from themselves and then banished from God's garden. This couldn't have been God's desire or intention, right? Rather, it was obviously a violation of His will. Humanity was punished, this was our great Fall, and since then we have been paying and suffering for our progenitors' primordial sin.

But as popular and pervasive as this rendition is, there's something troubling about it, isn't there? Is God's will so feeble and flimsy that it is defied and derailed within hours of its implementation? Is this what we think of the Creator of the universe?

'Let me generate a world,' we are to believe He said to Himself, 'of harmony and revelation. Let there be light, let there be heavens, let there be water that teems with life, and earth that sprouts forth vegetation and birds of the sky and beasts of the field. And finally, let there be humanity, glorious beings fashioned in My image who will work my garden. Let them walk with Me and know Me. Let them know themselves and be transparent. I will grant them free will, and I will give them everything but the fruit of the tree in the middle of the garden which I will instruct them not to eat." And He did just so. But there was a serpent, and the serpent was silver-tongued and it seduced them. And within hours of their formation, all of God's plans were laid to waste. Afterwards, for eons His creations would suffer and His world would languish.

This is a fairly pathetic version of history. The failure of Adam and Eve pales in comparison to the seeming failure of their Creator who envisioned something idyllic but was forced to accept and endure something far more infernal. Is it possible that God "failed" so miserably?

The Only One

Torah does not support the concept of Original Sin. Nor does Torah believe in "the devil," an evil force that is equal and contrary to God's power. Torah doctrine professes, rather, a concept known as

"Hashgacha Protis," which is translated as Individual Divine Providence, and which means that there is nothing that occurs in the universe that is contrary to the will of God. Every incident is an indispensable component of the divine tapestry and plan. A leaf does not blow in the wind if it is not precisely as the Creator intended it to be.[2]

This notion of "hashgacha protis" is predicated on the fundamental tenet of Jewish theology and ontology, which is the complete and exclusive unity of God. There can be nothing that occurs outside of God's will because *there is nothing that exists other than God*. This complete unity is stated succinctly in the expression "אֵין עוֹד מִלְבַדּוֹ/ain od milvado/there is nothing besides Him."[3] This tenet is so central to our existence that we declare this unity twice daily in the "Shema," a prayer that is known by most Jews, but understood by few. The prayer is derived from a verse in the fifth book of the Torah, Deuteronomy:

שְׁמַע יִשְׂרָאֵל יְ-הֹוָה אֱ-לֹהֵינוּ יְ-הֹוָה אֶחָד:

Shema Yisrael, A-donai E-loheinu, A-donai echad.
Hear O Israel, the Lord our God, the Lord is ONE!
(Deuteronomy 6:4)

Commonly interpreted as a statement of monotheism, this verse, like all of Torah, operates simultaneously on multiple levels. On the simplest level, the primary contribution of Torah to world history and culture was the notion of one God. The prevalent belief throughout the pagan world prior to the time of Abraham, the first Jew, was that the universe was influenced by a vast plurality of deities. Rather than a god of the sun, a god of rain, a god of wind, and a host of other idols that humanity fashioned and worshipped in pursuit of its needs and desires, Abraham came to understand that there was one God who controlled all of the forces and happenings that swirl around us. It was a revolutionary concept that would ultimately transform civilization and spawn at least

---

[2] Even free will, a subject that is beyond the scope of this work and treated in many volumes that are devoted to this issue alone, is accounted for in the doctrine of hashgacha protis; for even as God does not compel our decisions and actions, He is aware of them and inclusive of them in His infinite nature beyond time and space. For more on the subject of hashgacha protis, see Tanya Shaar HaYichud VehaEmunah, ch. 2, and Iggeres HaKodesh, Epistle 25.

[3] Deuteronomy 4:35

three of the world's foremost religious traditions: Judaism, Christianity, and Islam.[4]

Yet monotheism was only a part of Abraham's message. The revolutionary innovation that would be passed down through his descendants was not simply that there is only one God, as opposed to many deities. In its simple reading, the Shema prayer states 'Listen Israel, there is one God." But in its inner essence, it tells us something far more subtle and radical: 'Listen Israel, there is only One: God!'

This even more revolutionary message is discovered by analyzing the specifics of the prayer's wording: The verse begins, "Shema Yisrael/Hear Israel." It commands us to "hear" what it is about to instruct us rather than to know it, see it, ponder it, or understand it. Why is this something we must specifically "hear?" Because the forthcoming truth is too profound and abstruse to be seen or even clearly grasped intellectually. The custom is therefore to close one's eyes for the recitation of the Shema and to cover them with one's hand. We must rely on a more inward and ethereal type of perception for what the verse will go on to reveal because it is completely beyond the realm of both our sensate and intellectual experience.

The verse then mentions two terms, "A-donai E-loheinu/the Lord our God," which seem, at first blush, to be synonymous. But if they mean the same thing, then why does the verse mention both of them when it could have simply enlisted one or the other? In fact, "A-donai" and "E-lohim" are merely two of the many different names for God in the Hebrew language and liturgy, each of which signifies a different aspect of God's creation and manifestation. "A-donai" refers to God as He transcends the experiential world (the supra-natural God), while "E-lohim" denotes God in His detailed involvement in our daily lives (the immanent God). We tend to view these various components of our experience as distinct and separate, yet this is a basic misunderstanding of reality which this verse sets out to clarify.

---

[4] Torah itself suggests that the religions of the East were also significantly influenced by the Abrahamic tradition, as it explicitly states "And to the sons of Abraham's concubines, Abraham gave gifts, and he sent them ... eastward to the land of the East" (Genesis 25:6). The sages indicate that these "gifts" were secret divine names, one of which was the holy name "Ohm," one of the 72 three letter names of God mentioned in Kabbala.

It does so by continuing and concluding that "A-donai echad/ the Lord is One." It thus informs us not merely that there is one God as opposed to many, but even more significantly, that there is only one existence, and that is God. He is the one and only. There is no being or entity other than Him. Nature and the miraculous, earth and the heavens, body and soul - they are not multiple realities or coexisting creations. They are rather various aspects of the exclusive infinite reality of God.

Of course if this is the case, if the Shema is accurate and God is the only true being, then we are forced to wonder what this means about us. Twice daily, when we recite the Shema and thereby negate the existence of anything other than God, are we declaring that we don't exist? We close our eyes and nullify the plurality around us, and then we open them and are forced to function in a structure that we have seemingly just denied. How does this make sense?

Furthermore, if God is truly One, if there really is nothing other than Him, then what is this illusion of multiplicity, and why does He hide Himself behind it? Why does He allow it to seem as though His project has failed if in fact He is perfectly and completely in control?

The Face Of Death

To answer these questions, we must address the issue of human error. When God's creations fail to live up to His standards and expectations, is this an infraction of God's will? As we have discussed, the Torah's principle of "hashgachah protis/individual divine providence" insists that nothing can happen that is contrary to God's intention, because nothing truly exists other than God Himself. If so, then how are we to understand the concept of transgression?

The Torah is replete with stories of human error. A world in which the ultimate truth is concealed is bound to be a place of trial and miscalculation. Of all of the errors that are recorded in scripture, there are two that are considered to be so egregious that they influenced all of history in their wake. The first was the eating of the forbidden fruit, which we have been discussing already. The second was the worship of the golden calf.

As the story of the golden calf goes, Abraham's descendants were enslaved in Egypt. After several generations, God afflicted the Egyptians with ten plagues, forcing the wicked Pharaoh to let His people go. The fledgling nation fled into the desert, where they were then pursued by Pharaoh and his army. God split the sea so that the Israelites could escape, and He then led them to Mount Sinai, where their leader, Moses, ascended to retrieve the Torah. But Moses was on the mountain for 40 days, and the people grew impatient and feared that he would not return. They therefore built themselves a golden idol in the form of a calf, and they worshiped it in spite of all the miracles and wonders that God had performed for them in Egypt, at the Sea, and at the mountain.

On the simple level, what distinguishes these two most egregious "sins" - the eating of the fruit in the Garden of Eden and the serving of the golden calf at Mount Sinai - from all other instances of transgression, is their seeming brazenness and inconceivability. It is one thing for people to make the wrong decision when they are tempted and confused and dwelling in a realm of darkness with no moral clarity. But in both the Garden of Eden and at Mount Sinai, God had made Himself and His will extraordinarily clear. In Eden, He spoke directly to Adam and Eve. At Sinai, He had just performed not only the ten miraculous plagues that had rescued the Jewish nation of slaves from the superpower of Egypt, but He had split the sea and led the people through it on dry land. This was such a miraculous revelation of the divine that it is said that the most simple and lowly servant was granted more profound prophetic vision at the sea than the great prophet Ezekiel would experience in all of his communication with the divine.[5] With God so close and revealed to them, how could the nation err so dramatically just days later with the creation and worship of a golden idol formed in the image of a cow?

The eating of the fruit and the worship of the golden calf were similar not only in their gross defiance of a God who was revealed and available, but also in their subsequent effect on the entirety of the creation. The eating of the fruit plunged the world into exile and alienation from the divine. Two and a half millennia later, the giving of the Torah was intended as a corrective to that first fall. What God granted on Mount Sinai was not just a book of law and history, but rather a revela-

---

[5] Mechilta on Exodus 15:2.

tion of what had been hidden since the first day of Adam and Eve's creation and their expulsion from the garden. From Sinai, the nation was supposed to proceed to the promised land with their new gift of God's revealed word, and there they would usher in the messianic era.

Yet here again, on the verge of paradise, God's hopes were seemingly dashed by His rebellious creations. Just as His plan for revelation and unity had been derailed at the outset of creation by the first humans He formed, similarly His "chosen" nation, newly birthed after their redemption from Egypt, shattered His plans by building an idol at the foot of His holy mountain. Just as the idyllic existence in the Garden of Eden lasted only briefly, so now the elevation of the world and the revelation of the divine that had been created by the giving of the Torah would last only briefly. The "sin" of the golden calf immediately sent the creation toppling back again into a state of darkness and disconnection.

Why does this keep happening?!

If God wants us to see Him and experience Him, then why does He once again allow us to cast Him away so quickly and easily? In the immediate aftermath of the golden calf, God provides an answer to this perplexing question. Moses, clearly bewildered by the sequence of events, asks God to explain Himself to him.

וְעַתָּה אִם־נָא מָצָאתִי חֵן בְּעֵינֶיךָ הוֹדִעֵנִי נָא אֶת־דְּרָכֶךָ וְאֵדָעֲךָ:

V'atta im na matzasi chein b'einecha hodieini na es derachecha v'eidaacha.

If I have indeed found favor in your eyes, let me know Your ways, so that I may know You.

(Exodus 33:13)

God accedes to Moses' request. He invites Moses to come up once again onto the mountain, and there He will cause His glory to pass before him. But Moses will be granted only a vision of God's back, not His face.

וַיֹּאמֶר לֹא תוּכַל לִרְאֹת אֶת־פָּנָי כִּי לֹא־יִרְאַנִי הָאָדָם וָחָי:

Vayomer lo tuchal liros es panai ki lo Yirani ha'adam va'chai.

And He said to him, "You will not be able to see my face, for man shall not see Me and live."

(ibid 33:20)

Why is it that Moses is not permitted to see God's face? What does this mean that a person can experience God's back, but cannot perceive His face and continue to remain alive?

God's face represents His full and complete revelation, whereas His back represents a more shrouded and limited view and understanding of Him. The inability to see God's face informs us that if we were to experience the full, unimpeded revelation of His infinite reality, which is His complete unity, then we would understand that nothing else, including ourselves, truly exists at all. The verse does not read 'if man sees Me he will perish,' but rather "man shall not see Me and live." In other words, it is not that seeing God's face would cause one to die, but rather that in the presence of His "face" one does not, and never did, truly live. We cannot see His face because in the presence of His face, which is the manifestation of His infinite presence, there is nothing else, and therefore no "we" at all.

With this, we can answer our question of why God hides His unity - because if He didn't, we would cease to be. "Olam," Hebrew for 'world,' is related to the word "helam/hidden" because the act of the creation of the world was an act of concealment. *In order to allow for the existence of any seeming other, God had to allow Himself to be unseen.*

Intentional Error

We can now understand the story of Adam and Eve very differently from the version of God's failed experiment that we presented above. When we view the events with the assumption of "hashgacha protis" - God's complete providence and control - and we begin with the awareness of God's Oneness and His desire to create "others" with whom He could interact, the version of events plays more like this:

'Let me generate a world,' God thought to Himself, 'of concealment and plurality. Where there was originally only Me, let Me now withdraw and obscure Myself so that a creation can emerge. Let there be light and darkness, let there be heavens and earth, let there be life that does not know where it comes from or that it is not truly distinct and diverse. Let there be beings who resemble Me, who sense Me, who are capable of finding Me, but who do not know the full extent of Me. I will place them in My garden to give them a glimpse of their essence and my truth, and then I will allow them to lose themselves, to get lost, to lose sight of their Creator. They will stumble in the darkness, but I will never leave them, because there is no place that they can go where I am not already and always there." So He created the garden and placed Adam and Eve in it; He created the fruit and commanded them not to eat it; He created the snake and its silver tongue; and He set His plan in motion so that He would be unseen and a world could develop in His seeming absence.

Just as the eating of the fruit and the "expulsion" from the garden was therefore not a failure or an accident, we can similarly understand the story of the golden calf not as another frustration of God's plan, but as a necessary condition for it:

From the day of Adam and Eve's creation and exile, there were two millennia of concealment and spiritual darkness. At that point, after twenty generations, God determined that it was time for the gradual process of His revelation to begin. In the the year 1948 on the Hebrew calendar (1813 BCE), Abraham was born, and he became the first human to innovate and publicize the idea of one God. Abraham's grandson, Jacob, also known as Israel, descended to Egypt, and after the death of his 12 sons, the Bnei Yisrael (children of Israel) were enslaved. In the year 2448 (1313 BCE), God freed Abraham's descendants from Egypt and guided them, under the leadership of Moses, to Mount Sinai. Here, God performed a national revelation, manifesting Himself to the three million men, women, and children who were gathered at the base of the mountain. At this moment, He provided them a covenant and a scripture that would enable them to begin to light the darkness.

It was then that the children of Israel became the Nation of Israel, and then that they were given their mandate to be "אוֹר לְגוֹיִים/Ohr l'goyim," a light unto the nations. What this meant is that they were commissioned to go forth from the revelation that they had experienced, and to share, with all those they would encounter, the message that God is hidden beneath the fabric of creation. The darkness, they would report, is only a thin mask that conceals a breathtaking light beneath. God, they would declare, is One.

But in the radiance of God's oneness, it is difficult to negotiate the mundane imperatives of the material world. How can we leave the warmth and brilliance of the light on the mountain to venture into the darkness and coldness of the surrounding world? In the glory of His presence, all else becomes trivial, and ultimately illusory. How are we to function in a system that is not real? In the awareness of God's Oneness, we become conscious of our own nonexistence. How can we fulfill our mission and task if we believe that we are nothing?

Therefore, immediately after God's revelation, there was once again a reversion to His concealment. The worship of the golden calf precipitated Moses' immediate descent from the mountaintop and his shattering of the tablets that he had received from the hand of God. The channel that had been opened between the heavens and the earth was once again closed, and the clarity of vision which had been momentarily granted to every man, woman, and child was once again clouded and obscured. Here again, as in the garden of Eden, with every experience of intense exposure, there is a subsequent incident of withdrawal. This is imperative because the continued existence of the creation depends on it. If revelation would continue unimpeded, then God's absolute unity would be revealed and would preclude the presence and "survival" of anything other.

Darkness, we suddenly and shockingly realize, is not evil! It is not the province of some demonic force that is working against God's will. Darkness is God's as much as light is. It allows us to be. Astonishingly, concealment, we have come to understand, is an act of consummate divine love!

An Invitation

We can now understand that, as we suggested earlier, being lost is not our fault, but it is rather the nature of the existence into which we have been thrust. Far from the notion of blame and guilt, we can begin to free ourselves from the belief that our confusion and alienation are the result of our failings. We are not lost because we have been cast from God's loving embrace. Rather, it is in order to embrace us that God has created "distance" between us and Him - for otherwise, He would merely be embracing Himself.

Guilt is not a productive emotion. It has certainly proven to be a motivating force, and it may in fact account for the majority of what most humans do on a daily basis and throughout our lives. But that does not render guilt productive, nor does it make it positive or desirable. It could, in fact, be suggested that guilt is responsible for most of the destructive thoughts and actions that we visit upon ourselves and those around us. The sense that I am not as I should be, or that I ought to be better than what I have become, often leads us to the subconscious belief that we are deserving of the suffering that we experience. This can subsequently bring us to the self-defeating and self-fulfilling assumption that we are incapable of rectifying our previous missteps. This type of shame and despair embitters us, and when we are bitter, we tend to punish not only ourselves, but everyone else as well.

God did not create us to despair. He did not conceal Himself in order to deceive us or in order to watch us fumble about in the dark. He did not send us from the garden to live lives of anguish and regression. He does not look down upon us from somewhere on high and revel in our struggle. God is not vindictive or vengeful. These are not the traits of God, but of men who have created a god in their own image with which they can intimidate and control others. Shame, fear, and guilt are the weapons of those who are hungry for power. God has no hunger and needs no power. Though His ways are mysterious and our comprehension is limited, we know that just as creation was an act of love, so too all darkness is simply a concealment of His unity which enables us to exist as individuals who will ultimately reunite and recognize our inherent divinity.

None of this is to suggest that light and darkness do not differ within the framework of our reality, or that right and wrong cannot be established and distinguished. None of this absolves us from the responsibility to choose right action over wrong action. And none of this denies the reality that we often choose poorly. We are human, our world is a realm of hiddenness, and we stumble. Yet when we do, we can admit our failings without guilt. We can feel regret without the debilitating hobbles of shame. The regret is the awareness that we did not live up to our potential. We know we can do better, but we also know that it is not we who have created ourselves imperfect. It is not we who have hidden our true essence from ourselves. Our Creator did that. This does not free us from the task of finding the truth, but it relieves us from the disgrace of being lost and imperfect. The task is far less burdensome and far more achievable if we are not plagued with self-doubt and self-loathing.

"Where are you" is not an accusation, but an invitation. Prior to being lost, Adam and Eve were not aware that there was anything within them to be found. They were not looking for themselves - their true selves - because they had no self-consciousness. They were naked, and as they were unaware of their nakedness, they were unashamed. But they were also simply unaware. It was a paradise, a dream with no consciousness, a blissful ignorance. The fruit from the tree of the knowledge of good and evil woke them from their reverie. It shattered the placid glassy veneer of the dream, and revealed to them that there was a whole world of depths down there beneath the surface. "Ayecha," God said to them, "where are you?"

Come, He beckoned them, I did not create you to be unconscious in the garden like the other animals. I have a job for you to do. There is something that I've hidden that I want you to find and reveal. I have chosen you for the task because I love you and I believe in you. It will not be easy, but I will be with you. I am not sending you away - there is no 'away' from Me because I am everywhere. I am not punishing you - you have not failed by eating the fruit, you have simply created the distance that is necessary for your journey to be set.

With a backward glance at the garden, along with a fond remembrance of the ease and bliss that they had known and would not know again, Adam and Eve accepted the mission that their Creator had assigned them. And likewise we, lost and full of uncertainty, but free of guilt and confident in the One Who sends us, are ready to set out east of Eden on the arduous, awesome task of getting found.

Chapter 2: IN THE DARKNESS

Pre-Dawn Departure

We begin our journey in the dark. The sun may have risen already, but it is dark nonetheless. That is the nature of this world, as we have previously discussed - 'olam/world' is derived from 'helam/hiddenness.' Sunlight does not dispel the darkness, it only simulates illumination. The truth is as obscure at midday as it is at midnight. It is true that God created light on the very first day of the creation. "Let there be light,"[6] He said, and there was light. But the sages teach that this light was immediately hidden away, only to be accessed and utilized by "the righteous in the future."[7] This light that enables genuine vision is referred to as the "Ohr Haganuz/the hidden light," and it is generally inaccessible to most of us now. Physical light is only part of the illusion that enables us to believe that we can see.

---

[6] Genesis 1:3

[7] Rashi on Genesis 1:4

Admitting that we are lost and in the dark can be frightening. We're uncertain how we got here, or why we're here at all. We don't know what's lurking nearby, and we have no idea which way to go. Fear can stymie us, rooting us in our place, or it can make us want to run, aimless and mindless. But neither of these will help us to get found. This is not a time for panic. It is a time for courage and composure. It is time to assess our situation and gather what we know.

What we know at this point is that hiddenness is intentional, that it is not a result of failure or punishment, but rather it is a prerequisite for our existence. We have also established that we have been created with a purpose and a mission, and that is to find what has been hidden and lost. Yet this knowledge leaves us with several questions that we must address in order to help us navigate the journey from our current place of exile to the place of revelation and redemption that we seek.

Our first question is why God requires or desires our existence at all? We can understand that He must hide His infinite presence in order to allow finite creations like us to exist, but we have not yet determined why it is important for Him that we exist in the first place. If we are to suggest that there is a task that He assigned to us, we have to wonder how it is possible for there to be anything that we can do which He could not have done Himself. If we believe that He is omnipotent, and that, according to the notion of "hashgacha protis/individual divine providence," He determines everything that happens at every moment and in every place throughout the universe, then what could our creation possibly provide to Him that He did not already possess?

Our second question is that if this world was truly intended to be a realm of concealment, then why does God provide intermittent moments of revelation at all if they are only to be followed by a return to darkness? Why did we begin in the garden if we were inevitably to be expelled from it? Why did God reveal Himself to us at Mount Sinai and give us His Torah if we would quickly turn from Him and attempt to replace Him with an idol made of gold? Why do we have glimmers of clarity, connection, and inspiration throughout our lives, only to lose them the moment we try to grasp them? Again, according to our premise of "hashgacha protis/individual divine providence" and intentionality, there must be a purpose and necessity for both the light and the darkness. But which is it that God truly desires - an "olam/world" where He is shrouded in "helam/concealment," or a realm of light where the truth of His unity is revealed?

Our two questions are intertwined. The first asks why our existence is so important to God that it justifies His self-concealment and the creation of darkness, which is the root of all confusion and conflict. The second seeks to understand the flashes of stunning revelation that rip across the darkness like occasional lightning bolts throughout the long night. What is this interplay between revelation and obfuscation, how do we reconcile the two, and which is it that God primarily desires? In the dark before the dawn, as we prepare to set out on our journey, we attempt to familiarize ourselves as best we can with God's goals and motivations so that we can most successfully fulfill the mission that He assigns us.

Night And Then Day

Which came first, the chicken or the egg? The question has confounded multitudes, but in the creation story at the beginning of the Torah, the answer is clear. God created the animals fully formed, and then He commanded them to reproduce - so the chicken came first, and then came the egg. From the same creation story, in the very first verses of the Torah, we can address another profound order of precedence: which came first, the darkness or the light? The question may not be as catchy as the one about the chicken, but it is certainly significant and informative.

בְּרֵאשִׁית בָּרָא אֱ-לֹהִים אֵת הַשָּׁמַיִם וְאֵת הָאָרֶץ: וְהָאָרֶץ
הָיְתָה תֹהוּ וָבֹהוּ וְחֹשֶׁךְ עַל־פְּנֵי תְהוֹם וְרוּחַ אֱ-לֹהִים מְרַחֶפֶת
עַל־פְּנֵי הַמָּיִם: וַיֹּאמֶר אֱ-לֹהִים יְהִי־אוֹר וַיְהִי־אוֹר:

Breishis bara E-lohim es hashamayim v'es haaretz. V'haaretz haysa sohu vavohu v'chosehch al-pnei t'hom v'ruach E-lohim merachephes al-pnei hamayim. Vayomer E-lohim yehi ohr va'yehi ohr.

In the beginning of God's creation of the heavens and the earth. Now the earth was astonishingly empty, and

darkness was on the face of the deep and the spirit of God hovered over the face of the water. And God said, "Let there be light," and there was light.
(Genesis 1:1-3)

From these opening verses of Torah, we see clearly that darkness preceded light. First there was darkness "on the face of the deep," and then God said "let there be light." It is for this reason that on the Hebrew calendar, the date begins not with morning, but with nightfall. Describing the creation of each of the days of the first week, the verse states "Vayehi erev, vayehi boker - it was evening, and (then) it was morning."[8]

Like every detail of Torah, the sequence is consequential. God created darkness and only thereafter light because that is the progression that He designed and intended for this world. First there was to be darkness, because darkness serves an important function - it allows a world to exist, as we discussed in the previous chapter. But darkness is not the goal or the ultimate objective. After the darkness, there was to be light; and not just any light, but a light that could only be achieved after dwelling in the dark.

When a light is switched on in the darkness, we are momentarily blinded. It may be a dim light, a light that we could tolerate easily and comfortably at any other time, but in contrast to the darkness, it is glaring, and we are forced to blink or shield our eyes. Such is the reality that was expressed by the wisest man in history, King Solomon, when he wrote that wisdom is better than folly, just as light is better than darkness. The mystics wonder at this statement. Did it require the deep insight of King Solomon to understand that wisdom is superior to folly? Or, for that matter, that light is preferable to darkness? Yet a careful reading of the Hebrew original indicates that Solomon was alluding to a far more subtle and profound truth.

וְרָאִיתִי אָנִי שֶׁיֵּשׁ יִתְרוֹן לַחָכְמָה **מִן**־הַסִּכְלוּת כִּיתְרוֹן הָאוֹר **מִן**־הַחֹשֶׁךְ:

V'ra'isi ani she'yesh yisron la'chochmah **min** *hasichlus k'yisron ha'or* **min** *hachoshech.*

---

[8] Genesis 1:5

> I saw that there is an advantage to wisdom **FROM** folly
> like the advantage of light **FROM** darkness.
> (Ecclesiastes 2:13)

The mystics point out that the word "מִן/min" which appears before both the words "הַסִּכְלוּת/hasichlus/folly" and "הַחֹשֶׁךְ/ha-choshech/darkness" is commonly translated as "than," but it literally means "from." The verse therefore expresses not merely that wisdom is greater *than* folly, or that light is greater *than* darkness, but that the advantage of wisdom comes *from*, or *subsequent to*, folly, and the advantage of light comes *from*, or *subsequent to*, darkness. What King Solomon offers here, therefore, is not a simple statement of the obvious, but rather a profound insight into a) the nature of what wisdom and light are and how to attain them, and b) why the world we inhabit is filled with folly and darkness.

True wisdom, he informs us, comes from, and after, folly, just as the most blinding light is that light which follows darkness. One cannot be truly wise until s/he has made errors to learn from. One cannot come ultimately close to something until s/he has experienced distance, alienation, and longing which then drive her/him passionately toward that which s/he has lacked. One has never experienced true and blinding light until s/he has first dwelled in, and adjusted to, the darkness.

———————

Singing In The Dark

Every voyage begins with a single step.

We have taken our first step.

The first step is the understanding that there are steps. There are phases and stages to the world and God's plan for it. We cannot merely establish a polarity of light and darkness and ascribe to God a desire for one or the other. Such a simplistic conception does not recognize the inclusion of all aspects of creation within the divine unity. Any attempt to delimit God to one thing or another is inherently a failure to recognize His presence in, and therefore His intention for, everything that He has created. If something exists, then there is a reason it exists and a purpose for its existence. This is not to say that everything is "holy," desirable, or permissible, but rather that everything can and must be traced back to its origin, which is the ultimate truth that has been hidden within it. Darkness, as we have seen, is not evil. It is a veil with which God conceals Himself so that we are not obliterated in His infinite presence. While concealment is therefore a gift and an act of love, it is not an objective in itself. It is our point of embarkation. It is the beginning of a journey that will lead us to an unprecedented revelation of unimaginable light.

The recognition of steps is not only a prerequisite and jumping off point, it also assures that we are setting off on the right foot, so to speak. The journey will be long and arduous, but it need not be painful or unpleasant. The awareness of steps is the antidote to frustration, depression, and despair. It is the cure before the wound. Life, for many, is full of pain, but it needn't be. What is certain, in a world of darkness and concealment, is that there will be trial and struggle. However, these are not synonymous with pain. Pain is the result not of challenge, but of the assumption that there is no benefit in the challenge, and no purpose in its endurance. When, on the contrary, we are conscious of the underlying reason and productive function of a trying situation, we are able to endure it, and even pursue it, no matter how uncomfortable or troublesome it may be. As Freidrich Nietzche wrote, and as Viktor Frankl explained in his work *Man's Search for Meaning*, "He who has a why to live for can bear with almost any how." The recognition of steps enables us to set out in the darkness, to be unafraid and undeterred because we are aware that not only is there a purpose and reason for this concealment, but it is temporary and it is merely a dim passageway that will usher us to someplace luminous.

With such consciousness, we face the journey ahead not with trepidation and resignation, but rather we embrace the darkness because we know that it is not only a necessity, but a benefit. We venture into the darkness headlong because we know that our goal awaits us on the other side. We are even able to face the darkness with song, as the verse in Psalms declares:

עִבְדוּ אֶת־יְ-הֹוָה בְּשִׂמְחָה בֹּאוּ לְפָנָיו בִּרְנָנָה:

Ivdu es A-donai b'simcha, bo'u lefanav b'renana.
Serve God with joy, come before Him with singing.
(Psalms 100:2)

On this verse, The Zohar[9] teaches that "simcha b'tzafara, u're-nana b'ramasa/joy is in the day, while singing is in the night."[10] Singing, the sages indicate here, is specifically something that we do in the darkness. Joy occurs when we can clearly see, but we sing precisely when we are in the dark. When we are close to our beloved, when we have what we desire, we do not sing. Rather, we are silent, and we embrace. But when we are far, when we are in the dark, we sing our beloved's praises, we raise our voice and call out to our love and express our passionate desire.

We would not sing, however, if we were afraid, or if we were uncertain that our lover was somewhere nearby. It is the awareness that the darkness is not permanent, and the sense that the light and the object of our desire is imminent, that enables us and inspires us to sing. Yet without the darkness, we would not have the beauty of song at all. It is specifically the longing for something unattained that strums the deepest chords of the soul.

With this, we can now glean the answer to our second question, which is that if God created this "world/olam" as a place of "conceal-ment/helam," then why does He keep introducing these glimmers of light and revelation that gleam momentarily and then quickly fail. Why place Adam and Eve in the Garden of Eden if He knew that they were to eat the fruit and be exiled within hours of their creation? Why bestow the Torah on Mount Sinai if He knew we were to fashion a golden calf soon thereafter? Why build not one, but two Temples in Jerusalem which would later be destroyed? Why the cyclical rhythm of exile and redemp-tion? Why communicate divine edicts to prophets that would go un-heeded? Why the constant oppression of those who attempt to discern, discharge, and disseminate the divine will? Is it concealment that You desire, God, or is it revelation?

The answer, we now understand, is both. More specifically, as discussed above, the answer is one and then the other. He desires dark-ness and then light, and ultimately light that comes from darkness. The reason for the glimmers of unenduring light is to provide us glimpses of

---

9 Zohar is a seminal text of Kabbala, written by Rabbi Shimon Bar Yochai. Kab-bala is the mystic and esoteric dimension of Torah.

10 Zohar 1, 229

the truth so that we remain aware of the end-game and can thereby continue to withstand the challenges of this interim darkness and persevere. The goal is therefore light, but there is something that the darkness provides that the light does not and cannot. The darkness provides the distance that makes the subsequent light appreciable.

With this answer to our second question, we must now address our first. What is it that the darkness and concealment provide to God? If, as we have established previously, He concealed Himself so that we could exist, what is it that our existence does for Him that He could not have done Himself? What is it that a vast multiplicity of flawed and finite beings can accomplish that an omnipotent and infinite unity cannot?

***

All One, Alone

"In the beginning, God created the heavens and the earth."

This is the common translation of the first sentence of the Torah. We begin with the beginning, which seems to be a reasonable place to start. But this is not truly the beginning, because something existed beforehand. We know this not only because God Himself obviously predated the creation if He created it, but also, as the classical commentator Rashi[11] points out, the grammar of the verse makes it clear that this is not a reference to the very first moment of existence. The word "בְּרֵאשִׁית/ Breishis," the very first word of the Torah which is translated as "in the beginning," always modifies the word that comes after it, and therefore more literally means "in the beginning OF." As such, the verse does not mean "In the beginning, God created the heavens and the earth" as it is generally rendered, but rather "In the beginning OF God's creation of the heavens and the earth...."

The difference is subtle, but substantive. If the verse were truly intending to discuss the very beginning of all creation, then the proper Hebrew word would have been either "בראשונה/Barishona" or "בתחילה/ B'tchila," both of which means "at first." "Breishis," on the contrary, indi-

---

[11] Rabbi Shlomo Yitzchaki, 11th century French sage and the foremost commentator on Torah's "pshat" or "simple meaning." 1040-1105

cates that we are not talking here about the absolute beginning of all things, but rather the beginning of a particular stage in the larger context of existence. The process that is initiated at the opening of the book of Genesis is the creation of the world that we inhabit, but this is not the only world, nor is it the first. If this were truly the beginning, then we would not seek to understand what preceded it. But if, as the verse literally indicates, this describes only the dawn of our existence and the realm in which we exist, i.e. the heavens and the earth, then we will want to know what there was before we were. What preceded the creation of our world, which is what is recorded in the beginning of the Torah.

On the face of it, the Hebrew Bible, otherwise known as the "Chumash" or the Five Books of Moses, is focused on our world and our function within the context of this particular creation. Therefore, it does not explicitly concern itself with pre-history or the spiritual realms and alternate realities that coexist with ours. This Bible, beginning with Genesis and ending with Deuteronomy, is what most people understand to be the Torah. However, Torah more generally refers to far more than the five books of Moses. It comprises all of the divine wisdom that has been communicated to and by the sages, including the Talmud, or oral Torah, as well as the vast literature and tradition of Kabbala. Kabbala is the esoteric and hidden tradition which has been passed down through the ages. Among other things, it explores other worlds and the interplay between our reality and those which are beyond our immediate perception. The esoteric wisdom provides a glimpse of the ultimate beginning, prior to the creation of any world or any being, when there was only God.

At that point, God was One. God was All. God was All One, or Alone.

'Alone' generally connotes a state of isolation and separation. In God's case, of course, these terms do not, and cannot, apply. He is not isolated because He is everywhere at once. He is not separated, because there is nothing other than Him from which He can be distinct. 'Alone' in God's primordial sense means that there is no one, and no thing else. Oneness is a difficult concept to imagine, and though we meditate on it multiple times daily with the recital of the Shema prayer (as we discussed above), it continues to elude our mortal comprehension. We cover our eyes when we say Shema because vision is irrevocably tethered to the facade of plurality - the moment we look, we see so many things that seem to be separate from ourselves and from each other. But close your eyes and imagine for a moment an empty space that stretches infinitely in every direction. There are no walls that bound the space, no floor or ground below, or ceiling or sky above. The space just goes on forever. Now remove yourself from the space as well so that there is not even a distinct being observing the space, there is only space. Yet the space is not truly empty. Something fills and pervades it. It is the space itself. It is all there is, and it is everywhere. It is not dark, or light, and it has no hue, or sound, or weight, or scent. It is everything and nothing at once. It is all, it is one. It is alone.

'Alone' is often correlated with 'lonely,' but of course they are not the same. Loneness is not synonymous with lonesomeness. We often tend to associate negative feelings with being alone, but it carries no inherent emotional state. For some, the idea of being isolated may be frightful or sad, but for others, the privacy and tranquility of seclusion are desirable and pursued. For God, we cannot say that His singularity presented a lack, or any feeling of incompleteness, because these very terms cannot apply to something that is everything. Yet in some way, which is beyond the reach of our intellectual comprehension, there was a desire within God for something else, something other.

How could One who is all, and who has all, want or need? Infinite, omnipotent, and omniscient, God could have, or be, or know anything He desired. But there was one thing He could not do: He couldn't give. He couldn't give because there was nothing other to give to. One cannot truly give to Oneself, and even if One could, One cannot be given to when One already possesses and includes everything that is.

Good Nature

Why are we here? Why does the universe exist? We must all face the question eventually. Some will conclude that there is no why, no reason or intention. There were simply a series of random and colliding factors that precipitated a long and gradual evolution leading to where we are now. We will not debate such a conception. We will rather provide an alternative. We begin, as we have already begun, with the belief in God, and by God we mean the Being, or the Everything, that existed before existence as we know it. Therefore, the question for us is not simply why does the universe exist, but more specifically, why did God create the universe? What was His reason? What did He want? Further, as we have posed earlier, what could our creation give Him that He didn't already have? And even further, what was He seeking that was worth concealing Himself and initiating a world of darkness in order to have it?

Volumes have been written on the question of the divine why. One very concise, and simultaneously very profound, reason for the creation of our universe that has been provided by the mystics is:

טֶבַע הַטוֹב לְהֵטִיב.

Teva hatov l'heitiv.
It is the nature of one who is good to do good.
(Emek HaMelech, Shaar Aleph)

God, according to this explanation, created the world because He desired to give. Or to put it slightly differently: God did not simply desire to create the world, but rather His giving nature necessitated the creation of the world, so to speak, because there had to be an outlet for His inherent and essential nature to manifest His beneficence. It is the nature of one who is good to do good, and therefore in order to express His natural goodness, God required a recipient to whom He could convey His generosity.

But how could God find a recipient if He was the sole existence? He would have to create an "other." But where could this other be created if there was no place that God did not already inhabit Himself? He would have to withdraw Himself, so to speak, from some portion of infinite space in order to make room for this new realm of otherness. But can One who is infinite create a space that is empty of Him? Theoretically, God is omnipotent, and therefore, there is nothing that He cannot do. However, by suggesting that He can create a space that is devoid of His presence, we are bounding His infinity; yet, if we affirm his ubiquity and suggest that there can be no place where He is not, then we are challenging His omnipotence.

The mystics resolve this paradox with the concept of "צמצום/ tzimtzum," or contraction. God contracted Himself to create a void where His presence was not revealed. It's not that this space was truly

empty of God's presence, but rather that His presence here was concealed. By creating the world - "olam," again related to "helam" meaning
hiddenness - God is not truly withdrawing Himself, but He is rather
concealing His omnipresence. He does so in order to manufacture the
appearance of otherness so that He can express His irrepressible benevolence.

If there were a brief introductory paragraph before the first verse
of chapter one of the book of Genesis, it might read something like this:

In the beginning, the true beginning, before the beginning of the
Creation of heaven of earth, God was All One, and He desired to give. In
order to do so, He first needed to create an other, or many others, to be
the recipients of his giving. Yet there was no place for any other, because
He filled all space and place. Therefore, in order to fashion a creation,
first He needed to conceal Himself. Thus, the very first thing that God
created, before He initiated the Creation as we know it, was darkness,
which was not truly a creation, but rather a shrouding of His presence.
Darkness is not truly void of God, because He remains One, everywhere
and everything. Darkness is rather a concealment of the essential reality
of His Oneness.

From this preface, we can better understand the first verses of
Genesis: "In the beginning of God's creation of the heaven and the earth,
the earth was astonishingly empty, and darkness was on the face of the
deep, and the spirit of God was hovering over the face of the water. And
God said 'Let there be light,' and there was light" (Genesis 1:1-3). We can
now understand why there was already darkness and emptiness prior to
the establishment of our world - because these were prerequisites for this
realm of hiddenness. We can now comprehend "why the spirit of God
was *hovering over*" the space rather than pervading it - because He
"withdrew" Himself, so to speak, through the process of "tzimtzum" in
order to make room for otherness. We can also appreciate why His first
creative utterance was "Let there be light" - because darkness was only a
preparatory contingency, and since light was the ultimate end-game, He
announced and introduced its creation first. Darkness is concealment,
withdrawal, and restraint, while light is revelation, effusion, and lovingkindness. The sole purpose of the former in God's scheme of creation
was to enable the latter.

This reality has been explained with a simple but powerful analogy: There was a King with inexplicable capability, power, and wealth, but he had no one to share his gifts with because no one could tolerate the incredible force, immensity, and bliss of his presence. He possessed everything anyone could ever desire, but he wanted nothing more than to share his abundance with others. One day, as he sat alone at his tremendous table in the royal dining room, he had an idea. He took portions of himself, fashioned them into human form and outfitted them with various costumes and masks, and placed them in the chairs around the table. Each of them soon forgot that they were wearing masks and eventually came to believe themselves to be individuals rather than portions of the king himself. Delighted with his "guests," the king provided them every type of delicacy and "everyone" rejoiced in the royal feast.[12]

This dynamic is alluded to early in the creation narrative with the verse, shortly after the creation of Adam:

לֹא־טוֹב הֱיוֹת הָאָדָם לְבַדּוֹ:
Lo tov heyos ha'adam levado.
It is not good for man to be alone.
(Genesis 2:18)

On the simple level, this statement refers to the first man's solitary predicament. Because God saw that it was not good for Adam to be alone, He therefore created Eve to be his partner, as the verse continues "I shall make him a helpmate opposite him." But the Chassidic masters teach that, like all verses in the Torah, there is a mystic secret contained in these words, and that "haAdam/man" in this verse simultaneously refers to God Himself. Adam is the name that was given to the first human, but it also refers to "Adam Kadmon," a kabbalistic term that is best translated as "primordial Man" and which denotes the Godly "image" or "structure" that existed before the creation and to which the human image corresponds. Translated in this way, the verse is informing us of the very reason for the creation: 'It is not good for God to be alone, I shall make a helper corresponding to Him.'

This analogy has been offered by Gutman Locks, author of "There is One", "Coming Back to Earth" and other enlightening books.

When was God "alone?" Before He fashioned the creation. Why was it not "good" for Him to be alone? Because "tov/good," by its very definition, is the bestowal of kindness from one to another. If there is no one to be, or to do, good to, then there is no good at all. Therefore, it was not "good" for God to be alone, and thus in order for good to exist, God needed to create an other to whom good could be given. Therefore, "I shall make an ezer/helper k'negdo/corresponding to him" - God fashioned a being that was in His image, an Adam/man that was corresponding to Adam Kadmon/His primordial image, in order to "help" Him by enabling Him to express His goodness.[13]

With this, we have now answered both of our questions. We had previously established that our world was a realm of intentional concealment, and that the reason for the creation of darkness was to cloak God's unity so that something other - ie. we and all of the creation - could exist. But we wondered why our existence was necessary, and what it is that we can provide to God that He could not have provided Himself. And we now understand that we are here in order to provide God a recipient for His love and kindness.

But still we are lost. Still, we are in the dark. While these answers shed some glimmer of comprehension on the origin and nature of our being, and provide some ray of comfort in the awareness of our blamelessness for the darkness that surrounds us, they still tell us nothing of our objective or of the direction that we should pursue. As we set out on our journey, we need to know where we are going, why we are going, and indeed whether we should be going at all. If we are created simply to be recipients of divine charity, then can we not merely sit in our place and collect what God desires to give? Does this not fulfill our purpose? Or is there something that we were put here to do?

Adam and Eve were sent out of the garden. Moses and the fledgling Jewish nation were set free from Egypt, and then sent away from Mount Sinai. History has been a series of exiles and excursions through foreign and often oppressive lands. We are scattered throughout the globe and always yearning for a messianic eventuality that will deliver us from the darkness and usher us back to our home. Yet we are not simply waiting. We are not merely floating on the tides of history and allow-

---

[13] See Torah Ohr, Parshas Breishis, maamar "Lo Tov Hayos HaAdam Levado," where the Alter Rebbe discusses this idea.

ing ourselves to be buffeted by the stormy seas. We have a role to play and a job to do. We are lost and in the dark by Godly design, but we are not sitting idly by and awaiting rescue. We are sent out to find our way, to find ourselves, to find the Creator Who has hidden Himself in order for us to exist.

If darkness is concealment of God's oneness, then light is its revelation. The first divine proclamation, "Let there be light," is more than an act of creation, it is an indication of our mission and purpose. While we were created to be the recipients of God's love and kindness, our task is not simply to be passive receptacles. True love does not merely bestow, because passive receipt is not what is best for the beloved. True love provides one's lover the opportunity to be active and to give in return, because the dignity that one earns by giving is far more valuable than all the riches and gifts that one can passively receive. God therefore gives us the ability to be good and Godly ourselves by providing us a task that we can do for Him. What is that task? To illuminate the darkness, to shed light on what is hidden, to reveal Him in a realm in which He has concealed Himself.

What then does our creation provide to God? Not only the ability for Him to give, but also the revelation and publication of His presence in a world that is capable of denying His existence.

The Mission

As we head out on our journey, though there is darkness all around us, we can find clarity for our mission from a variety of sources. One is hidden in plain sight in the very first words of the Torah:

בְּרֵאשִׁית בָּרָא אֱלֹהִים אֵת הַשָּׁמַיִם וְאֵת הָאָרֶץ:
Breishis bara E-lohim es hashamayim v'es haaretz.
In the beginning of God's creation of the heavens and the earth.

(Genesis 1:1)

The chassidic masters have suggested that these words contain our ultimate mission statement and a concise expression of the very meaning of life. While we have previously translated this verse as "In the beginning of God's creation of the heavens and the earth," the richness and elasticity of the Hebrew language enabled the rabbis to intuit a profound message in these words. "Breishis," commonly rendered as 'in the beginning of," can also be read as "the first thing" or "the primary thing." "Bara" means "creation," and can also be rendered as "revelation" because creation is essentially an act of revelation, in that whatever is being created did not previously exist, and thus it has now come into a state of being and awareness. Translating the words this way, and adding the rest of the verse, we find in the very opening of the entire Torah, a clear and simple instruction:

> Breishis/the primary thing is bara/the revelation of
> E-lohim/God es hashamayim v'es haaretz/in the
> heavens and the earth.

"The primary thing is the revelation of God in the heavens and the earth." It is a simple statement, but its implications are deeply profound. When God gave us the Torah, a compendium of His will and wisdom, He provided an answer to our most fundamental question - what is the purpose of our lives - right in the opening words. **We are here to make the Creator known throughout His creation.**[14]

What does this mean? How exactly are we to reveal God in the heavens and the earth? Is it simply a matter of declaring "there is a God"? While such a statement and awareness is significant, and while there have always been those throughout history who have denied this reality, it hardly seems to be the sum total of our life's work and our very raison d'etre. Billions of people around the globe believe in God in some form or another and declare and demonstrate their allegiance daily. Can we say that each of us is fulfilling our personal mission and expressing the meaning of life simply by acknowledging God's existence or presence? Is believing in God the same as "revealing" Him? For that matter, is one "revealing" God simply by virtue of serving Him? In other words, is it possible that one can have faith in God, and beyond that s/he is

---

[14] See Kesser Shem Tov, Hosafos daled and hei

even dutifully devoted to fulfilling God's will to the best of her/his abilities, but s/he is still not "revealing" God and therefore not yet fulfilling the mission statement that is etched into the Torah's opening verse?

"The primary thing is the revelation of God in the heavens and the earth!"

How do we do that? What is He asking of us, and what can we do to fulfill it? How many of us are actually able to accomplish this "primary thing" for even a moment throughout the entirety of our lives? Most of us are not even aware that this is our purpose and directive. And now that we do know, what are we supposed to do to actualize it?

Seeing In The Dark

In order to "reveal" God, first we have to perceive Him. We must see God ourselves so that we can then disseminate the knowledge of Him around us. As we have been discussing, seeing God is no easy task, because He has, by design, not made it easy. The world we inhabit is a realm of darkness and concealment because otherwise we would be unable to exist. Yet He wants us to see through the darkness. He wants us to find Him where He is hiding. He wants us to divulge His presence under the shroud of His concealment, to unmask the blinding light that crouches silently and disguises itself in the shadows. In addition to embedding this mission statement in the opening verse of the Torah, God has also implanted this intention in the name of the nation to which He would give the Torah, Israel.

The name Israel, or "יִשְׂרָאֵל/Yisrael" in Hebrew, has many explanations. The most common and explicit is the way it is expounded by the angel who changes Jacob's name to Israel after the two have wrestled and Jacob has been victorious. As the story goes, Jacob is on his way back to the home of his parents after he has spent two decades abroad in order to distance himself from his murderous twin brother Esau. The night before he is to encounter Esau after all these years, he is visited by an angel who wrestles with him until dawn. Some say it is Esau's guardian angel, and others suggest it is Jacob's own angel who has come to test and strengthen him. As the sun begins to rise, the angel tries to return to the heavens, but Jacob refuses to release him until he will grant him a blessing. The blessing that the angel gives him is a new and holy name:

> וַיֹּאמֶר לֹא יַעֲקֹב יֵאָמֵר עוֹד שִׁמְךָ כִּי אִם־יִשְׂרָאֵל כִּי־שָׂרִיתָ
> עִם־אֱ-לֹהִים וְעִם־אֲנָשִׁים וַתּוּכָל׃
>
> *Vayomer lo Yaakov ye'amer od shimcha ki im Yisrael ki sarisa im E-lohim v'im anashim vatochal.*
>
> And (the angel) said, "It shall no longer be said that your name is Jacob, but rather Yisrael, for you have nobly contended with God and men and you have prevailed."
>
> (Genesis 32:29)

The name "יִשְׂרָאֵל/Yisrael" can be broken down into two words, "שׂר/sar," which connotes nobility and victory, and "א-ל/E-l," which is one of the names of God. Because Jacob struggled against the angel of God and was victorious, his name was changed to Yisrael, meaning "one who has wrestled victoriously with God." The "Children of Israel," Jacob's descendants, would wrestle with the divine throughout history, struggling to reconcile the physical and the spiritual, to understand the darkness and the light, to decipher God's intentions and overcome His tests and challenges. For this reason, "one who wrestles with God" is an appropriate name not only for Jacob, but for his progeny as well.

The Kli Yakar[15] provides an additional interpretation of the name Yisrael which applies more directly to our theme of finding and revealing God. Similar to the first explanation above, the Kli Yakar breaks the word down into its two component parts. But in this case, rather than "שׂר/sar" and "א-ל/E-l" as above, he renders it "שׁר/**shar**" and "א-ל/E-l." Because there are no grammatical markings in the Torah scroll, the second letter of the word can be read as a both a "שׁ/shin" (with the vowelized dot on the right side of the letter), which is pronounced "sh," and a "שׂ/sin," (with the vowelized dot on the left side of the letter), which is pronounced "s." While the angel translated the first segment of the word as "sar/wrestle" as discussed above, the Kli Yakar translates it as "shar,"

---

15 Torah commentary by the 16th century scholar and mystic Rabbi Shlomo Ephraim of Luntschitz

which means "to see." As such, the name Israel, according to the Kli Yakar, thus means "One who sees God."

Interestingly, the Kli Yakar further teaches that according to some opinions, the name of the angel that fought with Jacob was "סָמָאֵל/ Samael," which, according to Jewish mysticism, is the name of an angel otherwise known as "the satan." Though as explained in the first chapter, Torah does not believe in a devil that works against God's will, the concept of "satan" is derived from Torah sources and is a force created by God to provide an alternative option so that we can *choose* to do the divine will rather than being forced to accede to it by compulsion. As such, the satan is as much a part of God as everything else, and its ultimate will is that we should be strengthened by the challenges that it presents us. How does the satan challenge us? We see this through understanding its name, Samael. "סָמָאֵל/Samael" is a compound of the Hebrew word "סוּמָא/suma," which means "blind," and "א-ל/E-l", which, as we saw earlier, means God. As opposed to Yisrael, which means "one who sees God," Samael means "one who is blind to God." Satan/Samael is the force that tries to blind us to God's existence and presence.

The classical commentator Rashi points out that in the fight between Jacob and the angel Samael, the word for their struggle is "יֵאָבֵק/ ye'abek," which shares the same root as "אבק/avak" which means "dust." The Kli Yakar teaches that when Samael/satan struggles with us, he kicks dust up in our face in order to blind us and maintain our inability to see God's presence through the darkness. Furthermore, as the story continues, though he is unable to defeat Jacob, the angel reaches out and injures his thigh. Why is it Jacob's thigh specifically that the angel injures? Because, the Kli Yakar explains, the thigh represents concealment, the part of our body that we cover, as it says in the Talmud, "just as your thigh is hidden, so are the words of Torah hidden."[16]

From all of these details, we reinforce our new awareness that our mission is to see and reveal God. Simultaneously, we find that there are potent and persistent forces in the universe that will constantly battle us in order to keep us from fulfilling this mission. Yet with all this, we must remain cognizant of the fact that it is God Himself who created the darkness and our blindness. It is God who creates the environment in

---

[16] Sukkah 49

which it is difficult for us to see Him. It is He who sends His servant Samael to kick dust in our eyes, to injure our thigh, and to maintain our myopia. And yet He creates the nation of Israel as a force of vision and light in the darkness. He provides Israel the Torah, and instructs them to teach its wisdom to the other nations. In so doing, He provides us all the potential to be victorious over Samael, and to see what was heretofore invisible.

Double Darkness

We are now equipped with a distinct statement of our purpose - "the primary thing is to reveal God" - as well as some new insights into our nature and the nature of our reality. But in spite of the various clues that God provides us, the vast majority of us don't even realize that He has hidden Himself or that we are supposed to be seeking Him. This is because He is not only hidden, but furthermore, He has hidden His hiddenness. In other words, not only is God concealed, but He has concealed the fact that He has concealed Himself, and therefore many, if not most, of His creations are not even conscious of the fact that there is something that is missing.

This dynamic is alluded to near the end of the Torah in one of the final chapters of the book of Deuteronomy. God speaks to Moses before his death and informs him that he will soon pass from this world, and following his death the people will stray from the path he presented them and will worship the idols of their neighbors in the land. As we have seen before, it is known by God that the people will lose themselves in the confusion and distraction of the world. Even in the desert, where the divine presence was apparent daily in the provision of manna from heaven as well as other overt miracles, the people repeatedly erred and went astray. How much more so would they falter after Moses' passing and the cessation of the direct flow of divine transmission that Moses conveyed. As a result of the people's turning away from Him, God informs Moses, He will hide Himself from them.

וְאָנֹכִי הַסְתֵּר אַסְתִּיר פָּנַי בַּיּוֹם הַהוּא:

V'Anochi haster astir panai bayom hahu.
And I will hide My face on that day.
(Deuteronomy 31:18)

This is curious. Hasn't God just begun to reveal Himself to the people? After two millennia of complete concealment, He has identified Himself to Abraham, Isaac and Jacob, and then He has rescued their children from slavery and given them the Torah so that they can find Him and reveal Him throughout the creation. Furthermore, isn't their transgression (and all transgression) attributable to the fact that He has already hidden Himself too much? If He wanted their compliance and devotion, wouldn't it make sense to make Himself more apparent rather than less? Can He really blame them - and us - for turning to "other gods" when He has made it so difficult for us to detect Him in the darkness of this concealed realm? Why would He now decide to conceal Himself further?

What is also puzzling is the specific language of the Hebrew verse. It is simply translated as "I will hide my face," but the word for "hide," "אַסְתִּיר/astir," is repeated twice - "הַסְתֵּר אַסְתִּיר/haster astir" - so the literal reading is "I will hide hide my face." The common explanation for such repetition in Torah is that the word is doubled for emphasis, so the verse would read "I will certainly hide my face." But the mystics interpret the words more literally as, "I will *hide the hiding* of my face." With this reading, they identify a reference here to the primary existential quandary of this reality: not only is this world, "olam," founded on concealment, "helam," but this situation of concealment is itself concealed so that we are not even aware that the we are in the dark. We are so discombobulated that we have come to confuse the darkness for light, so blind that we don't even realize that we cannot see.

We might describe such a reality as a game of hide and seek where one player hides, but the others don't even know that they are playing, and therefore they don't look for him. Why would God create such a "game" in which the players are unaware that they are playing? We have already established why God hid himself, in order that we, and anything other, could exist. But why did He then choose to hide the very fact that He was hidden? Why make the darkness so dark that we don't even see our inability to see? Because, as we have established previously,[17] the darker the darkness, the greater will be the ensuing light. Therefore, with every glimmer of revelation, there is an increase of concealment that immediately follows. Yet within each of those glimmers resides the power and potential to overcome the darkness, as we find in the subsequent verses of this same conversation between God and Moses. Immediately after informing Moses that He is going to hide His face, God continues:

וְעַתָּה כִּתְבוּ לָכֶם אֶת־הַשִּׁירָה הַזֹּאת וְלַמְּדָהּ אֶת־בְּנֵי־יִשְׂרָאֵל
שִׂימָהּ בְּפִיהֶם לְמַעַן תִּהְיֶה־לִּי הַשִּׁירָה הַזֹּאת לְעֵד בִּבְנֵי יִשְׂרָאֵל:

V'atta kisvu lachem es hashira hazos v'lamda es bnei Yisrael
sima b'fihem l'maan tih'yeh li hashira hazos l'eid bivnei Yisrael.

And now, write for yourselves this song, and teach it to
the Children of Israel. Place it into their mouths, in order that this song will be for Me as a witness for the
children of Israel.

(Deuteronomy 31:19)

Now, God tells Moses, in order to combat the darkness that is ahead, teach the children of Israel to sing these words of my Torah. There will be darkness, God informs us, and this darkness will be so thick and so disorienting that we will be unable to recognize that we are in the dark at all. But there will always be a light, a remembrance, a song that is heard by our ears even when our eyes fail us and prove completely unreliable. Many will forget the song - either they will tune it out intentionally or lose it beneath the clamor of their appetites and distractions. But as God continues to assure Moses:

וְהָיָה כִּי־תִמְצֶאןָ אֹתוֹ רָעוֹת רַבּוֹת וְצָרוֹת וְעָנְתָה הַשִּׁירָה
הַזֹּאת לְפָנָיו לְעֵד כִּי לֹא תִשָּׁכַח מִפִּי זַרְעוֹ:

V'haya ki timtzena oso raos rabos v'tzaros v'ansa hashira
hazos lefanav l'eid ki lo tishachach mipi zaro.

It will be, when they will encounter many evils and
troubles, this song will bear witness before them, for it
will not be forgotten from the mouth of their offspring.

(Deuteronomy 31:21)

---

[17] In the section "Night and Then Day"

There will always be those, God promises us, few and scattered among the nations, who hum in the shadows and remind us that it is not too dark to see that we are in the dark. In other words, God has not hidden Himself completely. He has given us a lantern to penetrate the doubled and redoubled darkness. He has given us a song to guide us audibly and spiritually when our more external senses fail. He has given us a job to do, to find what has been lost, to remind those who have forgotten, to forge headlong through the gloom.

The first step then is to know that we are supposed to be looking for something. Before we can reveal what has been hidden, first we must reveal that there is something to reveal. Once we do that, then we can begin to search. And once we begin to search, only then can we find what we are looking for. If we are not looking, we will certainly never find it. Not only don't we know where to look, we don't know what we're looking for, and we don't know that we are lacking, and therefore looking, at all.

Most of us have some sense that we are missing something, some nagging sensation of emptiness deep within us. There is a void, a yearning, a thirst, but we don't know how to fill or slake it. So we try to ignore it. We distract ourselves with every manner of entertainment and diversion. Or we attempt to numb or drown our emptiness with substances, chemicals, or other addictions that may temporarily mitigate our angst, but which can never fully eradicate it. This is the darkness that conceals the darkness. The only solution is to admit and confront the presence of absence within us. There is something missing. I am deficient of something. That is not a defect or a shortcoming, it is the nature of the human condition. I need not panic in response to my lack. I needn't try desperately to deny and disown it. I am not abnormal or defective. On the contrary, it is how I and all of us were created. There is no one whole, but there is, rather, a hole within each of us. Our lifelong task is to fill it, but first we must acknowledge it is there.

Obligatory Happiness

Once we have established that we are intentionally lost and that God is intentionally hidden, once we have recognized that our task is to reveal Him and simultaneously find ourselves, once we have begun to understand the purpose of the darkness and our ability to see through it and eventually transform it, now we are just about ready to set out to fulfill our mission. But there is one thing more that we will need before we go. That is "שִׂמְחָה/simcha/joy." Without joy, we will surely fail. This is because joy is not simply a tool that will assist us along the path, nor is it the prize that awaits us at the end of the path, but rather joy is the path itself. Those who believe that they will only find happiness when they have traversed and transcended the darkness will forever find themselves in the dark. It is the ability to sense and experience joy *within* the darkness that will lead one where s/he needs to go.

As we quoted earlier,[18] in Psalms we are instructed "Ivdu es Hashem b'simcha - serve God with joy."[19] This is not a suggestion or an encouraging piece of advice, as if to say we must serve God anyway, so we may as well try to enjoy it. It's not even a blessing, assuring us that if we serve God, it will be with joy - the proof of this is that there are plenty who believe that they are serving God, and they may in fact be fulfilling His commandments diligently, but they are not joyful. "Serve God with joy" is a directive and an obligation. It is a principle that informs us that it is only through simcha/joy that we can serve God truly.

This is displayed in the book of Deuteronomy when Moses delivers to the people what is referred to as the "תּוֹכָחָה/tochacha/rebuke," a long list of "curses" that will befall them in the future if they do not pursue the proper path. This path that must be followed is not merely, as one may think, the fulfillment of God's commandments. Moses declares:

וּבָאוּ עָלֶיךָ כָּל-הַקְּלָלוֹת הָאֵלֶּה ... תַּחַת אֲשֶׁר לֹא-עָבַדְתָּ
אֶת-יְ-הֹוָה אֱ-לֹהֶיךָ בְּשִׂמְחָה וּבְטוּב לֵבָב מֵרֹב כֹּל:

---

[18] in the section "Singing in the Dark"

[19] Psalms 100:2

U'va'u alecha kol haklalos ha'eileh ... tachas asher lo avadta es A-donai E-lohecha b'simcha u'v'tuv leivav me'rov kol.
All of these curses will befall you ... because you did not serve the Lord, your God, with happiness and with gladness of heart, when [you had an] abundance of everything.

(Deuteronomy 28:45-47)

The mystics note that it does not say that the curses will be the consequence of failing to serve God, but rather failing to serve God **"with happiness and gladness of heart."** The implication here is astonishing: if one were to serve God fastidiously, to perform all of His positive commandments and to abstain from all of His prohibitions, yet s/he did so without joy, either begrudgingly or even simply by rote with no emotion whatsoever, then s/he is liable to the strict consequences that Moses has previously enumerated. We see from this that if we desire to pursue the path that God provides us, we must "ivdu es Hashem b'simcha/serve God with joy," for this is the only way to truly serve Him at all.

But this presents us a quandary. How can we be joyful in the dark? Even if we understand that God creates the darkness, and even if we are aware that it is only temporary, how are we expected to maintain happiness when we are lost and dwelling in a place of confusion and conflict?!

Perhaps if we were commanded to serve God with *hope*, it may be easier to understand and fulfill. Hope itself is not easy to maintain when we are presented with challenges and difficulties, but a consciousness of the big picture and the ultimate end-game can enable us to remain calm and confident even in the most trying circumstances. This is what we discussed earlier in quoting Nietzche's insight that "he who has a why to live for can bear with almost any how." Yet "bearing with" adverse conditions is certainly not the same as being joyful. Tolerating struggles is quite different from "serving with simcha/joy." It is the difference between surviving and thriving. We are not meant to merely survive or abide the darkness, we are commanded to rejoice within it, and this is the only way that it will be transformed.

How can we possibly do so?

The Joy Of The Search

True and lasting happiness is not an emotion, it is a practice. It is not something that happens to you, but something that you must sow and cultivate constantly. Moments of joy may be happened upon, but if so they are fleeting and unreliable. In order to maintain happiness, to "serve God with simcha," one must exercise joy and develop the proper "muscles" to grasp and hold onto it.

Every "מִצְוָה/mitzvah/commandment" is a practice. Torah is not simply a book of philosophy or a system of faith, it is a series of actions and meditations that enable one to develop her/his inner vision and thus ultimately fulfill the task of revealing God. One of the most essential and powerful components of the practice is prayer. Three prayer services a day invite one to step away from the facade of the physical world and to reconnect to the reality that is hidden beneath.

At the beginning of the morning prayer service, which is performed at the dawn of the new day before engaging in any other activities, one recites a prayer called "הוֹדוּ/Hodu." The third verse of this prayer reads:

יִשְׂמַח לֵב מְבַקְשֵׁי יְ-הֹוָה:
Yismach leiv m'vakshei A-donai.
Happy of heart is the one who seeks God.
(Psalms 105:3)

This statement is puzzling. Why is one happy if s/he is looking for something? If s/he is seeking it, then this means that s/he has not found it, so why would s/he be happy? Seemingly, it would make more sense if it read 'happy is the one who *finds* God.' But the one who is looking, who looks daily and constantly but does not find what s/he seeks, wouldn't s/he be more inclined to be frustrated or anxious rather than happy? We might say that such a person is passionate, or driven, or hopeful even, but why happy? Are we happy when we lack what we seek, or is it when we achieve our goal that we are truly joyous?

The message here is powerful, and it is placed at the beginning of the daily service because it is essential for one to remind her/himself of it as s/he sets out anew each morning: Joy is not merely in the achievement, but in the pursuit. It is not only in the reward, but in the attempt. It is not primarily in the afterlife, but in the lifelong exertion and toil, as the sages teach, "a single moment of repentance and good deeds in this world is greater than all of the world to come."[20] Why is this so?

We might understand how unrewarded labor is "great" from God's perspective, greater even than all of the rewards in the world to come, because such service is unselfish and altruistic. From God's perspective this type of commitment and perseverance may be praiseworthy and precious. But where is the joy for the one who must toil in the dark day after day? How can we truly say that "happy of heart is the one who seeks God?" The verse does not say that joy is brought to God by the one who seeks daily, but rather that the seeker's own heart is happy. What is the source of this seemingly unreasonable happiness?

It is the knowledge that that which one seeks is there to be found! One is happy when s/he believes wholeheartedly that s/he can find what s/he is searching for, and that s/he is on the right path. S/he sings in the dark because though s/he may be lost, though s/he has not yet discovered what s/he is after, s/he knows that it is close and that there is nothing that can ultimately keep her/him from it. S/he is happy because s/he knows that s/he was made to search, that this is precisely what s/he was placed in this realm of darkness to do.

Unhappiness is not the result of our goal being as yet unfulfilled. Unhappiness is the abandonment of the search, the resignation and despair that come when we convince ourselves that we will never find what we are after and we decide to try no more. God does not exist, we determine, or perhaps He is out there somewhere but I do not have the strength, wisdom, or wherewithal to find Him. The moment we give up, any joy we knew is gone. Further, this surrender will lead to a sense of failure and a deeper melancholy that stems from the sense that I am not good, I am not doing what I should be doing, I am not being what I should be. Unhappiness is guilt and shame, self-judgment and self-loathing.

---

20 Pirkei Avos 4:17

Happiness, on the contrary, is the sense that "this too is for the best"[21] - that the world, with all its imperfection, is just as it was created to be, and I, with all my imperfections, am just as I was created to be. I was created imperfect. I was placed into an "olam/world" of "helam/concealment." That is nothing to be ashamed of, and nothing to be afraid of. The darkness is not frightening, it is God hiding Himself because He wants me to exist so that He can give to me. He wants me to seek Him and find Him and reveal Him, and He created me with the ability to do so. He will not make it easy, because ease is not love. Ease will keep one small and feeble, while challenge will give one strength and confidence and dignity. Challenge provides the fortitude to withstand the darkness and find what we are looking for.

To have happiness in the darkness thus requires one to be strong, but one must be gentle simultaneously. We must be confident, but not cocky, and not critical. We must persevere, but we must be limber and agile and not hard. We will fall in the darkness - it is the nature of being unable to see clearly. If we are hard when we fall, we will break. If we walk gently and lightly, we will roll when we tumble. We may get bruises and scrapes along the way, but we will not break or crumble. We will smile at the obstacles rather than cursing them. We will laugh at our clumsiness rather than rage at our imperfection. God did not create us flawless, and He did not give us perfect vision or a clear, unobstructed path. We trip, and then we chuckle and get up - I see what you did there God, that was a good one. We learn, we grow, we proceed gently and carefully and gradually. We become patient, as we learn that God is patient. This is fine, this is progress, this is all He asks of us.

"Yismach lev m'vakshei Hashem" - happy is the one who seeks Him. We know that we may be forever seeking - as the subsequent verse of the "Hodu" prayer says, "bakshu panav tamid/seek His face always" - and that is okay, as that is what we were created to do. As long as we understand our purpose and we pursue it, as long as we recognize the root of our challenges and see the darkness itself as a condition for our existence and a precursor for the ultimate light, we will sing with joy as we venture into the unknown.

---

[21] "גַם זוּ לְטוֹבָה/Gam zu l'tova/this too is for the best" was the mantra of Nachum Ish Gam Zu, a first century Tanna and teacher of Rabbi Akiva.

On an even deeper level, the one who seeks God in the darkness is joyous because s/he knows a secret that those who believe that God is only to be found in the light do not know. S/he knows from the "Shema" prayer that, as we discussed earlier,[22] God is One, the one and only. Therefore, s/he recognizes that the darkness is God as much as the light is, and so no matter how dark it gets, God is always present and there is nothing to fear. This is what King David expressed in Psalms:

וָאֹמַר אַךְ-חֹשֶׁךְ יְשׁוּפֵנִי וְלַיְלָה אוֹר בַּעֲדֵנִי גַּם-חֹשֶׁךְ
לֹא-יַחְשִׁיךְ מִמֶּךָ וְלַיְלָה כַּיּוֹם יָאִיר כַּחֲשֵׁיכָה כָּאוֹרָה:

Vayomer ach choshech yeshupheini va'lyla ohr ba'adeini gam choshech lo yachshich mimecha va'lyla kayom yair ka'chashe-icha ka'ohra.

If I say, surely the darkness shall cover me, the light shall be night about me. Even the darkness is not dark for you; but the night shines like the day; darkness is as light with you.

(Psalms 139:11-12)

If we believe in the darkness, if we fear it and fail to recognize that it has no true existence other than its function in God's will to conceal the truth of His oneness so that we are able to exist, then even the light itself will be like night. In other words, if we don't recognize God's oneness and His presence in every single aspect of creation, then we will feel constantly anxious and alone because life itself will be devoid of sense and meaning and purpose. When, however, we recognize that the darkness is not truly dark, but rather it is only a place where Godliness is temporarily concealed, then the night itself will shine like day. With such consciousness, there is only joy.

Of course, this raises another question, which is that if one has already accomplished this level of awareness and joyousness, then has s/he not already found what s/he is seeking? If one knows that God is One and everywhere, then why is s/he referred to as "m'vakshei Hashem/ one who seeks God" when s/he already seems to know where God is? Furthermore, if s/he is happy, then what else does s/he need - after all, isn't happiness the goal?

---

22 In section "The Only One"

What we will understand from this is that, as mentioned previously, happiness is not the goal but the path to get there, and recognizing God's omnipresence is not the mission, but rather revealing it is. "Breishis bara E-lohim es hashamayim v'es haaretz" - the primary task is to REVEAL God in the heavens and the earth, not simply to be aware of His presence and oneness, but to make it apparent, visible, and undeniable. Consciousness of God's unity and the joyfulness that this engenders are prerequisites for the task at hand. Equipped with these, we are ready to set out, confident that, with divine intention and assistance, we will find what we have lost. We will rediscover ourselves and our Creator, and we will make them manifest and evident for all.

Chapter 3: GETTING FOUND

Exile

We are on our way. But which way are we supposed to go?

We have established that our task is to find and reveal what has been hidden, but now we must determine where we are supposed to look. If we are here to reveal God, we need to know where He hid Himself. Furthermore, we realized at the very outset that we, ourselves, are lost. How can we find anything else, if we do not even know how to locate ourselves? As it turns out, this is not a problem. The first step in getting found is recognizing that you are lost, even if, and especially if, you feel that you are at home.

The Torah begins with exile and ends on the doorstep of a homeland with the promise of exile's end. On the first day of our creation, we were expelled from the garden, and throughout our history, we have wandered and waited for the day when we will be able to return home. The very first communication that the Torah records between God and Abraham, the first Hebrew, is a commandment to leave his home.

וַיֹּאמֶר יְ-הוָה אֶל־אַבְרָם לֶךְ־לְךָ מֵאַרְצְךָ וּמִמּוֹלַדְתְּךָ וּמִבֵּית
אָבִיךָ אֶל־הָאָרֶץ אֲשֶׁר אַרְאֶךָּ:

*Vayomer A-donai el Avram lech lecha me'artzecha u'mi'mo-
ladetecha u'mi'beis avicha el ha'aretz asher areka.*

And the Lord said to Abram, 'Go forth from your land
and from your birthplace and from your father's house,
to the land that I will show you.

(Genesis 12:1)

Like his first forebears, Adam and Eve, Abraham's journey begins by being sent away. The primary condition of a relationship with
God seems to be displacement. Why?

Abraham would settle in the land of Canaan and raise his son
Isaac there. Isaac would live his entire life in his birthplace, but his son
Jacob would be forced to flee from Canaan to escape the murderous
wrath of his brother Esau. He would return decades later, but his son,
Joseph, would be sold by his brothers into slavery in Egypt. Later the
entire clan would be forced by famine to relocate to Egypt, and this
would mark the beginning of the exile that would stretch throughout the
vast majority of the Torah. Subsequent to the events recorded in the five
books of Moses, the young Jewish nation would enter the land of Israel,
where they would live for roughly a millennium before the brief Baby-
lonian exile, and then another half millennium before the Roman exile
which has left them wandering throughout the ensuing two thousand
years.

The fact that exile is such a central theme and trope in Torah is
no coincidence. It has been remarked by scholars and luminaries
throughout the ages that one of the most miraculous aspects of Jewish
history is the survival and longevity of this people living without a land.
For thousands of years, the Jewish nation has dwelled without a nation-
state, scattered and dispersed throughout the lands of others. More often
than not, it has been among others who are less than welcoming and
hardly tolerant. How is it possible that this tiny people, only a fraction of
a percent of the global population, has survived without a home to call
their own and a place where they can gather and huddle together? Can
we identify any other people that has similarly survived the millennia in
kingdoms around the globe that have tried to kill or convert them? The
empires and global superpowers have come and gone - Egypt, Babylo-

nia, Rome, Greece, Germany, Russia - but the small people that they enslaved or sought to eradicate continues to endure.

The 'how' of such a reality is mysterious and wondrous, but the 'why' of this dynamic is explained by what we have been discussing until now. Exile is the natural state of this 'olam', this world of hiddenness, that we inhabit. We have been exiled from paradise, alienated from the truth of who and what we are. We are never "home" in this world because this is not where we are from, it is not our origin or our destination. Wherever we may find ourselves, we are simply passing through, dwelling temporarily. We are looking for something, and as long as we do not find it, we are not settled or at ease. We cannot rest as long as we remain lost, and we are always lost because that is the very nature of this world that we inhabit.

The exiled "Jew" is aware constantly that s/he is *in* the world, but not *of* the world. This is not our true home. This exile appears to be a curse, but in fact it is a blessing. It keeps us from being comfortable here, from mistaking this for our proper habitat or environment. It reminds us that we have something to do, that we need to expose the truth behind the ruse. Those who are comfortable and "well-adjusted" in this false reality are not healthier or better off - they have actually bought into the lie. They have accepted, and adapted to, life in prison. The hiddenness is hidden from them, as we discussed earlier. This is far worse than if one feels the discomfort of being lost and therefore strives always to be found.

In examining that first instruction which God communicated to the first Jew - "Go forth from your land and from your birthplace and from your father's house, to the land that I will show you" - the Chassidic masters[23] identify the blessing that is hidden within this expulsion. "Go forth" is a translation of the Hebrew words "לֶךְ לְךָ/lech lecha," which literally mean "go to you." If God wanted simply to direct Abraham to go from his home, He could have more succinctly stated "לֶךְ מֵאַרְצֶךָ/lech me'artzecha /go from your land." The additional word, "lech *lecha* me'artzecha," can be translated the same way, but the sages teach that there is nothing superfluous in the Torah. Even the inclusion or exclusion of mere letters signify hints or allusions to profound additional insights. Therefore, an additional word is no accident or coincidence.

23 See *Likkutei Sichos*, parshas Lech Lecha by Rabbi Menachem M. Schneerson, the Lubavitcher Rebbe

"Go *to you* from your land" is God's intimation to Abraham, and to all of us after him, that exile is the first step in the quest that He has assigned us. You will not find yourself without leaving where you are comfortable, He tells us. Get up and begin the journey. You have to find yourself, and you have a long way to travel to do so.

Just as the verse begins with hidden guidance, so does it conclude. Where is it that we are going when we leave where we began? At first glance, the verse seems to leave that answer vague and unidentified - "to the land that I will show you." But once again, the Chassidic masters note that the Hebrew contains an allusion that provides us a deeper answer and a greater certainty. The final word, "אַרְאֶךָ," means "I will show you." In the simple translation, this modifies the previous word, so that we understand it to indicate that what God will show us is the land. However, the word can also be read by itself, as "I will show *you*" - not that I/God will show something else (the land) *to* you, but that the thing that I/God will show *is* you. The verse thus informs us that when we leave our place of origin and comfort, when we undertake the journey that God assigns us and we follow the way He designates, He will ultimately lead us to find precisely what we have been seeking all along - ourselves.

"Where are you," God had asked Adam at the very beginning of creation. For two thousand years, Adam's children remained lost and misguided. And then one of his descendants discovered the One and only God in an environment where all of his peers were worshiping any idol they could get their hands on. To this man, Abraham, God provided the beginning of the answer to the question that He had posed to his first ancestor. 'This world is a realm of concealment,' He told Abraham. 'From the very first days, humankind has been lost. But rise up and follow me, and I will take you from your exile to the place where you will be found.'

Where is this "land" where we will be found? Where is it that God is leading us? We have been wandering for millennia, and we still haven't found it. It is not on any atlas or map. It is nowhere that we can visit by plane, or boat, or any other means of transportation. It is not above us or below us, nor is it someplace foreign or exotic. It is not in the heavens and not across any sea. There is only one direction that will take us to God's land and to the ultimate 'you' that is hidden there.

That direction is *within*!

Inward Bound

It is no secret that if we want to find ourselves, we must look within. We have heard this from any number of teachers, spiritual guides, therapists, and healers from a diversity of backgrounds and ideologies. Over 3,300 years old, Torah has been directing us inward throughout the millennia. The Jewish nation's exile, enslavement, wandering, and longing to return home is one sweeping allegory for the existential dilemma of losing our connection to our essence, and our history-spanning effort to reconnect. As mentioned earlier, our first progenitors, Adam and Eve, were originally in perfect communion with their interior - so much so that their skin was translucent and there was nothing that separated their inner essence from their outer reality. With their eating of the apple, however, they grew opaque, they were subsequently exiled from the garden, and we have been looking for our true selves ever since.

The central Torah concept and practice of "תְּשׁוּבָה/teshuvah" reflects this constant movement back and inward. Commonly translated as "repentance," "teshuvah" literally means "return." Throughout our lives, we are working perpetually on this process of getting back in sync, or returning to our original state of purity and integrity. We have lost our bearing and our center. Our goal is not to find new uncharted ground, but to go back to the place and state from where we came. Our actualization comes not from becoming something different and better, but rather from simply getting back to, and manifesting, what we were created and intended to be.

"שַׁבָּת/Shabbat/the sabbath," which is the pinnacle of the week and a focal point of Torah time in general, is closely aligned with this concept of "teshuvah/return." The Hebrew words "תְּשׁוּבָה/teSHuVah" and "שַׁבָּת/SHaBbat" share the same root, "שׁ-ב/SH-V," which means "return."[24] The sabbath is the day when one is to cease all worldly labor and activity in order to relinquish her/his focus on the external reality

---

[24] In Hebrew, the letter ב is sometimes 'b' and sometimes 'v' depending on its attending vowel.

and redirect consciousness on her/his inner essence. This allows one to reconnect to her/his truer self, and then venture out into the workweek once again when the sabbath ends.

Because one day a week is not enough time to strengthen and maintain this consciousness, Jews pray three times daily. The Hebrew word "תְּפִילָה/tefilla" is commonly translated as "prayer," but the Chassidic sages[25] teach that its deeper meaning is "union" or "bond."[26] Torah prayer is not primarily about requesting one's needs, but rather about re-unifying one's being. The daily prayer services are, like the sabbath is to the workdays, opportunities to step off the spinning wheel of our mundane reality and remind oneself of one's more infinite potential. Furthermore, the entire system of 613 mitzvos, which create the backbone of Torah life and practice, is similarly predicated on this idea of reunification. Commonly translated as "commandment," the word "מִצְוָה/mitzvah," according to the mystics, is derived from the Aramaic word "צוותה/tzavsa," meaning "bond." Every one of the daily actions and prohibitions included in the 613 mitzvos that comprise Torah law - from the most global like "Thou shalt not kill" to the most picayune like washing hands before eating bread - is intended to reorient one to the awareness of, and attachment to, the soul which resides within her/him.

Torah practice is thus an attempt to reconnect, re-bond, and re-unify one's experience so s/he is not divided from her/his inner essence and cut off from who and what s/he truly is. Yet in spite of this ancient wisdom that counsels us to turn within, and in spite of a variety of more modern and popular wisdoms that echo this biblical call, this has not discouraged many of us from seeking satisfaction and relief everywhere except inside of us. We look to entertainment, to money and material gain, to fame and other markers of societal recognition, to gluttony and various forms of intoxication. This is perhaps because, as we discussed earlier, what we sense inside of us is a void, an emptiness, and we believe that the only way to fill it is to bring something in from outside of us. To compound our confusion, we have been taught to pursue material pleasure and distraction by a society that profits from personal dissatisfaction and external gratification. Furthermore, the interior search is de-

---

[25] *Likkutei Sichos*, Vol. II, pp. 409-411)

[26] See also Rashi on Genesis 30:8.

manding, requiring discipline, commitment and hard work, while indulgence and inebriation, on the contrary, are easy and quick.

Yet "deep down inside" we know that none of these diversions will work. Sooner or later, we will conclude that all of these schemes and strategies to quell our inner longing with something external will only increase the void. And then we will begin to look inside. When we do, what will we find there? With hard work, and a good guide, we will find what we have been looking for - ourself. But that's not all. Torah teaches that we will find far more. We will find, in the deepest recesses of our being, that the self that we were missing is very different from, and infinitely greater than, what we thought it was. A tremendous surprise is awaiting us!

The Face Within You

So what's in there?

What is it that we will find in that most inward place? We can call it our self, our essence, our core, our inner spark - but none of those terms help us to understand what it is. Religiously, we can refer to it as our soul, but what is a soul? In Hebrew, there are numerous words for soul: "נֶפֶש/nefesh," "רוּחַ/ruach," "נְשָׁמָה/neshama," "חַיָּה/chaya," and "יְחִידָה/yechida." We might wonder why there is such a variety of different expressions for the same thing. The anthropologist Franz Boas studied the Inuit people of Alaska in the late nineteenth century and discovered that the eskimos have dozens of names for snow. This is because they identified many different types of snow - dry powdery snow, wet slushy snow, hard icy snow, just to name a few - and when something is such an integral part of your existence, you learn to differentiate between its various forms. In Torah, the soul is like snow to the eskimo - it is not something that one encounters only occasionally, but rather one lives with it and interacts with it every moment. It is not simply a detail of our existence, it is rather the very crux of it. We are not merely beings with souls, but it is our souls that make us beings. There is no existence without the soul, and there is nothing that exists that does not have a soul of some form or other. Even inert matter, like stone or mineral, has a soul according to Torah. The soul is the spark of vitality that enables the creation to be.

The various names for the soul refer to its different aspects, functions, and manifestations. For example, the "nefesh" level of the soul manages physical action, while "ruach" guides one's emotional makeup, and "neshama" regulates intellect. Yet while this informs us, to some extent at least, what the soul *does*, it still does not tell us what it *is*. The soul governs us, and even more than that, it vitalizes us, gives us existence, and underlies everything that is. But where does it come from, what comprises it, and, perhaps most pertinent to our line of inquiry, how are we to identify it and reunite with it, particularly if we have no clear idea what it is that we are seeking?

To complicate matters further, we seem to be ignoring an apparent contradiction that makes our search all the more confounding. On the one hand, we are instructed "Lech lecha/go to yourself," which seems to indicate that the object of our investigation is our self, which we have otherwise identified as our soul. On the other hand, we have established earlier that our fundamental mission is "bara E-lohim," to reveal God. So which is it? Is our search directed at finding ourselves, or at finding God? If we are looking within, we would seem more likely to find ourselves. But is this search not distracting us from the larger objective that we are responsible for, which is finding and revealing God?

A verse from Psalms will help us to resolve this confusion and identify the ultimate target of our search:

לְךָ אָמַר לִבִּי בַּקְּשׁוּ פָנָי אֶת־פָּנֶיךָ יְ-הֹוָה אֲבַקֵּשׁ:

Lecha amar libi, bakshu panai, es panecha A-donai avakeish.
On Your behalf, my heart says, "seek my face." Your
face, O Lord, I will seek.
(Psalms 27:8)

This verse, like all of the verses of Psalms, is poetic, somewhat cryptic, and open to a variety of interpretations. Written by King David, and expressed by each of us who recites it, the verse addresses God and informs Him that our heart speaks to us on His behalf. There is a voice from deep within us, in other words, that speaks for God and instructs us to "seek My face." What is unclear, however, is whose face we are to seek - does "my face" refer to God's face or to our own? If the voice is ours, emanating from our heart, and it urges us to seek "my" face, then it seems to be our own face that is to be sought. If, however, the voice is speaking on God's behalf, as the beginning of the verse indicates, then "my" face may in fact be referring to the face of God. However, the voice may also be speaking on God's behalf and expressing His desire that we should seek our own face. Some clarity is provided by the second half of the verse, which indicates "Your face, O Lord, I will seek." Yet we are left with a question of which and whose face the first part of the verse refers to.

Before we can answer this question, we must understand what is meant by the word "face." What is this "face" that we are seeking, whether it is God's or our own? Can it be said that God has a face? And if it is referring to our own face, then why does it need to be sought when it is plainly visible, and all we need to do is look in a mirror? However, as we explained earlier in the first section of chapter one, the Hebrew word "פנים/PaNiM/face" is closely related to the word "פנימיות/PNiMyus/inwardness," and refers not only to one's physical visage, but also to one's innermost essence. While there would seem to be a great distance and difference between one's face (her/his outermost and most superficial attribute) and one's soul (her/his innermost core), we have explained earlier that they are ultimately supposed to be perfectly attuned and aligned. It is only on account of the "hiddenness/helam" of this "world/olam," that they are alienated from one another. And this is what the voice of our heart is telling us in this verse on God's behalf - that our task in the darkness of this world is to find the "Panim/face" that we have lost. That face is obviously not the one that stares back at us in the mirror, but rather our true face, our deepest inwardness, the "face" of our soul.

The first part of the verse thus declares "On Your behalf, God, my heart tells me to seek **my own** face," my own self and soul, from which I have become disconnected and lost. But if so, then why does the second half of the verse say that it is "**Your** face," God's face, that we are to pursue? The verse thus presents us with the seeming contradiction that we have noted above. We are instructed to seek our self, as God's instruction to Abraham, "lech lecha," denotes. But we are informed in the very first line of the entire Torah, "breishis bara E-lohim," that our fundamental mission statement is to seek and reveal God. Which is it, and how are we to focus on one when we are distracted by the other?

In his work *Tanya*, the Chassidic master Schneur Zalman of Lia-di,[27] also known as the Alter Rebbe, reveals the profound esoteric secret hidden in this verse of Psalms. Within our innermost interior, we will find not only our own soul, but we will discover what constitutes that soul:

נִיצוֹץ אֱלֹקוּת שֶׁבְּכָל נֶפֶשׁ מִיִּשְׂרָאֵל.

Nitzot Elokus she'bchol nefesh Yisroel.
A spark of God that is in every soul of Israel.
(Tanya, Igeres Hakodesh, Igeres 4)

The foundation of our soul, the Alter Rebbe informs us, is a portion of God that He has concealed within us. *We, and every component of our physical universe, are sparks of God that have been hidden within a material exterior in order to create a realm of multiplicity.* As we discussed in chapter two, God desires such multiplicity, and therefore He masks these fragments of Himself a) so that He can express His infinite nature to give, and b) because the light that is revealed subsequent to darkness is far more brilliant than the original light itself.

With this remarkable insight from the Alter Rebbe - that the soul is a veritable spark of God - we have answered several of our questions at once. We have asked what is the soul that we are seeking? We have simultaneously wrestled with the seeming conflict of goals and instructions: is it our own soul that we are to be looking for, or are we to focus our search on the discovery of God? Whose "face" is it that the voice of our soul directs us to seek, and how can we find either if our intention is unclear? Finally, we understand that the direction of our search is certain, and the goal of our search is not ambiguous or multiple. To find what we are after, we must move inward. And when we penetrate, with endless persistence and devotion, to our innermost interior, we will find our soul. And when we plumb the deepest depths of our soul, we will find not only our own face, but ultimately, the very face of God!

---

[27] Founder and first Rebbe of the Chabad-Lubavitch system of Chasidic philosophy in Russia. 1745-1812

The first portion of King David's verse, "Bakshu panai/seek *my* face," and the second portion of the verse, "es panecha A-donai avakeish/ *Your* face God I will seek," are not conflicting or confounding, because they are phases of the same search and aspects of the same reality. "Lech lecha/go to yourself," and "Breishis bara Elokim/the primary thing is to reveal God," are not contradictory instructions because our essential self and God are not distinct or separate, they are One!

The face of God is within you! It is your own inwardness and your deepest self!

———— ◆ ————

In Me?!

Where are you?

It was the first question with which we opened this book, and the first question - "ayecha" - that God asks Adam and Eve, and through them all of their descendants. It is the invitation with which He beckons us to seek and find what has been lost or hidden. We know now what we are looking for, and we know now where to begin our search. What we have lost is the awareness of what we are. What we are is pure Godliness that has been concealed and disguised. What we must do is uncover that reality. Where we must go is deep within ourselves to find the face of God so that we can allow it to be revealed.

Knowing that God's face is within us does far more than provide us a direction for our search. It also informs us of our fundamental nature and our inherent worth. It compels us to confront the reality that we are intrinsically Godly. It inspires us to express our infinite potential. It fortifies us with the ability to overcome all challenges. It reminds us that we are good even when we feel or act bad, and thus allows us to be better versions of ourselves than what we become when we forget our intrinsic greatness.

This is an extraordinary and intensely uplifting notion with tremendous ramifications which we will explore throughout the remainder of this book. But before doing so, it is important to admit that it is also an audacious claim that some may find uncomfortable or even objectionable. Reluctance to accepting such an idea may be predicated on a variety of considerations. The first may be the perceived burden that it confers - if I am Godly, then must I be perfect? What kind of limitations and restrictions does this inherent divinity impose on me, and what if I don't want the responsibility of such a lofty potential?

This type of rejection of divine potential and the personal accountability it demands has existed throughout the ages. But it was institutionalized in "The Enlightenment" of the 18th and 19th centuries when Reason and Rationality challenged notions of faith and intuition and cast doubt on all forms of mystic wisdom that could not be empirically demonstrated and proven. Great advancements resulted from the Age of Reason, but great losses were also incurred as the focus on physical and external experience and phenomena gained precedence over the spiritual and internal. The desire to rid oneself of the onus of godliness can be witnessed in a very frank admission by the novelist and philosopher Aldous Huxley. Grandson of Thomas Huxley, who was one of the original proponents of evolutionary theory and was known as "Darwin's bulldog," Aldous Huxley confessed that those who developed scientific and evolutionary theory were intentionally trying to find a way to rationalize and normalize their baser instincts.

> "I had motive for not wanting the world to have a meaning; consequently assumed that it had none, and was able without any difficulty to find satisfying reasons for this assumption. The philosopher who finds no meaning in the world is not concerned exclusively with a problem in pure metaphysics, he is also concerned to prove that there is no valid reason why he personally should not do as he wants to do, or why his friends should not seize political power and govern in the way that they find most advantageous to themselves. ... For myself, the philosophy of meaninglessness was essentially an instrument of liberation, sexual and political." (Huxley, A., *Ends and Means*, 1937, pp. 270 ff.)

By denying one's divine origin and essence through tracing one's roots to primitive creatures, one can view himself as an animal in order to justify and permit his egoistic and animalistic impulses. The prevailing view of the human's relationship to God had grown onerous, and armed with the demonstrable rigor of science, many were glad to dispatch the superstitious foolishness of faith and liberate themselves from the morality and virtue that it inspired. A century and a half later, generations have been raised on humanism, skepticism, and personal emancipation. So the idea of God in general, and in particular of God existing within us and expressing Himself through us, may understandably feel foreign and oppressive for some at first. Yet the desire to be Godless, or the inculcation of Godlessness, do not make it so. The sources cited so far, as well as those that are to be explored further on, offer an alternative understanding of what we are, and of what we are capable of being if and when we become cognizant of the truth that is hidden within us.

Resistance to the notion of inner Godliness may alternatively be based not on atheism or a desire to be free of the responsibilities of God, but rather on deep religious conviction and an image of the self that is far too base and lowly to contain, or even to compare to, the divine. Religious conditioning, particularly in western culture, has drawn a sharp contrast between the human and the Godly. The human is viewed as animalistic and sinful, and the Godly is seen as an external force that can rescue or redeem us from our inherent wickedness. Suggesting that God can be found within us would thus be demeaning to God, if not downright blasphemous. Many of us have been reared by religious leaders and teachers who have convinced us that we are weak and selfish and unworthy. Our "self," we have been told, is our ego, and our ego is what we must deny and transcend. God, in such a worldview, is surely not within us. We would certainly not identify God with ourselves, but rather we are exhorted to crush and eradicate our self in order to achieve a relationship with Him.

But what if my ego is not my true self? What if my ego is not what I ultimately am, but rather it is a disguise that has been wrapped over me in order to conceal my essential divine reality and unity?

Of course, there are valid reasons to make a distinction between the self and the divine, and there are real risks involved with identifying God with the self. To be sure, there have arisen within the past half century numerous modern "religions" and pseudo-spiritualities that have veered toward self-worship on account of various misunderstandings of the notion of a universal and internal Godliness. Mystical truths, in the wrong hands, have been twisted and perverted - sometimes deliberately, and sometimes inadvertently - to result in outcomes that are completely contrary to their intentions or origins.

For all of these reasons, and in light of all of these reasonable objections, it would be legitimate for one who is skeptical, or for whom the concept of the face of God within is new and uncertain, to say "prove it." At least give me some additional supports for this idea.

For those, on the other hand, who find the idea attractive and inspiring, it is also worthwhile to explore evidence and support for such a revolutionary and potentially life-altering claim. It is one thing to invoke pseudo-spiritual and pop-psychological platitudes to suggest that we are Godly beings. It is quite another thing to provide textual citations from ancient and authoritative sources which can reveal the existence of the very face of God within us. Furthermore, when the sources will be shown to exist within the framework of an age-old codified system, they will be understood in the context of a rich and established tradition of thought, and their implications and ramifications will not be left subject to haphazard interpretation or personal whimsy.

All of this is to say that we need to further explore the biblical sources for the claim that the face of God is within us. Is this truly supported by scripture and consistent with the tradition that has been transmitted throughout the generations from Mount Sinai until today? Where can we find authentic evidence for such a notion, and if it is so, then why does it seem so radical, questionable, and unfamiliar?

What we will find by digging even a little bit beneath the surface of the Torah text is that this reality is hidden in plain sight, and that the idea that the face of God is embedded within us is not what is shocking. Rather, with all of the indicators pointing to it, what is truly remarkable is that we have any doubt that it is there! What we will discover through the sources is not merely the existence and nature of our Godly essence, but we will furthermore come to know what we have been created to do, where we have to go to do it, and how we are to get it done.

Chapter 4: SOURCE

Face "In" Face

Moses, in describing the events on Mount Sinai when God gave the Torah to the Jewish nation, states that God spoke to the people "face to face."

פָּנִים בְּפָנִים דִּבֶּר יְ-הֹוָה עִמָּכֶם בָּהָר:
Panim b'panim dibber A-donai imachem bahar.
Face to face God spoke to you at the mountain.
(Deuteronomy 5:4)

It's difficult to understand what this could mean. Does it imply that the people saw the actual face of God as they stood at the foot of the mountain? This is problematic on a number of different levels. First, we know that God does not have physical attributes. How then could one suggest that His face was visible? Secondly, as we discussed earlier in chapter one, God informed Moses that "you will not be able to see my face, for man shall not see Me (God) and live."[28] If so, how could it be that He spoke to the entire nation "face to face" and they survived? Once again, the English translation is baffling, and we must look to the Hebrew original in order to clarify our confusion.

The wording used by Moses in the verse, "פָּנִים בְּפָנִים/Panim b'-panim," does not literally mean "face to face" as it is commonly translated. That would be the literal translation of "פָּנִים אֶל פָּנִים/panim **el** panim." The Hebrew word "אֶל" means 'to' (as does the letter "lamed/ל" by itself), while the Hebrew letter "beis/בְ," which Moses uses in the verse, means "in." The expression "פָּנִים בְּפָנִים/Panim **B**'panim" therefore literally means "face IN face," and the full verse would thus be translated "face IN face God spoke to you at the mountain." This is very odd, particularly because there are other verses in the Torah where the expression "face to face" is used, and in those cases the proper expression "פָּנִים אֶל פָּנִים/panim *el* panim" is employed. For example, after Jacob wrestles with an "angel of God," he exclaims:

וַיִּקְרָא יַעֲקב שֵׁם הַמָּקוֹם פְּנִיאֵל כִּי־רָאִיתִי אֱ-לֹהִים **פָּנִים אֶל־פָּנִים** וַתִּנָּצֵל נַפְשִׁי:

*Vayikra Yaakov shem hamakom Peniel ki ra'isi E-lohim **panim EL panim** vatinatzel nafshi.*

And Jacob named the place Peniel, for [he said,] "I saw an angel **face to face**, and my soul was saved."

(Genesis 32:31)

Here, the Torah utilizes the expression "panim *el* panim" as one would expect. Later, when the people are in the desert after the Exodus and after the events at Mount Sinai, the Torah describes Moses' relationship with God and his frequent communications with Him in the tent of meeting:

וְדִבֶּר יְ-הֹוָה אֶל־מֹשֶׁה **פָּנִים אֶל־פָּנִים**:

*V'dibber A-donai el Moshe **Panim EL panim**.*

And God would speak to Moses **face to face**.

(Exodus 33:11)

---

[28] Exodus 33:20

Once again the common expression "panim el panim" is used. Why in Moses' description of the interaction at Mount Sinai does it use the unusual expression "panim B'panim," and what could it mean that God spoke to us "face *IN* face?"

To reinforce our question further, in the chapter previous to the one from which this verse is taken, Moses warns the nation against the worship of idolatry by stating:

וְנִשְׁמַרְתֶּם מְאֹד לְנַפְשֹׁתֵיכֶם כִּי לֹא רְאִיתֶם כָּל־תְּמוּנָה בְּיוֹם
דִּבֶּר יְ-הוָֹה אֲלֵיכֶם בְּחֹרֵב מִתּוֹךְ הָאֵשׁ:

V'nishmartem m'od l'nafshoseichem ki lo re'isem kol tmunah bayom dibber A-donai Aleichem b'Chorev mitoch ha'aish.

But you shall greatly beware for your souls, for you did not see any likeness on the day Hashem spoke to you at Horeb (Sinai).

(Deuteronomy 4:15)

If it was not clear before from Moses' unusual wording, then from his admonition here it becomes obvious that we did not speak to God "face to face" as the English translation implies. Rather, the expression "panim B'panim / face IN face" denotes an experience of something at the giving of the Torah which has nothing to do with any physical or visual phenomenon.

As we have discussed on multiple occasions already, the Hebrew word for "face," **PaNiM** is closely related to the word **PNiMyus**, "inner essence," and can therefore refer to an experience of one's deepest interior as opposed to one's most surface features. As such, what Moses describes by utilizing the phrase "face IN face" rather than "face to face" is a mingling of "faces," an infusion of one inner essence into another. The giving of the Torah, we come to understand, was not simply the transmission of a book of laws and narratives. While the ten commandments and the Biblical text that Moses brought down from Mount Sinai contained a divine wisdom that would revolutionize the world, there was something even more profound that was conveyed at that moment. Many have missed the nuance of the language of the verse that we have been discussing, but a careful reading of the Hebrew text renders the secret that Moses is alluding to completely apparent:

"Panim b'panim dibber Hashem imachem bahar" - **at the mountain, God infused His face, His quintessence, into our face, our innermost core.**[29]

———◆———

The First Commandment

This provides an entirely new and earth-shattering context to the events at Mount Sinai and the understanding of what the Torah is. Far more than a rule book and a chronicle of historic events, Torah is a mechanism through which we can access the infinite potential that is embedded within us. Beyond Moses' intimation of this reality through his unusual language, we can also see this from the very first word of the ten commandments, which are the encapsulation of the entire Torah and the very words that Moses and the nation heard on Mount Sinai.

אָנֹכִי יְ-הֹוָה אֱ-לֹהֶיךָ אֲשֶׁר הוֹצֵאתִיךָ מֵאֶרֶץ מִצְרַיִם מִבֵּית עֲבָדִים:

Anochi A-donai E-lohecha asher hotzeisicha me'eretz Mitzrayim mi'beis avadim.

I am the Lord your God who took you out of the land of Egypt, out of the house of bondage.

(Exodus 20:2)

"אָנֹכִי / Anochi" means 'I', and it is the first word of the first commandment. But the common Hebrew word for 'I' is "אֲנִי / ani," and the sages ask why this far less common usage is employed here. One answer

---

[29] See *Likkutei Torah*, Parshas Reeh where the Alter Rebbe discusses this subject: "*V'hinei kasiv 'panim b'panim dibber Hashem imachem' ki b'shaas kabbalas haTorah nimshach l'kol echad v'echad m'yisrael bechinas Havaya b'bechinas panim shelahem b'kol nitzutz nishmoseihem v'zehu inyan kabbalas hadibbur Anochi Hashem Elokecha, peirush she'yihyeh bechinas Shem Havaya me'ir u'misgaleh b'cha.* / And behold it is written 'face to face Hashem spoke with you' because at the time of the receiving of the Torah there was drawn down into every single individual of Israel the aspect of Havaya into the aspect of their 'face' in every spark of their neshama, and this is the concept of receiving the statement 'I am the Lord your God,' the explanation of which is that the aspect of the name Havaya should shine and be revealed within you."

they provide is that the word "אָנֹכִי/A-No-CH-I" is an acronym for the phrase "אנא נפשי כתיבת יהבית/Ana Nafshi Chatavis Yahavis," which means "I wrote and gave Myself."[30] From this, we further understand that what God delivered to us through the giving of the Torah was not just His wisdom or His will, but it was His very self.

But where is this "self" that He gave us? Is it on the tablets that were engraved on the mountain and brought down to us by Moses? Is it on the parchment of the Torah scroll? Is it in the breath of the words that were passed down verbally through the oral Torah? The answer to this is found in Moses' statement "panim b'panim." The "Self" that God delivered to us is His "panim/face," and the place where He deposited it is in our "panim/inner core."

This contention is further supported by a deeper exploration of the first commandment. Beyond the first word, "Anochi," we must understand the introductory phrase "Anochi A-donai E-lohecha/I am the Lord your God." What is the commandment here, and what do these three words mean? Unlike the subsequent nine commandments that instruct us on various behaviors or proscriptions - you shall have no other gods but me, honor your father and mother, don't kill, etc. - this first commandment seems to lack a specific instruction. It seems to simply state a fact, that the one who is delivering these words is our Lord and our God, and furthermore, as the rest of the sentence states, He is the one who "took us out of the land of Egypt." Why is that considered a "commandment," and why is it the very first commandment no less? Furthermore, why does it need to state that He is both our "Lord" and our "God"? What is the difference between the two terms, and what makes them both necessary?

The mystics point out that each of the first three words of this verse refers to a different aspect of God. "Anochi," which as we pointed out above, means "I", refers to a level of God that is so lofty and inaccessible that it cannot even be captured by a name. A name is not the true essence of the thing that it signifies, it is rather a label by which other things can know it, grasp it, and relate to it. In itself, a being does not need a name; a name becomes necessary only when it is communicating

---

30 Talmud Bavli, Shabbat 105a

with something other. "Anochi," therefore, alludes to a level of Godliness that is beyond names and beyond a relationship with the world.

The second word of the verse, "הוה-י/Y-h-v-h," is a name of God that we do not pronounce as it is spelled because it is so holy. We therefore pronounce it as "A-donai" when we are praying or reading Torah, and we commonly speak of it as "Hashem/the name," or sometimes as "Havaya" which is a remixing of the letters to produce a word that is similar to the actual name and enables us to discuss it without explicitly mentioning it. This name refers to a transcendent level of God that is "above" the world but simultaneously related to the world in that it creates it and "surrounds" it. Though we use spatial words, like "above" and "surround" to describe the relationship between the levels of Godliness and the creation, these are only borrowed terms. For the name "A-donai" and the level of God that it represents, there is no space nor time, as these are merely constructs which God fashioned to manage and order this material creation. The very name "הוה-י/Y-h-v-h" alludes to its transcendent quality, as it contains within it the words "היה/hayah/was", "הוה/hoveh/is", and "יהיה/yihyeh/will be," and thus indicates that past, present, and future are all contained within it as one.

The third name "E-lohecha", is a form of the divine name "א-להים/E-lohim" which refers to Godliness that pervades the world and interacts with it. "E-lohim" conducts the moment to moment operations of the creation. It is the aspect of God that has lowered itself to the extent that the actions of humankind carry significance. While "A-donai" is not phased by our deeds and conduct because from such a lofty and removed perspective we are all one and unified, "E-lohim" is the force of God that distinguishes between right and wrong and administers judgment and consequence.

By invoking all three of these names and levels of God, the first commandment is informing us of one of the deepest secrets of our reality: the level of "Anochi," a Godliness that is so lofty and boundless that it cannot even be named, descends into "A-donai," a state of Godliness which creates but transcends the creation, and thereby comes down into "E-lohim," a divinity that can suffuse even the most picayune aspects of humanity.

Not only does the highest essence of absolute Godliness make this precipitous descent into our world, but furthermore, as the verse states, "Anochi A-donai E-lohe**CHA**/I am the Lord **YOUR** God!" If it had merely stated 'Anochi A-donai E-lohim/I am the Lord God,' this in itself would have been a profound disclosure informing us that God's sublime essence descends into the very details of the creation. But by utilizing the possessive form and specifying "E-lohe*cha*/*Your* God," the verse reveals that "Anochi" and "A-donai" permeate not only into the level of "E-lohim," but this level of "E-lohim" enables all of these degrees of Godliness to become *yours*, to literally penetrate within you and to be possessed and incorporated by you. Through this process of the giving of the Torah, God becomes not only the consummate, infinite Creator that is above you and beyond you, but He has made Himself yours. He can be accessed by you, emulated by you, and attained by you.

In other words, because He has implanted "Anochi" within us, because He has thereby revealed to us the secret reality that there is nothing other than His oneness - that all of creation is unified in His unconcealed essence - thereby each of us can be Godly, because we are Godly! This transcendence of our mortal limitations is the explanation of the words that finish the first commandment, "I am the Lord your God *who took you out of the land of Egypt.*" The Hebrew word for Egypt is "Mitzrayim" which literally means "restrictions" or "limitations." When we become aware of the fact that we are inherently Godly, there is nothing that can contain or restrain us.

Now we can understand why this verse is the first declaration that God conveyed to Moses on Mount Sinai. "I am the Lord your God" is not simply an introduction, or a prelude for the commandments that will follow. It is the very first commandment of the ten commandments because it is a statement of the deepest secret and purpose of our existence. My infinite essence, God informs us, trickles down through every fiber of My creation, and embeds itself within your core. It becomes yours to wield and to reveal. This is not only a proclamation or a statement of fact, but it is a commandment with a very specific instruction. It is commanding us to know and internalize the fact that God is not merely omnipresent and beyond the world ("Anochi" and "A-donai"), but He is simultaneously immanent within us ("E-lohecha"). With this knowledge, we are instructed to transcend all of our perceived limitations (to go out of Mitzrayim/Eypt), and then to externalize and publicize the truth of God's oneness throughout the creation. This is the first commandment because it is our entire   life work and raison d'etre.

———————◆◆———————

In Your Face

With this deeper understanding of the first commandment, we can see the correspondence between the first words of the entire Torah, and the first words that were delivered to Moses on Mount Sinai. It is taught in the Zohar that the world was created with ten utterances which are listed throughout the first chapter of Genesis, and these correspond to the ten commandments that God declared to Moses as an introduction to the giving of the Torah. The first of the ten creative utterances was "Breishis bara E-lohim ...,"[31] which we have discussed at length (see chapter two, section "The Mission"), and the first of the ten commandments is "Anochi A-donai E-lohecha ...,"[32] as we have just explored in the previous section. As we discussed earlier, the common translation of "Breishis bara E-lohim" is "in the beginning God created," but on a deeper level the words are instructing us that the "primary thing is to reveal God," and the Torah thus begins with a statement of our fundamental mission. As we just detailed in our explanation of the first commandment, the words "Anochi A-donai E-lohecha" assign us this very same charge. We are here to find the truth of God's absolute unity that is hidden deep within our core, and then to reveal that truth which is concealed by the veil of the creation.

It is important, particularly in our context, to highlight the parallel between the first commandment and the first creative utterance. This is because we may have been inclined, from our discussion of the first commandment, to mistakenly assume that the face of God was not within us prior to the giving of the Torah. If "I am the Lord your God" was declared on Mount Sinai, and if, as we discussed above, this verse indicates that "Anochi" was infused through "A-donai" into "E-lohecha" and our inner recesses, then one can reasonably wonder when this oc-

---

[31] Genesis 1:1

[32] Exodus 20:2

curred. Clearly the events at Mount Sinai marked a revolutionary moment in history and something new and profound was introduced into the universe, and into us, at that time. But what about the previous 2,448 years from the time of Creation until then? If, as we've noted earlier, the soul is the life force of all beings, and, as we quoted from the Alter Rebbe, that it is "a spark of God" that exists in each of us, then certainly God was within us from the moment of our creation. What then does it mean to say that the giving of the Torah marked the moment when God placed his "face/panim" into our "pnimyus/inner essence," as we discussed in regards to the phrase "panim B'panim/face IN face" above?

We will gain some further insight by exploring another verse that also expresses these themes. In the first verse of the fourth portion of the book of Deuteronomy (parshas "Re'eh"), God proclaims:

רְאֵה אָנֹכִי נֹתֵן לִפְנֵיכֶם הַיּוֹם בְּרָכָה וּקְלָלָה:
Reeh Anochi nosein lifneichem hayom bracha u'klala.
See, I give before you today a blessing and a curse.
(Deuteronomy 11:26)

Simply translated, this verse means that God is providing the nation on that day a choice between a blessing and a curse. The subsequent verses then go on to explain that the blessing will come if God's will is obeyed, and the curse will result from the opposite. Afterwards, the blessings and curses are laid out in detail. Like all of Torah, the verse operates on this basic level, but also reveals deeper truths beneath its surface. Its more hidden meaning is once again gleaned from examining the precision of the Hebrew text.

Two of the words in the verse bear particular relevance to the analysis that we have been pursuing. First, there is once again the word "אָנֹכִי/Anochi," which we have already identified as an unusual usage and a less common translation for the pronoun "I." Secondly, we find the word "פְנֵי/pnei/face," which we have been discussing at length, within the word "לִפְנֵיכֶם/lifneichem."[33] Neither of these word choices are haphazard or insignificant. The Alter Rebbe asks why "lifneichem," which is

---

[33] "פְנֵי/pnei" is another form of the word "פָּנִים/panim," both meaning "face." The Hebrew letter 'פ' can be pronounced either 'p' or 'f' depending on its vowelization. Therefore "face" can be vocalized as either "pnei" or "fnei."

translated as "before you," was used here rather than the more simple and straightforward "לָכֶם/lachem/to you." If God merely wanted to express that "I am giving *to you* today a blessing and a curse," then He could have more simply stated "Ani nosein *lachem* hayom…." Substituting "lifneichem" for "lachem" provides a far more profound implication, as does inserting "Anochi" instead of "Ani." "Lifneichem" can mean "before you," or it can be translated as "within you." Both meanings are a function of its root "pnei/face." "Before you" is an expression of something being 'in front of your face.' "Within you" is an expression of another connotation of "panim" which we have mentioned several times now, "pnimyus" or inwardness. In this sense, "lifneichem" would more literally mean "in your face" or inside your inner-ness.

Based on the use of these terms, the Alter Rebbe's translation of the verse reveals its mystic secret:

"See, I place 'Anochi' within you today, a blessing and a curse."

On this deeper level, the verse is not simply stating that God is placing a blessing and curse before us, but that He is placing His level of "Anochi," His deepest self, within us, and this can manifest as either a blessing or a curse. The "blessing" is when we are aware of this divine reality and we publicize it. The "curse" is when we remain ignorant of what we truly are, and we therefore neglect our duty to make it known to others and thereby transform the entire creation. Once again, as we found in the deeper understanding of the first commandment, we are presented with a shockingly blatant and succinct statement of God's insertion of His essence within us. Our task is laid out in the first word of the verse, "Reeh/See": we are instructed to perceive this hidden truth, and to then make it revealed so that others can see it as well.

Yet what remains to be understood in the verse is the word "הַיּוֹם/hayom/today." When is this "today" on which God implanted His level of "Anochi" into our "pnimyus/innermost core?" The verse is stated some time in the fortieth year that the nation is journeying in the desert, soon before they enter the land of Canaan.[34] However, it was not at this moment that God spoke to the nation "face in face." Rather, as the verse explicitly says, "face in face God spoke to you *at the mountain*." It was therefore on Mount Sinai, when He gave His Torah, that His "Anochi" was implanted "lifneichem/within you." This is supported by a principal in Torah analysis that is known as "gezeira shava" which means "identical terms." When identical words or phrases are utilized in different places in Torah, one is able to interpret them in one context based on how they are similarly used in other contexts. The word "Anochi" in the verse "I place *Anochi* within you…" connects it to the first of the ten commandments that we discussed previously, which begins with the same term, "*Anochi* Havaya Elokecha." Because of this linguistic correlation, the chassidic masters interpret the verse to be referring to that same moment when the commandments were communicated to Moses on Mount Sinai. This verse, then, in which God informs us that He places His "Anochi" within us, is consistent with the first commandment, reiterating and reinforcing the momentous innovation of that day.

But the sages point out that the principal of "gezeira shava/identical terms" can be applied to another word in the verse as well. The word "hayom/today" aligns the verse with another significant date in history. The Zohar, discussing the verse "Atem nitzavim *hayom*/you are standing *today*,"[35] comments that the word "hayom/today" in that verse is a reference to the first day of Adam and Eve's creation. This is because the same word is found in the phrase from the talmud, "zeh **hayom** techilas maasecha zichron l'yom rishon/this day is the beginning of your works, a remembrance of the first day."[36] If we read "hayom/today" in our verse ("See, I place Anochi within you *today* …") as a reference to the day of humanity's original creation, then we find that the time when God instilled His inner essence into our innermost core was the very

---

[34] Rashi informs us that the blessing and curse which the verse alludes to were given on Mount Gerizim and Mount Ebal, two mountains that stand in the land of Canaan on the other side of the Jordan River, which was not crossed until Moses's death at the end of the fortieth year. The event is described in more detail in Joshua 8:30-35.

[35] Deuteronomy 29:9

[36] Tractate Rosh Hashana 27a; Ramaz, Zohar Chadash beis 32,2

moment of our inception. Humanity was conceived and created with God's level of "Anochi" as our crux and foundation. It is what we are in essence and in fact!

If this is the case, then what was the innovation at the giving of the Torah? How is it, as we discussed in the previous section, that we and the world were dramatically transformed when we stood at Mount Sinai after we went out of Egypt two and half millennia after our creation? If the soul, which is God's "face," was in our "face" all along, then what did we gain with the receiving of the Torah? What is the significance of the fact that God spoke to us "panim **B**'panim/face IN face" at this point if He had already embedded His face within us thousands of years earlier?

While we might be tempted to suggest that He gave us "more" of His face at Mount Sinai than He had given us at our creation, this is untenable because there cannot be more or less of the infinite. However, there can be a greater revelation of something that already existed in a more hidden way. And this is precisely the additional dimension that became manifest when the Torah was given. At that point, with the giving of the Torah, humanity was provided a far greater ability to locate the face that God had already hidden within us at our creation. The Torah was, and is, a way for us to relate to and reveal the infinite that was previously too blinding for us to detect. The "Anochi" that He gave with the giving of the Torah was a mechanism for us to see the "Anochi" that was already in there but was previously impossible to grasp and maintain. In this sense, Torah can be seen as an eyepiece that allows us to perceive, and even stare without being blinded, into the blazing infinite light that shines from within our hidden nucleus.

In *The Ethics of the Fathers*, it is taught: "Precious is man for he was created in the image of God. Even more precious is that it was made known to him that he is formed in the image of God."[37] The face/image of God was always within us, but we weren't aware of that and truly able to know what that meant until we received the Torah. The Torah's inner dimensions enable us to plumb our depths to understand and express our true nature and potential.

---

[37] Pirkei Avos 3:14

Not So Fast

We have answered a number of our questions at this point, but another question, which is perhaps even more troubling, now confronts us.

Our initial question, and, as we have pointed out, God's initial query in the Bible, was "ayecha", **Where are you?** The question itself led us to the awareness, which we often try to ignore, that we are lost. And this prompted us to ask our second question: **Why are we lost?** To this, we responded that we are lost because this is precisely how God intended it. This prompted the obvious follow up: **Why would God create us to be lost?** And here, we explained that this "olam/world" was to be a realm of "helam/concealment" so that we, and anything "other" than God, could exist (or at least perceive itself to be existing). This existence was necessary in order for God to express His infinite giving nature - "teva hatov l'heitiv/it is the nature of the good to do good."

We then asked: **What is our task in this darkness?** And we concluded that we are here to find what has been lost and concealed, and then to reveal it in order to manifest a light that would shine extraordinarily bright in comparison to the darkness that preceded it. Ready to set out in order to undertake this search, we next pondered: **Where are we to look?** We recognized our propensity to seek satisfaction and fulfillment in a wide variety of places where we know it will never be found, and concluded that the proper direction can only be within.

At this point, turning inward, and anxious to be on our way, we paused to clarify some confusion about the ultimate object of our search: **Were we to be looking for ourselves** - "lech lecha/go to you" - **or for God** - "Breishis bara Elokim/the primary thing is to reveal God"? The startling and exhilarating response was that we are seeking both simultaneously, and that the one is hidden within the other: "panim B'panim dibber Elokim" - God instilled His essence into our core. Inspired by the new awareness of our personal divinity, we inquired: **How can we find the face of God within our own inner face deep within us?** And we were encouraged as we learned that there is a map which we have been given that will lead us there. That map is the Torah.

With all of these questions and their respective answers, we have penetrated a good way into the darkness already. However, we are now presented with a quandary as we rest to catch our breath. As we realize that our goal and destination is still not at all apparent to us, the obvious and unsettling question creeps up on us: **if we have the Torah which is to serve as our guide, and if we have had it for nearly three and a half millennia already, why are we still lost, and why does God remain concealed?**

For those who have not devoted any significant amount of time to learning Torah, the inclination would now be to turn to those who have, and to determine whether they, through their labors, have already discovered what we continue to seek. If they have, then our next step is obvious: we will simply begin studying the Torah ourselves so that we too will know where and how to search in order to find and reveal the face of God within us. But as we consider this notion further, we would have to wonder why those who have studied the Torah, and thereby found themselves and God in the darkness, have not shared their discovery with the rest of us. Indeed, the goal is not merely to discover the face of God within oneself, but the primary responsibility, as we have come to understand from the first verse of the Torah, is to "bara Elokim es hashayim v'es Haaretz/to reveal God throughout the heavens and the earth." This is the very essence of what it means to be "ohr l'goyim/a light unto the nations." If God is not openly revealed, as He does not seem to be, and if we are still lost, as seems to remain the case for the vast majority of us, then we might assume that either a) those who have utilized the Torah to find what we are all seeking are shirking their responsibility of sharing their findings and dispelling the world's darkness, or b) that the Torah does not deliver on its promise of guiding us to find what it has commanded us to reveal.

For those, on the other hand, who have indeed devoted themselves to learning Torah, perhaps years or even decades of assiduous study, the question is no less confounding. If the Torah demands us to be a light unto the nations, and it requires us to reveal God throughout His creation, then why does the world continue to be so dark? If we are doing what is expected of us, and if we know that "A-donai echad/God is One," then why does the majority of creation seem to be so godless? Have we failed? Have our countless hours of Torah study taught us nothing and contributed little if anything to our ultimate purpose? Where have we gone wrong?

The answer, to both the questions of those who have studied Torah and those who have not, is that it is no fault or error which has resulted in the continued darkness. As we touched on in chapter one, this is precisely what God intended when He created this "olam/world" to be a place of "helam/concealment." As we elaborated in chapter two, He created darkness prior to light - "it was evening and then morning" - because there is a benefit in the progression from the one to the other. That is that light which comes after darkness is more brilliant than light by itself. Therefore, every moment that there is continued darkness and concealment, we are building toward an ever greater eventual revelation. It was never God's intention that we should quickly move from exile to redemption. If He had desired that to be the case, then, as we have discussed regarding the principal of "hashgacha protis/divine providence" and God's complete control of everything that happens, it would have been so. The fact that the nation of Israel has languished in exile for the majority of its history, and the fact that human existence has been marked by consistent conflict, confusion, and frustration, is not an accident or an indication of either divine or human failing. Rather, it is the precise process through which God's ultimate goal of the meticulous transformation of darkness to light will be accomplished. And though it may seem to be moving too painfully slow from our perspective, we must remind ourselves that everything must and will move at God's pace, which is precisely the right pace.

The advent of the Torah was not meant to immediately usher in an age of total revelation. It was not intended to overturn the creation or eradicate the laws and systems that God had previously put in place and set in motion. The complete disclosure of God's essence and reality would cause the world to revert to nothingness in the face of His absolute oneness. This would be utterly contrary to His initial intent in the creation of a multiverse where His unity would be concealed and otherness could exist. Therefore, He provided a tool with which bits of light would be gradually revealed within the darkness. Every "mitzvah/commandment" prescribed in the Torah would create an individual act of illumination, a breaking of a small shell which contained and concealed a morsel of divine light. Through the aggregate performance of innumerable such acts throughout history, the darkness would slowly be transformed and an age of unprecedented radiance would evolve. The end of this process is known as "יְמוֹת הַמָּשִׁיחַ / yemot hamashiach / the days of the Messiah," the messianic era when "the earth will be filled with the knowledge of God like the oceans fill the sea-bed."[38] At that point, all of the world and its creations will recognize the face of God within them. Until then, we remain in the dark with the lantern of Torah which lights the path in front of our feet and urges us forward step by step.[39]

From 'Knowing' To 'Showing'

The fact that the world we inhabit was created to be a realm of concealment does not absolve us from our task of working toward illumination and revelation. The fact that the possession of the Torah does not enable us to instantly actualize all of its insights does not diminish its truth or our responsibility to pursue and manifest it. The fact that we are unable to clearly see and reveal the face of God within us does not render us less Godly or free us from the opportunity and duty to exercise our inherent Godliness.

Another way to state all this is to acknowledge that **knowing that the face of God is within us does not mean that we have found it**. Rather, it simply gives us an indication of where to look. Having a map with an 'x' on it to mark where the treasure is hidden is obviously different from finding and possessing the treasure that the 'x' represents. Yet

---

[38] Habbakuk 2:14

[39] There have been many predictions and forecasts throughout history as to when the messiah will come, but none of this is relevant to our daily purpose and labor. A person's job is to work toward it constantly. One of the "13 Principles Of Faith" of the Rambam is to expect and precipitate the messiah's coming every day, for we never know when God will decide to end this final exile. In the meantime, it is established that the world will exist for seven thousand years, and the seventh millennium will be the age of the messiah. The six millennia of this world parallel the six work days of the week, and the seventh millennium parallels the sabbath, the time of rest. We are currently in the last quarter of the sixth millennium, corresponding to the afternoon of the sixth day when the sabbath can be inducted early.

there is tremendous value to the map, for without it, we may spend all of our days hunting for the treasure in all of the wrong places, or worse yet, not knowing that the treasure exists at all. Torah provides us the map. It informs us that there is a priceless and infinite fortune awaiting us, and it offers us instruction on how and where to find it. But it gives us no guarantee when we will reach our destination. That is dependent, in part at least, on the effort that we are willing to exert. It is also, and primarily, dependent on when God chooses to bring the final redemption and take the world out of this last period of exile. The Sages teach that His decision to do so is contingent on our deeds. We never know which mitzvah, or act of illumination, will be the one that finally puts us over the top and completes the requisite amount of light that will overcome the prevailing darkness. Until then, we are working constantly to move from knowledge to revelation, from intellectual and spiritual awareness of the existence of God's presence within us, to the clear and universal perception and experience of this reality.

For some, however, including many who are reading this, knowledge and awareness of Godliness are not a starting point, and maybe not even a certain goal. We have, after all, provided no proof that the face of God is within us. Rather, we have merely provided sources from the Biblical text - "panim B'panim dibber Elokim", "Anochi Havaya Elokecha", "Reeh Anochi nosein lifneichem Hayom" - which the mystics have interpreted to reveal the secret of this latent dynamic. But the face remains hidden, and there is no empirical proof that can settle the issue definitively. For those who do believe, or who find the sources compelling, this is precisely the task and the objective - to transform their beliefs into something perceptible and irrefutable. In other words, as we have stated already, the entire project of life is to first admit God's unity into one's constant awareness, and then to make His presence conspicuous and undeniable throughout every part of His creation.

We can refer to this as a progression from "knowing" to "showing," and we can witness this dynamic in the words of the daily prayers. In the Hebrew "siddur/prayerbook," each day begins with a declaration of acknowledgment of God's presence, and then proceeds with prayers requesting the ability to expose this truth and render it perceptible. The first of these two stages is expressed in the very first words in the prayerbook, which one recites immediately upon awakening every morning:

מוֹדֶה אֲנִי לְפָנֶיךָ מֶלֶךְ חַי וְקַיָּם, שֶׁהֶחֱזַרְתָּ בִּי נִשְׁמָתִי בְּחֶמְלָה רַבָּה אֱמוּנָתֶךָ.

Modeh Ani lefanecha melech chai v'kayam, shehechezarta bi nishmasi b'chemla, rabba emunasecha.

I offer thanks to You, living and eternal King, for You have mercifully restored my soul within me; Your faithfulness is great.

Simply understood, this prayer is an expression of gratitude to God for restoring one's life this new morning and allowing one to live another day. Sleep, according to the sages, is one sixtieth of death,[40] in that the soul partially abandons the body and ascends to the heavens when one sleeps. When one awakens, the soul is restored, and therefore one gives thanks to God for its return and for entrusting her/him with such a precious endowment yet again. Gratitude and appreciation for the gift of life are certainly valuable principles with which to begin every day, but there is an even deeper message hidden within this initial declaration that is uttered within the first moments of consciousness.

The third word in the prayer, "לְפָנֶיךָ/lifanecha," should look familiar to us by now. It is similar to the word "לִפְנֵיכֶם/lifneichem" which we recently discussed from the verse "Reeh Anochi nosein *lifneichem* hayom." In that verse, "lifneichem" was simply translated as "to you" in the plural, or in other words, 'to all of you.' "Lifanecha" is the same word, but it means "to you" in the singular - one is offering thanks "to you" God, for restoring her/his soul. Regarding "lifneichem," we explained that its root is "pnei/face" and its literal meaning is "to your face" or "in your face." Similarly, "lifanecha" in this initial morning prayer literally means "to your face." In the verse from the Torah that we analyzed, the Alter Rebbe asked why the term "lifneichem" was chosen rather than the more common and straightforward "lachem/to you." He then explained that its more literal meaning provided us the secret that God had instilled His deepest level of "Anochi" within us. Here too, if the intent of the prayer were simply to express our gratitude to God, the word "lecha/to you" could have been employed. The use of "lifanecha" tells us that we are

---

[40] Talmud, Berachot 57b

84

simultaneously referring to something more, which is once again some allusion to God's "panim/face."

To understand what we are saying here about God's face, we must also explore the first word of the prayer, "מוֹדֶה/modeh", which is translated plainly to mean "give thanks." The common Hebrew word for thank you, "תּוֹדָה/todah," shares the same root. But the word's root, "הוֹדָאָה/hodaah," also means to confess, to admit, to submit, to acknowledge, and to bow. Understanding "modeh" in this sense, and reading "lifanecha" in its more literal translation, the prayer takes on a very different implication. Rather than "I give thanks to you," we can now read the beginning of the phrase as "I acknowledge your face" or "I admit/submit/bow to your face." Translating the entire prayer in this context, we can render it as follows:

"I acknowledge your face, living and eternal King, which You have returned within me, my soul; with great mercy is Your faithfulness."

Understood this way, the first utterance as one begins every new day is an acknowledgement and admission of the face of God which He has placed within us. One reminds her/himself that this is what the soul is - we live and are sustained only by virtue of the fact that God infuses His innermost essence into us. We recognize the tremendous extent of His mercy and His faith in us that leads Him to entrust us with such a precious part of Himself.

Imagine awakening daily with this affirmation and this resolve. The recognition of our core divinity and the proclamation of what we ultimately are will certainly transform our consciousness and positively influence the day ahead. This is the purpose and underlying meaning of prayer in general. As we explained earlier,[41] the Hebrew word "tefilla" that is commonly translated as "prayer" derives from the root meaning "union" or "bond." The thrice daily prayers are intended to be primarily about pausing from one's daily routine in order to meditate on one's Godly essence and thereby reunite with her/his source.

Yet with all of this profound awareness and acknowledgement, one must 'admit' and 'submit' to this truth rather than perceive it. This is

---

[41] See chapter three, section "Inward Bound"

the implication of the word "modeh," according to the Alter Rebbe.[42] It is an admission and submission to something that one cannot see clearly, but which he recognizes to be true nonetheless. The term is used in this context in the Talmud where it is stated that "modim chachamim l'Rabi Meir/the sages were "modeh" to Rabbi Meir."[43] This means that though these other rabbis disagreed with Rabbi Meir's position on certain issues based on their own understanding of the given factors, nevertheless they acceded to his opinion because they recognized his superior intellect and insight. "Modeh" thus describes an act of submission to something that is beyond one's intellect or perception on account of one's admitted limitations. Just as the rabbis were "modeh" to Rabbi Meir's superior understanding, so too we are "modeh" to God's perspective of reality even though we are unable to perceive His truth with our limited human senses.

"Modeh ani lefanecha" is thus our daily admission, the moment we awaken, that God's face, "panecha," is within us though we don't yet see it clearly. We are furthermore submitting to the reality of our divine essence, even if we are not feeling particularly Godly. And we are committing to doing our best to make that Godliness visible through our actions throughout the day ahead.

Yet our goal is not to stay at this level of "modeh/admission" where the truth is hidden but acknowledged. While we are charged with the task of expressing Godliness through our actions within this time of exile and concealment, our ultimate goal is not to remain in the dark, but to eradicate and transform the darkness. This means that while our daily prayer begins with an admission of an unperceived truth, this is only a first step - albeit an extremely profound first step - and we do not stop here. From here, we move immediately to an impassioned request for the truth to emerge from its obscurity and to become overt. We will find this expressed in the next verses of the liturgy of the daily morning prayers.

---

[42] Likkutei Torah, Devarim p.1, Tzion B'mishpat Tipadeh

[43] Baba Kama 29a

Blessed Are You

After the recitation of "Modeh ani" with the first glimmer of consciousness upon awakening, one rises from bed, washes one's hands and attends to one's bodily needs. It is then time to recite the morning service before turning attention to one's daily pursuits. The service begins with the "E-lohai neshama" prayer, which reads as follows:

אֱ-לֹהַי נְשָׁמָה שֶׁנָּתַתָ בִּי טְהוֹרָה הִיא, אַתָּה בְרָאתָהּ, אַתָּה
יְצַרְתָּהּ, אַתָּה נְפַחְתָּהּ בִּי, וְאַתָּה מְשַׁמְּרָהּ בְּקִרְבִּי, וְאַתָּה עָתִיד
לִטְלָהּ מִמֶּנִּי, וּלְהַחֲזִירָהּ בִּי לֶעָתִיד לָבֹא. כָּל זְמַן שֶׁהַנְּשָׁמָה
בְּקִרְבִּי, מוֹדֶה אֲנִי לְפָנֶיךָ אֲ-דֹנָי אֱ-לֹהַי וֵא-לֹהֵי אֲבוֹתַי, רִבּוֹן
כָּל הַמַּעֲשִׂים, אֲדוֹן כָּל הַנְּשָׁמוֹת. בָּרוּךְ אַתָּה אֲ-דֹנָי, הַמַּחֲזִיר
נְשָׁמוֹת לִפְגָרִים מֵתִים.

E-lohai neshama shenesata bi tehora hi, attah barasa, atta yetzarta, attah nefachta bi, v'attah m'shamra b'kirbi, v'attah atid litla mimeni, u'l'hachazira bi l'atid lavo. Kol zman shehaneshama b'kirbi, modeh ani lefanecha, A-donai Elo-hai v'Elo-hai avotai, Ribon kol hamaasim, Adon kol haneshamot. Baruch attah A-donai, hamachazir neshamot lifgarim meisim.

God, the soul that You have given within me is pure, You created it, You formed it, You blew it into me, and You guard it within me, and You will take it from me in the future and return it to me in the time to come. All the time that the soul is within me, I will thank you my God, my Lord, and the God of my fathers, Master of all works, Lord of souls. Blessed are you God, Who restores souls to dead bodies.

As we can see, with the continued discussion of the soul that is given into the body, there are similarities here to the "modeh ani" prayer that was recited recently upon awakening. But now with the commencement of the the formal prayer service, the verses elaborate on some of the ideas that were touched on briefly in the first moments of consciousness. The prayer begins with an acknowledgement of the soul and its investiture within us. However, this time it is not enough to merely state that God "restored my soul within me" as was said in the "modeh ani" prayer. Now it goes further to comment on the soul's nature

87

("the soul that You have given within me is pure"), its creation and investment within the individual ("You created it, You formed it, You blew it into me, and You guard it within me"), and its destiny ("You will take it from me in the future and return it to me in the time to come"). While it is beyond the scope of our discussion, the mystics explain that this one sentence describes the entire progression and devolution of the soul from its source in the highest spiritual realms through the four "worlds" and into our physical reality.[44]

The second sentence then begins "Kol zman shehaneshama b'kirbi/all the time that the soul is within me," and then it employs the exact same language that was uttered as one awoke, "modeh ani lefanecha/I will thank you God." The simple meaning of the phrase is that one will thank God for the soul as long as it continues to vitalize the body. In other words, as long as I am alive I will give thanks to You, God, for my life. However, if we apply the deeper implication of the phrase "modeh ani lefanecha" that we discussed above in the previous section, we understand that one is not merely expressing gratitude, but one is "modeh" to "panecha," or one "submits" to the hidden reality of "Your (God's) face." What is "panecha/Your face" and where is it? It is, as the beginning of the phrase articulates "haneshama b'kirbi/the soul that is within me." Interpreted in this way, the prayer expresses the following recognition:

"Kol zman/throughout time" - in this realm where the superficial construct of time delimits the eternal, "shehaneshama b'kirbi/when the soul is within me" - while the infinite soul is contained and constrained within my finite physical form, "modeh ani lefanecha/I admit to Your face" - I acknowledge that it is Your face and essence that is hidden within me.

So far, the prayer has essentially reiterated, with some elaboration, the concept that was expressed in the more brief "modeh ani" verse that was recited upon awakening in bed. This is the "knowing" that we

---

[44] "Tehora hi" refers to the world of Atzilut, "barasa" refers to the world of Beriah, "yetzarta" refers to the world of Yetzira, and "b'kirbi" refers to this world of Asiyah. For a further exploration of this subject, see *Likkutei Torah*, Devarim p.1, "Tzion B'mishpat Tipadeh." In short, we are to meditate with these words on the great loftiness of the soul in its unity with God's deepest essence, and the great descent through a variety of levels that it undergoes to inhabit this place of tremendous limitation and concealment within us.

identified above as the first stage of our process. However, it is the conclusion of this "E-lohai neshama" prayer, and its subsequent blessings, which develop our theme and carry it to the second stage of "showing." The final phrase of the prayer begins "בָּרוּךְ אַתָּה אֲ-דֹנָי/Baruch atta A-don-ai," and here we are introduced to a well known refrain that is found throughout the Hebrew prayer liturgy. "Blessed are You, God," is the conventional translation of these words, but we must try to understand what the expression truly connotes.

What does it mean to say "Blessed are You God"?

Who is blessing God, and what is the implication of God's being blessed? Are we suggesting with this expression that we are blessing Him? Isn't it, rather, we who are blessed *by* God? Does God need our blessing, and is He not already blessed whether we bless Him or not?

In general, to bless something means to confer on it some sacredness, or alternatively to bestow upon it a prayer for some desired benefit or divine assistance. God, who is already sacred, and who can have whatever He desires, does not require our blessing in any of these senses. To bless can also mean to proclaim that something is holy, and in this sense, though God is holy whether or not we proclaim Him to be, there is some value in our proclamation. However, the Hebrew word "baruch" has a much deeper implication, the understanding of which can literally transform one's entire practice and consciousness.

The root of "baruch," ב-ר-ך, is found in the Talmud in the word "מַבְרִיךְ/mavrich," which means "to draw down," as in the phrase "*hamavrich es hagefen*/to draw down a vine"[45] and plant it in the ground so that it grows a new plant. It is also found in the word "בְּרֵיכָה/breichah," which means "pool." Both of these derivatives provide us a more thorough understanding of what it means to "bless." Just as "mavrich" means to draw down, and just as a pool is a place where rain has gathered after falling from above, a blessing is an attempt to draw

----

[45] Sotah 43a

down, consolidate, and manifest something in this lower realm which originates in a loftier source above.[46]

Understood in this sense of "drawing down," the phrase "baruch atta A-donai" becomes both a request and a mechanism for God to be revealed in this world of concealment. Rather than "blessed are You, God," it is now rendered, "may You be drawn down and revealed, God." This forms the introduction to manifold prayers and blessings in Torah practice, because this is the ultimate intention of the variety of actions and meditations which one performs throughout the day. "May You be revealed" through my eating of this food; "May You be revealed" through my lighting of these candles; "May You be revealed" through the washing of my hands. Each of these acts becomes a way for one to manifest the Godliness that is concealed within her/him, or within the item that s/he is about to consume or utilize. And each prayer one recites beginning with these words is an entreaty to God to assist her/him in the task that God assigned each of us with the first words of His Torah, "breishis bara Elokim/the first thing is to reveal God." We recognize that this is no easy job, and we, therefore, ask Him frequently for His help to fulfill it.

With this, we can now understand the progression within the "E-lohai neshama" prayer that serves as the launching point for the formal morning service. One begins with "modeh," which, as step one, is acknowledging and admitting the divinity within us and all of creation even though it is concealed. From here, one proceeds to "baruch," which is the second step, the attempt to move from "knowing" to "showing" and thereby revealing God and transforming the darkness of this world to light. This prayer initiates the morning service because it establishes the entire objective and strategy for the day ahead. Directly following its completion, the service continues with a series of fifteen short blessings that all begin with the phrase "baruch atta A-donai." This demonstrates that as soon as one has stated her/his mission and purpose, s/he immediately jumps directly into the task at hand. That is, by repeatedly "bless-

---

[46] Above and below, higher and lower, up and down and other such terms do not refer here to physical space or location. Rather, they are borrowed terms that allude to a thing's closeness to, or distance from, the revelation of its Godly source. While God is everywhere and therefore equally close to all things, the "higher" something is in the hierarchy of realms, the more its divine reality is revealed, and the "lower" something is, the more this reality is concealed.

ing" God so to speak, one works to draw Him down and reveal Him in all the places that He is not yet seen.

———————◆———————

The Great Name

We have now explored several of the biblical sources for the indwelling of God's essential presence within us, as well as citations from the daily prayer service which are intended to focus us on this divine reality and our task of exposing it. Before we move on, it is worthwhile to identify two other pieces of the liturgy which serve a similar purpose. Though there are many more prayers or terms that could be added to this list, the following two, similar to "baruch atta A-donai," are very common phrases which are recited repeatedly throughout the prayer service. They are therefore familiar to many, but their inner meaning is not commonly understood. Beneath their surface, they also convey this idea of drawing down and revealing one's inner Godliness. The first is the phrase "יְהֵא שְׁמֵהּ רַבָּא מְבָרַךְ לְעָלַם וּלְעָלְמֵי עָלְמַיָּא/ y'hei shmei rabba m'vorach l'olam u'l'almei almaya," and the second is the term "הַלְלוּיָ-הּ/halleluy-ah."

"יְהֵא שְׁמֵהּ רַבָּא מְבָרַךְ לְעָלַם וּלְעָלְמֵי עָלְמַיָּא/y'hei shmei rabba m'vorach l'olam u'l'almei almaya" is the response that the congregation recites aloud during the "Kaddish" prayer. "Kaddish" is a prayer that is repeated multiple times throughout each of the three daily services. It is recited both by the prayer leader to separate and demarcate between different sections of the service, and also by mourners who commemorate the passing of their loved ones with this prayer for a year after their passing and each year on the anniversary of their death. During the "kaddish," which can only be recited when there is a quorum of ten participants, the prayer leader or mourner chants several verses of praise, and then the congregation responds with this verse that is commonly translated "May His great name be blessed forever and ever." Most Jews are at least somewhat familiar with this phrase because it is recited at funerals and throughout the mourning period, and it is repeated so frequently in each service. An even greater number of people - Jews and non-Jews - are familiar with the word "הַלְלוּיָ-הּ/halleluy-ah," which has even crept into the English language as an exclamation of gratitude or an interjection that is commonly understood to mean "Praise the Lord!" However, both of these expressions, while familiar to many, convey far more than their surface translations disclose.

On the simplest level, "Yhei shmei rabba m'vorach.../may His great name be blessed forever and ever," seems to be a wish that God will be acknowledged and praised throughout time. But probing the language a bit more deeply, several questions arise. If the intent is that God should be glorified, then why does it refer to "His great name" rather than simply saying 'May *God* be blessed' or even 'May *He* be blessed'? What is "His great name" and why is it referenced here? Furthermore, as we asked earlier, what does it mean that He or His name should be "blessed"? The word used here is "מְבָרַךְ/m'vorach," which is another form of "ברך/baruch" that we discussed above. How can we apply our new understanding of the term to this verse as well? And finally, what does the phrase "forever and ever" communicate that would not be conveyed more simply by the word "forever" alone? Is there some time beyond "forever" that the additional words "and ever" will include that would not be included without them? We might suggest that these linguistic choices are simply poetic or stylistic embellishments. But as we have seen already, with Hebrew scripture and liturgy, there are always deeper meanings alluded to by the specificity of the language.

"Blessed," as we have discussed at length, means "drawn down" and revealed. When we say "baruch atta A-donai/blessed are You God," we are praying that God should be revealed in this place of concealment. "Yhei shmei rabba m'vorach/may His great name be blessed," is similarly entreating that He should be drawn down into actuality. But here we are specifying that it is His "great name" that needs to be accessed. What is this "great name"?

There are many names for God in the Torah - A-donai, E-lohim, E-l, Sha-dai, and others. As we mentioned earlier in our discussion of the first of the ten commandments, three words are listed in succession which all refer to God in various levels of manifestation: "Anochi A-donai Elokecha/I am the Lord your God." The name "Anochi" alludes to such a lofty level and aspect of God that it means simply "I." As names are generally relevant only when we are relating to others and not when we are alone, "Anochi/I" denotes that essential unity of God in which there is nothing other. And yet the miraculous paradox of our creation, as we explained, is that this infinite level of God was infused into each finite one of us - "Reeh Anochi nosein lifneichem / see that I have placed Anochi within you." It is this "great name," Anochi, which is even more lofty than the name A-donai, that we are praying to be "m'vorach / revealed" when we recite "Yhei shmei rabba m'vorach / May His great name be blessed" over a dozen times throughout the day.

However, the end of the phrase is still puzzling. Why do we ask that this name should be blessed or revealed "לְעָלַם וּלְעָלְמֵי עָלְמַיָּא/l'olam u'l'almei almaya / forever and ever"? The word "לְעָלַם/l'olam" has multiple connotations. Its root, "olam," is a word that we have mentioned repeatedly already. It means "world," and as we have explored at length, it is etymologically linked to the term "helam," which means "hidden," because this world was intended to be a place of concealment. Thus, in addition to "forever," "l'olam" literally means "to the world." By extension, it can also be interpreted as "to the hiddenness." Translated as such, the phrase is a supplication that the essence of God should be revealed to the world and to the places where it is currently concealed.

The final two words of the verse, "וּלְעָלְמֵי עָלְמַיָּא/u'l'almei almaya" are simply different forms of the same root word "olam." When "l'olam" is translated as "forever," these additional words are rendered simply as "and ever." This, as we questioned above, makes little sense, as 'forever' implies eternity and needs no further augmentation. If we translate "l'olam" as "to the world" or "to the hiddenness" however, the last two words would mean "and to all the worlds," or "and to all the hidden places," and would add additional detail and implication. With all of these elements, the phrase "Yhei shmei rabba m'vorach l'olam u'l'almei almaya" will be interpreted as follows: "May the essence of God be revealed in all the hidden places of the world." Once again, in an expression that is recited frequently and commonly, we find a succinct statement of our most basic objective and duty.

According to the chassidic masters, the words "l'olam u'l'almei almaya" carry an additional significance, as they refer to the three elemental garments of our soul: thought, speech, and action. These are referred to as "garments" because they are the way that our soul appears and is expressed in this world. The phrase "yhei shmei rabba" is thus fundamentally a prayer to God that He should assist us to make His essence, which is hidden within us, manifest in all of our thoughts, words, and deeds. This is the true goal of our labor in this world, that we transform our body from something that conceals God to something that reveals and expresses Him. Through refining ourselves constantly and diligently, we can eventually make ourselves a channel for what we truly and ultimately are. At that point, every action we perform, every word we speak, and even every thought we conceive, will expose our Godly essence. This will be the fulfillment of the charge in the Torah's opening words: "Breishis bara Elokim/the primary thing is to reveal God."[47]

Halleluy-ah!

The word "הַלְלוּיָ-ה/halleluy-ah" is similar to "y'hei shmei rabba..." in that it also refers to God's name and its exposure. It is actually a compound of two Hebrew words: "הַלְלוּ/hallelu," which means "praise," and "יָ-ה/Y-ah," which is another name of God. Together, the word "halleluy-ah" literally translates as "praise God." But what does it mean to praise God? Just as we asked earlier what it means to "bless" God, now we must explore what "praising" Him connotes. What exactly is one declaring when s/he says "halleluy-ah/praise God" dozens of times throughout the prayer service?

To praise something generally means to express approval of it. When we praise a person, we mention his or her positive qualities, indicating our feeling of admiration or appreciation. To praise God is likewise a statement of recognition and gratitude. We acknowledge His greatness and His generosity. But why do we do so? God does not need our praise. He does not have an ego or a longing for congratulation or validation. Our intention in mentioning His sublimity may be to remind ourselves of the source of our blessings, to publicize His sovereignty to those who are not aware of it, and to express our gratitude and allegiance to Him with the hope that He will continue to favor us with His

---

[47] For more on this interpretation of "Y'hei shmei rabba m'vorach" and this correlation of "l'olam u'l'almei almaya" to the garments of thought, speech and action, see *Likkutei Torah*, parshas Reeh.

guidance and kindness. While all of this provides plenty of good reason to extol God, the word "halleluy-ah" carries an additional nuance which can elevate our "praise" to a far more profound level.

The chassidic masters point out that the word "hallel/praise" derives from the root "ל-ה/hil" which means to light or ignite. This is evidenced in the following verse from the book of Job:

בְּהִלּוֹ נרוֹ עֲלֵי רֹאשִׁי לאוֹרוֹ אֵלֶךְ חֹשֶׁךְ:

BeHILo nero alai roshi l'oro yeilech choshech.
When **He lit** His candle over my head; by His light I
would go through the darkness.
(Job 29:3)

In this sense, "halleluy-ah" means to ignite the "יָ-ה/Y-H" or to make it shine. What is this "Y-H" that we desire to kindle and irradiate? We indicated above that "יָ-ה/Y-ah" is another name of God, but more specifically, it is the first two letters of the divine name "יְ-הוה/Y-H-V-H" (which is articulated as "A-donai" in order not to pronounce the holy name). This first half of the name, "יָ-ה/Y-ah," alludes to the concealed aspect of God, and the second half of the name, "ו-ה/V-H," alludes to the aspect of God that is more revealed in the world. The expression "halleluy-ah" is thus a supplication for the "Y-H" to be illuminated and emblazoned throughout the darkness. It is yet another affirmation of our goal, which is to make our hidden Godliness shine. The true "praise" of God is the revelation of His oneness. Nothing we can say or do can possibly express His greatness more than the simple manifestation of His essential hidden truth.

Where is this essence concealed? As we have illustrated, it is within our essence. It is buried beneath our flesh and all of the layers of this "olam/world" of "helam/hiddenness" that were created to conceal it. The "panim/face" of God is buried in our "pnimyus/core." We want it to shine so that we can see it and find our way back to it. It is a beacon that we strive to light so that we know how to get back home. Each "halleluy-ah" is the striking of the flint, the blowing on the spark to help it glow, the stoking of the flames so that they grow into a blaze that can no longer be concealed, ignored, or denied.   In this sense, we can understand why Moses' face shone with beams of light when he descended from Mount Sinai:

וַיְהִי בְּרֶדֶת מֹשֶׁה מֵהַר סִינַי וּשְׁנֵי לֻחֹת הָעֵדֻת בְּיַד־מֹשֶׁה בְּרִדְתּוֹ מִן־הָהָר: וּמֹשֶׁה לֹא־יָדַע כִּי קָרַן **עוֹר פָּנָיו** בְּדַבְּרוֹ אִתּוֹ:

*Vayehi b'redes Moshe me'har Sinai u'shnei luchos ha'edus b'yad Moshe b'ridto min hahar u'Moshe lo yada ki **karan ohr panav** b'dabro ito.*

And it came to pass when Moses descended from Mount Sinai, and the two tablets of the testimony were in Moses' hand when he descended from the mountain and Moses did not know that **the skin of his face had become radiant** while He had spoken with him.

(Exodus 34:29)

As a result of his intimate contact with God throughout his forty days and nights on the mountain, the light within Moses glowed so brightly that it could no longer be restrained. The "face" of God which was implanted within him burst forth and radiated from his own face. So bright was this radiance that Moses wore a veil in order that those around him would not become blinded. This expression of one's inner Godliness is what we aspire to ourselves, and this is precisely what we are praying for with each utterance of "halleluy-ah."

On the surface, one is offering thanks and devotion to a God that is somewhere beyond us, in an effort to bring Him close, or to convince Him to continue to care for us. But on a deeper level, the intention of terms like "halleluy-ah," "Baruch atta A-donai," and "y'hei shmei rabba m'vorach," is not to praise something outside of us, but to remind ourselves to express what is within us. Prayer, and religious service in general, is commonly understood as means of requesting favor and benevolent treatment from a distant, superior being who looks down upon us with judgment and frequent displeasure. Yet as we have seen from these examples, the goal of Torah prayer is to arouse the Godly face that is within us, to awaken the ultimate us, and to enable it be expressed.

We could even go so far as to suggest that all of Torah practice - the entire system of study, worship, and ritual observance - is a series of meditations and practical actions intended to constantly redirect one's consciousness and awareness to what s/he truly is, pure Godliness, and to help one to remove the darkness and crust that conceals this holy truth. The prayer that underlies every prayer is that wherever I go and whatever I do, may I be conscious of my divine reality, may I express it, and may I live according to it. As we conduct our lifelong search and mission, as we move through the darkness, may we be aware that the light that we seek is within us. May we conduct ourselves and our search in the way of dignity and integrity that befits a divine being. And may our light burst forth to illuminate our way and the way of those around us.

This revolutionary consciousness will change our life and significantly assist us in our search and on our journey. We have come a far distance already, although our odyssey has barely begun. We now know where we need to go, and we have lit the inner torch to guide us through the darkness. This is not to suggest that the path ahead will be easy however. Even as we catch glimmers of how holy we ultimately are and how infinite our potential, we remain in a thick shadow that obscures our vision and clarity. We frequently wonder, "if I am Godly, then why don't I feel Godly; and on the contrary, why do I feel so ungodly so often?" The darkness does not give way readily because it serves the divine purpose of maintaining the illusion of multiplicity which allows for our individual existence. Therefore, we must live in the dark and carry the light.

The constant remembrance of the infinite Godliness within us will enable us to continue on our way even as our surroundings threaten to overwhelm us with fatigue and despair. In the following chapter, we will move further along our pathway as we begin to explore how the consciousness of the inner face of God will transform our every moment from one of uncertainty and human frailty, to one of determination, dignity, and fully exploited potential.

Chapter 5: INFINITE POTENTIAL

The Next Question

We began this book with one question, and now we are ready to introduce another. The initial question was "Ayecha/ where are you?" It is, as we discussed, God's first and eternal question. It is our invitation to undertake the search that will involve us every moment of our lives. It is our safeguard against complacency, and our reminder to never allow ourselves to be lulled into the trance of this world's deceptive facade. It is our mission statement, to constantly seek that deepest aspect of ourselves which is not apparent and not fully actualized.

Throughout the previous chapters, we have addressed this first question and have begun to provide an answer, or at least a path that will lead us to the answer. Where are you? You are within. "You," the true and ultimate you, is the face of God that is embedded within your innermost core. That is what we are seeking, and that is what we are challenged to reveal. This answer is a tremendous step, but it is only the beginning of the journey. The proposition of "Ayecha" is not merely to know where "You" can be found, but to eventually render this "You" unhidden so that the question need no longer be asked. Our goal, as we explained, is to move from "modeh" to "baruch," from the stage of acknowledgement in which we admit to our truth though it is concealed, to the stage of revelation in which this truth is seen and no longer merely a matter of faith or belief. This is our daily and lifelong labor.

In the process of addressing the question "where are you," we have also touched on several other questions: 'what are you,' 'who are you,' and even 'why are you.' You are pure Godliness that has been placed in a world of concealment and covered in flesh so that God can express His infinite love to an "other," and so that there can be a light which proceeds from darkness which is more brilliant than the original light itself (to summarize in one long sentence what we developed at length in the first three chapters). Now that we've devoted some time to 'where,' 'what,' 'who,' and 'why are you,' we're ready to ask the next question:

How are you?

The question here is not 'how' as in 'how did you come to be,' or 'how is it possible for you to exist as an individual being when God is a complete and singular unity.' We addressed both of those questions briefly in our previous discussions, and a more thorough exploration of these issues are beyond the scope of this book. The mechanics of creation and the devolution of distinct physical matter from a nonmaterial celestial unity are treated at length in Kabbala and some of the more esoteric works of Chassidus. It is a fascinating and complicated subject, but it is not what we are concerned with here. The 'how are you' that we are asking at this point is 'how are you doing,' or 'how are you feeling?' It is an inquiry of your well-being, and an expression of interest and concern.

One might wonder if this question is as pressing as the others. After all, God does not ask it as clearly and directly as He asked the first. While "where are you/ayecha" is explicitly mentioned in the Torah text, 'how are you' is not. Therefore, one might be left with the false impression that God does not care how we feel, and that our feelings are irrelevant to our pursuit of the mission He assigns us. This could not be further from the truth, nor is such an attitude at all conducive to assuring our mission's success. God loves His creations infinitely, and He wants nothing more for us than to experience His love and care. This, as we have discussed,[48] is one of the fundamental reasons that He created us and all of the framework in which we exist, in order to have someone(s) to whom He could express His love - "teva hatov l'heitiv / it is the nature of the good to do good." This idea is similarly expressed in a phrase from Psalms:

עוֹלָם חֶסֶד יִבָּנֶה:

Olam chesed yibaneh.
The world is built on lovingkindness.
(Psalms 89:3)

We see here that "חֶסֶד / chesed / lovingkindness," is not just one of the building blocks of creation, it is its very foundation. To illustrate the degree to which God adores His creations, and to enable us to relate to this love in some fashion that could make sense to us, the Baal Shem Tov[49] taught that God loves each of us more than parents love an only child who was born to them in their old age after they had been unable to bear children throughout their youth. Furthermore, while some mistakenly assume that this love is predicated on obedience or compliance, we will see that it is not, in fact, conditional or contingent. This is demonstrated in the prayer in the daily evening service which is said just prior to the recitation of the Shema:

אַהֲבַת עוֹלָם בֵּית יִשְׂרָאֵל עַמְּךָ אָהָבְתָּ: תּוֹרָה וּמִצְוֹת חֻקִּים וּמִשְׁפָּטִים אוֹתָנוּ לִמַּדְתָּ:

Ahavas olam beis Yisrael amcha ahavta. Torah u'mitzvos chukim umishpatim osanu limadta.
With eternal love You have loved your people the house of Israel. Torah and commandments, decrees, and laws You taught to us.

The order of these two sentences is significant. First God's love is recognized, and only thereafter are his commandments mentioned. This order is intentional in order to assure us that God loves us not because,

---

48 See chapter 2, section "Good Nature."

49 Rabbi Israel Baal Shem Tov, 1698-1760, the founder of the Chassidic Movement.

or only when, we fulfill His law. But rather, on the contrary, He gave us His law because He loves us. The law is thus not a prerequisite for God's love, it is a result of it. It is something He provides us to enable us to connect with Him, to embrace the infinite and to be embraced within it. We don't earn God's love, we are a manifestation of it. The question is not whether or not we are loved by Him, but whether or not we are aware of His adoration.[50]

With all this, there will still be many who question or doubt God's love and concern for them. If God loved me, they will contest, then my life would not be so difficult. If He loves me, they will ask, then why does He not make this love obvious? What kind of love is it that is unseen and disputable? If He truly loves me, then why can I even question the existence of His love?

To these questions, the sages have offered a variety of answers, but their first response is empathy. This empathy comes with the awareness and the admission that life is not easy and its challenges are many. The questions are not only valid, they are not only normal, but they are healthy and even holy. The tears that all of us have shed in our moments of loneliness and uncertainty are sacred tears. They are not signs of our weakness, but of our humanity. Being human means being lost, as we have discussed at length. Being in this world of concealment means being uncertain, as we seem to be separated from our source and our truth. The greater our feeling of distance from God, the greater is our yearning for Him, and the greater will be our efforts to find and reunite with Him. So the questions and doubts are not only understandable, but they are productive.

After empathizing with our questions and the feelings of alienation and forsakenness that they reflect, the sages then address the questions themselves. On the simplest level, they urge us to question our assertion that God's love is not obvious. Look at our lives, the very gift of life itself - the ability to exist, and grow, and learn, and love, and see the sun rise and set, etc. Are these precious gifts not blatant expressions of God's love for us? Such appreciation of our blessings, or the refocusing of our vision and consciousness on all that we have rather than all that

---

[50] For a wonderful discussion of this topic, see "Is God Always Angry" by Rabbi Yossi Jacobson at www.theyeshiva.net

we lack, this cultivation of gratitude will enable us to begin to recognize and sense God's love.

But this does not answer our question about the difficulties and pain that we encounter. If God loves me, then why is life so hard? To this, the sages ask us to consider whether challenges truly reflect a lack of love. Is it true that our lives would be only easy and pain free if God adored us? Would we be showered with everything we desired? Or is it possible that the distress, deficiencies, and discomforts that we experience are also expressions of divine beneficence and care? Can we grow without challenge? Do we not grow complacent when we have no incentive to shift and flex and move in a new direction?

Love, we come to understand, is not expressed only in giving, but sometimes in restraint. When a child asks for candy, it is sometimes more loving to withhold it than to supply it unstintingly. While the child may not understand our refusal to gratify all of her/his desires, it is clearly our love for her/him that compels us to deny these requests. When our desires are not automatically fulfilled, we are forced to adapt and to reconsider our needs, all of which enables us to mature and grow and further refine our conception of what we are and why we are here. Small and fleeting pleasures give way to more profound and lasting understanding and appreciation, and we will eventually realize that it was the frustrations and disappointments that proved to be God's greatest gifts.

As for our question of why God allows us to be uncertain of His love, we have addressed this subject at length already. The only way that God can love us is to conceal Himself from us. If He were to be revealed, if the full nature and glory of His being were to be manifest without the contraction, limitation, and obscuration that He has imposed on Himself, then nothing other would continue to exist. Ultimately, this awareness is the most compelling confirmation of His love for us. God loves us because He IS us. Love is generally understood in human terms as one's deep affection for another. However, quintessential love is the absolute fusion that results from the recognition that there is no other. This concept of complete unity is abstruse and challenging for the human mind due to the elaborate mechanics of creation that God has constructed to conceal it. However, unlike human vision, God's vision is never deluded by the illusions of this world. He loves us even if we do not recognize our oneness with Him, and even if we fail to love Him back.

Loving us in such a way, God certainly cares how we are feeling and doing. Though He may not ask us "how are you" as explicitly as He asks us "where are you," His concern for us is implicit in His love for us. Though He allows us to struggle, this is in order for us to grow and succeed. Though we have suffered as individuals, as a people, and as a species throughout our history, this must not be seen as a sign of God's disinterest or His absence, but as a part of His plan and His concealed presence. As we discussed in chapter one, the doctrine of "hashgacha protis/divine providence" indicates that there is nothing that occurs anywhere or at any time in God's creation that is beyond His purview and His concern. He cares for every one of His creations and is involved with our every step and our every movement. Though He provides us free choice and does not control our thoughts or compel our conduct, He has given us an intricate system of rituals and practices that will enable us to maintain awareness of His constant presence. He has revealed to us His way and His wisdom, and through study and practice, we can achieve the spiritual and emotional health that He desires for us. In effect, He asks us about our welfare constantly, urging us to evaluate our being and existence at every moment and offering us the opportunity to change our course if we are moving in a direction that is not one of joy and meaning and deep satisfaction.

So how are you?

Be honest. Do not be afraid to ask yourself this question, and do not think that you are not supposed to focus on your feelings or your well-being. God wants to know. Or rather, He knows, of course, but He wants you to pay attention to your inner state. This is not self-indulgence, it is self-awareness. It is not for the sake of self-service, but for the sake of self-improvement, self-transcendence, and ultimately self-actualization. How do you feel - not just at this moment, but in your life more generally? If you were to stop at multiple random moments throughout the day and spot check your emotional state, what would you find? There would undoubtedly be a range of emotions at various times and in various circumstances, but if we were to aggregate these moments in order to create an average, what would your baseline be? By and large, do you feel fulfilled and positive? Do you feel clear and confident? Do you feel pleased with who you are and what you have done with the time you have been allotted? Or do you feel uncertain? Do you feel adrift and alone? Do you feel anxious, or ashamed, or inferior, or blemished, or unworthy?

We will find that our answer to the question "how are you" will be inextricably linked to our first question, "where are you," and to its subsidiaries "what," who," and "why" are you, which we have been addressing. With the proper approach to those initial questions, the answer to the question of our feelings will be tremendously positive. Asked "how are you," we can consistently respond 'I'm great!' Such a response is possible when it is not merely a statement of how one feels, but a recognition of how one IS. I AM great, and therefore, I feel great. know where the ultimate me is to be found; I am aware of the true nature of my essence; I see the "Pnei Hashem/face of God" within my "pnimyus/ inner core," and I subsequently appreciate my enormous value and capabilities. This awareness will foster not only profound joy and confidence, but it will enable us to act in accordance with our inherent greatness.

Feeling Great, Being Great

Earlier, in chapter two, we identified our goal and purpose in life as it is disclosed in the very first verse of the Torah: "Breishis bara Elokim es hashamayim v'es haaretz/the primary thing is to reveal God in the heavens and the earth." In chapter three, we then discussed God's first command to Abraham, "lech lecha/go to yourself," and we learned that our lifelong task is to discover our true self which is hidden deep within us. We wrestled with this seeming contradiction, asking whether our ultimate task is the revelation of God, or the discovery of our self. We reconciled the two directives with the insight that God is hidden in our core, and therefore, finding the one will allow us to find and reveal the other. But what does not seem to be included in either of these statements of our life's work is the imperative to be happy or to feel good. Therefore, it would be reasonable to wonder what role, if any, happiness plays in the pursuit of our mission and goal. Perhaps it would be possible to suggest that as long as we are working to "lech lecha," i.e. find ourself, and "bara Elokim," i.e. reveal God, it is not relevant whether we are joyous, miserable, or somewhere in between.

To forestall any such conclusion, the Torah commands us "ivdu es Hashem b'simcha/serve God with joy." As we discussed in chapter two,[51] this is not a suggestion, but a demand and requirement. The point of life is not to suffer in servitude, or even to merely obey stoically and mechanically, but to serve with pleasure and delight. It could be said that if we are not serving God with joy, then we are not serving Him properly at all. This is because proper service will necessarily bring us joy. It is not that being happy is the goal, but rather that joy is the inevitable bi-product of pursuing our goal of finding our true self and revealing God.

We saw this earlier in the verse from the morning prayers, "yismach leiv m'vakshei Hashem/happy of heart is the one who seeks God." What is it about this search that makes one joyous? It is the knowledge that the face of God is within us even if we cannot see it clearly, and even if we have yet to make it revealed. It is the awareness of our inherent and essential greatness that makes us feel great. And it is this sense of our tremendous potential, and the feelings of incredible optimism and elation that arise from it, which will ultimately enable us to manifest the greatness that is hidden within us. From all this, we begin to understand that the awareness of the Godly face within us is both the source of our joy and its outcome: knowing our Godly essence and core creates immense positivity, and then that positivity enables us to fulfill the arduous task of withstanding and overcoming the darkness so that we can finally bring God's face to a state of revelation.

It is no secret that one's attitude is a major determinant of her/his reality. One's self-image will significantly shape the figure that s/he projects. It is not surprising, then, that a society which downplays the inherent goodness and interconnectedness of its members will produce a culture that is, at best, individualistic and libertarian, and at worst, decadent, narcissistic, and cruel. To understand why modern culture has veered into stark divisiveness and increasingly frequent violence, we need only recognize the angst and despondency of several generations that were reared on notions of existentialism, atheism, nihilism, and naturalism. These and a host of other 'isms' have encouraged them, either

---

[51] Section "Obligatory Happiness"

subtly or more blatantly, to question their intrinsic worth and their fundamental goodness.

Even in homes and communities that clung to "traditional" and "religious" values, the prevailing concepts are not much more encouraging or optimistic. Adherents have been inculcated, again either subtly or more vehemently, with the belief that they are sinners by nature. They are convinced that they have been conceived and born in lust and immorality, and that they must constantly do their penance and strive against their backsliding inclination. It is hard to blame those who turned to the 'isms' and turned away from these dogmas that constantly pressed them down and tried to convince them that they were base and degenerate beings who could only be redeemed if they complied with various strictures and requirements.

But whether one is a "believer" or a skeptic, the conceptions of self that have characterized modern humanity - be it a weak and wayward brute, a mannered animal, or a fleeting figment of nothingness - have often left us less than inspired or empowered. This would be sad but inevitable if the truth were as bleak as these ideologies portrayed them. But as we are, in fact, divine, and as the face of God does indeed reside within us, therefore, these misconceptions of our being and misrepresentations of our nature have been responsible for so much avoidable suffering, heartache, and squandered potential.

Human Nature

To appreciate the profound difference between the Torah's conception of a person and other non-Torah views, it is helpful to compare and contrast the terms that are used to describe humankind. The word with which the Torah designates humanity is "אָדָם / Adam." Though the term is also the proper name of the first man, it is employed more generally to refer to the species of beings of whom Adam was the first. Eve, too, was included in the name Adam, as we can see in the verse that introduces them:

וַיִּבְרָא אֱ-לֹהִים אֶת־הָאָדָם בְּצַלְמוֹ בְּצֶלֶם אֱ-לֹהִים בָּרָא אֹתוֹ
זָכָר וּנְקֵבָה בָּרָא אֹתָם:

Va'yivra E-lohim es Ha-Adam b'tzalmo, b'tzelem E-lohim bara oso, zachar u'nekeiva bara osam.

And God created man (ha-Adam) in His image; in the image of God He created him; male and female He created them.

(Genesis 1:27)

"Adam" here is used to refer both to "him" and to "them." In English, we see a similar duality in the word "man." While the term more specifically refers to a male person, in a more general sense it can be employed as a reference to "mankind." In such a usage, it is a shortened form of the term "human," which categorizes the entire species. The derivation of "human," and of the Latinate "homo," which classifies an even wider range of primate species, is from the Proto-Indo-European term "(dh)gomon," which means "earthling" and is itself a derivative of the root "dhghem," which means "earth." A human being, according to the etymology of the term, is an "earthling," one who inhabits the earth and who derives from the earth.

The Hebrew "adam" shares this connotation of earthliness. The word "אֲדָמָה/Adama" means "earth" or "ground." On the simple level, it is because the human being was formed from the dust of the ground that s/he is called Adam.

וַיִּיצֶר יְ-הֹוָה אֱ-לֹהִים אֶת־**הָאָדָם** עָפָר מִן־**הָאֲדָמָה** וַיִּפַּח
בְּאַפָּיו נִשְׁמַת חַיִּים וַיְהִי הָאָדָם לְנֶפֶשׁ חַיָּה:

*Va'yitzer A-donai E-lohim es Ha'**Adam** afar min ha-**Adama** vayipach b'apav nishmas chayim vayehi ha-Adam l'nefesh chaya.*

And the Lord God formed **man (ha'Adam)** of the dust from the **ground (ha'Adama)**, and He breathed into his nostrils the soul of life, and man became a living soul.

(Genesis 2:7)

However, the sages teach that there is another reason why humanity is referred to as 'Adam.' While the term links the human to her/his earthy origins, it has an additional connotation as well. 'Adam' is also derived from the word "adameh," which means 'like' or 'similar.' The rabbis[52] teach that humanity was given the name "adam" because we are "adameh l'Elyon/similar to the Most High."[53] In this sense of the word, our name indicates our loftiness and our resemblance to our Creator.

This comparison to God is also emphasized in the verse from the first chapter of Genesis quoted above which states that we were created "in His image." What does it mean to be created in the image of God? As we know, God has no form or image per se. The expression conveys that there is something about the human creation that carries God's likeness within it. However, as God is one and all, then would this not be true of every one of His creations? Yet it is stated explicitly and exclusively in regard to mankind. This is because the human being is the entity in which God infused Himself most distinctly. The human has the ability to know that God is within him/her, to comprehend that s/he is created in God's image, and to make that image manifest.

The human being, according to Torah, is thus "Adam," a fusion of opposites, as we see from both of these connotations of her/his name. S/he is comprised of both the "earth/adama," and of Godliness, "adameh l'Elyon/similar to the Most High." The English/European 'human,' on the contrary, is strictly a creature of the earth. Nothing in her/his name suggests any relationship to the celestial. What has been lost in translation is the duality - the presence of holiness within the profane.

We can further see this limited view of mankind in the usage of the term "human" to express deficiency and weakness. We say that one is "only human," to explain his/her frailty and to excuse her/his fallibility. We invoke "human nature" to describe our selfish tendencies and baser inclinations. When "human" is utilized in such a pejorative fashion, it is not only a justification and rationalization for our misbehavior, but it is a self-fulfilling prophecy. We cannot help ourselves, we assume, because it is simply the way we are. But when we are "Adam," on the contrary, when we are both "adama/earth" and "adameh l'elyon/similar to the Most High," then we cannot say that we are "only human." Unlike "human," "Adam" is a term of great esteem. It would make no sense to

---

[52] Including the Shelah Hakadosh in his introduction to "Toldos Adam." The Shelah, Rabbi Isaiah Horowitz, lived in Israel from 1555-1630 and was a renowned mystic known by the acronym of his work "Shnei Luchot Habris."

[53] Isaiah 14:14

say one is "only Godly" as an excuse for reprobate behavior. When one realizes that s/he is "adam,' and not merely human, then s/he will not continue to be satisfied with being only earthly and failing to express the Godliness within her/him.

When we explore the nature and essence of what we truly are, we will carve through the misconceptions and deceptions, and we will ultimately reveal our true grandeur and holiness. We will find that we are tremendous and full of infinite potential. We have a purpose and every ability to fulfill it. This awareness imbues incredible self-esteem and dispels all of the insecurity and angst that has characterized so much of human existence until now. It removes the sackcloth of self-recrimination and self-flagellation and enables us to change into the robes that are fit for our royalty. We will expect more of ourselves when we understand our true selves, and when we see ourselves as nobles rather than brutes. We will live our best lives when we realize that our lives are precious and divine.

Being And Becoming

There is an idea that we are not 'human beings,' but rather 'human becomings.' The notion is that we are ever evolving, and that we must never limit ourselves to the state in which we find ourselves at the moment. Rather, we must always allow ourselves, and push ourselves, to grow and progress further. In Torah, this idea is expressed frequently. As we discussed in chapter three, God's first direction to Abraham was "lech lecha/go to yourself." The process of self-discovery is one of constant going. We must travel "me'artzecha/from your land," in other words from the place where we began, and we must wander through the desert, through a variety of exiles, throughout the millennia, in order to approach our eventual destination. From the first day of human creation, we were exiled from the garden, and we have been trekking and "becoming" ever since.

As a matter of fact, it is our ability to move and progress that distinguishes us from angels and places us on a higher level than they can achieve. Angels are referred to as "עֹמְדִים/omdim / standing ones," while humans are known as "מַהְלְכִים/mehalchim / walking ones":

כֹּה־אָמַר יְ-הֹוָה צְבָאוֹת **אִם־בִּדְרָכַי תֵּלֵךְ** וְאִם אֶת־מִשְׁמַרְתִּי תִשְׁמֹר וְגַם־אַתָּה תָּדִין אֶת־בֵּיתִי וְגַם תִּשְׁמֹר אֶת־חֲצֵרָי וְנָתַתִּי לְךָ **מַהְלְכִים** בֵּין **הָעֹמְדִים** הָאֵלֶּה:

Koh amar A-donai Tzevaos **im b'drachai teilech**, v'im es mishmarti tishmor, v'gam atta tadin es beisi v'gam tishmore es chatzeiri v'nasati lecha **mehalchim** bein ha'**omdim** ha'eileh.

So said the Lord of Hosts: **If you walk in My ways**, and if you keep My charge, you, too, shall judge My house, and you, too, shall guard My courtyards, and I will give you free access among **those who stand by**.

(Zecharia 3:7)

God refers to angels here as "those who stand by," and he promises that we humans will be able to move freely in the realm of the angels if we "walk in (His) ways." It is not simply the fulfillment of God's will that earns a person this lofty privilege, for that is implied by the expression "keep my charge" which is also mentioned in the citation. In addition to this basic level of performance signified by "keep my charge," one must also "walk in my ways," constantly proceeding and progressing, in order to raise her/himself to the heavens. Once there, s/he is not merely on par with the celestial beings, but even higher than they. Angels are called "omdim/those who stand" because while they inhabit a very lofty level of spirituality, they are incapable of growth or change. They are unable to deviate from their assigned trajectory and become more or less than what they already are. We, on the contrary, have the potential to fall or to rise, and when we choose to elevate ourselves in spite of the difficulties in doing so, we display the unique greatness of human existence.

This idea of the power of growth and movement can also be seen in the following statement of the sages:

מָקוֹם שֶׁבַּעֲלֵי תְשׁוּבָה עוֹמְדִין צַדִּיקִים גְּמוּרִים אֵינָם עוֹמְדִין:

Makom she'baalei teshuvah omdin tzadikim gemurim einam omdin.

In the place where penitents stand, the perfectly righteous do not stand.

(Talmud, Brachot 34b)

While one may be a "tzaddik," one who is perfectly righteous
and never swerving from her/his divine service, it is the "baal teshuvah,"
the one who has fallen and then chosen to pick her/himself up and return to God's way, who demonstrates the true immensity of human potential. Ultimately, the human was designed to be one who is constantly
moving and advancing.

But while this notion of "human becoming" expresses the imperative for perpetual progress and improvement, there is a truth to the
concept of "human being" that is also profound and frequently overlooked. Because we are "adam," and thus "adameh l'elyon/similar to the
Most High," we are already, by our very nature, that which we aspire to
being. The idea of 'becoming' implies that we are not yet what or where
we are supposed, or destined, to be. We must do something, change
something, or create something that doesn't already exist. However,
Torah teaches that we need not become something different, other, or
new in order to fulfill our mission and purpose. Rather we must simply
return to what we inherently are. This, as we mentioned in chapter
three,[54] is the concept of "תְּשׁוּבָה/teshuvah." Although the word is commonly translated as "repentance," the Torah's notion of self-improvement and self-actualization is not that one must punish her/himself for
who s/he is, or turn away from where s/he has come. This punitive approach to the self is the implication of the word "repent," the root '-pent'
deriving from the Latin 'poenitire' meaning 'make sorry.' 'Teshuvah,' on
the contrary, literally means "return," and our work is not to suppress or
eradicate some wayward nature, but rather to constantly peel away the
things that have covered and concealed our essence so that we can express and expose the purity and brilliance that has always existed within.

In the above-referenced citation from the Talmud, it is said that
the "tzaddik," who is perfectly righteous, cannot stand in the place of the
"baal teshuvah," who has strayed and returned. This is because the true
"baal teshuvah" is the one who has mastered this process of return - s/he
is the "baal/master" of "teshuvah/return." One who is completely right-

---

[54] See section "Inward Bound"

eous may comply with all of the laws and may never stray from the pre-scribed path, but this is not yet the apex of human existence. We are not here to simply follow rules and avoid transgression. We are here, as we have discussed at length, to find our true selves and to reveal God in a place where He is hidden. It is true that we manifest Godliness in the world through performance of "mitzvos" (more on this later), but it is also true that one can be fully compliant with Torah law, and simultane-ously fully ignorant of her/his potential and responsibility to manifest Godliness in everything s/he touches and affects. The "baal teshuvah," in the ideal and ultimate meaning of the term, is one who has dug so deeply into her/his core that s/he has discovered the face of God that is buried there. S/he knows that just as it is Godliness that underlies her/his inherent being, so too this Godliness underlies all being. When we "return" to the source and essence of all things, we find the simple and sublime truth that there is only one thing. We need not become some-thing else, we need simply to revert to this singular truth and to allow ourselves to be what we have always been.

The difference here is not merely semantic. One's basic concep-tion of humanity, and of the universe more generally, is fundamentally different when we are aware of the goodness and Godliness that is lodged in our own center and in the center of every component of exis-tence. Rather than a dark, difficult, and malevolent world that needs to be battled, conquered, and redesigned, we find ourselves in a realm of obscured luminescence which merely needs to be stripped of its screens and shrouds. Rather than laboring arduously and endlessly to construct something that does not yet exist, our task is simply to uncover the bril-liant and intricate edifice that has been built into us and around us and which is waiting to be unveiled. What's more, the veil itself is not wicked or destructive - its purpose, as we have seen, is to protect us from a light so bright that we cannot withstand its infinite gleam.

None of this is to suggest that our task is easy or that there are not real and profound challenges that we face daily. Yet our ability to meet and overcome these challenges will be significantly augmented when we are cognizant of both the Godliness that is within them - i.e. the divine wisdom and benevolence that is, as yet, beyond our line of vision - and the Godliness that is within us - i.e. our immeasurable strength and potential. We can see this in an expression that is commonly used to encourage those who are facing a daunting endeavor: "you have it in you," we tell them, assuring them of their ability to succeed. What we are reminding them with this reassurance is that the capability and fortitude that they require is not something that they need to obtain or manufacture, but rather it is something that they already possess and embody. The implication, of course, is that it is easier for us to access something that we own than it is to acquire something that we lack. And while it is not always simple for us to tap the deep stores of power and aptitude that are contained within us, we are far more likely to draw upon them and harness them when we know that they are there.

In short, while some would suggest that our goal in life is to express our human potential, what we are proposing here is that our task is to reveal that we are not actually "human," but we are rather "adam," and thus we are inherently divine. We are not created to 'become,' but to shed those things that conceal what we already are. We need not create or generate light, we need simply to stop suppressing and impeding the infinite light that crouches within us. Our work is not creation or even transformation; it is release, expression, and revelation. We must let go of the mask and let it fall away, and we will eventually understand that wearing it, or holding it in place, is more exhausting than allowing it to drop.

The Lubavitcher Rebbe[55] used to greet people outside of his Brooklyn headquarters on various special occasions. Long lines would form, and people would wait for hours to see the Rebbe in person and to receive from him a word or two of blessing. It is said that the Rebbe had the most penetrating eyes, and standing in his presence one would have the sensation of being seen through and through. People from various walks of life would queue up in front of his headquarters at 770 Eastern Parkway. Some of them were the Rebbe's devoted chassidim, some were Jews from other denominations who had heard of the Rebbe's salutary blessings, and some of them were secular and unaffiliated individuals who weren't quite sure what had drawn them there. On one of these occasions, one of those in line was a young man who had been struggling for years with various internal challenges. He had recently begun to pull his life together and to turn away from the self-destructive behaviors that

---

[55] Rabbi Menachem Mendel Schneerson, the seventh Rebbe of the Chabad chassidic dynasty, 1902-1994.

had dogged him until now. He came to the Rebbe with one of his relatives who, when they reached the front of the line, gestured to the young man and said to the Rebbe, "he's becoming a good boy." The Rebbe looked at the young man and smiled. He then turned to the relative and corrected him: "he's always been good, he just didn't know it."

Not In Heaven

Knowing what we are will render us far more capable of expressing our true potential. It is true that we are still in the darkness. We still have a long way to travel and much to accomplish. As long as we are in this "olam/world," we are still immersed in a place of "helam/hiddenness," and we have yet to complete the task of revealing the light that is concealed within us and within everything. However, the awareness that the "Pnei Hashem/face of God" is embedded in our "pnimyus/inner core" is crucial for our lifelong task of taking it from a state of being known (modeh) to a state of being shown (baruch). This awareness is not merely the first step of the process, it is the lantern that lights the way for every step that follows. The question and challenge of "ayecha/where are you" is still on the table. However, with the question of "how are you," we have begun to feel a bit lighter and more buoyant, and this lightness makes the darkness a bit less oppressive and foreboding.

It is interesting that the term 'light' in one sense describes the quality of weight or weightlessness, and in another sense, it describes the quality of illumination and visibility. The two are related of course. The less heavy one feels emotionally, the more bright her/his surroundings seem to be. The more despondent and immobile one feels, the less her/his inner light glows, and the less luster s/he is able to share with her/his environment. Therefore, the awareness of our inner Godliness, even as it remains concealed in our deepest depths, has made us both more agile and more radiant, and the path ahead as we continue is thus less treacherous and intimidating.

We can now move along the path with purpose, direction, and even urgency, but without pressure, guilt, or anxiety. The darkness is not our fault, but it is our responsibility. It is our concern, but not our worry.

We are good, we are Godly, and furthermore we recognize that the God-liness within us is the same Godliness that enwraps us. The darkness is not evil, for there is no true evil. There is only the One God (A-donai echad) and the various mechanisms through which He allows Himself to be either hidden or revealed. Seeing the world as such, we are able to pursue our mission not as a burden or a trial, but as an opportunity and a purpose. Seeing oneself as such, we replace self-recrimination with self-esteem. We lose our ego as we find our infinite essence. We harness the strength of something so much larger than ourselves, and we are thus humbled in the enormity of our task, but we are simultaneously confident in the One who has sent us and who dwells within us.

As our optimism continues to swell with the recognition of our tremendous potential and our inherent worth, concurrently we are bolstered by the realization that our goal is far closer than we had once imagined. It is so close, in fact, that it is within us:

כִּי הַמִּצְוָה הַזֹּאת אֲשֶׁר אָנֹכִי מְצַוְּךָ הַיּוֹם לֹא־נִפְלֵאת הִוא מִמְּךָ וְלֹא־רְחֹקָה הִוא:לֹא בַשָּׁמַיִם הִוא לֵאמֹר מִי יַעֲלֶה־לָּנוּ הַשָּׁמַיְמָה וְיִקָּחֶהָ לָּנוּ וְיַשְׁמִעֵנוּ אֹתָהּ וְנַעֲשֶׂנָּה:וְלֹא־מֵעֵבֶר לַיָּם הִוא לֵאמֹר מִי יַעֲבָר־לָנוּ אֶל־עֵבֶר הַיָּם וְיִקָּחֶהָ לָּנוּ וְיַשְׁמִעֵנוּ אֹתָהּ וְנַעֲשֶׂנָּה: **כִּי־קָרוֹב אֵלֶיךָ הַדָּבָר מְאֹד בְּפִיךָ וּבִלְבָבְךָ לַעֲשֹׂתוֹ:**

*Ki hamitzva hazos asher Anochi mitzavecha hayom lo niflas hi mimcha v'lo rechoka hi. Lo bashamayim hi leimor mi yaaleh lanu hashamayma v'yikacheha lanu v'yashmieinu osa v'-naasena. V'lo maaver layam hi leimor mi yaavar lanu el eiver hayam v'yikacheha lanu v'yashimieiny osa v'naasena. **Ki Karov eilecha hadavar meod b'picha u'vilvavcha laa-soso.***

For this commandment which I command you this day, is not concealed from you, nor is it far away. It is not in heaven, that you should say, 'Who will go up to heaven for us and get it for us, to tell it to us, so that we can fulfill it?' Neither is it beyond the sea, that you should say, 'Who will cross to the other side of the sea for us, and get it for us so that we may hear it and fulfill it?' No, **the thing is very near to you; it is in your mouth and in your heart so that you can fulfill it.**

(Deuteronomy 30:11-14)

Here, God assures us that what He asks of us is not as distant or difficult as we believed it to be. It is, in fact, right here inside of us! Yet in the subsequent verse, God goes on to inform us that He has provided us a choice whether to recognize His closeness and accessibility, or to remain mired in the illusion that He is elsewhere and far:

רְאֵה נָתַתִּי לְפָנֶיךָ הַיּוֹם אֶת־הַחַיִּים וְאֶת־הַטּוֹב וְאֶת־הַמָּוֶת וְאֶת־הָרָע:

Reeh Nasati lifanecha hayom es-hachayim v'es hatov, v'es hamaves v'es hara.

See, I have placed before you today life and good, and death and evil.

(Deuteronomy 30:15)

The "life and good" that we can choose is the awareness of His immanence, while the "death and evil" is the delusion that He has secluded Himself in the distant heavens and that we are cast away from Him in a wasteland that is devoid of His presence. The simple translation of the opening words of the verse, "Reeh Nasati lefanecha," is "see I have placed before you." However, as we have seen earlier with a similar verse - "Reeh Anochi nosein lifneichem/See, I give before you" - the use of the word "lefanecha/before you" is not the simplest or most obvious choice. As the Alter Rebbe commented on that verse, if God's intent were merely to indicate that He was giving something *to* us, then the Hebrew word "lachem/to you" would have been more appropriate. "Lifanecha," as we noted, can mean "to you" or "before you," but it also literally means "to your face." And "panim/face," the chassidic masters explain, is a reference to one's "pnimyus/inner core." Just as we saw in the earlier verse that God was indicating that He placed His level of "Anochi" within our "panim" - His essence within our essence - so too here we find that He has placed the choice of "the life and the good or the death and the bad" within our deepest depths. We choose "the life and the good" when we see Him within us and manifest Him through our deeds, and we choose "the death and the bad" when we fail to sense and express Him. When we are conscious of the "Pnei Hashem/face of God" within our "pnimyus/innermost core," when we become aware of the fact that it "is very near to you, in your mouth and in your heart so that you can fulfill it," we select "hachaim v'hatov/the life and the good." In other words, we are then full of life, and we are able to experience the great good that is available to us at every moment.

This closeness - the fact that what we seek is "not in heaven" and "neither is it beyond the sea" - provides us tremendous hope and inspiration. We are "inspired" in the true sense of the word - we are up-lifted and invigorated by the "spirit" that is "in" us. While it is true that God has hidden Himself from us in this "olam/world" of "helam/con-cealment," and it is therefore the case that we may spend the entire span of our life here seeking Him, the primary question that will determine the nature of our search and the quality of our time is whether we are searching around us or within us. If our search for Him is always leading us to far flung places or ideas that are perpetually somewhere other than the mundane reality in which we find ourselves, then we will forever be reaching for something just beyond our grasp. But when we recognize that He is within us, that He is with us wherever we go and no matter how debased our surroundings, then our quest to find Him is no longer so daunting and difficult.

We need not climb tremendous mountains or perform monu-mental feats. We need not journey to a remote monastery or decipher some cryptic and forgotten language. He is right here. We need not ac-quire Him because we already have Him, and He already has us. We are in His loving arms, and He is in our core. We simply need to be aware of God's presence and permanence within us and then to allow Him to manifest and express Himself through our being. This is true "teshu-vah/return." It does not mean that we must return to some place that we have strayed from and left behind. We must only stop looking and mov-ing outside of ourselves for the thing that is always right there within. We must be still and delve inward, returning to where we begin and where we have always been. There we will find that everything we have ever needed and desired has been awaiting us in the One place that we have never truly left. This process of opening and releasing will not be without effort and travail. But it will be far less grueling than the fleeing, fighting, crushing and reconstructing that we believe to be necessary when we conceive of ourselves as inherently flawed, empty, or forsaken, or when we locate God somewhere outside of us.

Chapter 6: WRAPPINGS AND TRAPPINGS

Skin And Light

The journey, as we have discussed, is not to some distant, remote land or some elusive, exotic locale. The journey is not outward at all, it is within. The "you" that we are directed to seek is buried in our core, where it is fused with the "Pnei Hashem," the essence of Godliness that we were created to reveal. In the previous chapter, we clarified that while this inward voyage will be lifelong and will present frequent challenges, it need not be dismal or painful. With the proper understanding of our essential nature and potential, it can (and therefore must) be joyous. At this point, in order to travel to the destination at our innermost depths, we must open a path, and we must shed the layers of plaque and crust that we have built up around our core. To do so, it will be worthwhile to further explore the nature of, and reasons for, these coverings, and to understand why the process of removing them has spanned the entire course of history.

In chapter one, we explained that our first forebears, Adam and Eve, were created diaphanous. Their skin was translucent because there was no barrier between their interior and their exterior. In that Edenic realm, there was a complete harmony in the creation, and there was no split dividing the Godly essence of things from the casing that contained and expressed it. With the eating of the fruit of the tree of knowledge of good and evil, however, Adam and Eve internalized a duality - good AND evil - and they were now forced to inhabit a world of division and opposition. Immediately after consuming the fruit, they hid. This reaction was a result of their sudden fear and shame, neither of which exist in a state of unity and holism. Self-consciousness and guilt only materialize when we conceive of ourselves as distinct and, therefore, incomplete or defective. "Where are you?" God called to them, and Adam answered:

אֶת־קֹלְךָ שָׁמַעְתִּי בַּגָּן וָאִירָא כִּי־עֵירֹם אָנֹכִי וָאֵחָבֵא:

Es kolcha shamati ba'gan va'ira ki eiram anochi va'eichava.
I heard Your voice in the garden, and I was afraid because I am naked; so I hid.
(Genesis 3:10)

God knew that they had eaten the fruit. He knew that they would. It was a necessary part of the process that began with His complete oneness and culminated in a complex system of otherness and multiplicity. This world was not meant to be translucent and to constantly manifest the Godly essence that resided in its core. It was time to clothe Adam and Eve and conceal their naked truth.

וַיַּעַשׂ יְ-הֹוָה אֱ-לֹהִים לְאָדָם וּלְאִשְׁתּוֹ **כָּתְנוֹת עוֹר** וַיַּלְבִּשֵׁם:

*Vayaas A-donai E-lohim l'adam u'l'ishto **kasnos ohr** vayalbisheim.*
And the Lord God made for Adam and for his wife **coats of skin**, and He dressed them.
(Genesis 3:21)

In the simple sense, this verse indicates that God fashioned "kasnos ohr/coats of skin," which we understand to be garments of leather. But the sages explain that on a deeper level, the skin with which God covered them was not animal hide, but rather their own flesh. Prior to eating the fruit, Adam and Eve were clothed not in skin, but in garments of light. This is taught in the Midrash[56] which states that "in the Torah Scroll of Rabbi Meir, we find that it (the verse cited above) is written "כָּתְנוֹת אוֹר/kasnos ohr," where the word "ohr" is spelled with a letter "א/aleph" rather than the letter "ע/ayin," as it is spelled in the Torah today. The Hebrew word "ohr" can be written either "אוֹר" or "עוֹר." The two spellings are pronounced the same, but with an "א/aleph" - "אוֹר" - the word means "light," and with an "ע/ayin" - "עוֹר" - it means "skin."

The discrepancy of spelling in Rabbi Meir's Torah scroll teaches us that before the eating of the fruit, the human body was composed of glowing light which projected the luminescence that radiated from its Godly core. Afterwards, the "א/aleph" was replaced by an "ע/ayin," and the "light/אוֹר" was replaced by an opaque fleshy "skin/עוֹר." The interior was cut off from the exterior, and the source was hidden away. Subsequently, Adam and Eve were sent from the garden of Eden, and we have been lost ever since. As we explained in chapter one, it is not simply that we have lost our way geographically, but rather the perpetual wandering and seeking throughout our history is a reflection of our inner exile. We have lost our way because we have lost our self. With the installation of a skin that partitions our interior from our exterior, we have been divided from our essence, and we are therefore unaware of who and what we are.

While this state of concealment and exile can be challenging, it is, as we have pointed out repeatedly, precisely God's will and intention. He created a world in which His unity would be concealed so that otherness could seemingly exist, and love and kindness could thereby be expressed.[57] The first garment that enclothed and obscured our core was therefore crafted and placed upon us by God. It was holy and purposeful. Though it cloaked our inner light and thereby resulted in darkness, it was not undesirable or antithetical to the divine plan. There is sometimes need for withdrawal, limitation, and restraint.

However, God's intention with the concealment of His infinite light was not that it should remain trapped and forgotten inside of us in perpetuity. On the contrary, this state of estrangement was only to be

---

[56] Breishis Rabba 20:12

[57] As explained in chapter two, section "Good Nature"

temporary. With the exodus from Egypt and the liberation of the nascent nation of Israel, a new period would begin in which the barriers would be broken and the truth of our existence would begin to be revealed. The Torah's narratives provide a metaphor of the spiritual drama that plays itself out within each of us. We had been enslaved - in other words, our spiritual substance had been restrained and repressed by the confines of our physical bodies and our animal instincts - and now it was time for that inner truth to be liberated. Weeks after the exodus from Egypt, the nation arrived at Mount Sinai where the Torah was given as a tool with which one could penetrate and dismantle the screen that separated the outer and inner worlds. Throughout the ensuing millennia, we have been engaged in that process.

But why has it taken us so long? Is the skin that God wrapped us in so thick that it requires thousands of years to be infiltrated and re-moved? Is the Torah so ineffectual that it cannot instruct us how to fulfill its intent? Is God Himself so passive and detached that He cannot re-move the covering that He had applied now that it is no longer serving His ultimate purpose and intention?

Of course, the answer is that the flesh is not impenetrable, the Torah is not ineffective, and God is not disinterested or uncaring. If the goal were to separate the soul from the body, that could, and can, be done instantaneously - it is called death. However, the process of revela-tion was never intended to be contrary to life or to negate the world of limitation and concealment in which life exists. The divine aim has al-ways been to bring about revelation *within* the creation itself. In other words, the goal is not to divorce the body and soul, but to fuse them so that the physical will not oppose or obscure Godliness, but it will rather express it. This is why the Midrash discusses the consonance of the words "אוֹר/ohr," meaning light, and "עוֹר/ohr," meaning skin. Ultimate-ly, as we discussed in the previous chapter, the human being, "adam," is supposed to be both "adama/earthy" and "adameh l'Elyon/Godly." S/he is supposed to be garbed in flesh, "עוֹר/ohr," that comes from the earth, and that flesh itself is meant to beam with the light, "אוֹר/ohr," of the Godly core that it contains and conveys.

According to the doctrine of "hashgacha protis/divine providence"[58] and the complete and constant dominion that it presupposes, it
is clear that if He so desired, God could remove the covering with which
He enveloped us at any moment. However, His will is not for us to be
disembodied spirits hovering in some ethereal realm. Nor is it His will
that He should once again be 'alone/all one' as He was before the creation. Nor is it His intention to contravene the process that He has established for His creations. The objective is that we ourselves should become cognizant of the spark that burns within us, and we should then
fan the flame of our Godly core so that it glows so brightly that it will
permeate our fleshy skin and burst forth to flood our surroundings with
its gleam. Therefore, God leaves the task to us, and He also supplies us
with the Torah that lays out our mission and informs us how we can fulfill it.

If so, then why does it remain so difficult for us, and why do we
continue to languish in the dark? The unfortunate answer is that rather
than uncovering our core and opening a pathway so that it can be accessed and revealed, we tend to spend our lives doing precisely the opposite. We add layers to the husk that encases us, and we close off the
passageways to our inner depths so that they will not be breached.

Why do we do that?

Shame

While the original layer of flesh with which we were enwrapped
was installed by God, the countless layers that have been added over it
were imposed by ourselves either consciously or unintentionally. The
original casing was fashioned by God in order to serve the piece of Himself that He invested inside of it. It would do so by distinguishing the
Godly spark, housing it, and carrying it. The additional coverings that
we have added have served either to hide and protect our core from external threat, or to repress what is within us in order protect the outside
world from the (supposed) darkness that seethes beneath our surface.

---

[58] Discussed in chapter one, section 'The Only One'

From the time of Adam and Eve's "fall," we are subject to constant fear and shame, afraid of either what is around us, or what is within us, and often both.

It is therefore the basic misconception of our essence and being which has led us, throughout the majority of our history, in the opposite direction from our goal. Rather than probing inward and working to remove the strata that we have built up over and around our center, we have moved ever outward to seek gratification externally. We have simultaneously wrapped ourselves in an ever-increasing mantle of garments in order to bury and conceal our core. The misconception is predicated on one of two errors: we have mistakenly believed that our essence is dark and malevolent and it must be repressed, or we have mistakenly believed that it is weak and vulnerable and needs to be protected. Neither of these conceptions of our inner foundation is even remotely accurate. Our "pnimyus/inner core" is the "Pnei Hashem/Face of God!" It is pure Godliness, and as such it is both infinitely good and impregnable. How and why did our image and appraisal of ourself come to be so far from the truth?

The misreading and misinterpretation of the story of Adam and Eve have played no small part in our fundamental misunderstanding of our nature and our reality. As we discussed at length in chapter one, Torah does not support the notion of 'original sin.' On the contrary, it propounds the doctrine of "hashgacha protis/divine providence" which compels us to recognize that nothing can be done that it is ultimately contrary to God's will. Therefore, the eating of the fruit and the subsequent expulsion from the garden were not obstructions to God's plan or violations of His will, but rather manifestations of His design and fulfillment of His intention. If so, then why is the simple understanding of the story so easily misperceived? Why did God allow it to be regarded as a contravention of His design? Why has He allowed us to wallow in the shame and guilt of our perceived transgression and the assumption that we are intrinsically weak and deeply flawed? The answer, as we explained in the first chapter, is that the very nature of this creation in which we live is concealment. This "world/olam," is a realm of "hiddenness/helam" and dissimulation. "Vayehi erev, vayehi boker/it was evening, and it was morning" - we begin with darkness, and only then can we proceed to the most radiant light.[59] By virtue of participating in this world, we are subject to obscurity and misperception.

Darkness and concealment, however, do not equate with sin and guilt. The fact that mankind was forced to leave the garden does not mean that we are inherently sinful. It means, rather, that God intended for us to exist in a realm where our essential nature, and His essential unity, would be veiled. But if God's intention was for His creations to inhabit a world of concealment, then could He not have introduced us directly into such a world? Instead, we were formed and initiated in the Garden of Eden, a heavenly realm where our skin was made of light and our Godly essence was apparent. We dwelled in this paradise for only a matter of hours, and then we transgressed the one and only commandment that we were given - do not eat from the tree of the knowledge of good and evil. As soon as we did so, we were chastised and expelled. Only then did we enter this framework of concealment which He intended us to inhabit for the course of human history. Why did God structure it this way rather than simply bypassing Eden and creating us outside of the garden in the first place?

He did so because there is a crucial value to both stages of the process. First we were to be created with the truth of our essence, and then that essence needed to be concealed so that we would appear to be "other" in order for God's ability to give and love to be expressed.[60] In order to mask our intrinsic Godliness, God couched our origins in the framework of transgression and expulsion. In other words, we had to believe that we were ungodly in order to forget that we are nothing but Godliness enclothed. This means that through the commission of "sin," we would view ourselves as sinful, and thus less than divine. We would become conscious of our nakedness, and become clothed in a concealing garment. This garment would separate us from our interior and hide from us our inner truth.

However, if this was God's aim, if He wanted us to believe that we are not Godly, that we are separate beings that exist distinctly from Him (and therefore we are "others" who He can love and give to), then could He not have simply created us without any consciousness of our

---

[59] See chapter two, section "Night And Then Day"

[60] See chapter two, section "Good Nature"

Godliness? Why was it necessary to begin with complete connectedness, purity, and revelation in Eden, and then to be thrust out of there with the stigma of sin and the loss of our exalted status? Because by beginning in Eden, we have a record of our true origin. We have evidence that we do not exist with "original sin," but with original purity and Godliness. Our origin story is that we were at first completely Godly. Subsequently we "sinned" and our Godliness became concealed. But that sin is not what or who we originally and essentially are. It is merely a cloak that obscures what is beneath it.

For two and a half millennia, from the time of the exile from Eden until the giving of the Torah, Adam and Eve and their progeny were mired in the belief that they were sinners. The aspects of darkness and deception within us are easy to see - they are right here on the surface. The Godliness is much harder to perceive - it is buried deep down within our core. Therefore, when we consider ourselves, we see our facade rather than our true "face/panim/pnimyus," and we feel shame. This shame compels us to cover up further, constantly running from ourselves and trying to forget what we are. Yet if we knew what we really were, we would stop running and stop feeling shame. We would dig and work incessantly to uncover what is in there.

God knows what is in there. He allowed it to be hidden from us for thousands of years after we left the garden. Throughout these generations, the darkness solidified, and we lost all memory of that time and place where we began. And then it was time to remind us. With the giving of the Torah, He provided this recollection. The intention of the Torah's reminder of our origins is not to admonish us that 'you have been bad,' but to inform us that 'you have been hidden.' God assures us that this concealment and forgetfulness are not our doing, but rather His. I created you as a pure reflection of Myself, He tells us. I sent you forth from the garden to populate a world in which you and I are hidden. Now I am calling on you to remake that world, to transform it from a place of darkness to a realm of revelation. In the thousands of years since the giving of the Torah, there have been those who have been working on that project. However, the darkness has been difficult to penetrate. There are a variety of reasons for this difficulty, but primary amongst them is the resistance that so many of us have developed to the recognition and admission of our inherent Godliness.

When we are in denial of our divinity, whether we are truly ignorant of it or we are unwilling to admit it, we are susceptible to the hazards to which shame and self-doubt expose us. These include destructive habits and patterns of self-sabotage. When we believe we are worthy of punishment, we hold on to pain and suffering. We create illness and failure subconsciously, as mechanisms to punish ourselves for our wrongdoing and purge us of our guilt. In addition to these internal abuses, we subject ourselves to external manipulation and mistreatment. When we recognize our tremendous worth, on the other hand, we are strong and invulnerable to exploitation. When we feel guilt and self-recrimination, we are weak and lost and desperate. We become vulnerable to those who offer us salvation and security and all of the things that will fill the void within us and enable us to control our "evil" nature. Therefore, throughout history, "leaders" who would subjugate us and dominate us have labored to convince us that we are debased and needy. For it is far easier to maintain power when one's subjects are disenfranchised and burdened with shame.

Beyond those who crave superiority and control, there have been countless other leaders who are less self-serving and malevolent, but who simply want to maintain order and security. They have witnessed greed and perversion around them and within them, and they have therefore become convinced of their inherent wretchedness and sinfulness. True believers, they truly believe that the path to redemption is through self-flagellation and the embracing of an external savior who will harness their innate barbarity and rid them of their sins. Whether it is therefore with malicious intent or sincere devotion and desire for a connection to the divine, these figures and institutions in our lives have convinced us to suppress and cover over precisely what we need to pursue and release.

God's response to all of these forces that generate shame and steer us outward rather than inward is consistent throughout His Torah: "Panim b'panim dibber Hashem imachem bahar/face to face God spoke to you at the mountain" - He infused His face, His quintessence, into our face, our innermost core.[61] "Anochi Havaya ElokeCHA/I am the Lord YOUR God" - My infinite essence, God informs us, trickles down through

---

[61] See chapter four, section "Face to Face"

every fiber of My creation, and embeds itself within your essence.[62] "Reeh Anochi nosein lifneichem/See, I give Anochi within you" - God has placed His level of 'Anochi,' an aspect of Himself that is so internal that is beyond a name other than 'I', within our 'panim/pnimyus,' our innermost nucleus.[63]

I am within you, and you are Godly, God informs us repeatedly. It is time for us to discard the erroneous ideas of original sin and human inadequacy, and to accept what we truly are and thereby begin to reveal it.

Sin

None of what we have discussed so far negates the fact that we are imperfect.

Recognizing our Godly essence does not preclude the awareness of those aspects of ourselves that defy and conceal our higher instincts and deeper nature. Just as God created light, He also created darkness, and as we discussed in chapter two,[64] darkness was created first, and it currently predominates in this world of hiddenness. It is vital for us to be cognizant of the fact that darkness is no less Godly than light. To assume otherwise would be to propose a duality which is completely contrary to the fundamental thesis that "A-donai echad/God is one" and there is nothing other than Him. The darkness serves God's desire to conceal Himself and create otherness, as we have discussed at length. This, however, does not absolve us of the responsibility to choose light over darkness. While God created darkness, He charged us with the task of dispelling it through the revelation of the light that He hid within us and within every aspect of the creation. However, He simultaneously garbed us within a casing that enables us, and even inclines us, to choose wrong at times. It is no surprise or secret to God that we are fallible. He created

---

[62] See chapter four, section "The First Commandment"

[63] See chapter four, section "In Your Face"

[64] Section "Night And Then Day"

us that way. His love for us is not contingent upon our perfection. If it were, He would not have formed us with the ability and proclivity to violate His will.

We therefore need to understand the nature of sin and why God allows it to exist. We have addressed the latter question in part in our discussion of the first sin, Adam and Eve's eating of the forbidden fruit. Sin, we explained, allows God to maintain the illusion of something distinct and contrary to His unity. If there were no sin, no free will, no ability for us to choose anything other than God's way, then it would be difficult, if not impossible, to attest to our differentiation and independence. If we were simply automatons that were programmed to perform a strictly delineated set of actions, then we would not serve the purpose of being others to whom God could give and show love. One can have affection for a doll or a toy, but if it is unable to feel and choose, then it cannot experience love no matter how much we may try to express it. The goal of God's darkness is to allow for the existence of beings that are "in His image" - with a full complement of desires, will, and capabilities - but who are able to perceive of themselves as being distinct from their source.

"Sin," then, as counterintuitive as this may sound, is part of the divine plan. This is certainly not to say that God wants us to sin, but He created us with the capacity to do so, and He is not shocked or caught off guard when we do. To take it a step further, contrary to popular belief, *God is not injured, insulted, or even angry when we sin!* How can we make such a claim? Is it not in opposition to explicit verses from the Torah like, "They have angered Me with their vanities,"[65] and, "And G-d's anger will flare?"[66] Will such a claim, furthermore, not encourage one to flaunt God's will and therefore bring more darkness to the world than light?

Indeed, we are treading on precarious ground here, and there is a genuine risk that the presentation of these concepts, taken out of context and divorced from the explanations that will follow, can result in the very opposite of their intention. For this reason, we must proceed here with great caution. There is good reason why such discussions of the Torah's inner depths have been restricted and sequestered. Throughout

---

[65] Deuteronomy 32:21

[66] Deuteronomy 11:17

the majority of our history, the study of Kabbala and the Torah's esoteric secrets was limited exclusively to those who were tested and deemed thoroughly versed in the revealed dimensions of Torah. Furthermore, one was required to reach the age of forty before he would even be considered for such initiation. This is because insights such as the ones we are discussing here could be confusing and even harmful to those who did not already have a strong foundation in Torah study and practice, as well as the life-experience and maturity to understand the wiles of the ego and one's baser inclinations. The analogy has been given to one who, while walking in a field, falls into a pit because her/his eyes were directed at the stars rather than what is in front of her/his feet. First, we must be very familiar with the ground around and before us, and then we can begin to gaze up to study the heavens above us.

In spite of these valid concerns, the latter mystics, beginning with the Baal Shem Tov in the 18th century, determined that the time had come to begin revealing the Torah's secrets to the masses. This was, in part, in order to combat the coming "Enlightenment" and the age of rationalism that would tear so many away from their faith and their connection to God. Only through a deep and thorough understanding of God's unity and our place in His creation can we withstand the temptations and attractions of the modern age and recognize that they will not lead us to joy, peace, and freedom, but rather to insatiability and anguish.

In this light, we can appreciate a parable that was told by the Alter Rebbe. It had come to his attention that there was a heavenly charge against his teacher, the Maggid of Mezeritch, for the crime of spreading the precious secrets of Torah to the masses, where they were squandered and frequently misunderstood. In response to the charge, the Alter Rebbe told the parable of a great king whose son, the prince, was deathly ill. All of the kingdom's doctors were summoned, but nothing would remedy the lethal illness. One wise man came and informed the king that the only possible cure was an elixir that could be made from the dust of an exceedingly rare gem, the only one of which was embedded in the king's crown. The jewel was priceless, but the king did not hesitate to have it removed from his headpiece. As it was about to be ground to dust, some of the king's advisors tried to dissuade him. We don't know if the elixir will work, they told him, and even if it does have the proper healing properties, the prince is unconscious and it is possible

that none of it will make it down his throat. Even if only one drop penetrates, the king replied, and even if there is only a minute possibility of
saving my beloved son's life, it is worth far more than the most priceless
gem. He ground the stone and made the elixir. A mere drop was ingested
by the prince, but it was enough to save his life. So too, the Alter Rebbe
taught, his teacher's efforts to save God's lost and ailing children with
the secrets of the Torah were justified in spite of the priceless gems that
were squandered in the process.

With this preface, we can return, with great care and discretion,
to the subject of sin, and the audacious - and potentially dangerous - assertion that God is not ultimately "angered" by our transgression of His
will. So far, we have approached this notion from the perspective of the
utility and benefit of sin in God's ultimate plan. Though sin itself may be
undesirable, as part of the process of the larger divine end-game, it
serves a purpose that is ultimately positive, in spite of its seeming and
temporary negativity. That is, it enables God's creations to be fully
fleshed-out beings, as opposed to mere robots who are programmed to
do only what our Creator demands. Just as we saw in chapter two that
darkness was created in service of the more brilliant light that would
eventually follow it,[67] so too sin, understood in this way, is a stepping
stone that can ultimately be evaluated properly only in the context of the
broader timeline of history.

We can even take this idea a step further and demonstrate that
not only is God not angered by our misdeeds, but in the deepest sense
(as opposed to the surface reality of this earthly plane), He is not affected
by our actions at all. The sages have found support for this divine impas-
sivity in the following verse:

אֲנִי יְ-הֹוָה לֹא שָׁנִיתִי:
Ani A-donai, lo shanisi.
I am God, I have not changed.
(Malachi 3:6)

The implication of this statement is that the temporal and finite
world has, and can have, no impact on the eternal and infinite God. Just
as He was One before He created the world, so is He One after the cre-

---

[67] Section "Night And Then Day"

ation. This is difficult to comprehend from our human perspective, but we must remember that God is not subject to time or space or any of the other "natural laws" which He created and in which we function. From our viewpoint, pre-creation and post-creation represent an enormous change - it is the difference between existence and non-existence. But from God's perspective, the entire span of history and the entire expanse of space is not even as proportionate to His ultimate reality as one drop of water in comparison to the sea. For while one drop is an infinitesimal amount in relation to all of the 26,640,000,000,000,000,000,000,000 drops that mathematicians have determined to be contained in the earth's oceans,[68] it is still one part of that number. In relation to infinity, however, even numbers in the septillions like the one above do not account or amount to even a minute fraction of a fraction. It is in this regard that we can come to the conclusion of the insignificance of our deeds. Scripture verbalizes this reality as follows:

אִם־חָטָאתָ מַה־תִּפְעָל־בּוֹ וְרַבּוּ פְשָׁעֶיךָ מַה־תַּעֲשֶׂה־לּוֹ:
אִם־צָדַקְתָּ מַה־תִּתֶּן־לוֹ אוֹ מַה־מִיָּדְךָ יִקָּח:

Im chatasa mah tifal bo, v'rabu pishaecha mah taaseh lo? Im tzadakta mah titen lo, o mah miyadcha yikach?

If you sinned, what effect do you have on Him, and if your transgressions are many, what do you do to Him? If you are righteous, what do you give Him, or what does He take from your hand?

(Job 35:6-7)

What can our trivial actions amount to, Scripture asks. Can our sins truly have any effect on God in the grand scheme of His infinite Oneness? For that matter, does our righteousness actually impact Him in any way?

It is a sobering line of reasoning, and one that does not necessarily bring us comfort. While we can find some solace in the notion that our errors and misdeeds do not anger God and do not provoke in Him a desire for punishment or vengeance, the suggestion that our deeds are meaningless and irrelevant certainly is not inspiring and, on the contrary,

---

[68] with an estimated 1.332 billion cubic kilometers of sea on Earth and 0.05 ml of water in a drop

it can feel extremely defeating. If this is the case, then what meaning is there in our existence, and what difference does it make what we do or how we conduct ourselves? Furthermore, how do we reconcile either of these ideas with the verses from the Torah which, as we quoted earlier, explicitly refer to God's anger and vengeance?

Layers

To address the previous questions, we must begin with the awareness that everything in life is comprised of various levels and layers. The Torah is said to have many "faces":

שִׁבְעִים פָּנִים בַּתּוֹרָה:
Shivim panim laTorah.
Torah has 70 faces.
(Midrash Bamidbar Rabba, 13:16)

This means that a single Torah concept can be understood on seventy different levels, all of which are valid and true even as some may be conflicting or contradictory. Rabbi Yitzchak Luria, the holy Arizal,[69] taught that there are actually 600,000 various interpretations for every Torah idea. In general, Torah study is referred to as walking in an orchard, the Hebrew word for which is "פַּרְדֵּס/pardes." In addition to meaning orchard, "פַּרְדֵּס/PaRDeS" is also an acronym for four words:

"פְּשָׁט/Pshat," which means "simple meaning."
"רֶמֶז/Remez," which means "allusion."
"דְּרוּשׁ/Drush," which means "homily."
"סוֹד/Sod," which means "secrets."

Torah is called a "pardes/orchard" because it can be experienced on all four of these general levels of interpretation.

---

[69] 1534-1572, one of the foremost Kabbalists in history, who created the system of Lurianic Kabbala.

Very generally speaking, we can break this down to two primary categories: there is the revealed surface of things, and then there are the hidden depths beneath and within. We have been speaking primarily in this book about these two levels of "pshat," the simple and surface level of understanding, and "sod," the secret depths that are concealed beneath the surface. Throughout our discussion, we have made frequent reference to the "panim/pnimyus," which is the "sod" or secret inner dimension, and the 'olam/world' (derived from the world 'helam /hiddenness') which is the "pshat" or the simple visible reality in which we operate and beneath which the secrets are concealed. While the secrets are more "true" in the ultimate sense, the surface also represents a truth and reality that we must recognize and negotiate. While these levels are starkly different, and they can even contradict one another, nevertheless they can, and do, exist simultaneously. It is taught that one of the highest levels of wisdom is the tolerance of paradox. The sages state it this way:

אֵלוּ וָאֵלוּ דִּבְרֵי אֱ-לֹהִים חַיִּים:
Eilu v'eilu divrei E-lokim chayim.
These and these are the words of the living God.
(Talmud, Eruvin 13b)

The implication is that though concepts or perspectives may diverge dramatically, they can both be true depending on the perspective and level of reality that they reflect. We have seen this repeatedly already in our discussion of God's complete unity, and our simultaneous existence and independence. On the one hand, there is nothing but God; but at the same time, He created us as others, and we therefore exist. On the deepest level, there is only One, but on the level of this world, there is vast multiplicity. We have seen this also in our exploration of the story of Adam and Eve in the garden. On the revealed and simple level, they sinned by eating the fruit, and they were therefore punished and expelled. On the deeper level, their act was precisely what was necessary in order to further God's design, and their journey from the garden was not a downfall, but rather an opportunity to bring the light that God had implanted within them out into the surrounding darkness.

On the level of "pshat," the revealed surface of our existence, sin does indeed "anger" God. While it is ultimately true that in relation to His infinite reality our actions may be minuscule and meaningless; nevertheless, He has created a realm in which every aspect of our lives is significant and impactful. Simultaneously, on the level of "sod," the hidden depths of the ultimate existence, there is nothing we can do which is contrary to God's consummate unity, and there is therefore never an occasion in which He experiences frustration or displeasure. This dynamic of the conflicting reality of sin can be seen in a section of the Torah which is known as the "tochacha/rebuke." In the book of Leviticus, in the portion of "Bechukosai," God lays out a lengthy list of punishments that will result if the people choose to violate His will. He begins:

וְאִם־לֹא תִשְׁמְעוּ לִי וְלֹא תַעֲשׂוּ אֵת כָּל־הַמִּצְוֹת הָאֵלֶּה:

V'im lo tishmiu li v'lo taasu es kol hamitzvos ha'eileh.

If you will not listen to Me and you will not fulfill all of these commandments.

(Leviticus 26:14 - 15)

He then proceeds with a litany of curses that will ensue from this disobedience. But He begins these consequences with a very strange verse:

וְנָתַתִּי פָנַי בָּכֶם וְנִגַּפְתֶּם לִפְנֵי אֹיְבֵיכֶם:

V'nasati panai bachem *v'nigaftem lifnei oyveichem.*

I will set My attention against you, and you will be smitten before your enemies.

(Leviticus 26:17)

What is odd about this statement is the literal translation of the Hebrew words. Though the first phrase is commonly rendered, "I will set My attention against you," the literal meaning of the words "v'nasati panai bachem" is, "and I placed my face in you." This language confounds the sages. How is it that God's 'placing His face in us' is a consequence for our disobedience?

The Maharal,[70] in his classical commentary Gur Aryeh, points out in response to this anomaly that the expression "God's face" is always positive. "Kol 'panim' hu l'tova/all reference to God's face is for the good," he asserts. Therefore, he changes the word "פָּנַי/panai," which

---

70 Rabbi Yehuda Loew, sixteenth century Kabbalist from Prague.

means "my face," to "פְּנַאי/pinai," which means "my attention." As such, he explains the verse to mean "I will set my attention against you," as it is commonly understood. Rashi, the primary expositor of the Torah's plain meaning, concurs with the Maharal's suggestion that the intention of the verse is that God will focus His attention on those who transgress His will. He adds that the word "פָּנַי/panai/my face" also shares the root of "פּוֹנֶה/poneh" which means "to turn." The verse, according to Rashi, is thus indicating that God will turn (פּוֹנֶה) His attention (פְּנַאי) to those who disobey Him in order to punish their misdeeds.

While these interpretations suit the context, they rely on a maneuvering of the language in order to do so, and they do not address the text's literal meaning. They fail to do so because the literal translation of the words provides us an insight that goes far beyond the surface of the Torah to its very depths. Rashi establishes early on in his commentary on the Torah that his purpose is only to explain the simple level of the text:

וַאֲנִי לֹא בָאתִי אֶלָּא לִפְשׁוּטוֹ שֶׁל מִקְרָא.

V'ani lo basi elah l'pshuto shel mikra.
I have come only [to teach] the pshat/simple meaning
of Scripture.
(Rashi on Genesis 3:8)

While Rashi's intent is only to explain the surface layer of the Torah and not its deeper mystic implications, the verse itself reveals a "sod/secret" that is mind-blowingly profound. As we saw from the Gur Aryeh above, "all reference to God's face is for the good." Therefore, if we do not change the word from "פָּנַי/panai/my face" to "פְּנַאי/pinai/my attention," and we read the verse precisely as God Himself actually wrote it, then we realize that even when one transgresses God's will, He still "places my face in you." This brings us to the shocking and counter-intuitive conclusion that ultimately, *even our negative actions will only bring us positive results!*

The illogic and seeming injustice of such a conclusion is what led the sages to alter the language for the sake of the simple understanding. However, the deeper truth is that God, at His essential level, is not compelled by logic or motivated strictly by justice. It is true that within the realm of "pshat" and the limited structure of the "olam/world" in which we live, logic and justice are paramount. However, beyond this realm of "helam/hiddenness," *when God's essential nature is revealed, His love, forgiveness and unity transcend the rules of reason and judgment.* At such a level, whether we go in God's ways or we turn away from His commandments, ultimately His response is the same! Either way, "וְנָתַתִּי פָנַי בָּכֶם/ v'nasati panai bachem," He has placed His face within us. *Regardless of our actions and our conduct, we are Godly at our core and nothing can change that!*

It is essential to reiterate that this does not mean that there are not laws or consequences for our actions within this temporal realm in which we currently exist. But it means that in our ultimate reality, all of these distinctions and repercussions cease to exist. God's love for us is not dependent on our compliance. He "turns" to us, and "faces" us regardless of our conduct. He cannot help but face us because His "panim/ face" is lodged in our "pnimyus/core." The only real question is whether *we* are facing *Him* or turning away - whether we are conscious of His love and unity, and thus responding to it with love, or we are unaware of His existence at the base of our existence, and therefore turning away from Him to pursue other avenues that we mistakenly believe to be in our best interest.

Obstruction

The choice is ours!

We can choose which layer of existence we prefer to inhabit and manifest. We can opt to live in a world of "pshat," where justice and judgment reign supreme, and where compliance is rewarded and defiance is penalized. Or we can decide to peel back the layer of the "pshat/ simple level" to uncover the "sod/secrets," thereby dwelling in a reality where God's infinite love and unity transcend the superficial distinctions that subject us to division and valuation. This is not to say that we can rest exclusively in the layer of our choosing and ignore the others or pretend that they don't exist. We have, after all, been placed in this world with a mission and a purpose to fulfill here. We can, however, determine whether we are going to remove the veil and expose what is beneath, or add to the coverings that conceal our essence and confine us to the surface.

This brings us back to the beginning of the chapter. There we explained that the first garment in which we were enclothed and concealed was fashioned and applied by God, but the additional layers that have been added over that initial covering were created by us. Rather than working to reveal our core, we have labored to further obscure it for the variety of reasons that we went on to discuss (shame, fear, etc). This, we will now come to understand, is the true nature of what we refer to as "sin." Commonly understood as an evil deed or a crime, we conceive of sin as an affront to God, a disrespecting and disobedience. We feel guilt for having broken His law and His trust. We feel fear for having exposed ourselves to His wrath and punishment. We feel remorse for having proven ourselves weak and flawed. We beg for forgiveness and mercy, knowing that though we are unworthy, He is nevertheless compassionate. We admit our wrongdoing, and we appeal to His tolerance. He chastises us, repays us with the consequences of which He had given us more than ample warning, and then He forgives us and grants us another chance to grow and do better. In this "pshat" dynamic, God is just. He has forewarned us; He is disappointed by our failure, and saddened at least, and perhaps even angered, by our disobedience. He disciplines us, but He is forbearing and does not hold a grudge.

However, according to our new "sod" perspective and the awareness that ultimately God is neither offended, nor even affected, by our misdeeds (as we explained above, "im chatasa mah tifal bo/if you sin what effect do you have on Him"), then we must refine this understanding of transgression. What is sin truly, and what is its impact if it does not ultimately impact God? We can find an answer in the words of the prophet Isaiah:

עֲוֹנֹתֵיכֶם הָיוּ מַבְדִּלִים בֵּינֵכֶם לְבֵין אֱ-לֹהֵיכֶם:
Avonoseichem hayu mavdilim beineichem l'vein E-lokeichem.
Your iniquities have separated between you and your God.
(Isaiah 59:2, beginning)

The prophet seems to suggest here that our sins cause us to be separated from God. But this raises an obvious question: how is it possible for anyone or anything to be separate from God?! If He is One, and thus He is everywhere and everything at once, then how can we be distinct or distant from Him? In truth, we cannot. And in fact, we never were. At the level of "sod," we know that "A-donai echad/God is one" - there is nothing but Him alone. Sin, therefore, does not, and cannot, separate us from God from His vantage. It can, however, create an obstruction from our perspective and in the realm of "pshat." Understood this way, sin is the layer of interference and concealment that we create between ourselves and our Creator. As such, sin is that which renders us less perceptive of, and receptive to, God. It is the curtain or barrier that we erect 'between' us and Him which makes it more difficult for us to perceive and reveal the truth of His infinite light. Though we are ultimately no more 'distant' from God after we have sinned than before - because God is everywhere equally - nevertheless, each sin encrusts us in another layer that makes us less capable of seeing the Godliness within us and around us.

Why do we sin? Why do we create these barriers? Because we believe ourselves to be separate already. We have forgotten what we truly are, and each "sin" takes us further and further from ourselves. As the verse from Isaiah quoted above continues:

וְחַטֹּאותֵיכֶם הִסְתִּירוּ פָנִים מִכֶּם:
V'chatoseihem histiru panim mikem.
And your sins hide the face from you.
(Isaiah 59:2, end)

The first half of the verse indicates that our sin separates us from God. This second half adds that sin hides "panim/the face" from us. It does not indicate whose face is hidden - is it our face or God's face that sin hides from us and makes it more difficult to sense? The answer is both. Our misdeed creates an additional layer of covering that we drape over our own "panim/inner essence;" and since the "Pnei Hashem/ face of God" is embedded within our "pnimyus," therefore when we further obscure our own essence, we increase our separation from Him as well.

Seen in this light, sin is not an "evil deed" for which we deserve punishment. It is rather a self-defeating act for which we deserve sympathy. God desires to avail us of His light and of the peace and bounty that comes with the revelation of His infinite presence. We can choose to accept and receive that or to refuse it. When we choose the latter, it is not because we are wicked, but because we are misguided and unaware of what we have spurned. No one would intentionally trade infinite benevolence and abundance for the limited and ephemeral delights of this world unless s/he were incapable of clearly seeing and understanding the comparison between the two options. It is God Himself who has obscured our vision, and as a result of our myopia we have made decisions that are not in our best interest, further diminishing our ability to see and choose properly. God's reaction to our errors and our predicament is therefore not anger or righteous indignation, but rather compassion and the desire for us to "see the light" that is within us. He knows our weaknesses - He created them - and yet He believes in us nonetheless. He does not want to do the work for us, but He provides us His Torah so that we can utilize its wisdom to delve inward, remove the coverings, and thereby allow His blessings to flow freely and abundantly.

When we come to God in prayer, therefore, it is with remorse, but not shame or self-flagellation. We are sorry not because we have harmed or hurt Him - He cannot be harmed or hurt - but because we recognize that we have denied ourselves His love and denied Him the opportunity to fully express that love. We ask for forgiveness, but what that means is not that He was angry at us or distanced from us and we want to be reconciled. ForGIVEness means that we want to remove the barriers that have temporarily interfered with His GIVing. We ask Him to help us to clear away the blockages that we have created, and to help us to refrain from erecting these blockages again in the future. Help me to open to You, we pray. Help me to peel off the many layers that I have clad myself in, and to access and uncover the channels through which You give Your infinite benevolence to me, and through me to all of Your creation.

The root of all "evil" and negativity in the world is this blockage that exists between our consciousness and our essence. In a discourse on the giving of the Torah, the Alter Rebbe states:

גַּסוּת הוּא שׁוֹרֶשׁ כָּל הָרָע.

Gasus hu shoresh kol harah.

Arrogance/Coarseness is the root of all evil.

(Likkutei Torah, Bamidbar, Inyan Shenitna haTorah)

140

The word "גַּסּוּת/gasus" literally means "coarseness." It is commonly used in the phrase "gasus haruach," which is translated as "coarseness of spirit," but it is understood to mean haughtiness or arrogance. On the simple level, the Alter Rebbe's statement is teaching us that ego is the source of all transgression and conflict. This is an important lesson, but it is not particularly unique or revolutionary. However, on a deeper level, we can glean from the Alter Rebbe's statement something far more profound and particular to the Torah's secrets and its unique approach. All evil, the Alter Rebbe informs us, is the result of "gasus," a coarseness that obstructs between our surface and our core. The coarseness of our existence - our physicality and the "helam/hiddenness" that is the nature of this "olam/world" - this is what separates us from our source and essence and hides from us our true infinite nature. All negativity in life is the result of the obstruction that conceals from us what we ultimately are. Arrogance, pride, and self-consumption are all the result of our inability to see and sense our infinite greatness. Because we are unaware of how Godly and vast we are, therefore we feel the need to protect, project and aggrandize ourselves. These, and all negative traits, are the product of the barriers that hinder us from seeing and understanding our authentic reality.

The Alter Rebbe goes on to state that the Torah was given in order to counter this coarse obstruction:

וְעִיקַר הַתּוֹרָה הוּא לִהְיוֹת בִּבְחִינַת **בִּיטוּל**:
V'ikar haTorah hu l'hiyos b'bchinas **bittul.**
And the main point of Torah is to be **humble/nullified.**
(ibid)

The word "בִּיטוּל/bittul" is commonly used to mean "humble," but its literal meaning is "nullified." At face value, the Alter Rebbe teaches here that the Torah was given in order to teach us how to be modest and self-effacing, and to counter the arrogance that he had identified as the root of all evil in the previous sentence. On a deeper level, we can understand that the point of Torah is to enable us to "nullify" the "gasus/coarse obstruction" that interposes between our surface and our core, and thereby to reveal our true essence. Torah is the mechanism through which we can see through the thick layer that conceals our ultimate truth. It instructs us how to reveal our Godly foundation even as it is housed within the coarseness of the body and the world.

———◆———

Yadecha

Once we understand the nature of the obstructions that we have placed between our surface and our core, we are now ready to remove them. This removal will enable us to:

a) answer the first question that God asked humanity, "ayecha/where are you,"

b) comply with the initial command that God made to Abraham the first Jew, "lech lecha/go to yourself,"

c) fulfill the mission that was assigned in the opening words of Torah, "Breishis bara Elokim/the primary thing is to reveal God."

It will also enable us to transition our reality from a state of hiddenness and darkness to a state of revelation and light, and thereby to be the "light unto the nations" that we were created to be. This divesting of the layers that "separate between you and your God" and that "hide the face from you" is precisely the process of "teshuvah/return" that we are working on daily and throughout our lives. While "teshuvah" is commonly understood as repentance for sin, with our new understanding of "sin" as the layers we place over our essence and the face of God that is hidden within us, we will now recognize "teshuvah" as the efforts we make to shed those layers and expose what is beneath them. When we accomplish this "teshuvah/return," we will reveal the level of "sod/secrets," which is the ultimate truth of God's unity. At this level, our sins are meaningless and there is only divine love. In such a reality, we will align ourselves with God's will not because we are coerced to or because we fear to do otherwise, but because God's unconditional love arouses within us a reciprocal love. In other words, we cannot help but love the one who loves us so completely. *Finally, we will come to understand that we are nothing other than Godliness, and therefore it is our very nature to act Godly.*

With this, we will come to a deeper appreciation of one of the central verses from the daily prayers which is repeated multiple times throughout the day. The prayer known as "אַשְׁרֵי / Ashrei" is comprised of chapter 145 of the book of Psalms along with two other verses appended at its beginning and one additional verse at its end. It is included three times in the daily prayer services - twice in the morning service and once in the afternoon service - in accordance with a teaching in the Talmud that states, "Rabbi Elazar said in the name of Rabbi Avina: Anyone who recites 'Tehilla l'David' (psalm 145, here identified by its opening words) three times every day can trust that he will merit the world to come."[71] The Talmud then asks why this chapter has such power, and one of the reasons provided is because it contains the following verse:

פּוֹתֵחַ אֶת־יָדֶךָ וּמַשְׂבִּיעַ לְכָל־חַי רָצוֹן:
Poseach es yadecha u'masbea l'chol chai ratzon.
You open Your hand and satisfy every living thing's desire.
(Psalms 145:16)

On the simple level of "pshat," the importance of this verse is its acknowledgment that all of our needs and desires come directly and exclusively from God's hand. This indeed is a foundational principle that we must repeat regularly in order to engrave it into our constant awareness. Doing so three times a day, according to the sages, will enable us to lead a meritorious life and will thereby earn for us a precious reward in the afterlife. However, as we explained above, "Torah has 70 faces," and therefore this verse, like all of Torah's verses, has additional levels of meaning that are hidden beneath the surface. The "sod / secrets" of this verse reveals even deeper reasons why it is to be recited three times daily and why doing so will lead us to heavenly states.

In Tikkunei Zohar, it is stated that the third word of our verse, "יָדֶךָ / yadecha," can be read alternatively because the verses of scripture themselves were not recorded with vowels. The simple rendering of the word, "yadecha," means "Your hand," as translated above. But without

---

[71] Talmud Berachos 4b

vowels, it can also be read as "y<u>u</u>decha," as the Tikkunei Zohar explicitly states:

אַל תִּקְרֵי יָדְךָ אֶלָּא יוֹדֶיךָ.

Al tikrei yadecha elah yudecha.
Don't read 'yadecha' but 'yudecha.'
(Tikkunei Zohar 7b)

Discussing this verse, the Alter Rebbe explains that it can also be read "y<u>i</u>decha." What are "yudecha" and "yidecha"? What do these alternate readings do to the verse, and what are the secrets that they reveal? The suffix "-echa" means "your," and this does not change. It refers here to something belonging to God. The variant readings of the word determine whether we are speaking about God's "yad," His "yud," or His "yid." God's "yad/hand" is easily understood, as we have explained it above. His "yud" and His "yid" are somewhat more complex, as the Torah's secrets tend to be.

Yidecha

"Yid" means "Jew." It is the root of the word "Yiddish" which is the name of both the language and the culture of Jews in Europe and elsewhere throughout their exile. The word "Yid" itself is a shortened form of the Hebrew word "Yehudi," which means a member of the tribe of "Yehuda." The English word "Jew" is an abbreviated version of the anglicized version of this name, Judah. "Yehuda/Judah" was one of the twelve sons of the Patriarch Jacob. Though the Israelite nation was comprised of twelve tribes - corresponding to Jacob's twelve sons from whom the nation descends - the entire nation became known as "Yehudim" or members of "Judah-ism" (Judaism) for two reasons. Historically, it is because when the kingdom of Israel split in the 8th century BCE, ten of the tribes were eventually lost and the remaining nation was ruled by kings from the tribe of Judah. It is decreed that the ultimate king, the Messiah, will come from Judah as well. Because the tribe of

Yehuda/Judah ruled, and would rule, the remnant of the people, the entire nation came to be known and Yehudim, or Jews.

On a more homiletic level, it is taught that the nation is known by the name of Yehuda because of the significance of the term itself. The root of the name Yehuda is the word "hod" which means both humility and gratitude.[72] Leah, Jacob's wife, named her fourth son Yehuda because as a prophetess she knew that Jacob would have twelve sons. As one of Jacob's four wives, she assumed that each wife would bear him three sons. When she was privileged to give Jacob a fourth son, she knew that she had been blessed with more than her share. She therefore expressed her deep appreciation to God by naming her fourth son "gratitude." The entire nation would eventually become known by this term because fundamental to Torah philosophy and practice is the awareness that we have been given by God far more than we have earned.

"Poseach es YIDecha" thus means "You open Your Jew." What is the implication of this statement, which we are to make three times daily? And what does it mean that when God "opens His Jew," He thereby "satisfies every living thing's desire" (as the verse then concludes)? We can begin to understand this in context of the process of unwrapping which we have been exploring throughout this chapter. Our mission, as we have discussed repeatedly, is to find ourselves and to find and reveal God. The path that we must travel in order to do so is inward. And in order to access this path, we must open ourselves and peel away the layers of crust that conceal the various points of entry and obstruct our passage. This is precisely what we are verbalizing and meditating on with our recital of the verse "poseach es yidecha" repeatedly each day. We remind ourselves that everything we need is within us, not around us or beyond us: "Poseach es yidecha" - When God opens His Jew, i.e. me, "umasbea l'chol chai ratzon" - every desire of my life will be satisfied and fulfilled. All we need to do is open the packaging and discover the gifts that God has already provided within us. Meditating on this notion thrice daily will ensure us access to heaven (as we quoted above from the Gemara's teaching) because with this awareness, we realize that we already have heaven. It is not something we need to achieve or acquire, it is already possessed by us and contained within us.

---

[72] See chapter four, section "From Knowing to Showing," where we discussed the word "modeh" which derives from the same root.

As we repeat this mantra to remind ourselves of this elusive truth three times daily, we are simultaneously speaking to God, asking Him for His assistance in this difficult task. Please open your Jew, we beseech Him. Help us to become open, to remain open, and to negotiate the obscure and circuitous paths that will lead us to Your "panim/face" within our "pnimyus/inner core." We need God's help because the nature of the world is concealment. Even as we discover an opening, it quickly closes. Even as we are aware in the morning of the inward direction we need to travel, by afternoon we have become mired in our external reality and our physical drives and imperatives. We must therefore remind ourselves again, and we must once again plead to God for clarity and strength. We cannot achieve our goal without great effort and without divine assistance. We recite this verse repeatedly throughout the day in order to continually open ourselves and focus our attention inward.

On an even deeper level, the verse informs us of the unbounded potential within each of us to satisfy not only our own needs and wants, but also the requirements of the entire creation. "Poseach es yidecha/ when You open your Jew," then "u'masbea l'chol chai ratzon/the desire of **EVERY LIVING THING** will be satisfied." The implication here is that when any of us is truly opened, we will find such abundance within us that it will be enough to provide all of the world with all that it requires. Each of us contains such infinite wellsprings that if we are simply able to access them, we can supply everything that the creation lacks. How is this possible? Because it is the "Pnei Hashem/face of God" that is hidden within us. Therefore, when we open ourselves up fully, we will find an infinite abundance that we can then release to the world. We open what seems to be a small, limited package, and what pours out is boundless.

This is the miracle of our being - we are infinity encased in a gauze of flimsy mortal flesh. "Poseach es yidecha" - open us God, and enable us to satiate Your entire creation with the divine energy that You have implanted within us.

Yudecha

Reading the verse as "Poseach es YUDecha/open Your Yud" (as the Tikkunei Zohar quoted above suggests) provides an even deeper implication. What is "yudecha?" "Yud/י" is one of the 22 letters of the Hebrew alphabet. The Hebrew letters, Kabbalah explains, are not merely symbols that correspond to the sounds of speech. Since God created the world with speech, the Hebrew letters are the building blocks of creation, and their written forms are visual representations of the various creative energies. This can be seen through an analysis of God's name "הֲוָה-י/Y-H-V-H,"[73] which begins with the letter "י/yud." While this name can be translated to mean 'the One who brings into being,' the forms of its letters also provide a visual map of the process by which God creates being from non-being: The letters "י-ה-ו-ה" depict the creative process as follows:

1) The first step of creation is an idea, a sudden flash of inspiration which is a kernel that has not yet been developed in depth or breadth. This is called "chochma/wisdom'" and it is represented by the letter "י/yud," which is the smallest of the letters, depicted as little more than a simple dot. It is a simple primordial building block from which everything else will grow.

2) The second step is the consideration and gestation of that initial spark through which it can then expand into a dimensional form that can be comprehended and conveyed. This is called "binah/understanding," and it is represented by the letter "ה/hei," which has now broadened the "י/yud" into multiple dimensions of length and width.

3) Once the idea has been developed and concretized in the realm of God's thought, so to speak, it is now ready to be brought down into the world of actuality, from the heavens to the earth. The letter "ו/vav" represents the drawing down

---

[73] As noted earlier, this name is articulated "A-donai" in order not to pronounce the holy name.

of this insight, as we can see that the "ו" is simply a "י" that is extended downward from above to below.

4) The final letter is another "ה/hei," which depicts how the concept is then broadened and fleshed out further once it has been transmitted down into this world.

We can see parallels of this system of creation in the process of birth. We begin with a simple seed, corresponding to the "י/yud." This seed then gestates in the womb to become a fetus with limbs, corresponding to the "ה/hei." This fleshed-out being is then drawn down from the uterus and into the world, corresponding to the "ו/vav." Once it is born in this world, it will then grow and mature further, corresponding to the final "ה/hei."

While this process of divine creative evolution is a fascinating subject and is worthy of far more study that is beyond the scope of this book,[74] we have presented this brief introduction in order to understand the "yud" and the implication of its "opening" in the verse "poseach es yudecha/open Your yud." As we have explained, the "yud" represents the level of "chochmah/wisdom" which is the beginning and conceptual foundation of all creation. It thus stands for the intellectualization and systemization which enable a creation to exist and persist. "Opening the yud," the Alter Rebbe explains, is moving beyond the confines of this limited creation to access a realm that transcends it. The world we inhabit which proceeds from the "yud" is predicated on logic and is therefore governed by the laws of rationality and intellectual discernment. In such a measured and orderly framework, there is a clearly established binary structure of right and wrong, good and evil, and reward and punishment. Our world is systematic and regulated because it begins with the "yud", and is thus founded in "chochmah/wisdom," which is based on reason. Opening the "yud" and moving beyond it therefore represents superseding the bounds of intellect and moving to a place where the dictates of logic no longer reign supreme.

What is this place that is higher than "chochmah" and reason? If "chochmah" is the highest level of our world, how can we move beyond

---

[74] For a more thorough exploration of the building blocks of creation knowns as the "Sefirot," see "Mystical Concepts in Chassidism" by J. Emmanuel Schochet.

it? If "yud" is the first letter of God's name, then what is there prior to the "yud"?

In the first of the ten commandments, three words are utilized to refer to God: "Anochi," "יְהֹוָה/A-donai," and "Elokecha." While "יְהֹוָה/A-donai" is the highest of the names of God, there is something higher than God's name, and that is the level of "Anochi" which simply means "I" because it references a level of God that is so lofty that it cannot be encapsulated in a name. When we move beyond the "י/yud" of "יְהֹוָה/A-donai," we access "Anochi," this level of God that completely transcends this creation, and is thus even higher than "chochmah/wisdom." What can be higher than wisdom? The Sages explain that prior to wisdom there is "will," or "ratzon" in Hebrew. "Ratzon/Will" is the level of innermost desire. Prior to any conception or creation, there is a will which desires for something to be. Once the will exists, then there must follow a way for that will to be enacted. "Chochmah/wisdom" is the beginning of the process by which God translates His desire for a world into actuality. In the realm of desire, prior to "chochmah," there is no reason or logic. There is simply the will to give, as we discussed earlier in chapter two,[75] "it is the nature of the good to do good." "Ratzon/will" is not subject to thought, evaluation, or judgment. It is God's "nature," so to speak. It is primal and foundational and beyond the realm of inquiry or discernment. This is the level of "sod", the hidden inner dimension where God's essential love, forgiveness, and unity transcend the rules of reason and judgment. This is the aspect of God that is so lofty and so all-encompassing that it is not affected by our deeds, as we saw above in the verse "If you sinned, what effect do you have on Him."

This level of will is what we are trying to access when we recite the verse "poseach es YUDecha, u'masbea l'chol chai RATZON/open Your Yud, and satisfy all that lives with Your WILL" repeatedly throughout each day. We are acknowledging that when God 'opens His yud' - that is, when He goes beyond His level of "chochmah" or reason - then 'He will satisfy all that lives' through His level of "ratzon/will." At the level of "chochmah," not all things are satisfied because there are limits and qualifications. But at the level of "ratzon," there is no judgment or justice, there is only the will to love and to give. Meditating on this con-

---

[75] Section "Good Nature"

cept reminds us that our ultimate relationship with God is based not on "chochmah/wisdom," but on "ratzon/will" - not on logic and justice, but on a will that is supra-rational. This informs us that we are not confined to the limits of what we deserve or what we have earned, but rather our bond with God is essential, and not transactional. If we can simply access that level of God, then we can leave behind the trail of "sins" and misdeeds that exist in our wake, and we can instantly be wholly purified and renewed.

How do we do this? How do we access this exceedingly high and deep level that is beyond the world? How do we remove the blockages that we have created which separate us from God?

Part of this process is simply being aware that this reality is available to us. When we recognize that this is our true and ultimate nature, we therefore ask Him, with sincerity and humility, to "poseach es YIDecha/open your Jew." We request His help in enabling us to open ourselves and finding that which He has hidden within us. But why would He help us with this? Are we deserving of His help? Are we not guilty of turning away from Him and creating the distance between us? On the surface, at the level of "pshat," this is true - "avonoseichem hayu mavdilim beineichem l'vein Elokeichem/your iniquities have separated between you and your God."[76] On the level of "chochmah" and justice, we are liable and not deserving. But we now understand that this is not God's essence or limit, nor is it our own. We know further that it is not God's desire for us to be distant from Him. Rather, He has created boundaries and darkness only so that we could exist in order for Him to express His infinite love. We know that in this realm where the ultimate reality is concealed, He has assigned us the task of finding and revealing Him within the darkness. Therefore it is our reconnection to Him that is His deepest "ratzon/desire." And therefore when we ask Him to "poseach es yidecha" - open us so that we can find You within us - and "poseach es yudecha" - move beyond Your "chochmah" to Your ultimate "ratzon" - there is nothing more that He desires to do.

As this is His true and deepest will, our task is to truly make it our will as well. In other words, our task is to remove the blockages that we have erected so that His will can be manifest within us and through

---

[76] See the section entitled "Obstruction" above.

us. Our responsibility is simply to make a small opening, and He will respond exponentially, as He tells us:

פִּתְחוּ לִי פֶּתַח אֶחָד שֶׁל תְּשׁוּבָה כְּחֻדָּהּ שֶׁל מַחַט, וַאֲנִי פּוֹתֵחַ לָכֶם פְּתָחִים שֶׁיִּהְיוּ עֲגָלוֹת וּקְרוֹנִיּוֹת נִכְנָסוֹת בּוֹ.

Pischu li Pesach echad shel teshuvah k'chuda shel machat, va'ani poseach lachem pesachim she'yihyu agalos u'kronos nichnasim bo.

Open for me one opening of teshuvah like the eye of a needle, and I will open for you a great entranceway that wagons and carriages can pass through.

(Midrash Shir Hashirim Rabba 5:2)

The process of opening ourselves and finding the "Pnei Hashem" within our "pnimyus" is not easy, but we need not do it alone. The truth, we realize, is that we are never alone; we are, rather, 'all one.' With such awareness, the obstructions begin to fall away of themselves. There is nothing that can separate us from God because there is nothing but God.

Before

Throughout this chapter, we have been discussing the process of unwrapping and opening. This process will enable us to pursue the journey inward that will lead us to our lost self and to the Godliness that we are tasked to reveal. We have explored the layers of crust that impede our path, how they came to be, and how we can remove them. We found that we are capable of reaching beyond the creation, which begins with God's name "יְהֹוָה / A-donai," to access the level of God's will, "ratzon," which transcends all of the accounting and evaluation of logic and justice and in which all division ceases to exist. Accessing this level of God is the path of "teshuvah / return," and it is the process through which we can remove the many layers of obstruction that interpose between our surface and our essence.

With this, we can understand a Torah verse that describes the holiday of Yom Kippur and the complete purification and atonement that is achieved on this holiest day on the Jewish calendar:

כִּי-בַיּוֹם הַזֶּה יְכַפֵּר עֲלֵיכֶם לְטַהֵר אֶתְכֶם מִכֹּל חַטֹּאתֵיכֶם לִפְנֵי
יְ-הֹוָה תִּטְהָרוּ:

Ki ba'yom hazeh yechaper aleichem l'taher eschem m' kol chatoseichem lifnei A-donai titharu.

For on this day He shall effect atonement for you to purify you. Before the Lord, you shall be purified from all your sins.

(Leviticus 16:30)

Yom Kippur is the Day of Atonement, and it is said that on this day one's slate is swept clean. Whatever sins one committed in the past are now absolved, as the verse indicates, "you shall be purified from all your sins." How does this cleansing happen, and what does it truly mean? On the simple level, it indicates that all of the acts that we have performed throughout the past year which have offended God will now be expunged from our record. We beg forgiveness, and in His great mercy, God grants it. Yet on a deeper level, we have come to understand that God is not truly offended or affected by our deeds - "im chatasa mah tifal bo/if you sinned, what effect do you have on Him." We have come to recognize "sin" as the layers of crust and obstruction that separate between us and our ability to see and connect to God. "Teshuvah," we now appreciate, is the process through which we remove the obstruction. "Atonement" is, as its name indicates, "at one-ment" - the reunification that we experience when the walls and veils that divide us are removed.

In such a light, we are now capable of understanding how this reconciliation and reconnection is accomplished. The verse itself tells us explicitly with its wording "lifnei A-donai titharu." This phrase is translated as "before A-donai you will be purified." On the level of pshat, "lifnei/before" means "in the presence of," and the verse is understood to say that we will be purified as we stand in God's presence. However, as we have mentioned previously, the chasidic masters point out that "lifnei" means not just "before" as in "in the presence of," but also "before" as in "prior to" or "preceding." Understood in this sense, we find that the key to our purification is, as we discussed above, accessing a level that is "lifnei A-donai/higher than A-donai." Because God has created an orderly world of structure and law, we are subject to the rules of that order. When we transgress the laws, we are blemished, according to the rules of that system. But because of His love for us, God gives us the ability and opportunity to be purified by going beyond the limits of the system. He does not want us to be blemished or punished, and therefore, He allows us to reach "lifnei A-donai/ higher than A-donai" so that we can then be "titharu/purified." What is it that exists "lifnei A-donai"? It is a realm of ultimate unity where there are no distinctions, no right or wrong, no good and evil. There are no rules at this level and no transgression. There is no order or structure. There is only Godliness. When we access this level, every blemish simply dissolves.

To go one step further, "lifnei," as we've discussed at length,[77] also literally means "to the face." It is understood as "before" or "in the presence of" because it means "facing" something or being in front of its face. Taken at its literal level, we can render the phrase "lifnei A-donai" as "to the face of God." We can thus understand the concept of "lifnei A-donai titharu" to mean that we become purified when we reach the place or level of God's face. When we find the "Pnei Hashem," we are completely cleansed of any and all blemish in its presence. How does this work, and why is this so? Because the "Pnei Hashem" is found within our "pnimyus," our innermost core. Therefore when we reach that level, when we penetrate to our deepest essence, we become aware that we are nothing other than Godliness. The level that is "beyond A-donai" is not somewhere outside of us and outside of this world, but rather it is the face of God that is embedded deep within each of us. When we peel off the many garments that cover our core, we are able to delve inward and arrive "lifnei A-donai." This then transports us far beyond all of the "helam/hiddenness" of this "olam/world."

It is important to note that this ability to reach "lifnei A-donai" and to thereby be purified and absolved of all past wrongdoing is one of the Torah's deepest and most sensitive secrets. There is the possibility, of course, that there will be those who view this accessibility to instant forgiveness and guiltlessness as a license to ignore or transgress the laws that God has established within the world. It is for this reason that many sages fought against the proliferation of the teachings of Chassidus and

---

[77] See chapter four, section "In Your Face"

insisted that the Torah's mystic secrets should remain confined to a select few. But the Baal Shem Tov and his followers knew that the awareness of God's limitless love, along with one's inherent accessibility to the boundless realms beyond this world, would ultimately be positive. Our recognition of God's unity and of our complete inclusion in that unity will not lead to distance from God. On the contrary, it will activate alignment with His will in the recognition that it is truly our very own will. When we recognize our Godly potential and essence, we respond to the Torah's teachings and edicts not with obedience and acquiescence, but rather with communion and consociation. *We perform God's will not in hope of reward or for fear of punishment, but in love of the One who loves us so infinitely, and in recognition of the reality that we are each intricate instruments of His expression and simple portions of His being.*

Chapter 7: BEING GODLY

Revolution

At this point, we have established that the destination of our journey is within, and we know that in order to continue this journey and reach "lifnei A-donai" - to the face of God where all impurity, darkness, and plurality cease to exist - we must remove the coverings that we have amassed over our center and open a path in order to penetrate to our inner depths. We know that when we access this space we will avail ourselves of a constant flow of Godliness and goodliness that will not only provide us everything we need, but will also enable us to endow the entire creation around us with everything it lacks. The next question, then, is how specifically we can remove these coverings. Fortunately, Torah provides us an intricate practice in order to help us do so. As a matter of fact, this is precisely Torah's purpose and intent, and we will explore this subject in depth in the coming chapters.

However, before we do so, we must pause on our path and return to the question that we began to address in chapter five. There, we introduced the question "how are you," and we touched on the self-esteem that comes with the recognition of the Godliness within. We explored the Torah's conception of the "Adam/human" as one who is not only from the "adama/earth," but is also "adameh l'Elyon/similar to God." We explained that what we are seeking is therefore not far from us but already in our inherent nature and in our grasp. We saw that this tremendous sense of self-worth lightens our load and brightens our journey through the darkness of this world. In chapter six, we then went on to analyze the coverings that obscure the light within us, the reasons they exist, and the ways in which we reinforce them rather than divest ourselves of them. Before moving onward, it is worthwhile to backtrack a few steps and further discuss how illuminated one becomes, and how beautiful life can be, when we are opened and our inherent Godliness is expressed.

As we deduced earlier, the answer to the question "how are you" will depend on our answer to our first question, "ayecha/where are you" and its corollaries "what are you" and "why are you." If we locate ourselves in this physical realm - if we identify ourselves as the body that fumbles around in the darkness, and if we conceive of our purpose as the accumulation of material possessions and the satisfaction of our body's passions and urges - then most certainly our answer to the question of "how are you" will be not well. It is not possible to be well in the long run in a realm of entropy where everything decays other than the appetites which consistently grow. If, on the other hand, we locate ourselves within, if we identify ourselves as the "Pnei Hashem" that is hidden in our "pnimyus," and if we realize that our purpose is the revelation of our Godly light within the darkness, then we will answer "how are you" with the humble recognition that "I am great." I am great because that which I truly am is pure and unadulterated Godliness.

This is a profound and potentially life-altering concept, but how do we take it out of the realm of the conceptual and bring it into the actual so that we truly feel great and we truly actualize our greatness? If I read this book and then put it down and move onward with some vague intellectual notion that God is within me, what have I really gained? Has my life truly changed in any significant way? Do I feel different? Do I act differently? Do I treat the people around me differently? The recognition of one's inherent Godliness is not simply a nice idea, or an inspiring spiritual insight. It is a revolution. It is a complete transformation of one's life from a condition of limitation, mortal frailty, and fallibility, to a brand new reality of vastness, transcendence, and boundless potential.

The ramifications of God's complete unity compel us to admit that not only is God within me and the ultimate essence of what I am, but He is similarly the core and ultimate reality of all else. In other words, not only are we ourselves nothing but Godliness, but furthermore everything we encounter is nothing but Godliness. Even the darkness and the layers of concealment that disguise this truth are nothing but Godliness! Imagine if you were conscious of this reality at every moment. How would your life be different? How WILL your life be different when this becomes your constant mindset?

Self Image

The first thing that will change with the awareness of God's absolute unity is the relationship one has with her/himself. It is no secret and no surprise that the vast majority of us dwell in a state of constant insecurity, self-consciousness, and self-critique. For some of us, our relationship with ourself is even more problematic. We tend toward self-loathing, displaying consistent behaviors that are self-defeating and self-destructive. Some of this negativity in our self-concept can be attributed to the shame that we discussed in the previous chapter. This shame is partially derived from a misunderstanding of our origins, and a misinterpretation of the concept of sin and Adam and Eve's "fall from grace" in the Torah's opening chapters.[78] Even those who are not interested in theological issues or religious involvement are subject to the pervasive cultural conception of the inherent sinfulness of the human being. This is perpetuated, in part, by those who have always sought to exploit our discontent in order to keep us under their control. Regardless of the sources and perpetrators of this toxic self-regard, its ultimate cause is the basic unawareness of what we are and why we exist.

Have you ever felt okay? Be honest. When was the last time you had a sense, deep down inside of you, that you are completely acceptable

---

[78] See section entitled "Shame" in chapter 6.

just as you are? Have you ever in your adult life experienced the conviction that you are fine and good and there is nothing wrong with you? Do you ever feel an absolute guiltlessness, a confidence that there is nothing you should be doing or being at this moment that you are not? This is not to say that you are perfect or complete - because we are not perfect or complete in this realm - but that you are complete in your incompleteness? Such a sense of worth and self-acceptance is extremely rare. Even those whom we deem to be "successful" and "accomplished" rarely exude the kind of contentment and serenity that would characterize this type of self-assurance. Accomplishment in our modern societies is usually identified with the amassing of material assets, the acquisition of power, and/or the achievement of renown. But all of these are generally the result of a drive for validation and recognition. Their possession usually only increases the appetites and renders the self more hungry and restless, and less satisfied and calm. How many people have you met in your life who truly seem to be fulfilled and happy with who and what they are?

Because we don't know who or what or where we are, we are constantly questioning our existence and calibrating our worth. This incessant self-evaluation and critique leaves us anxious and insecure. We feel judged and dissected, and the 'self' that we view in the mirror is flawed and blemished and unable to stand up to such persistent and excruciating scrutiny. The judgment comes from those around us, but even more frequently and damningly, it comes from ourselves. Most damagingly, we believe that the perpetual critique comes from God, the One who created us and who is ashamed of how far we are from what He had intended us to be. This assumption of God's criticism and ire is the very root of so much unhappiness and heartache, and it is so heartbreakingly unnecessary, because it is simply untrue! *God does not disdain us. He does not focus on our faults or look for opportunities to judge and condemn us. God IS us!* He therefore relates to us, understands us, appreciates us, roots for us, and loves us completely. Simultaneously, He challenges us, He hides Himself from us, and He allows us to be unaware of His absolute unity and His absolute love. But this concealment and its challenges are, as we have explained throughout this book, only a function of His love. Without it, we could not exist as seemingly separate beings, and He would have no "other" to whom He could express His infinite desire to give.

God's desire to overlook our faults and His disinterest in judgment and censure is stated explicitly in Torah:

לֹא־הִבִּיט אָוֶן בְּיַעֲקֹב וְלֹא־רָאָה עָמָל בְּיִשְׂרָאֵל:

Lo hibit aven b'Yaacov v'lo ra'ah amal b'Yisrael.

(God) does not look at sin in Jacob, and He has not seen crookedness in Israel.

(Numbers 23:21)

Here, the wicked prophet Balaam is forced to declare that not only does God not *seek* faults in His children, but furthermore He does not even *see* our shortcomings. It is not merely that He is not looking for opportunities to blame and shame us, but that even if He were, He would find none. This is because He does not view our acts as sin at all. This is reinforced by a verse from Psalms which states:

אַשְׁרֵי אָדָם לֹא יַחְשֹׁב יְ-הֹוָה לוֹ עָוֹן:

Ashrei adam lo yachshov A-donai lo avon.

Happy/fortunate is man, God does not consider His sin.

(Psalms 32:2)

On the simple level, this verse is commonly translated as "happy is *the* man whose sin is not considered by God." However, the literal reading of the verse reveals a deeper and more internal truth. It does not say "ashrei *ha'*adam/happy is *the* man" but rather "ashrei adam/happy is man." On the level of "pshat," the verse seems to refer to a certain type of person who is deserving of God's overlooking of His sins. But according to its "sod," it refers not to a particular person or people whose sins are not considered, but rather to mankind in general - all people - for God does not consider our sin. Why does He not do so? Because, as we discussed in the previous chapter, our misdeeds do not affect Him. They only create another layer of covering that obscures our view of Him and our recognition of His presence within our core. Ultimately, "lifnei A-donai," at the level of God's face, we are not judged. And as we find and experience this level of our essential reality, we need not judge ourselves.

We can actually begin to experience life, and experience ourselves, without constant self-recrimination and critique.

If we conceive of God as one who is constantly counting and accounting our sins and merits, and we want to emulate Him and be Godly, then we too will perpetually be judging everything around us and within us. But we must pause and ask ourselves if God is truly so, or if we are making Him in our image. Did He create us with this tendency and imperative to be constantly judgmental? Is this what He wants from us, to be always on guard, always tense, always afraid that we will fall or fail and then be punished? As we have quoted previously, Torah tells us "ivdu es A-donai b'simcha / serve God with joy."[79] How can we possibly serve with joy if we are always afraid? We can perhaps serve Him with fear, but is it truly possible to be joyous when we are incessantly critiquing our performance and dreading our inevitable failure?

God knows that we are fallible. He created us imperfect, and He situated us in the dark. He not only accepts our imperfection, but establishes it as a condition of our existence. It is what distinguishes us from Him and enables us to be the "other" that He desires. Therefore, we can accept our imperfection and strive for improvement without hating our deficiency. We can feel motivated to grow without feeling inadequate. *We can act Godly because we are Godly, and not simply because we want to avert retribution.*

If we view God as a strict and exacting judge who sits above and eternally assesses His creation, then our lives will be focused on right and wrong, good and evil, reward and punishment. We will view ourselves and our surroundings through this lens, and we will feel guilt when we err, and pride when we comply. We will judge and critique and forever struggle to negotiate this duality that bifurcates our existence. But if we view Him as the sole existence and the very essence of our being and all being, then we will stop evaluating ourselves and believing we are deserving of consequence and rebuke. Then we will stop struggling with life, and we will learn to navigate the currents without being angry that they don't always flow the way we wish. We will trust in God and know that He is here always; that everything is so because He makes it so; that I am so because He has made me so; that I can accomplish anything with His help when I stop limiting myself and limiting Him.

---

[79] Psalms 100:2

When we focus on the divisions that God has created, we live in division and limitation. When we focus on His unity, we unite with Him and transcend all of our constraints. Torah refers to God by multiple names which, as we have mentioned, allude to various aspects of His being. He is both "A-donai" and "E-lohim." "E-lohim" is His judgment, His manifestation within the world of division and plurality. "A-donai" is His infinite transcendence, His aspect beyond limitation and delineation. We and the world exist on multiple levels simultaneously: the physical reality and the spiritual essence. The question is not which aspect of God, of us, and of the creation is true, because they each have their truth. The question is in which aspect we choose to exist. We can dwell in the realm of limits, physicality, and judgment, or we can choose to transcend this space and live a life of expansiveness, patience, and infinite growth.

A recognition of our Godliness and the love that God feels and displays for us will revolutionize our self-image and transport us from an outlook of self-consciousness to one of God-consciousness. It will carry us from a state of self-judgment to one of intense self-esteem. When we recognize that the "Pnei Hashem" is lodged in our "pnimyus," then we can finally love ourselves and treat ourselves with the patience and kindness that we deserve. Even as we recognize that the casing that encrusts and conceals our ultimate self is less 'lovable' per se, we are aware that that exterior is not what we essentially are; therefore, we needn't be self-critical because that is not a representation of our truest "self" at all. Yet because "A-donai echad/God is One," we understand that even this bodily shell is Godliness, serving His purpose of allowing each of us to exist. With this awareness, we can come to value that part of ourselves as well.

We can begin to appreciate every aspect of creation, even as we work to refine it, transform it, and reveal it for what it truly is. We can love even those things that we must battle, even those things that have no awareness and no manifestation of their Godliness. If so, then we can certainly know that we are okay and fine, even as we are imperfect. I have work to do, but that need not hinder me from having genuine sympathy toward myself. Equipped with this self-directed sympathy, I can then sympathize with the entire creation. With this perspective, our angst and shame will begin to melt away, and we will begin to experience a buoyancy, clarity, and serenity that will transform our lives and our world completely.

Peace

After one's self-image changes, everything else begins to change as well. With the abandonment of self-consciousness and self-critique comes a tremendous release of pressure and tension. The transformative potential of this release and relief cannot be overestimated. It is the difference between a life of subtle, but endless anxiety, and an experience of liberation that many of us cannot even fathom because we are not conscious of our captivity or the possibility of its cessation. The stress in our lives is like an incessant, irritating hiss that we fail to hear or address because of its constancy. It is like a chronic ache that we eventually resign ourselves to because we become convinced that it is inevitable. It is a sad reality that the vast majority of us accept this type of torment, unaware that there is an alternative.

It is difficult to describe peace to one who has not experienced it. It is perhaps like trying to describe color to one who is blind. Yet it is important to explain this state to the best of our ability, because it is incredibly precious, and it is freely available despite the fact that it is so lacking in common experience. The hope is that we will work harder to seek and discover it if we grasp even some vague sense of its profound value and its attainability.

If we would be asked to define peace, we might characterize it as the absence of battle or conflict. By such a definition, much of the world today can be said to be "at peace" in that the zones of war and regions of armed conflict are relatively few. But it would be difficult to contend that most places in the world today enjoy true peace. We would be hard pressed to find many places where the majority of its inhabitants (or even a minority for that matter) would honestly assert that they are at peace. Real peace is a rare commodity in this world. It is not simply a matter of an absence of physical violence. What then is it?

We might suggest that peace is the absence of not only tangible and material violence, but also emotional and psychic conflict. One who is at peace would therefore not be plagued by thoughts and feelings that are troublesome or confounding. Yet while this may be true of someone at peace, it would be hard to argue that peace is merely the lack of challenge, contention, and variance. If that were the case, then could we say that anyone or anything that is not challenged is experiencing peace? Would we suggest that a cow is at peace, for example? Or a boulder? Or one who has suffered a brain injury and therefore is no longer in touch with her/his mental and emotion faculties?

Peace would seem to be more than a simple lack of conflict. Furthermore, the absence of conflict tells us nothing of one's ability to maintain composure and tranquility if and when conflict does inevitably present itself. Genuine peace will not only precede discord, but it will even preclude it. It will enable one to endure challenges and stress without panicking or crumbling or responding to disturbance with reciprocal disturbance. Peace is therefore not merely the absence or avoidance of tension, but rather it is something that provides us the ability to tolerate and abide the vicissitudes of life with a state of equanimity, acceptance, and constructiveness. What is this magical or mystical thing called peace that affords us an almost superhuman stability and poise?

As we work toward an understanding of this concept, it will be useful to point out something that peace is not. In Torah, peace is not a goal in and of itself. In some spiritual systems, the attainment of peace is the end game. Life is not considered to have significance beyond its experience, and therefore the objective is to attain a level of surrender and acceptance which can make our existence not only tolerable, but even beautiful. Peace, in such a framework, is not simply a tool to enable one to achieve some other aim, but it is the aim itself. There are certainly worse things to aim for, and one cannot be blamed for setting something as wonderful as peace as her/his target. But doing so, according to Torah, will not fulfill one's potential or discharge the holy duty that s/he was created to perform.

Similar to this idea is the concept of happiness in Torah. Happiness, or "שִׂמְחָה/simcha" in Hebrew, is not merely a Torah ideal, but it is a commandment, as it is written "ivdu es Hashem b'simcha/Serve God with joy."[80] Yet while Torah requires happiness and stresses its necessity, the objective is not the happiness itself, but the service that it facilitates

---

[80] Psalms 100:2. As discussed in chapter two, section "Obligatory Happiness"

and engenders. The verse from Psalms is not only telling us to serve God joyously, but it is instructing how we can achieve the service of God: "Ivdu es Hashem/serve God" - how do we do so? - "b'simcha," with, and through, simcha/joy. Without happiness, it is difficult to focus on anything but our own quandary or misery. When we are happy, however, we are able to move beyond ourselves and focus on how we can be of service to others and to the world around us.

Similarly, peace is a means to a greater end. The goals in Torah, as we have mentioned repeatedly, are to find oneself - "lech lecha/go to yourself" - and to reveal God in the realm of darkness and concealment in which He has hidden Himself - "breishis bara E-lokim es hashamayim v'es haaretz/the primary thing is reveal God in heavens and the earth." Peace is both a mechanism to help us reach these goals, and a product of their accomplishment. If we do not have peace, then we will be in constant turmoil, whether we are conscious of it or it afflicts us subconsciously. We will be occupied with so many ancillary battles that we will be unable to focus on the task at hand. Life presents us with endless diversions and enticements that heighten our tension and rob us of the ability to be in touch with what is truly important and significant. Peace is the clarity that comes with the elimination of these distractions, and it is the ability to ignore all of those things that vie for our attention. In one sense then, peace is the capacity to focus on what we are here to do.

Focus is the discipline to direct consciousness on a designated thing and shut out the many other things that surround it and compete for one's attention. It is the peeling away of all extraneous and superficial factors and details in order to pinpoint what is principal and essential. This is both the path to peace, and the essence of what peace is. When we succeed in shucking away all of the layers that cover our core, we will arrive at a place within us that is untouched and imperturbable. It is a dimension of incredible light and lightness. There is no tension there or conflict, because there is nothing else there at all. It is a mere point, but it is endless. Once we touch it, it envelops us. We find that it is not merely within us, but we are within it, and we always have been. It is the face of God, and God is One and all.

Oneness is the basis and foundation of true and ultimate peace. The Hebrew word for peace is "שָׁלוֹם/shalom," which derives from the root "שלם/shalem," which means "whole." Peace, quite simply, is the awareness that we are whole, and the eradication of all those deceptions in our lives that swarm around us and try to convince us otherwise.

The torment and angst of life is disconnection, division, and individuality. We feel alone and alien. We see ourselves as small and insignificant, hopelessly flawed, and irreparably broken. "Shalom/Peace" is the consciousness that God is within us and that we are within Him; that He is the fundamental and solitary truth of us and of all creation. The "world/olam" that we inhabit is a realm of "helam/concealment" that hides the reality of God's wholeness for all of the reasons that we have already discussed. Our task is to penetrate the concealment, to illuminate and eliminate the darkness. When we do so, we will experience the peace and euphoria of reuniting with everything we thought we had lost and lacked. The sense of alienation, the agony of not belonging in a cold world that does not know you or care about you, all of this will suddenly fade away, and we will experience the ecstatic intertwining of the billions of souls that are ultimately singular and undifferentiated.

When we realize that we are whole and one, there are no boundaries or limitations. We flow through and with everything as we are all kindred and synergistic. There is no fear, or trepidation, or bias. There is no need to explain oneself, or justify, or beautify. We need nothing, and we lack nothing, because we have everything, and we are everything. There is no tension or awkwardness, no self-consciousness or defense. There is no need to find the right words or wear the right clothes. There is no vanity, or jealousy, or envy. There is only amity, and empathy, and community in its truest sense.

On the subject of community and the interrelation of its members, there is a well-known Talmudic phrase:

כָּל יִשְׂרָאֵל עֲרֵבִים זֶה בַּזֶה.

Kol Yisrael areivim zeh bazeh.
All Israel is responsible for one another.
(Talmud, Shavuot 39a)

The word "עֲרֵבִים/areivim" means "guarantor," and the simple understanding of the verse is that we must all guarantee each other's well-being. However, the word "areivim" also means "mixed" and "intermingled." On a deeper level, we therefore glean that the reason we are responsible for others is not merely because we have a duty to them, but because we are inextricably co-mingled with one another. We are one soul, one being. Peace is not simply an alliance between us in which we agree to do no battle; it is the recognition that we are fundamentally one, and that any conflict between us is only a battle with oneself.

Ultimately, words will do this no justice. The peace that we are trying to describe here is more than simply the communion of all human souls. It is the absolute unity of all existence. This cannot be adequately transmitted in black ink on a white page. It must be experienced with a sense that is not visual or tactile or sensible. This is why we close our eyes when we recite "Shema Yisrael, A-donai E-loheinu, A-donai echad/ Hear Israel, the Lord our God, the Lord is One!" To attain this complete and euphoric oneness we must remove ourselves from the constraints of our six senses and our intellect, and we must shut out everything we know and think we understand. It is supra-rational, and supra-sensual, but it is palpable. You can feel it if you reach for it deep within you. And when you feel it, even a tiny twinge of it, it will send a type of spiritual shudder throughout the entirety of your being. There will be a tickle at all of your edges, a subtle pins-and-needles sensation in your toes, and your fingers, and your scalp, and then your entire skin, as all of your extremities begin to give way. You will feel a sudden weightlessness, and gravity will momentarily release its hold on you. You will wonder if you are about to float away or dissolve. And if you don't panic, if you resist the urge to grasp on to something solid in order to anchor yourself to the familiar, then you will eventually be overcome with the ecstasy of the harmony, integrity, and unity of all things.

It will require focus and concentration to attain this consciousness and this level of peace, but each of us is capable of doing so. This is one of the primary goals of Jewish prayer - to reconnect to the essence and unity of all things. As we have explained previously,[81] prayer is commonly relegated to the simple requesting of one's needs, but the concept of "tefilla/prayer" according to Torah is more about reuniting with one's source. The rich tradition of Jewish meditation has been an integral aspect of Torah practice for millennia. One of the primary focal points of meditation in the prayer service is the recitation of the "Shema," which

---

[81] See chapter three, section "Inward Bound"

we explored in the first chapter,[82] and which focuses us on the reality of God's sole existence. Unfortunately, many are accustomed to rushing through the prayer service, fulfilling their duty of pronouncing the proper words and phrases, but failing to take advantage of the profound transformation and liberation that is available through even a short but devoted meditation on the words and concepts they utter.

To experience the sense of oneness and the peace that meditative prayer can offer, try the following: Find a quiet room and sit in a chair. Close your eyes and breathe in through your nose and out through your mouth. Imagine that each inward breath brings cleansing air down into your abdomen and up into your mind. In your abdomen it collects tension, and in your mind it collects extraneous thoughts. When you exhale, allow yourself to feel the tightness drain from your body as the commotion slips from your brain, and begin to relax in the chair. Feel your weight in the chair and your feet on the floor, and let everything else go - the room and all that is in it, the house or building and the environment in which it is situated, let it all slowly vanish. It is now just you sitting in a chair, which rests on the ground, in an open expanse with absolutely nothing around you as far as the eye can see.

Keep breathing in and out, and now let the ground fade away. It is now just you on your chair, floating in space, with nothing around you, or below you, or above you. There is only a dull light or a glowing darkness that surrounds you as you sit comfortably on your floating chair. As you continue to breathe, slowly and calmly inhaling and exhaling, you realize that there is nothing holding the chair, and the chair is not holding you, so you let the chair go as well. And now it is just you, floating, weightless, alone but not lonely.

There is a stillness and quietness all around you that makes you feel calm and at rest. You realize that the body does you no good here, and so you let it disappear just like everything before it. And you are still here in the space, but you cannot be seen. You are not missing or lacking, you are everywhere now that there is nothing to confine you to one part of the space. You no longer struggle to be seen, to be recognized, to be special, because the "you" that yearned for those things was so small, and this everything which you are now suffused within is so complete and full and infinite. The tension that coursed within you is released,

---

[82] Section "The Only One"

dispersed, and set free. The static that was in you has become ecstatic, an energy that uplifts you and enthralls you. You feel it, but you don't contain it. You share it, and you can move with it across the expanse and back. You are here and there and everywhere at once. You are free. There is no in and no out. You breathe, but it is not you breathing, it is the universal breath moving like a great tide in the expanse. You move with it because you are mingled with it. There is no resistance, no fear of drowning, no struggle to float. There is no surface and no depths. It is all depth, and you are deep within it, and around it, and of it. You are of everything, "in Of" with it. Love is when you desire to bond with something separate from you. "Of" is when you understand that there is nothing separate from you. You lack nothing, and desire nothing. You are whole and holy. You are "in of" - at one, and at peace, with everything.

This is the "shalom/peace" and "shleimus/wholeness" that we can experience when we access the face of God within us and we shed all of the layers that clothe, surround, and conceal it. It is not easy to do so, because the default of this "olam/world" is "helam/concealment," and the crust that divides and individualizes us does not stop growing on us for a moment. This is why peace is so rare and fleeting. And this is why we must seek the face of God constantly, as we recite each morning in the "Hodu" prayer that begins the daily service, "bakshu panav tamid/seek His face always."

Peace will never come of its own or settle on us without effort. It is not the lack of work or a state of rest. In Torah, peace is not a passive affair. It is the labor of consistently delving inward and penetrating the barriers that alienate us from our essential self and the identical essence of all things. We must make peace with exertion and challenge, conscious that all of the trials and obstacles we face are also elements of God's infinite oneness. There is nothing that blocks or hinders us, because the blockages and hindrances are composed of precisely the same stuff that we are. With the consciousness that we are whole and one, we can alleviate the tension and stress that pervades and surrounds us, and thereby completely transform our lives and our world.

Bittul

There is a term that the mystics use for this concept of 'being one with everything' which we have described above. It is "הִתְכַּלְלוּת/ hitkallelut/interinclusion." The root of the word is "כל/kal," which means "all," and the term "hitkallelut" thus means to be included in all. But interestingly, the root "כל/kal" also means "expiry" as in "כִּלָּיוֹן/ki-layon/annihliation." We can understand this duality of meaning because if something is subsumed in everything, then it no longer maintains its own individual existence. Like a drop of water that falls into the ocean, it no longer exists as an individual drop as it becomes mingled with the entirety of the sea. This duality exists in the term "שלם/shalem" as well. As we have seen above, "shalem" means "whole," but it can also be translated as "complete" or "finished." From this linguistic nuance we can approach another subtle level in the concept of "shalom/peace." Peace, we will find, can be achieved not only by seeing one's greatness and perfection in the enormity and entirety of the whole (as we discussed in the previous section), but also on the contrary, by letting oneself go completely. By releasing the pressure of striving to exist and individuate, one can thereby allow oneself to relax into the reality of her/his ultimate "nothingness."

This is known in chassidic teachings as "בִּיטוּל/bittul," which literally means "nullification" but is often translated in this context more specifically as "self-nullification" or "self-abnegation." At first glance, this notion of self-nullification does not seem desirable or productive as it is completely contrary to the instinct for self-preservation. But while the body, or animal aspect of humanity, strives for self-preservation and self-aggrandizement, the soul knows that its greatest accomplishment is not asserting itself, but rather giving itself completely. The soul is not concerned with itself because it is not a self; it is a component of the all-encompassing and exclusive reality of God. Therefore, by surrendering itself, it simply reunites with the infinite. "Bittul/self-nullification" is the end of the self, but it is not the end of the soul. For the soul there is no end. Its only limits are when it is individualized, so to speak, and confined to the physical restraints of the body. The more it gives itself -

through acts of self-sacrifice and surrender even as it remains within the body - the more it is united with its infinite reality.[83]

The sacrifice of one's self does not truly result in nothingness therefore, but rather in "everythingness." One does not become nothing through self-nullification; rather s/he becomes unified with everything. Individuality is not what makes me something, it is what separates me from everything. I do not cease to exist when I let go of my boundaries, I cease to be small and limited. I begin to truly exist when I stop insisting on my individual existence. In this sense, the choice is not the existential quandary of "being or nothingness," as Jean Paul Sartre phrases it; it is rather being or "everythingness." Shakespeare's classical dialectic in Hamlet's soliloquy, "to be or not to be," is not the authentic question. In our framework, the option would be "to be or to truly be." In other words, one can decide whether to be small by insisting on one's particular being and thus holding on to finitude, or to be limitless by letting go of one's self and thus entering eternity and infinity. Surrender and self-nullification, therefore, will lead to both "nothingness" and "everythingness" simultaneously. What is nullified and eradicated is not the true self, but those wrappings and trappings that we erroneously believe to be the self. These wrappings actually conceal the "Pnei Hashem," which is our ultimate self and the essence of all things. With "bittul/self-nullification," these coverings become nothing, and then it is revealed that we are truly everything.

Though it is known as "self-nullification," this negation of the self does not mean that one has no sense of dignity or worth and therefore allows the world to mistreat and trample her/him. On the contrary, through "bittul" one is conscious of her/his infinite worth as a veritable part of God. One knows that the truest expression of her/his value and preciousness is the transcendence of the ego and its self-concern. This secret of the inestimable value of nothingness is identified by the mystics in several places in Torah. In the book of Job, we find the following:

וְהַחָכְמָה מֵאַיִן תִּמָּצֵא:
V'chochmah me'ayin timatzei?
And wisdom, **from where** will it be found?
(Job 28:12)

---

[83] More on this in the following chapter, see section entitled "Death."

Simply translated, the verse is read as a question, asking where wisdom is to be found. The word "אַיִן/ayin" is rendered in this reading as "where." However, the term also means "nothing." Therefore, the verse can simultaneously be read as a statement rather than a question: "and wisdom from nothingness will be found." True wisdom, the chassidic masters teach, is the awareness that we are "nothing" in and of ourselves, and we are only expressions of Godliness. In fact, the very word for "wisdom" in Hebrew, "חָכְמָה/chochmah," is an articulation of this understanding. "Chochmah," the Chasidic masters teach, is a compound of two words, "כח/koach/power" and "מה/mah/what." Wisdom is thus "the power of what." In other words, wisdom is the enlightened capability to ask 'what am I' - what is my ultimate essence and ultimate worth - and to recognize that I am nothing in and of myself. This intense wisdom and humility was expressed by Moses in the desert when he exclaimed:

וְנַחְנוּ מָה:
Ve'nachnu mah?
What are we?
(Exodus 16:7)

While the phrase is read as a question in the plain sense, it can also be read as a statement: "we are what!" In other words, we are nothingness. Though he was the leader of the nation, the one man who had spoken to God face to face and had stood up to Pharaoh and the entire army of Egypt, he recognized that he was nothing but an instrument through which God expressed Himself in the world.

The value and power of nothingness is also articulated in Psalms. There King David exclaims:

מֵאַיִן יָבֹא עֶזְרִי:
Me'ayin yavo ezri?
From where will my help come?
(Psalms 121:1)

On the simple level, once again reading the word "ayin" as "where," David is asking where is the source of his help. However, on a more subtle and mystic level, reading "ayin" in its translation of "nothing," the verse is David's statement of precisely where his help will originate: "from nothingness will my help come." What does this mean? How does one's help come from nothing? David is informing us that through accessing the lofty level of "bittul/self-nullifcation," he will no longer be subject to the perils of which he has been afraid. By recognizing that he is truly and ultimately "ayin," i.e. nothing other than Godliness, and furthermore that there *is* nothing other than Godliness, he realizes that there is therefore nothing to fear. His deliverance from all trouble, therefore, derives from this awareness of his fundamental non-being.

The Baal Shem Tov finds this lesson similarly hidden in a common expression from "The Ethics of the Fathers." One of the most frequently quoted verses from this collection of wisdom is:

אִם **אֵין** אֲנִי לִי מִי לִי:

*Im **ain** ani li mi li?*
If I am not for myself, who is for me?
(Pirkei Avos 1:14)

Usually cited to express the need for self-reliance and independence, the verse is understood to mean that I must have the courage to stand up for myself, because I cannot rely on others to fight my battles. While this lesson is both true and important, the Baal Shem Tov detects the "sod/secrets" in this verse which express an even more subtle truth. The word "ain/not" in the verse is the same word as "ayin/nothing" - both are spelled אין in Hebrew. Therefore, in addition to its plain meaning "if I am not for myself," the phrase can be rendered "if I am nothing to myself." The second part of the verse, "mi li," is commonly translated "who is for me?" But the words literally mean "who to me," and therefore the Baal Shem Tov reads it as "who can get to me." Together then, the two phrases are interpreted, "if I am nothing to myself, who can get me?" In other words, if I am nothing, then there is nothing that can harm me. If I exist and I am a substantial and solid target, then I am subject to attack. But if I don't exist, because I am one with the infinite, then the blows and projectiles that are launched at me will fail to land and will move right through me. When I am not trying to assert and establish myself because I am nothing in my own estimation, then nothing can harm me because there is no 'me' to be harmed.[84]

Fearlessness

One of the most significant impediments to peace is fear. Even if one is not at war or in battle, if s/he is afraid, then s/he is certainly not at peace. Previously, we had discussed the fact that self-consciousness and self-condemnation are obstacles to an experience of self-worth and contentment, and that the discovery of the face of God within us would bring us to the realization of our wholeness and integrity and a resultant mindset of peace. In the case of fear, it is the recognition of our immateriality which will enable us to overcome any worry of attack or violence. There is nothing to fear because there is not only no object of attack - for I am nothing substantial and therefore all aggression will move right through me - but furthermore there is no attacker - for just as I am "ayin/nothing" so is my assailant "ayin/nothing." Therefore, anything and everything that is hurled in my direction has no substance either. There is not only no target, but there are no arrows. There is no bow and no archer, no aggressor and no victim.

The pervasiveness of fear in our lives is not surprising. For as we have discussed from the very first pages of this book, we have been created in a realm of darkness, and we are lost from the moment we are born. In addition to this, Torah characterizes life as a constant battle. In his work *Tanya*, the Alter Rebbe describes the conflict between the Godly and animal aspects of our soul as two rival armies which are fighting for control over a city.[85] Each of us is the "city," and our two opposing inclinations - our Godly nature and our animal nature - vie for dominance over our being. With this battle raging perpetually within us and around us, it is no wonder that we are ravaged by fear. The Zohar similarly depicts our spiritual reality as a battle:

---

[84] Tzavaas HaRivash 62

[85] *Tanya*, Likkutei Amarim, chapter 9

כַּד אָתֵי צַפְרָא, בָּעֵי לְנַקָּאָה גַּרְמֵיה בְּכֹלָּא, וּלְמֵיזַן זַיְינֵיה.

Kad asei tzafra, ba'ei l'naka'ah garmei b'chola, u'l'meizan zay'nei.

With the dawn, one should cleanse himself of every-thing, and then arm himself for battle.

(Zohar III, 260a)

Each new day, the Zohar tells us, confronts us with a series of skirmishes as the various aspects of our existence wrestle with one an-other. Even seemingly simple daily processes present us with constant conflict and confrontation:

שעתא דקרבא היא שעתא דצלותא.

Sha'ata d'krava hi sha'ata d'tzlosa.

A time of war is the time of prayer.

(Likkutei Torah, Ki Teitze)

Prayer, which is allegedly to be a time of peace and calm, is in fact a time of war. As we attempt to focus and clear our mind, we are barraged by distractions and temptations, and our quietude and clarity are perpetually challenged. Even things as mundane and simple as con-suming food present us with friction and contention:

שעתא דמיכלא שהיא שעתא דקרבא.

Sha'ata d'michla she'hi sha'ata d'krava.

The time of eating is a time of battle.

(Zohar III, 188)

The act of eating inflames our animal instincts and provokes our baser nature. In effect, every moment of life is a struggle between our hidden inner essence that wants to express itself, and our outer material housing which wants only to further sate and pleasure itself, and there-fore strives to keep its Godly origins suppressed.

Because of the nature of this ongoing conflict between the spiri-tual and physical forces of our existence, we are constantly confronted with the violence and cacophony of battle. However, our response to this warfare need not be fear. The question is how we prepare for the battle, and how we engage the "enemy." If, as the Zohar states, we begin the day with the battle of prayer, then we can glean from the prayer service the strategy and methodology with which we should face the combat that threatens us.

Most soldiers and forces prepare for war by girding their bodies in protective armor and readying their weapons. They cover themselves with gear that will reinforce and guard their flesh so they will not be harmed and their ranks will not be diminished. The more shielded and impenetrable they are, the greater their chance of victory. However, Torah prayer prepares for battle in a diametrically opposite manner. The service begins with the recital of "קָרְבָּנוֹת/karbonos/sacrifices," in which one reads verses that narrate the order of the animal sacrifices that were offered in the Temple. The intention of these sacrifices was the consumption of the flesh and the eradication of the animal casing that conceals the spirit within.[86] Through meditating on this act in the beginning of the daily prayers, the Godly essence that is hidden beneath the flesh is empowered and prioritized.

Yet this is counterintuitive. As the enemy fortifies itself in armor and equips itself with weaponry, Torah urges one to take her/his flesh, her/his animal and physical strength, and place it on the fire. As the enemy approaches in full regalia, one burns away her/his garments, armor, and all of her/his material might. One does so with the realization that these trappings make one vulnerable, not secure. We come to understand that muscle and metal don't protects us, but rather they contain us. They isolate us and make us small and frail. Beneath them, within them, free of them, we are only light and fire. We are spirit, which is impenetrable and untouchable. We are one with the spirit all about us, and therefore we are unified and infinite. We enter the battle unencumbered and unafraid. We move through the field undetected. We leave the skirmish unharmed. The weapons of mankind destroy the flesh, but we have shed the flesh and can be neither felt nor felled. "Me'ayin yavo ezri" - from nothingness will come my help. "Im ain ani li, mi li" - if I am nothing to myself, then who can get to me?

The battle is over when there is no one here to fight. When we give up our animal, our fleshy and material self, we become invincible, and the enemy ceases to exist. Prayer is meditation on this self-transcendence and its subsequent oneness. Through prayer, we peel off the gar-

---

[86] More on this to come in chapter nine, section "Uncovering and Uniting."

ments that constantly grow on us like a crust. Our daily experience in the world convinces us that our physical individual reality is paramount - that I am the center of the universe, and that the weight of the world presses on me every moment. We pray to disentangle ourselves from this lie, to disrobe from this costume, to remind ourselves that we are united with everything else. The struggle then ends, and the fear melts away. Our blood pressure stabilizes, and we face the day with peace and confidence. The war does not end, but we are at peace even in the midst of the battleground. This sentiment is expressed by King David in Psalms:

לְדָוִד יְ-הֹוָה אוֹרִי וְיִשְׁעִי מִמִּי אִירָא יְ-הֹוָה מָעוֹז חַיַּי מִמִּי
אֶפְחָד: בִּקְרֹב עָלַי מְרֵעִים לֶאֱכֹל אֶת־בְּשָׂרִי צָרַי וְאֹיְבַי לִי
הֵמָּה כָּשְׁלוּ וְנָפָלוּ: אִם־תַּחֲנֶה עָלַי מַחֲנֶה לֹא־יִירָא לִבִּי
אִם־תָּקוּם עָלַי מִלְחָמָה בְּזֹאת אֲנִי בוֹטֵחַ:

L'David A-donai ori v'yishi mimi ira A-donai ma'oz chayai mimi efchad. Bikrov alai m'reiim le'echol es-bisari tzarai v'oyvai li heima kashlu v'nafalu. Im tachaneh alai machaneh lo yira libi, im takum alai milchama b'zos ani boteach.

Of David. The Lord is my light and my salvation; whom shall I fear? The Lord is the stronghold of my life; from whom shall I be frightened? When evildoers draw near to me to devour my flesh, my adversaries and my enemies against me -they stumbled and fell. If a camp encamps against me, my heart shall not fear; if a war should rise up against me, in this I trust.
(Psalms 27:1-3)

What is it that instills this confidence in David and frees him from all fear? We find the answer in the subsequent verse:

אַחַת שָׁאַלְתִּי מֵאֵת־יְ-הֹוָה אוֹתָהּ אֲבַקֵּשׁ שִׁבְתִּי בְּבֵית־יְ-הֹוָה
כָּל־יְמֵי חַיַּי לַחֲזוֹת בְּנֹעַם־יְ-הֹוָה וּלְבַקֵּר בְּהֵיכָלוֹ:

Achas shaalti me'es A-donai osa avakeish shivti b'veis A-donai kol yimei chayai lachazos b'noam A-donai u'l'vaker b'heichalo.

One [thing] I ask of the Lord, this I seek - that I may dwell in the house of the Lord all the days of my life, to see the pleasantness of the Lord and to visit His Temple.
(Psalms 27:4)

The simple understanding of the verse is that David asks God for one thing. However, he then proceeds to list a number of things: that he should dwell in God's house, that he should see the pleasantness of God, and that he should be able to visit His Temple each morning. The chassidic masters explain that if we read the verse more literally, we will understand its deeper secret and discover the key to David's peace and calm in spite of the warfare around him.

"Achas shaalti me'es A-donai / One I ask from God." It is not one *thing* that David asks from God, but rather he asks God for "achas/one." He is requesting from God that He bestow on him the consciousness of His complete oneness. With this consciousness, nothing worries him. With this consciousness, he will then be able to dwell in the house of the Lord all of his days, because wherever he may be, he knows that it is all the place of God's dwelling. He will be able to constantly see the pleasantness of God, and he will be able to visit God's hall each day because He is forever in God's presence.

Peace, and the transcendence of all fear, are possible when we become aware that the two enemy forces clashing within us are not truly enemies, and are not truly 'two' at all. The Godly and animal aspects of our being are not, in fact, opposites, because there are no opposites, and there is no opposition at all. There is only one. The goal is therefore not to overcome, to conquer, or to vanquish. It is rather to unify. It is to recognize that we are all inter-included, and to lose ourselves - and thereby find ourselves - in the uncompounded infinity that is hidden within our core.

Spiritual growth, Torah teaches us, is thus a lifelong process of disrobing. We begin naked, vulnerable, and afraid. We spend our days seeking shelter and acquiring garments. We lose ourselves inside our clothing and structures. With Torah's wisdom, we will come to understand that the fortifications we have constructed around us do not protect us, instead they imprison us. We will then work to dismantle and discard these structures in order to uncover what we have buried within them. With God's help, we will finish and once again find ourselves "naked," but now we will be unashamed, untouchable, and unafraid.

Letting Go

Inner peace, we have seen, is achievable through a process of release and surrender. Surrender is a term that is generally misunderstood in our culture. It connotes a sense of weakness and loss in a world that is concerned primarily with strength and victory. But Torah's conception of surrender is related to the concept of "bittul" that we have been discussing above. It is a positive nullification, if such a thing can be said. It is the result not of frailty or cowardice, but of tremendous power and fortitude. It is a liberation rather than a submission, and an accomplishment rather than a failure.

Surrender in this context is not giving up, but rather we can refer to it as "giving in." We are giving expression to what is within us, opening a path to the "Pnei Hashem/face of God" that is in our "pnimyus/inner core" and allowing it to become manifest. We are relinquishing not our true self, but the external construct that contains and restrains our true self. We are not submitting to some foreign force, but we are rather sloughing off the alien force that has been controlling and limiting us. We are thereby allowing our authentic essence to finally be expressed. This surrender is not a defeat but an overwhelming victory. In a sense, it is a victory over the need to be victorious. While the ego desires to fight and win, the "Pnei Hashem" has no ego, and it surrenders to One because it is One. There is no struggle, no fear, and no shame. There is only release and realignment, reunification and peace.

To achieve such a surrender, along with the serenity and bliss that it engenders, seems to be a prodigious task that is beyond the grasp of the vast majority of us. It is the spiritual masters and mystics who can attain such lofty levels, we convince ourselves. But what if we are all capable of reaching such heights? What if doing so is not a matter of scaling precipitous peaks or spending decades learning to decipher the most abstruse and esoteric texts, but simply learning to let go? We touched on this idea earlier in chapter five[87] where we cited God's insistence that "the thing is very near to you; it is in your mouth and in your heart so that you can fulfill it."[88] The peace and bliss of unifying with His pres-

---

[87] Section "Not In Heaven"

[88] Deuteronomy 30:14

ence is therefore not something that we must chase or create, but it is something we can simply allow.

The question that we must ask ourselves is whether it is easier to continue living on the surface of this existence and contending with all of the stress and tension that is found here, or to relinquish our hold on this superficial layer in order to experience a more authentic and sublime reality. It would seem to be easier to remain here - otherwise why would the vast majority of us do so our entire lives? Why would we allow ourselves to be freed from this realm of conflict and anxiety only when we die? It would seem that most of us don't have the strength, the wisdom, or the ability to transcend our current circumstances and embrace our Godly truth. But what if we are actually holding on to this realm rather than being held by it? What if the effort we are expending in grasping who and what we believe ourselves to be is much greater than the energy it would take to relinquish our grasp and let go? What if we are hanging on to our lives - and hanging on *for* our lives - so intently that we don't even realize that we can simply stop and set ourselves free?

Imagine, for a moment, releasing that tight grip that you constantly maintain on being you - that tension that begins somewhere behind your sternum or beneath your shoulder blades which exerts incessant gravity on all of the particles that distinguish you from everything that is not you. Imagine letting it go, and dissolving. Imagine the relief of ceasing to pull everything inward in a desperate attempt to be you as long as possible; ceasing to protect all that you perceive to be you from all that you believe to be not you. Imagine the ecstasy of unwinding after being so tightly wound; of finally being unguarded and unafraid; of coalescing with everything and clinging to nothing. What if you release your hold and find that you won't actually fall apart or fall to pieces? The world will not actually tear apart at the seams, because there are no seams. There are no parts or pieces. It is all one, and it's all fine, and it will all be fine.

This incredible relief cannot be described in words. It must be felt. The feeling is utter relaxation. It is the rest that comes when you set down a tremendous weight that you have been straining to hold your entire life. You are so accustomed to the strain that you have come to ignore it, but you can release it. You can put it down and sit down and let every ounce of pressure drain from your body.

Prayer is precisely this process of letting go. As we discussed earlier in the chapter, prayer is pausing from our daily routine to reconnect to what we truly are, and to disconnect from what we are not. When we begin each morning with prayer, we literally begin anew. We let go completely of who we were the previous day. We abandon all of our worries and thoughts and suppositions, allowing ourself to be completely emptied. As we begin reciting the order of the "karbonos/sacrifices" in the Temple in Jerusalem, we allow our flesh and body to be burned away in the fire on the altar. With them, all concerns and responsibilities melt away - if they are important, they will be there when we return after our prayer. Thoughts will try to impose themselves, insisting that they are urgent, but we will not let them. We challenge our suppositions and the weight we lend to things. How dire is it? How grave and important? What will happen if I let this feeling go? Does it really matter if this person thinks this of me, or if I don't win this argument, or if I don't have this item? What if I release these worries and needs - will I not be okay? Will I not, in fact, be more okay? What if I don't satisfy this urge or desire? What if I just let them go? What if I let go of all the anger and tension and desire - will I fail to be as great or strong as I was, or will I simply be lighter and more nimble and less tethered?

When we allow everything to dissolve, we can experience the bliss of weightlessness and stillness and timelessness. We will not die when we stop striving to exist and accomplish. We can experience moments of non-being, bathe in those moments, and then come back. All of the things that we need to do and be will be here waiting for us when we return. But those few, precious moments of nothingness and everythingness and oneness will make the world we return to less onerous and oppressive. We will know that all of these things that press us and stress us are not as solid and absolute as we had imagined. We are not defined by them or grasped by them. We can let them go whenever we choose.

This is not to shirk or abandon our responsibilities. Nor is it to suggest that there are not significant duties and issues in our life - our job, our relationships, our financial concerns - which may not be easy. But they are all one with us. They are all part of God, as are we. Seen in this light, they need not trouble us or worry us. It's not that we ignore them or wish them away, but we train ourselves to release them at various times throughout the day in order to remind ourselves that they do not own us, control us, or define us. We re-contextualize them, uniting with them and knowing that they are all elements of something universal and benevolent and mysterious. Through this, we can approach one of the most profound secrets in all of Torah: "הִשְׁתַּוּוּת/hishtavus/equanimity."

Equanimity

In his 16th century work "Shaarei Kedusha/Gates of Holiness," Rabbi Chaim Vital[89] tells the story of a sage who wanted to join one of the mystic circles in order to study the deep secrets of Kabbala. Induction into such esoteric societies was granted only to those who had already mastered the revealed and exoteric teachings of the written and oral Torah. This was a prerequisite because a fluency in the common ways of the world was necessary before delving into the mysteries of the universe. Therefore, when the sage approached the head of the society and asked to be admitted to his inner circle, the Kabbalist administered a thorough test of the sage's Torah knowledge. After the sage answered all of the questions posed to him, the Kabbalistic master confirmed to him that he had indeed amassed an impressive understanding of Torah, and that he must answer only one more question: one person honors you, and one person insults you, how do you respond to them? The sage answered that he would respond to them no differently, though his feelings for the one who shamed him would admittedly be less favorable than for the one who showed him honor. The master did not admit him to his circle, instructing him to go continue his learning and return when there is no difference to him whatsoever between being honored or shamed.

This lofty level of spiritual development is known as "הִשְׁתַּוּוּת/hishtavus," which in English is translated as "equanimity." The root of the Hebrew word is "שוה/shaveh," which means "equal," and the idea of "hishtavus/equanimity" is that all happenings and eventualities in one's life are valued equally regardless of their apparent benefits or detri-

---

89 1543-1620. Renowned Kabbalist from Safed who was the foremost disciple of the Arizal.

181

ments. This attitude and quietude is a result of one's ability to recognize the divine unity that underlies all things. In spite of surface and temporal differences, each and every experience is understood to be a facet of a Godly reality that is not only universal and infinite, but is also indispensable and beneficent. The Baal Shem Tov[90] expounds on this concept through a deeper understanding of a common phrase from Psalms:

שִׁוִּיתִי יְ-הֹוָה לְנֶגְדִּי תָמִיד:
Shiviti A-donai l'negdi tamid.
I place God before me always.
(Psalms 16:8)

This verse is often identified as a fundamental tenet of the Torah lifestyle. On its simple level, it alludes to one's constant awareness of God and the necessity to consider Him and His ways before deciding how to act in any given situation. But the Baal Shem Tov explains that the word "shiviti" in this verse, translated traditionally as "I place," shares a root with the word "shaveh/equal" which we identified above. The first word of the phrase can therefore be rendered "it is equal to me," and the Baal Shem Tov thus reads the verse on the level of "sod" as follows: "all is equal to me, (because) God is before me always."

When one becomes aware that everything "before me" is simply another manifestation of Godliness, and that all of the multifarious aspects of creation are not only connected, but actually unified in purpose and essence, s/he will no longer be afraid, agitated, or confused. S/he will rather be confident, content, and resolute, and all will be equally good in her/his estimation. This "hishtavus/equanimity" is one of the highest levels of spiritual development. It can be attained only by consistent meditation on God's unity and the awareness of God's presence within everything.

When one reaches this elevated consciousness, life transforms completely, and one can experience a state of freedom and tranquility no matter what challenges confront her/him. In such a context, the story is told of a man who once approached the Maggid of Mezeritch[91] with the question of how it is possible to fulfill the Torah's edict to thank God for everything that happens to him whether it is good or bad, as it is written "a person is obligated to bless upon the bad just as he blesses upon the good."[92] The Maggid told the man that in order to find the answer to such a question, he should travel to the home of the chassid Reb Zusha of Anipoli. The man followed the Maggid's directions through the forest and came eventually to a ramshackle cabin. He knocked on the door and was warmly greeted by Reb Zusha, who invited him in. The shack's interior was even more shabby than it had appeared from outside. There were no furnishings other than a crude wooden table and bench, and few supplies other than some basic necessities. Nonetheless, Reb Zusha's demeanor was warm and upbeat, and he offered his guest everything he had. After observing the poor chassid for some time and realizing that he had never met anyone so destitute, the man posed his question. He explained to Reb Zusha that the Maggid had recommended he travel here to ask him how it was possible to be grateful to God even in the face of severe suffering. Reb Zusha considered, and finally responded that it was an excellent question, but he couldn't understand why the Maggid had sent the man to him, as he had never suffered a day in his life.

This type of acceptance and serenity in the face of hardship and deprivation represents a sublime level of faith. Yet the chassidic masters describe even greater heights of equanimity in which the experience of adversity is not simply tolerated or even unnoticed (as in the case of Reb Zusha), but rather overturned or transformed completely. The Lubavitcher Rebbe distinguishes in this context between the concepts of faith and trust. Faith, "אֱמוּנָה/emuna" in Hebrew, is the belief that God controls everything and is capable of anything. If circumstances present themselves in a given way, then that is precisely as God wills it, and therefore there is no reason to worry or complain. God can, of course, change the situation if He chooses to do so, and so it is reasonable to request His assistance if one desires a different outcome. However, recognizing that all is in God's hands, one therefore never despairs and accepts everything that comes to him with patience and tolerance.

In contrast to this attitude of "emuna/faith," the Lubavitcher Rebbe defines trust, "בִּטָחוֹן/bitachon" in Hebrew, not merely as the

---

92 Mishnayos, Brachos 9:5

awareness of God's omnipotence, but furthermore as the certainty of His complete benevolence and the resultant assuredness of only positive outcomes. In other words, "emuna/faith" is the awareness that God CAN effect salvation, while "bitachon/trust" is the knowledge that He WILL do so. To demonstrate the difference between these two concepts, the Rebbe cites two well known expressions from the Gemara:

כָּל דְּעָבֵיד רַחֲמָנָא לְטָב עָבֵיד:

Kol d'aveid Rachamana l'tav aveid.
Everything that God does, He does for the best.
(Brachos 60b)

and

גַם זוּ לְטוֹבָה:

Gam zu l'tova.
This too is for the best.
(Sanhedrin 108b)

At first glance, the two phrases seem to be nearly synonymous, but the Lubavitcher Rebbe explores the subtle but profound difference between them. The first expression, "everything that God does, He does for the best," is attributed to the famed Rabbi Akiva.[93] Once Rabbi Akiva was traveling, and he approached a village to seek lodging for the night. He was turned away and was forced to sleep in a field outside the village. Nevertheless, he said "everything that God does, He does for the best." He had with him a donkey on which he would travel, a rooster to wake him in the morning, and a candle so that he could study Torah at night. In the night, a wind blew and extinguished the candle, a cat came and ate the rooster, and a mountain lion devoured the donkey. In spite of all this, Rabbi Akiva said again, "everything that God does, He does for the best." In the morning, he found that bandits had attacked the village in the night and taken the villagers captive. Had he been granted lodging, he would have been captured. Had his candle not been extinguished, the bandits would have seen his light. Had his rooster and don-

---

[93] 50-135 CE. One of the great sages and early teachers of Mishna, the redacted Oral law.

key not been eaten, the bandits would have heard the animals' sounds. Indeed, every seeming setback turned out to be a tremendous blessing, just as Rabbi Akiva knew it would.

The second expression, "this too is for the best," was the frequent saying of Rabbi Akiva's teacher, Nachum Ish Gam Zu.[94] He repeated the phrase so often that it eventually became a part of the name by which he was known, Nachum, the man of "Gam Zu/This Too." As the story goes, the Jewish people wanted to send a gift of gems to the emperor in Rome, and they selected Nachum Ish Gam Zu as the emissary to convey it. On the way, Nachum slept at an Inn where he placed the chest full of precious stones beside his bed. In the night, the Innkeeper crept into his room and stole the gems, replacing them with dirt. When Nachum presented the chest to the emperor the following morning, the emperor was highly insulted when he found the dirt inside, and he ordered his guards to execute Nachum Ish Gam Zu. Nachum's response was "gam zu l'tova/this too is for the best." As he was being taken away, one of the princes suggested to the emperor that perhaps the dirt was like the special dirt with which Abraham had defeated his enemies. Abraham would throw the dirt and it would become swords. The emperor tested the dirt, and indeed it miraculously transformed into swords. Thrilled with this incomparable gift, the emperor released Nachum Ish Gam Zu and sent him back to his people with great riches.

The Rebbe teaches that the difference between the two stories, and thus the two sayings, is that in the case of Rabbi Akiva, negative occurrences transpired, and he nevertheless accepted them with faith that they were ultimately for the best. Regarding Nachum Ish Gam Zu, on the contrary, there was no hardship to endure even temporarily. Whereas Rabbi Akiva was forced to sleep in a field with no light and his possessions were taken from him, Nachum Ish Gam Zu suffered no loss or adversity. Rabbi Akiva's faith assured him that the events could only be for the best as everything comes from God and God is only good, but the benefit was not immediately manifest. He was able to perceive the gain in his loss only after the fact. Nachum Ish Gam Zu, however, was never forced to suffer and never left to wonder how the events would eventually reveal their silver lining. As a matter of fact, the events were indeed for the best because the gift of jewels would not have been nearly as pre-

94 First century sage and teacher of Mishna.

cious to the king as the gift of the miraculous dirt. The statement "this too is for the best" expresses this immediacy and certainty - *this*, right here and right now, is for the best. Rabbi Akiva's statement, "everything that God does, He does for the best," does not convey this same certitude. It is a wondrous level of "emuna/faith," but it does not carry quite the same degree of clarity as the "bitachon/trust" of his teacher Nachum Ish Gam Zu.

This subtle difference may seem academic. The "emunah/faith" of Rabbi Akiva and the simple acceptance of Reb Zusha are tremendously high levels of spiritual development which one can spend an entire lifetime working to achieve. However, the Rebbe is teaching us that even the extraordinary "bitachon/trust" of Nachum Ish Gam Zu is accessible to each of us, and we can truly live a life in which all of our experiences are positive and "for the best." This consummate degree of equanimity is not simply a matter of accepting and enduring the bad now, and believing that its benefits will eventually be revealed either later in this life or at least in the next. It is rather the ability to assure that the good that God intends for us will be manifest now. This attitude was expressed by the Tzemach Tzedek[95] in his mid-19th century yiddish saying:

טראכט גוט וועט זיין גוט.
Tracht gut vat zein gut.
Think good and it will be good.

Referencing Torah wisdom from millennia prior, this ancient (and generally unattributed) source and precedent of modern theories of "the law of attraction" asserts not only that positive thinking will result in positive outcomes, but it also provides an explanation for why this is the case. *"Positive thinking" in the Torah context is not merely a matter of envisioning, and thereby manifesting, something that one desires. It is meditating on the ultimate reality of God's complete oneness and absolute benevolence.*

"Tracht gut vat zein good/think good and it will be good" does not mean visualizing personal goals or rewards, but rather ruminating to the point of complete internalization on the truth of God's utter goodness and oneness. It is living with the constant awareness that "this too is

---

[95] 1789-1866, Rabbi Menachem Mendel of Lubavitch, the third Rebbe of the Chabad/Lubavitch chassidic dynasty.

for the best" because every "this" is purely and simply another expression of Godliness. When one "tracht gut/thinks good" in this way, then it will necessarily "zein gut/be good" because s/he will have broken through all of the barriers that conceal the face of God within her/him and around her/him. The darkness that conceals the light will give way, and there will only be radiance and warmth and peace. This is the equanimity that we can achieve when we recognize the "Pnei Hashem" in our "pnimyus." This is the power that each of us possesses to remake our reality and transform the universe.

━━━━◆━━━━

Radiating Love

We began this chapter with the assertion that the recognition of the face of God within us could, and must, change our lives completely. The first shift, we noted, will be a revolution in the way we perceive ourselves as we move from guilt and self-recrimination to dignity and self-sympathy. From here, we begin to experience peace and fearlessness. Releasing our hold on the limited versions of ourselves and our world that we have previously clung to, we become acquainted with the transformative power of equanimity. With it, we are able to not only accept our reality, but to embrace it, and ultimately to shape it and actively participate in the process of "tikkun/transformation" for which we were created. Yet beyond all of these seismic life-shifts which we have explored throughout this chapter so far, there is an even greater revolution that occurs.

As one allows her/his Godliness to be manifest, there begins to well within her/him something even more ineffable, overwhelming, and phenomenal than self-acceptance, contentment, and peace. S/he begins to experience an extraordinary synergy and affinity with everything s/he encounters. Where there was once a pervasive air of separateness and alienation, one now begins to feel a stunning sense of belonging, empathy, and intimacy as s/he recognizes that the essence within is identical with the essence of everything without. With the revelation of the "Pnei Hashem" in one's "pnimyus," one will suddenly access a rapturous sensation of love that is unlike anything s/he has experienced before.

Love is the most powerful force in the universe. It is also, perhaps, the most misunderstood. It is desired by all, and apprehended by few. It is abundantly available, but it is tragically lacking in the lives of so many. The concept of love has been so distorted and misrepresented that we don't have any idea how to find it or hold onto it. It slips through our fingers though it is right there in our grasp. We have become so confused about what love is that as we struggle to attain it, earn it, or fall into it, we don't realize that it is, and always has been, nestled in our core. Love is not something to be found or to receive. It is entrusted to us at our creation. It is the essence of what we are, and it is waiting to be tapped, released, and shared.

This reality is expressed in the Hebrew word for love, "אַהֲבָה/ ahava," the root of which is "הב/hav," which means to give. From this derivation, we glean a profound insight about the nature of true love. It is not simply a yearning we have for those to whom we are attracted, or an affection for those from whom we have received kindness or other benefits. Love, in the Torah's sense of the word, is an intrinsic desire to give to an other. This jibes with the concept of God's love that we have discussed repeatedly. He created the world because He desired to give - "teva hatov l'heitiv/it is the nature of the good to do good."[96] He gives to His creations because He loves, and He loves His creations because we enable Him to express His giving nature. His creations, in turn, desire to give. The more in touch we are with the Godliness within us, the more we yearn to express our giving nature.

In addition to the comprehension of a term that is reflected by its etymology, the Hebrew language provides additional insight to a term's meaning from its *numerology*. Referred to as "gematria" in Hebrew, the numeric value of Hebrew words is based on the fact that each letter of the aleph-bet is also a number. The first letter, "א/aleph," is one, the second letter, "ב/beis," is two, and so on. The tenth letter "י/yud," is ten, and then each of the subsequent eight letters represent multiples of ten - the eleventh letter, "כ/chof," is twenty; the twelfth letter, "ל/lamed," is thirty etc. The nineteenth letter, "ק/kuf," is 100, and then the subsequent and final three letters represent hundreds, so that the twenty-second and last letter, "ת/tav," is 400. Based on the numeric value of words, which are determined by tallying the values of their letters, we can find correspondences with other terms of equal value, and thereby deduce additional meaning and relevance.

The letters of the word "אַהֲבָה/ahava/love" equal the number thirteen: "א/aleph/1" + "ה/hei/5" + "ב/beis/2" + "ה/hei/5" = 13. Thirteen is also the value of the word "אֶחָד/echad," which means "one": "א/aleph/1" + "ח/chet/8" + "ד/daled/4" = 13. The "gematria/numerology" of terms is a more hidden and esoteric expression of its meaning, and from the numerical equivalence of terms we can learn their deeper implication. The parity of the terms "ahava/love" and "echad/one" inform us that love, at its essence, is a unity that eliminates all distinction between lover and beloved. The profound secret is not that we become one with that which we love, but that we love those things with which we are inherently one. In other words, true love does not cause unification, it is rather a result of the fact that we are already and always united. When we recognize God's absolute oneness and our consequent unity with all things, an adoration for every aspect of our reality wells and radiates from within us.

This explains one of the Torah's most well-known, but least comprehended, verses:

וְאָהַבְתָּ לְרֵעֲךָ כָּמוֹךָ:
V'ahavta l'reiacha kamocha.
You shall love your fellow as yourself.
(Leviticus 19:18)

So fundamental is this verse that it has been identified by Rabbi Akiva, one of the most renowned Torah sages, as the "klal gadol ba-Torah/all-inclusive principle of Torah."[97] Beyond Jewish tradition, this concept has been referred to as "the golden rule," an ethic of kindness and empathy which urges generosity of spirit. It is said that every major religion or philosophy contains some version of the golden rule. But while the Torah verse is equated with similarly themed statements in other traditions, these comparisons fail to identify nuances which differentiate the Torah's specific language and which reveal an additional lay-

---

[97] Torat Kohamim 19:45

er of meaning that provides us not only ethical guidance, but also a profound mystic truth.

The ancient Greek admonition "Do not do to others that which angers you when they do it to you;"[98] the Christian "Do unto others as you would have them do unto you;"[99] the Hindu "One should never do that to another which one regards as injurious to one's own self;"[100] and the Muslim "As you would have people do to you, do to them; and what you dislike to be done to you, don't do to them"[101] - all of these bear thematic similarities to the Torah's verse from Leviticus. However, they are more similar to a line from the Talmud in which Hillel the Elder responds to a man who asks him to teach him the whole Torah while standing on one foot:

דַּעֲלָךְ סָנֵי לְחַבְרָךְ לָא תַּעֲבֵיד - זוֹ הִיא כָּל הַתּוֹרָה כּוּלָהּ,
וְאִידַּךְ פֵּירוּשַׁהּ הוּא, זִיל גְּמוֹר.

*Da'alach s'nei l'chavrecha la ta'aveid. Zo hi kol haTorah kula,
v'idach peirusha hi, zil g'mor.*

That which is hateful to you, do not do to your fellow.
That is the whole Torah; the rest is the commentary; go
and learn.

(Talmud, Shabbat, 31a)

The statement from Leviticus differs from all of these in that a) it refers specifically to love, which they do not, and b) it is a commandment, not a maxim or even an ethical advisory. This raises two obvious questions: First, how can one be commanded to love? While it is understood that actions can be legislated - for example, treat others, or do not treat others, in such and such a way - it is difficult to comprehend how an emotion like love can be mandated. Secondly, how is it possible to fulfill such a commandment? Can one truly love another as much as one loves her/himself?

---

[98] Isocrates

[99] Matthew 7:12

[100] Mahabharata Book 13

[101] Kitab al-Kafi, vol. 2, p. 146

One who takes these questions seriously must conclude that "V'ahavta l'reiacha kamocha/love your fellow as yourself" is more than a simple directive. As the Lubavitcher rebbeim point out frequently, the word "תּוֹרָה/torah" is derived from the term "הוֹרָאָה/horaah," which means learning or instruction. Though Torah is often viewed primarily as a book of law, it is in fact an instrument of development and connection. Therefore, it is not only impossible that the Torah would issue an edict that we would be unable to fulfill, but additionally, as a book of instruction, the Torah would not require us to do something without providing insight into how that requirement can be satisfied. "Love your fellow as yourself," therefore, is not merely commanding us to love, but it is furthermore revealing the deep secret of love's nature and essence. The verse tells us not only *that* we should love our fellow, but also *why* we should do so and *how* we can do so.

Why should one "v'ahavta l'reiacha/love your fellow" - because s/he is "kamocha/as yourself." How can one "v'ahavta l'reiacha/love your fellow" - by recognizing that s/he is "kamocha/as yourself." The key here, and the key to love in general, is to understand that "kamocha/as yourself" in this verse does not merely mean 'similar to you,' or even 'identical to you,' but also 'one with you.' On the simple level, the verse may be exhorting us to love others because they are just as desirous, or deserving, of love as we are. On a somewhat deeper level, it is encouraging us to love others just as generously and forgivingly as we love ourselves. But on its deepest level, the verse is instructing us that it is possible to *truly* love an other only when we recognize that that other is not simply *like* ourself, but that s/he is veritably the same as oneself because in essence we are one!

Just as our ultimate self is nothing but Godliness, so too, our fellow is only Godliness as well. "Ahava/love," as we have explained previously, is equivalent to "echad/one." When we recognize that the other is truly one and the same as myself, then love will arise effortlessly. It is not difficult to love another as oneself when we identify that the other is undifferentiated from oneself. In fact, this is the only way to achieve love in its most true and ultimate sense. We can desire an other. We can sympathize and empathize with an other. We can even give altruistically to an other. But the Torah is teaching us that *we can only truly love, in the most profound and divine sense of the term, when we understand that the other is not in fact an other at all.*

The commandment of "love your fellow as yourself," therefore, is not compelling an emotion, for you cannot demand one to *feel* a certain way. It is rather obligating us to meditate on the reality of our unity and to cultivate this awareness so that love will arise naturally and constantly. This is one of the primary functions of prayer. We have discussed previously that the Torah's concept of prayer is not merely requesting our needs from God, but rather reconnecting with Him through deeply contemplating our essential Godly nature. This contemplation similarly enables us to reconnect with one another and with the entire creation when we meditate on God's oneness and the inter-inclusion of all things. It is for this reason that the prayer service begins with the very verse that we have been discussing. After the morning blessings, at the very opening of the morning service, there is a line in the prayer book that reads:

נָכוֹן לוֹמַר קוֹדֶם הַתְּפִלָּה: הֲרֵינִי מְקַבֵּל עָלַי מִצְוַת עֲשֵׂה שֶׁל וְאָהַבְתָּ לְרֵעֲךָ כָּמוֹךָ:

Nachon lomar kodem hatefillah: Hareini mikabeil alai mitzvas asei shel v'ahavta l'reiacha kamocha.

It is proper to say before prayer: I hereby accept upon myself the positive commandment of you shall love your fellow as yourself.

(Siddur Tehillat Hashem, p.12)

As we commence our morning prayer, which is to set the tone for everything we will do throughout the coming day, we are instructed to meditate on this verse and to accept it upon ourself. Why this particular verse? It is certainly an important commandment, and it is, as Rabbi Akiva declared, an "all-encompassing principle of Torah." But we are not learning Torah at this moment, we are praying. What does this verse have to do with prayer, and why is it established as the very first line of our prayers? It is so because the essence of prayer is moving inward to find the "Pnei Hashem" within our "pnimyus," and recognizing that this Godly face is likewise within the "pnimyus" of everything that we will encounter in the day ahead. With this, love will surge from our core and will radiate from us to embrace and enflame all of those around us.

One Voice

Prayer, according to Torah's conception, is thus our opportunity to remind ourselves of what we are, to find the love that is hidden in our essence, and to allow it to suffuse us and emanate outward. This will also enable us to understand a legal ruling regarding prayer. There is a question in Jewish law about how we are to pray: should it be a silent devotion, or an audible pronouncement? The daily prayer service is comprised of both - communal songs and responsive verses at times, and then "silent" prayers in which we communicate only to God. But the most central prayer, as we have discussed previously, is the "Shema," which means "to hear," and the law dictates that it must be loud enough that "you make your ears hear what you emit from your mouth."[102] This is a strange law, particularly considering the fact that God does not have ears, or any bodily form for that matter, and He can "hear" our thoughts as easily as our words. The Alter Rebbe therefore teaches[103] that this law is not simply instructing us what the volume of our prayers should be. On a deeper level, it is informing us what prayer essentially is.

The Alter Rebbe notes that Torah law is very precise, with every word denoting a profound truth. He asks why the law is worded to say that one must "hear what *you emit* from your mouth," rather than more simply stating that one must "hear what comes from one's mouth." He explains that the Zohar identifies the word "atta/you" with the source of all souls, the primordial unity from which we all come and of which we are all a part. The law regarding the volume of prayer is worded specifically as it is, the Alter Rebbe teaches, in order to instruct us that the point of prayer is to enable us to "hear" and understand that it is "atta/you," the one soul from which all individual souls derive, that is being emitted through each of our mouths when we speak. In other words, while we generally assume that it is our own voice that emanates from within us when we open our lips, the truth is that it is the voice of the one and only soul - ie. God - that is expressed through us. There is only one voice, but

---

102 Talmud, Brachos 13a

103 *Likkutei Torah*, Shir HaShirim

it is intoned through many throats. There is only one wind, but it blows through many vessels. We are all instruments plied by the same hand, and played with the same breath.

With this, we will understand the verse from Psalms that one is instructed to utter under her/his breath before beginning the "amida," the standing silent prayer that is the culmination of each service:

אֲ-דֹנָי שְׂפָתַי תִּפְתָּח וּפִי יַגִּיד תְּהִלָּתֶךָ:
A-donai sifasai tiftach ufi yagid tehillasecha.
Lord open my lips and let me declare Your praise.
(Psalms 51:17)

On the simple level, this phrase is a request to God to assist us with our prayers. On a deeper level, it is an acknowledgement that it is not we who open our lips, but rather it is God who provides us the ability to do so, just as every capability we have is from Him and in His hands. On an even more esoteric plane, we are expressing the profound awareness that the words that we express are actually *His* words - "Your praise" - which He communicates through our lips. We are not simply asking for the ability to praise Him; we are inviting Him to express the praises that He wants to offer through our vocal chords. While "Your praise" is simply understood as 'praise *of* You,' it can also be interpreted as the 'praise that You express.' As we discussed earlier,[104] God does not need our praises. The word "tehilla/praise" is from the root "hil" which means to light or ignite, as in the phrase "beHILo nero/He lit his candle."[105] When God expresses praise, therefore, He is illuminating the darkness with His light. When we allow Him to open our lips and vocalize *His* praise through our mouth, we are participating in the process of enlightenment and revelation for which He created us. The ultimate meaning of this verse then is that we are asking God to let us be the vessel for the message and the light that He desires to deliver into His creation. Let me be conscious of the fact that this is all that I am. Let me align myself with Your will so that You can flow through me without obstruction or resistance. This is the secret of prayer, the Alter Rebbe ex-

---

[104] Chapter four, section "Halleluy-ah"

[105] Job 29:3

plains - "to hear what YOU emit from your mouth" - to know that it is "YOU/God" that moves and operates through each of us.

This understanding will, as we have discussed previously, lead to the awareness that the God that moves through me is the very same God that moves through everyone else. Each of us is purely and simply a vessel for One unique and unified reality. We are the same stuff, expressed through various forms. We are one soul that has been temporarily divided into "pieces" and dressed in different clothes.[106] In our deepest essence, there is no distinction between us - we are "echad/One." Imagine how different life would be if we lived with this awareness; if we could transcend our limited perspective of me and you and understand that you are only another manifestation of what has manifested in me as me. This has been described as water that has been poured into different containers, or light that shines through different shades of glass. Though it is the same water or the same light, it appears and exhibits differently depending on that which contains or conveys it. If we can understand each other this way, then would it not be foolish to resent one another, or envy one another, or harm one another? We would only be hating or hurting ourself. It would be as if one accidentally smashes his finger while hammering a nail, and then grabs the hammer with the injured hand and smashes the hand which held the hammer first.

Each of us often does things that are imperfect. Sometimes we berate or hate ourselves for doing so, but we generally forgive ourselves or at least make excuses for our errors. When we understand that the other is our same self expressed in a different vessel, then we will similarly grant that other the benefit of finding reasons for her/his actions. Think of the person that you like least in the world, someone with whom you have had an ongoing feud or who is currently making your life difficult. Now put yourself in her/his shoes, literally. Imagine that it is you in that body, the very same you that is in your body, but with a completely different set of traits and experiences. How did you become you and s/he become her/him? Is there a different soul in each of you, or is there simply a different framework for precisely the same soul?

Is it possible that the identical essence, placed in a vastly different context and environment, could produce such distinct and conflicting

---

106 See chapter two, section "Good Nature" where this analogy was explained.

individuals? It is not only possible, it is precisely what has happened! If we trace us both back to our beginning, prior to our lifetime of experiences and challenges, there is no difference. If we peel back the surface, all the way down to the life force that vivifies and animates us, we will find absolutely no distinction. It is the same face of God within each of us.

When I see the me in you and the you in me, I cannot hate you. I can only love. As the superficial and temporal exterior falls away, all of my anger melts away, and I see only what unites us rather than all of the surface elements that divide us. Being Godly thus begins with seeing God within all of us and within everything. This is what the mystics see, and this is what each of us will see when we hone our vision. Everything opens, all of the veils fall away, and our world is suddenly filled with great light. When we come to the awareness that we are all limbs of a single being, our feelings of resentment, competition, and antagonism fade away. What remains is a remarkable sense of consonance, harmony, and love that will radiate from us and ignite all of those with whom we come in contact.

Acting Like God

Throughout this chapter, we have discussed the various ways that one's life will transform when s/he recognizes the face of God within her/him. S/he will find self-respect and peace. S/he will recognize the good in all things. S/he will feel and exude tremendous love. But the ultimate outcome of recognizing one's Godliness is more than experiencing positive emotions. It is becoming Godly. By this, we do not mean acquiring power or obtaining all of one's needs or desires (though this all becomes possible, as we have discussed). Being Godly in this sense is a matter of becoming a truly positive and productive force in the universe. It is dwelling constantly in a divine consciousness which perceives the underlying harmony and resonance of all things. It is shaping and refining reality instead of being shaped and confined by it. When we realize that we are Godly, we will act Godly. This means that we will allow our highest nature to become our daily conduct.

This shift will indeed change everything if we allow it. It will not be a sudden and instant transformation, but with the constant awareness of our Godly essence, we can begin to infuse every decision and reaction with the patience, clarity, and generosity that characterizes the Godly perspective. Rather than responding to daily circumstances from the limited, vulnerable, and self-protective attitude of a "merely human" individual being, we will remind ourself that we are not small and powerless. We are rather a vessel for God's expression, and we need not be afraid and self-concerned. As soon as we begin to feel reactivity welling within us, we will learn to pause and to consider how God would act in such a situation. Though the tension and stressors of life may not abate, we will become habituated with breathing deeply and reminding ourself that God is in there, and that we can let Him out, so to speak. Don't keep Him hidden and unexpressed, we will whisper inwardly. Don't mistake yourself for the frail and needy organic matter that conceals your essence. Don't let that guide you and roil you and destabilize you. Rather be what you ultimately are. Let your Godly soul pervade you, steady you, and project through you.

In this way, we will become exceedingly giving and forgiving. We will find ourselves willing to give and forgive far beyond what we previously considered comfortable. We will constantly transcend our "normal" human tendency to be strict and exacting. Even when we are wronged and outrage is justifiable, we will overcome justice with kindness, as God does. Just as we ask Him to continually forgive us, so we will continually forgive others. Is this superhuman? Perhaps. Is it more than should be expected of us? No, because we *are* superhuman. We are Godly. We can choose to ignore or suppress our essence and be "only human," but we will choose rather to express our Godly reality.[107] When we choose to do so, the world will not buffet us. We will disarm all triggers, and we will no longer be prone to all of the provocations that have

---

[107] To be clear, this does not mean that we will allow others to trample on us or violate our dignity. Generosity and forgiveness do not mean self-neglect or being permissive of abuse. They mean the transcendence of ego. We can, and must, distinguish between being insulted or offended and truly harmed. If it is only our ego that is being bruised, we can tolerate this because we have let our ego go. Yet we will not tolerate danger or abuse. Being Godly is not being naive or sacrificing our dignity. It is knowing our true value and worth and letting unimportant things pass through us.

traditionally set us off. All of the many stimuli that used to infuriate us will no longer have any effect. We are even. Our breath is a constant and steady flow. Nothing can harry us or disturb our rhythm. We remain centered, which means that we are constantly conscious of what exists in our center and the center of all things.

With such an attitude, even small things begin to take on meaning and value. Every moment is precious, because it is a Godly moment, an opportunity for us to express our Godliness. Every action is carried out with intentionality and dignity - not only "important" or public activities, but even private and ordinary things like the way we eat, the way we speak, the way we dress. There is nothing mundane because it is all Godly, and therefore holy. We begin to appreciate and savor everything. No longer a hamster wheel of banal and meaningless moments, life becomes a series of sacred encounters. The taste and texture of this food on my tongue; this chance and momentary interaction with a stranger on the bus; the dance of leaves in the wind. When we come to see all of these as a reflection of God and an element of the same holistic unity of which we are a part, life then becomes a constant meditation. We begin to move more carefully and deliberately, considering each step and each outcome. We treat nothing as if it is extraneous. We value each person, and we make it our business to help her/him recognize the dignity within her/him as well. Suddenly, each interaction has a purpose and a meaning. If we don't perceive it, then we pause to find it. Why am I in this particular situation now? What is awaiting me in this moment that I am here to extract and beautify? Each experience offers tremendous significance and worth, and we approach every moment as an opportunity, a mission, and a gift.

We may know few people who truly live this way, but we have all heard stories of those rare individuals who exude an almost otherworldly aura of peace and generosity and wisdom. They are often humble servants who are not seeking notoriety or power. Yet on account of their rare insight and dignity, there have gathered around them those who seek their guidance and crave their leadership. In spite of their formidable influence and their ability to lead legions and move mountains, they are gentle and sensitive. They speak quietly, displaying remarkable patience, and espousing empathy and nonviolence even in the face of brutal opposition. This is because they do not confuse force with power.

They know that the most potent energy in the universe is love, and that the most effective means of achieving one's goals is through peace and union rather than conflict and compulsion. Therefore, they have no need to demonstrate their strength, because they are confident that if they simply allow their Godliness to radiate, it will stimulate the Godliness of those around them.

These remarkable people are referred to as "tzadikkim," or "saints," or even "angels," but they are human like the rest of us, and they are not as distant or different from us as we may believe. The distinction is that they can see the Godliness within them and around them, and therefore, they radiate clarity, love, and acceptance. They provide a beam of light in the darkness, and people flock to them because we are all attracted to light. Each of us is capable of similarly discovering our essence and unmasking it. It is not only the few or the select who have the potential to manifest their divine reality. Every one of us has this potential, and therefore every one of us has the responsibility to do so. This is our life goal and our assigned task.

We "reveal God in the heavens and the earth" when we unleash the Godliness that is embedded within us. We are all "saints." We are all God's agents and emissaries in the truest sense of the terms, because we are all fragments of God which He has disseminated throughout His creation. The question for each of us is not "am I truly Godly," but rather "am I expressing my Godliness?" Am I revealing it or concealing it? Is the "Pnei Hashem" broadcasting and irradiating through me, or is it obscured by all of the garments and barriers that I have imposed over it? If I am wracked with self-doubt, disharmony, and enmity; if I am reactive and I find myself battling life rather than embracing it, then I have not yet fully accessed or released the Godly essence that animates me and awaits me. When I am able to do so, I will begin to experience all of the sublime transformations that we have discussed throughout this chapter.

Part Two: Practice

Chapter 8: LIFE-CYCLE

Intention

We are far enough along our journey now to know where we want to go and why we want to go there. We are traveling inward to discover the infinite truth of God - His "panim/ face" - that is hidden within our "pnimyus/inner core." We do so because that is our mission - "lech lecha/go to yourself" and "bara Elokim/ reveal God" - and also because, as we have discussed at length in the previous chapter, the awareness of our inherent Godliness transforms our lives completely and brings us profound joy, peace, and love. The question for us at this point is "how."

We began our journey with the question "where are you?" We then moved on to "how are you?" We now continue with "how *can* you?" How will you be able to continue onward and penetrate the many veils and impediments that block your inward progress? A consciousness of our goal, direction, and potential is a valuable first step. An understanding of the barriers that we have erected and a desire to remove them will aid us on our path. Awareness of God's unbounded love for us and of the infinite and reciprocal love that wells within us will inspire us with enthusiasm and tenacity. But the obstructions are thick and persistent. They will not vanish simply because we want them to. Furthermore, they regenerate quickly from one moment to the next on account of the coarseness and darkness of the world we inhabit. Therefore, even if we are able to succeed in making meaningful progress beyond our limitations today, we may find ourselves right back where we started tomorrow.

Fortunately, Torah provides a holistic and integrative practice that enables us to remove the barriers consistently and cumulatively. This, in fact, is the very goal and essence of Torah, as we learned in chapter six[108] with the statement of the Alter Rebbe that "ikar haTorah hu l'hiyos b'bchinas bittul/the main point of Torah is to be in the aspect of nullification." Recognizing that the "gasus/coarseness" of this world is the root of all of our confusion and misdirection because it conceals our essential Godly reality, Torah offers a systematic approach to the identification and elimination of these boundaries in every aspect of our lives. This approach combines both consciousness and action, both awareness of the nature of our current reality and practical procedures that will enable us to transcend and transform it. *Torah practice is, in essence, a series and system of rituals and reminders to keep us conscious of what we truly are - pure Godliness - and to help us remove the darkness and crust that conceals this truth.*

To understand Torah properly, we must recognize that it is simultaneously a work of philosophy and a book of law. What Torah imparts to us is not only profound ideas and insights which plumb the very depths of our existence, but also detailed directions on how to apply its wisdom and manifest its truths in a realm where they are concealed. Throughout Torah, six hundred and thirteen "mitzvos/commandments" are legislated which provide detailed guidelines of conduct for every aspect of one's life. The Torah lifestyle is thus highly regimented and minutely regulated. From a superficial perspective, the many "mitzvos," along with the many more customs and behaviors that Torah observance promotes may be viewed as excessive or even oppressive. However, we will come to understand that every one of the many rituals and regimens that are mandated by the Torah are elements of an intricate **liberation**

---

[108] end of section "Obstruction"

practice. Each of these picayune details and behaviors are mechanisms through which the practitioner can peel away another layer of darkness and dismantle the fortifications that block her/his inward progress. This vital work is not relegated to particular periods of each day, certain days of each week, or special observances each year. It is the purpose of every moment of life, and therefore it is a discipline that one engages in constantly. Through this practice, one infuses consciousness of her/his mission and potential into every mundane activity, whether it is the way s/he dresses, the way s/he eats, sleeps, bathes, conducts business, interacts socially and interpersonally, etc.

Many spiritual systems concern themselves primarily with consciousness, i.e. the focusing of one's thought on the nature of her/his existence through meditation and retreat from the hustle and bustle of daily life. Torah practice, on the contrary, intends to instill that consciousness into every action and into a complete engagement with the world rather than a removal from it. The question, of course, is whether one will infuse the Torah's many actions, rituals, and practices with the mindfulness that will provide them their power to transcend and transform one's reality, or whether s/he will simply go through the motions. In the latter case, the mitzvos are reduced to a series of restrictions rather than a system of liberation. The mindfulness that is meant to underlie every mitzvah is called "kavana/intention." Though one can fulfill a mitzvah without the proper "kavana/intention," in doing so s/he has not exploited its full potential, nor has s/he performed it as it was intended by God to be a tool for our emancipation. The Alter Rebbe teaches that a mitzvah without "kavana" is like a bird without wings.[109] Such a bird is still kosher, but it cannot fly and ascend to the heavens. A mitzvah without "kavana" is similarly grounded - it maintains its existence as a Godly act on this physical plane, but it cannot rise up and have its intended effect in the spiritual realms, nor does it enable the one who performed it to open and penetrate her/his depths.

The Baal Shem Tov teaches that the dual nature of every mitzvah is evidenced by the words "asher kidshanu b'mitzvosav/Who sanctifies us with His commandments" that are included in the standard prayer that is recited prior to many mitzvos.

---

[109] *Tanya*, chapter 40

בָּרוּךְ אַתָּה יְ-הֹוָה אֱ-לֹהֵינוּ מֶלֶךְ הָעוֹלָם **אֲשֶׁר קִדְּשָׁנוּ בְּמִצְוֹתָיו**
וְצִוָּנוּ...

*Baruch atta A-donai, E-loheinu melech haolam, **asher kidshanu b'mitzvosav**, vitzivanu...*

Blessed are You, Lord our God, King of the universe,
Who sanctifies us with His commandments, and
commanded us...

The end of the blessing differs depending on which mitzvah is
going to be performed. If one is reciting this blessing over the lighting of
candles, s/he concludes with "and commanded us to light candles,"
whereas if it is recited before one puts on the tallis (prayer shawl), he
concludes with "and commanded us to wrap ourselves in tzitzit." Regardless of the mitzvah to be performed and the corresponding conclusion to the blessing, the Baal Shem Tov points out that the word
"mitzvosav/His commandments" in the prefix of the blessing is plural
even though it is referring to one particular commandment that the person is about to perform. The reason for this, he teaches, is because there
are actually two mitzvos in every mitzvah. There is the specific action
that is being performed within the physical realm, and there is the metaphysical outcome that is effected by each physical deed. This spiritual
result is brought about by one's "kavana."

Without "kavana/intention," each mitzvah is like a body without a soul, or a shell that is lacking its contents. With the proper "kavana,"
however, the Torah's directives will enable us to open and to connect to
our innermost dimensions. The most basic "kavana" for each mitzvah is
thus that it is an exercise which God has provided us to train us in the
process of opening and moving beneath and beyond the surface. With
this general consciousness in mind, we can then explore each aspect of
Torah practice to understand how it contributes more specifically to that
project and mission.

Torah's liberation practice includes a) a system of routine mitzvos
that are to be performed throughout the course of each day, b) calendrical observances that mark the weekly, monthly, and yearly phases, as
well as c) milestone rituals that span the duration of the entire life-cycle.
One is thus provided opportunities to open and delve inward each day,
each week, each month, each year, and throughout the complete term of

her/his life. We will examine the intricate daily regimen that Torah offers in the following chapter. But first, an exploration of the lifecycle events will give us an overview of Torah's lifelong approach to the process of opening and revelation. We will find that each of the observances that mark the birth, development, and major transitional periods of the soul's journey in this world are focused very clearly on this theme of removing the veils that cover our core and expressing the Godliness that is hidden within.

Bris Milah

The very first ritual that a male engages in after birth is "בְּרִית מִילָה/Bris Milah," or circumcision, which is the removal of the foreskin that covers the head of the male reproductive organ. It is no coincidence that the lifecycle begins with an action that is so clearly and graphically connected to this concept of opening and uncovering. Birth itself is an act of incarnation, which literally means to infuse and contain something within a covering of flesh, and from this moment on, every aspect of life is part of the process of revealing what has been enclosed and enclothed inside the body. For this reason, we begin life with the removal of flesh in order to signify that this new being will be devoted throughout his time in this world to this sacred process of uncovering his inner essence, just as his forebears have been before him. Throughout his life, he will bear the sign of the covenant on his body, and in particular on his sexual organ, in order to remind him that it is not the world of the flesh that is most important, but rather what lies beneath it.

While circumcision is practiced throughout much of the modern world for hygienic reasons, the Torah ritual focuses more on one's spiritual integrity and well-being than his physical health. For this reason, the practice is not referred to in Torah simply as "מִילָה/milah," which means 'circumcision,' but rather as "בְּרִית מִילָה/bris milah," which means *"covenant of circumcision."* A "bris/covenant" in Torah is something that transcends all considerations and conditions. It is not a simple agreement or contract that can change based on fluctuating circumstances. It is a bond that is entered into which is unbreakable and everlasting. It transcends the vicissitudes of time or fortune or mood. Parties enter into a "bris" when they wish to signify the eternality and essentiality of their relationship. This is the implication of this ritual at the very beginning of life - it conveys that while the lifespan in this casing will be finite, and while the body will change and eventually fail, that which is beneath the flesh is infinite and immortal. While the bond between the soul and God may be hidden temporarily, it will never be broken. No skin, no matter how thick, can ultimately interpose between the soul and its source. They will always be united even if they are seemingly divided.

This unity and immutability, which is reflected in the word "bris/covenant," is also expressed in the fact that circumcision, according to Torah, is not to be performed immediately at birth but on the eighth day:

וּבֶן־שְׁמֹנַת יָמִים יִמּוֹל לָכֶם כָּל־זָכָר:

U'ven shmonas yamim yimol lachem kol zachar.
And at the age of eight days, every male shall be circumcised.

(Genesis 17:12)

The number eight represents the supernatural realm, which is the realm beyond nature, or the divine. Seven denotes the natural order - as evidenced from the fact that there were seven days of creation and correspondingly seven days in a week, earth has seven continents and seven seas, there are seven colors in the rainbow. Eight is that level which is higher than nature. By performing "milah/circumcision" on the eighth day, we acknowledge that our "bris/covenant" is not subject to the limits and laws of the natural world that the soul has now entered. We cut away a layer of skin to indicate the impermanence of the flesh and, as we stated above, to begin the lifelong process of exposing the essence that lies beneath it.

The term "מִילָה/**mil**ah/circumcision" is not employed in the Torah only in reference to the removal of the foreskin of the male reproductive organ. It is mentioned also to refer to a concept known as the "circumcision of the heart." In Deuteronomy, God instructs Moses to command the nation:

וּמַלְתֶּם אֵת עָרְלַת לְבַבְכֶם:

U'maltem es arlas levavchem.

You shall circumcise the foreskin of your heart.
(Deuteronomy 10:16)

Later in the book, Moses repeats the phrase:

וּמָל יְ-הֹוָה אֱ-לֹהֶיךָ אֶת-לְבָבְךָ וְאֶת-לְבַב זַרְעֶךָ לְאַהֲבָה
אֵת-יְ-הֹוָה אֱ-לֹהֶיךָ בְּכָל-לְבָבְךָ וּבְכָל-נַפְשֶׁךָ:

U'mal A-donai E-lohecha es levavcha v'es levav zarecha l'ahava es A-donai E-lohecha b'chol levavcha u'b'chol naf-shecha.

And the Lord, your God, will **circumcise** your heart and the heart of your offspring, [so that you may] love the Lord your God with all your heart and with all your soul.
(Deuteronomy 30:6)

The sages explain that the circumcision of the male foreskin and the circumcision of the heart are two components of the same mitzvah. As we explained in the last section according to the teachings of the Baal Shem Tov, every mitzvah has two dimensions - the physical action and the spiritual intention, or "kavana." The "circumcision of the heart" is the inner dimension of the act of "bris milah." The "nitzot Elokus," which is the spark of God that is the innermost point of our soul,[110] is contained within our heart, so to speak.[111] But the heart is closed, and the spark is thus concealed within. Throughout our lives, we must therefore work to circumcise the heart, to remove the "flesh" that encloses the spark in order to allow it to become manifest. In this sense, this circumcision of the heart is precisely the opening that we are asking God to assist us with when we pray "poseach es yudecha/open Your yud," as we explained above.[112]

---

[110] As discussed in chapter three, section "The Face Within You"

[111] We are speaking here not of the physical organ of the heart, but the spiritual concept of the heart as the core of our being.

[112] Chapter six, section "Yudecha"

The Alter Rebbe takes this concept one step further. He explains that the Torah's two references to the circumcision of the heart refer to two different stages of circumcision. In the physical circumcision of the male organ, there are two layers that must be removed. The first is the thick foreskin, and the second is a thin membrane that adheres to the glans. In both ritual circumcision and medical circumcision, both of these coverings are removed. In ritual circumcision, if the foreskin is excised but the membrane is left in tact, then the "bris milah" is not deemed kosher and the child is not considered to be circumcised. The Alter Rebbe relates these two physical layers to two stages in our spiritual development. First, we must eliminate the coarse and obvious impediments that hinder the expression of our Godly essence. Afterwards, we must seek and peel away the subtle blockages that garb and inhibit our soul like a thin and almost imperceptible membrane.

Significantly, the Alter Rebbe points out, the first reference to the circumcision of the heart states "**You** shall circumcise the foreskin of your heart," while the second indicates that "**the Lord, your God,** will circumcise your heart." From this distinction, he explains that our task is to work diligently throughout our lives to eradicate the thick foreskin, i.e. the daily challenges that suppress our spiritual growth and expression; when we do so, God will then respond to our efforts at self-refinement by assisting us in dissolving the more subtle forces which are difficult for us to perceive and uproot.[113]

It is important to note that the circumcision of the heart is as applicable to females as it is to males. If so, then why is it that females do not require the physical act of "bris milah"? This is not because they lack the male reproductive organ, but on the contrary - the fact that they do not have a male organ is because they are not in need of physical circumcision. The male is more directed to the external, physical, and superficial - this is reflected by his sexual organ which protrudes from his body and extends to the outside. The female is born with a greater connection to the interior and less susceptibility to becoming mired in the coarseness of the material world around her. Her sexual organ is within her, and through the intimate union, she draws even the male externality inward.

We can see the greater spiritual sensitivity of the female in the relationship of Abraham and his wife Sarah. When Abraham is instruct-

---

[113] *Torah Or*, Lech Lecha, B'etzem Hayom Hazeh Nimol Avraham

ed by Sarah to send away his son, Ishmael, who was attempting to harm his brother Isaac, Abraham objects. However, God instructed Abraham:

כֹּל אֲשֶׁר תֹּאמַר אֵלֶיךָ שָׂרָה שְׁמַע בְּקֹלָהּ:

Kol asher tomar eilecha Sarah Shema b'kola.
Whatever your wife Sarah tells you, listen to her voice.
(Genesis 21:12)

The sages note from here that Sarah was greater than Abraham in prophecy, and that women possess a spiritual sense that men do not. Because of their inherent natures, the male is in need of circumcision and the female is not. Nevertheless, the "helam/hiddenness" of our "olam/world" affects even the more spiritually attuned female. Although she does not require the "bris milah" at the outset of her life in this world, she is charged with the circumcision of the heart, and she, too, will spend her life working to peel back the layers of concealment that cover the face of God within her.

Shearing And Shining

Like the "bris milah," the subsequent major life-cycle rituals designated by Torah mark significant phases in the development of the soul's relationship to this world and its embodiment and expression within the physical realm. Birth, as we mentioned, is the induction of the soul into a corporeal form. But Torah teaches that this coupling of the body and soul is not a single event. It is rather a process that plays out throughout the span of several decades, and in some ways, throughout one's entire life.

The soul, according to Torah, is a completely singular entity, as we have discussed previously. But as it descends into this world of multiplicity, it takes on various dimensions and becomes a compound of a variety of parts. As we mentioned in chapter three,[114] there are a number of different names for the soul in Hebrew - "nefesh," "ruach," "neshama,"

---

[114] Section "The Face Within You"

"chaya," and "yechida" - and these refer to various levels and functions. Additionally, it is taught that each being is comprised of two different soul components, the "nefesh Elokis/Godly soul," and the "nefesh habehamis/animal soul." The animal soul is also referred to as the "nefesh hachiyunis/the vitalizing soul," and it is the force within us that makes us live and drives us to perpetuate our existence within this physical world. It therefore includes our impetus to eat, to procreate, to protect ourselves, and all of the other natural instincts that are common to all forms of sentient life. The Godly soul, on the contrary, is unconcerned with physicality and self-preservation on an ego level. It is focused on the spiritual reality that exists beneath and beyond the physical. It exists before and after the soul's connection to this particular body.

As we mentioned briefly in the previous chapter, the Alter Rebbe in *Tanya* describes life as a constant battle between these two aspects of our soul. They are like two rival armies, he teaches, which are fighting for control over a city. The city, and thus the prize, is our body and being within this world. If the divine soul is victorious, then our body will perform Godly actions and engage in activities that promote a revelation of Godliness within the world. If our animal soul conquers the city, on the other hand, then our body will be utilized for the pursuit of its more base and animalistic urges and tendencies. This battle rages constantly for most of us, and the tides of war are constantly turning. Sometimes the Godly soul gains control of the city, and at other times the animal soul surges and takes over.

In context of the human lifespan and the Torah's rituals that mark the major life-cycle events, it is essential to understand that these two aspects of our soul do not introduce themselves into our body at the same time or at the same pace. The animal soul arrives within the person from the moment of birth. Without it, one could not live. It is like the electricity that turns a machine on and enables it to function. The Godly soul, however, does not reside within us immediately. This is evident from the actions and behaviors of an infant, which do not differ significantly from other newborn species. It eats, it sleeps, it excretes waste. It pursues its desires and instincts and does not display any complex intellect or morality. The Godly soul begins to introduce itself into the person later, and its investment is gradual. Unlike the animal soul, it does not enter all at once, but it takes many years from the time it begins to present itself to the time it is fully incorporated. Just as we saw earlier,[115] light comes after darkness - "it was evening and it was morning."[116] First the stage is set, with all of its limitations and concealment. Then the light emerges from the darkness to reveal itself with blinding brightness in comparison to what preceded it.

The life-cycle events that the Torah marks with special rituals correspond to the various stages in the Godly soul's infusion and embodiment. The "bris milah" on the eighth day is the moment when the Godly soul begins its entry into the child. While the first seven days represent the natural world, as we explained above, the eighth day activates the supernatural aspect of existence. It is therefore at this point that the Godly soul initiates its affiliation with the physical realm. The removal of flesh at this point, in addition to all that we stated above, can signify the weakening of the animal force as its rival enters the fray and the battle for control of the "city" begins.

The next life-cycle ritual is when the child reaches the age of three. For the boy, the third birthday is marked by an event called the "upsherin," which is yiddish for "shearing" because on this day, the child is given his first haircut. A girl's third birthday marks the beginning of her lighting of the shabbat candles every Friday before sundown. Both of these practices represent a new phase in the life of the child and her/his induction into the rituals of Torah observance. By this time, there has been an investiture of the Godly soul that enables the child to begin to express it through the performance of mitzvos. The girl's lighting of candles is an explicit demonstration of her ability (and therefore her concomitant responsibility) to begin to transform the darkness around her. For the boy, the cutting of his hair is, like the "bris milah," another physical symbol of the work he will have to do throughout his life to remove the coverings that continually grow over him to conceal his core. While the majority of the hair on his head is cut short, the "peyot," or earlocks, are left slightly longer (or significantly longer in some sects), and additionally, he begins to wear a "yarmulke" (head covering) and "tzitzis" (ritual fringes) full time. All of these practices are reminders that even as

---

[115] Chapter 2, section "Night And Then Day"

[116] Genesis 1:5

we shear away the barriers, there remain coverings which we must be conscious of constantly if we are to fulfill our worldly mission.

Taken together, the rituals of "upsherin" and candle lighting represent the work that we have been discussing and which each of us is tasked with throughout our lives: to remove the superficial layers and to reveal the Godly light that radiates from within. As we will soon see, the efforts of the male and female will eventually fuse in order that they will provide each other assistance in that life work. But before we can achieve the fusion of the male and female in the ritual of marriage, there must first be the completion of the investment of the Godly soul in each of them individually.

Bar/Bat Mitzvah

It takes over a decade for the Godly soul to become fully incorporated in the body. To be more precise, it is a twelve year process for a girl and a thirteen year process for a boy. It is at this point, on the girl's twelfth birthday and the boy's thirteenth, that the "bar/bat mitzvah" is celebrated and one transitions from the Torah's definition of childhood to adulthood. A child in this sense is one who is not fully invested with its Godly soul, and adulthood is reached at the moment that the Godly soul completes its embodiment. Until now, the animal soul has maintained its advantage. But now the Godly soul culminates the process that it had begun at the "bris milah" for the boy and at birth for the girl. "Bar mitzvah" literally means "son of mitzvah", and "bat mitzvah" means "daughter of mitzvah." "Mitzvah," means "commandment," and one who reaches the age of bar or bat mitzvah is now a son or daughter of the commandments. What does this mean, and why is this happening now?

On the simple level of "pshat," the "bar/bat mitzvah" is the moment when the new "adult" becomes liable for the fulfillment of the commandments. Prior to that time, s/he was a child, too young, immature, and inexperienced to bear the responsibility for the mitzvos and the culpability for their violation. Throughout the past decade, it has been the parents' responsibility to teach the child how to perform the mitzvos properly. Now the training wheels are removed, so to speak, and the young adult is deemed mature enough to take responsibility for her/his actions.

On a deeper level, we understand that it is not simply time and practice which have brought one to this new status. If that were the case, then there would be those children who, through either their inherent refinement or their diligence and/or the diligence of their parents, would be ready to reach this level of preparedness before they arrive at this age. Conversely, there would be those whose immaturity could persist for years beyond their twelfth or thirteenth birthday. Furthermore, we might expect to find differences in the timing of "bar/bat mitzvah" between those who were raised in homes that were steeped in Torah and those whose families and forebears knew nothing of the Torah's teachings and could therefore not prepare them. Nevertheless, the fact is that the timing of bar/bat mitzvah is not determined by one's knowledge, experience, or maturity, but simply by arriving at the designated age. This is because, as we stated above, there is a spiritual evolution which has now reached a tipping point in the life of this person. She or he is now fully equipped with the ability to counter the animal soul and to express the Godliness that is hidden within. This is facilitated through the fulfillment of the mitzvos, and this is why it is at precisely this moment that one becomes responsible to abide by them.

Mitzvos, as we have discussed, are not simply "commandments," or actions that we are required to fulfill for the sake of some other being who rules over us. They are not labors that we are assigned in order to enrich some master and/or to simply demonstrate our allegiance. They are exercises that we have been provided which enable us to open the pathway inward and connect to our infinite essence. While the word "mitzvah" is indeed derived from the word "tzivui/command," it also relates to the Aramaic "tzavsa/bond." A "bar/bat mitzvah" is therefore not only a 'son/daughter of the commandments,' but a 'son/daughter of the bond.' Understood in this sense, the "bar/bat mitzvah" celebrant is one whose essential bond with God has reached a new level of revelation.

Of course, we are all bound with God from the moment of our creation. "Hashem echad/God is one," and there is nothing other than Him. However, at birth, the spark of God that is our soul descended into this realm of concealment and buried itself within a casing of flesh. Our life work, as we have discussed at length, is the revelation of that spark and its unity with all of the other sparks that have likewise embedded and obscured themselves. There are times in our life when our ability to express that unity is augmented. The "bar/bat mitzvah" is the moment that we are now granted the full strength of our Godly soul so that we can begin to make it manifest. The method through which we can do so is the mitzvos - they are the actions that we can perform within this physical world that enable us to tear open the camouflage and transform concealment into revelation. Now that we have arrived at the completion of our Godly soul's embodiment, we are granted the full complement of the mitzvos in order to perform our earthly task of transformation and revelation. The "bar/bat mitzvah" can therefore be understood as the induction of the individual into the ranks of the special corps for which s/he was created, and the moment that s/he is endowed with the treasure chest of riches, resources, and implements with which s/he will pursue and accomplish the mission ahead.

Marriage/Fusion

The soul, we have seen, is comprised of many different components. There are the five levels of the soul - "nefesh," "ruach," "neshama," "chaya," and "yechida" - which refer to various functions and degrees of engagement of the Godly force within the body. There are also the two inclinations of the soul, the "nefesh Elokis/Godly soul" and the "nefesh habehamis/animal soul, which oppose each other and battle constantly for control of the body. Yet all of these pieces together still do not constitute a complete soul. A complete soul, according to the Zohar, is not contained by any one individual. Each person represents a half of a soul, and it is only through marriage that the two halves, which had been separated prior to birth, are reunited. The evolution of the soul that we have been discussing, therefore, is not completed at the stage of "bar/bat mitzvah," though that was the moment when the Godly soul finished its transmission into the body. The "bar/bat mitzvah" marks, on the contrary, a new beginning, the formal commencement of the person's mission and journey. But s/he is still incomplete, and there is another beginning ahead. At marriage, one rejoins the other half of her/his soul in order to embark on the lifework of self-discovery, self-transcendence, and procreation that can only be accomplished in partnership with one's "zivug" or soul-mate.

As we saw earlier, the male and female souls are not identical. They develop differently and they reflect various qualities. When they join, they complement one another and they are able to accomplish far more than either could accomplish individually. We might wonder why God established it this way. Why was each soul unit divided into two and invested in separate bodies only to reunite later? Could God not have left the soul intact and embedded it into a single body that incorporated all of its qualities and potentials? In fact, the Midrash tells us that it was not only possible for God to do so, but this is precisely what He originally did.

אָמַר רַבִּי יִרְמְיָה בֶּן אֶלְעָזָר בְּשָׁעָה שֶׁבָּרָא הַקָּדוֹשׁ בָּרוּךְ הוּא אֶת אָדָם הָרִאשׁוֹן, **אַנְדְּרוֹגִינוֹס** בְּרָאוֹ, הֲדָא הוּא דִכְתִיב (בראשית ה, ב): **זָכָר וּנְקֵבָה בְּרָאָם.** אָמַר רַבִּי שְׁמוּאֵל בַּר נַחְמָן, בְּשָׁעָה שֶׁבָּרָא הַקָּדוֹשׁ בָּרוּךְ הוּא אֶת אָדָם הָרִאשׁוֹן, דְּיוֹ פַּרְצוּפִים בְּרָאוֹ, וְנִסְרוֹ וַעֲשָׂאוֹ גַּבִּים, גַּב לְכָאן וְגַב לְכָאן.

*Amar rabbi Yirmiyah ben Elazar b'shaah she'bara Hakadosh Baruch Hu es Adam harishon, **androginus** b'rao, hada hu dichtiv (Breishis 5:2): **zachar u'nekeiva b'raam.** Amar rabbi Shmuel bar Nachman, b'shaah shebara Hakadosh Baruch Hu es Adam harishon, dyu partzufim b'rao, v'nisro v'asao gabbim, gav l'chan v'gav l'chan.*

Said Rabbi Yirmiyah ben Elazar: In the hour when the Holy One created the first human, He created him **androgynous**, as it is said, '**male and female He created them**.' Said Rabbi Shmuel bar Nachmani: In the hour when the Holy One created the first human, He created him double-faced and sawed him and made him backs, a back here and a back there.

(Breishis Rabba, 8:1)

The Midrash here informs us that Adam was not created first followed by Eve's subsequent creation. Adam and Eve were created simultaneously in the form of one being with both genders and two faces or fronts. Subsequently, God split this single being into two, each with its own gender, and its own front and back. This secret is revealed in the very text of the Torah itself, which the Midrash cites:

זָכָר וּנְקֵבָה בְּרָאָם וַיְבָרֶךְ אֹתָם וַיִּקְרָא אֶת־שְׁמָם אָדָם בְּיוֹם הִבָּרְאָם:

Zachar u'nekeiva braam vayivareich osam vayikra es shemam Adam b'yom hibaram.

Male and female He created them, and He blessed them, and He named them Adam on the day they were created.

(Genesis 5:2)

The simple reading of this verse from Genesis seems to indicate that God created both male and female beings. But the Midrash reveals that the deeper meaning of the verse is that this was a single being that was created both male and female. "He named *them* Adam," the verse states, indicating that Adam, the first human, was not merely a "him," but rather a "them" that included both genders and all of their various capacities. This condition did not last long however. Soon after the creation of Adam, God separated 'them' into Adam and Eve, him and her, and thereby established two complementary individuals who would partner together.

What is the meaning of all this? Why did God create a single, androgynous being and then cleave it into separate male and female parts? Was His original creation an error?

In the first chapter of this book, we asked a similar question about the other seeming "errors" of our origin story. Did God not know that we would sin and therefore be exiled from His garden? If not, then what does that tell us about His wisdom and His control? If He did know, then why would He have allowed us to sin, setting us up for failure and exiling us with the shame of our 'original sin'? We have answered these questions at length, both in the first chapter[117] and the sixth.[118] As we have explained according to the central Torah doctrine of "hashgacha protis/divine providence," God does not make errors. There

---

[117] Section "Intentional Error"

[118] Section "Shame"

is no force that competes with Him, and there is nothing that occurs in the universe that is contrary to His will. Therefore, there is a precise intentionality in every aspect of the process of our creation, and just as there are powerful reasons that we were first created in the garden with diaphanous skin only later to be garbed in opaque flesh and exiled from Eden, so too there is a profound lesson for us to learn from the fact that we were originally one androgynous being that was then divided into separate genders and forms.

We can begin to understand this with the concept that God created Adam "in His image." The verse quoted from Genesis above, "male and female He created them," is immediately preceded by the phrase "in the likeness of God He created him."[119] God is neither male nor female. He is one. He comprises all qualities, including both genders, and He is limited by none.[120] Creating humanity in His image thus necessitated that it included both male and female form. Just as Adam/Eve's translucent skin and placement in the Garden of Eden were indicative of their original perfection, so too their androgyny was a symbol of their wholeness and integrity. However, perfection and unity were not the conditions for the world that God would now create. This was to be a realm of concealment and division. Why? In order that there should be the existence of others to whom God could express His love, as we have explained previously in chapter two.[121] There, we quoted a verse from Genesis in which God contemplates Adam's solitary condition and decides upon the creation of his mate.

וַיֹּאמֶר יְ-הֹוָה אֱ-לֹהִים לֹא-טוֹב הֱיוֹת הָאָדָם לְבַדּוֹ אֶעֱשֶׂה-לּוֹ
עֵזֶר כְּנֶגְדּוֹ:

*Vayomer A-donai E-lohim lo tov heyos **ha'Adam** levado, e'eseh lo ezer k'negdo.*

And the Lord God said, "It is not good that man is alone; I shall make him a helpmate opposite him.
(Genesis 2:18)

---

[119] Genesis 5:1

[120] We utilize the male pronoun "He" only as a matter of grammar, and not to indicate any gender designation or limitation.

[121] Section "Good Nature"

We explained that while on the surface this verse is referring to Adam, the first man, on a deeper level the word *"ha'*Adam/*the* man" alludes to "Adam Kadmon," primordial man. This is the image of God Himself that precedes the creation and in the likeness of which the earthly Adam is fashioned. This verse is therefore a statement of God's reason for the creation - it is not good for *God* to be alone. "Good" is defined by the bestowal of kindness or caring from one to another. If God is alone, as He was prior to the creation, there can be no "good" because there is no one to whom He can express it. Just as this verse therefore explains why God decided to make divisions in His infinite unity in order to create otherness (so that there would be an outlet for His essential goodness), similarly it provides His rationale for splitting Adam below and forming male and female from the single being that He had originally created. It was not "good" for Adam to be alone, i.e. all one. "Good" would be effected only if there were separate beings who could express love and kindness to one another. Therefore, God hewed Adam in two:

וַיַּפֵּל יְ-הֹוָה אֱ-לֹהִים תַּרְדֵּמָה עַל־הָאָדָם וַיִּישָׁן וַיִּקַּח אַחַת מִצַּלְעֹתָיו וַיִּסְגֹּר בָּשָׂר תַּחְתֶּנָּה: וַיִּבֶן יְ-הֹוָה אֱ-לֹהִים אֶת־הַצֵּלָע אֲשֶׁר־לָקַח מִן־הָאָדָם לְאִשָּׁה וַיְבִאֶהָ אֶל־הָאָדָם: וַיֹּאמֶר הָאָדָם זֹאת הַפַּעַם עֶצֶם מֵעֲצָמַי וּבָשָׂר מִבְּשָׂרִי לְזֹאת יִקָּרֵא אִשָּׁה כִּי מֵאִישׁ לֻקֳחָה־זֹּאת:

Va'yipol A-donai E-lohim tardeima al ha'adam va'yishan va'yikach achas mitzalosav va'yisgor basar tachtena. Va'yiven A-donai E-lohim es ha'tzela asher lakach min ha'adam l'isha va'yivieha el ha'adam. Va'yomer ha'adam zos ha'paam etzem ma'atzmi u'basar mi'bisari l'zos yikarei isha ki me'ish lukacha zos.

And the Lord God caused a deep sleep to fall upon man, and he slept, and He took one of his sides, and He closed the flesh in its place. And the Lord God built the side that He had taken from man into a woman, and He brought her to man. And man said, "This time, it is bone of my bones and flesh of my flesh. This one shall be called ishah (woman) because this one was taken from ish (man)."

(Genesis 2: 21-23)

These verses describe the surgery that God performed on both Adam and Eve. Prior to this, they were both referred to as "Adam," as we saw above, "He named *them* Adam." He then determined that they should be individuals who would later reconnect. Therefore, He put them to sleep and performed the surgical procedure that severed them, and then healed the flesh where they had been conjoined.

Marriage, we see from this, is the allegory for the entire purpose and project of creation! God divided His unity to create the semblance of multiplicity in order to express His love to one who believed itself to be separate and distinct from Him. Ultimately, His beloved, in response to the love that God bestowed upon her/him, would recognize that s/he was not truly separate from her/his lover at all. Their unity would be revealed even within the framework of their seeming diversity. God's limitless light would thus glow within the darkness of this world. So too, God formed a single being in His likeness, and then divided it into pieces that would consider themselves independent. Eventually, these two beings, who seem to be individual and distinct, would come together and overcome their differences to fuse and coalesce. Through this process, they would recognize the transient and illusory nature of the flesh that confines and divides them, and they would become aware of the inner reality that unites them and ultimately defines who and what they are.

We have been detached and dispersed in order to reassemble and reunite. When we do so, we find the essential adhesive that is at our core. That is the face of God which is within each of us. It binds us to one another, to our Creator, and to every aspect of His creation which is only another disguise in which He hides Himself.

Wedding

Many more pages, and indeed chapters, could be devoted to the Torah's conception of marriage and the many opportunities it provides us to uncover the layers that encase us and to find the face within. Torah teaches that the marriage between husband and wife is an allegory for the relationship between God and humankind. Therefore, the exploration of the dynamics of the marriage bond will bring us as close as we can come to understanding the interconnection of our soul and its Creator. However, to explore this subject in the depth that it deserves is beyond the scope of this book. Nevertheless, before moving on, it is worthwhile to shift from the concept of marriage more generally and focus briefly on the protocol of the wedding itself. As we have been discussing, Torah provides not only a conceptual arena for inward exploration and spiritual growth, but also an intricate practice that promotes and supports self-discovery through very specific actions which carry profound meaning and significance. As such, the wedding rituals convey the aforementioned themes and ideas of marriage through the performance of very particular physical procedures and customs.

The wedding ceremony is incredibly rich with rituals and symbolism. The process begins long before the "chosson/groom" and "kallah/bride" walk down the aisle. One week prior to the wedding day, the couple separates and will not see one another until a very special moment just before the formal ceremony begins. The wedding is divided into two parts, known as the "Kabbalat panim" and the "chuppah." "Kabbalat panim" is translated as "reception," but it literally means "receiving faces." "Chuppah" means "canopy" or "covering" in reference to the bridal canopy under which the couple stands throughout the formal ceremony. It is no coincidence that these terms, and the rituals that they name, relate to the concepts of 'face' and 'covering' which we have been discussing in this book. For the wedding, like all of the milestone events throughout one's life, is a practice designed to assist us in the process of uncovering our "pnimyus/inner core" and finding the "Pnei Hashem/face of God" that exists there.

On the surface level, the term "kabbalat panim" is rendered simply as "reception," and this is a more informal phase of the wedding where the bride and groom are situated in separate rooms as guests begin to arrive and are "received" (the meaning of "kabbalat") or greeted. Various legalities are performed at the groom's reception, including the signing of the "ketubah/marriage contract" by the officiating rabbi and two witnesses, and the reading of the "tena'im," or the conditions of the engagement. Following the completion of these legal documents, together the mothers of the couple break a plate to symbolize the irreversibility of the contracted terms. At this point, the "badeken" takes place - a powerful ceremony that will provide a far deeper meaning to the term "kabbalat panim."

"Badeken" means "covering" in Yiddish, similar to the English term 'bedeck,' which means to adorn or dress up. The groom, followed by his guests, proceeds from his reception room to the hall where the bride is seated on a throne, and the couple comes face to face for the first time since their separation a week earlier. It is at this very emotional moment when the couple greets one another that we understand that the "faces" (panim) which are "received" (kabbalat) during this stage of the wedding are not simply those of the arriving guests, but more particularly the faces of the bride and groom themselves. It is a brief, but profound and often tear-filled moment, and then the groom places a veil over the bride's face in preparation for the "chuppah," the formal marriage ceremony which will shortly commence. The derivation of this custom is from the first meeting of the matriarch Rebecca and her intended husband, the patriarch Isaac.

וַיֵּצֵא יִצְחָק לָשׂוּחַ בַּשָּׂדֶה לִפְנוֹת עָרֶב וַיִּשָּׂא עֵינָיו וַיַּרְא וְהִנֵּה גְמַלִּים בָּאִים: וַתִּשָּׂא רִבְקָה אֶת־עֵינֶיהָ וַתֵּרֶא אֶת־יִצְחָק וַתִּפֹּל מֵעַל הַגָּמָל: וַתֹּאמֶר אֶל־הָעֶבֶד מִי־הָאִישׁ הַלָּזֶה הַהֹלֵךְ בַּשָּׂדֶה לִקְרָאתֵנוּ, וַיֹּאמֶר הָעֶבֶד הוּא אֲדֹנִי וַתִּקַּח הַצָּעִיף וַתִּתְכָּס:

Vayeitzei Yitzchak lasuach basadeh lifnos arev vayisah einav vayar v'hineh gemalim ba'im. Vatisah Rivkah es-eineha vatireh es-Yitzchak vatipol me'al hagamal. Vatomer el ha'eved mi ha'ish halazeh haholech basadeh likraseinu, vayomer ha'eved hu adoni, vatikach hatzaif vatiskas.

And Isaac went forth to pray in the field towards evening, and he lifted his eyes and saw, and behold, camels were approaching. And Rebecca lifted her eyes, and saw Isaac, and she let herself down from the camel. And she said to the servant, "Who is that man walking in the field towards us?" And the servant said, "He is my master." **And she took the veil and covered herself.**
(Genesis 24:63-65)

Rebecca's act of veiling herself when she first encountered Isaac has been expounded on many different levels. In one sense, it is an expression of her modesty. In another sense, it is the declaration that now that she has met her betrothed, her beauty will be reserved for him exclusively. On a deeper level, it is Rebecca's statement to her future husband that it is not her superficial beauty which he marries, but the tremendous worth within her which cannot be seen with the physical eyes. On an even more esoteric level, it is explained that just as Moses was forced to cover himself with a veil when he descended from Mount Sinai because of the beams of Godly light that radiated from his face after his intimate interaction with God,[122] so too the bride emits the glow of her divine essence at the time of her wedding.

In this last explanation, we see that as marriage is an allegory for the relationship between God and humanity, so too the wedding is represented by the events at Mount Sinai. Moses, as a representative of the entire nation, is the bride, and God is the groom. When the bride and groom come face to face and unite - in other words when there is a "kabbalat panim" and they truly receive one other's "pnimyus" or inward essence - there is an inevitable overflow of the divine light that dwells within them. It beams from the bride's face so blindingly that it must be covered in order for the "olam/world" of "helam/hiddenness" to continue to exist.

After the "badeken," which again means "covering" in Yiddish, the ceremony continues with the "chuppah," which also means "covering" in Hebrew, and in this second phase of the wedding this symbolism continues. The groom proceeds first to his place under the bridal canopy, or "chuppah," which is generally a prayer shawl (tallis) or other embroidered cloth that is held aloft by four poles. The bride then follows, and when she arrives, before standing at his side, she first walks around the groom seven times. He then places a ring on her finger, encircling her reciprocally. The marriage contract is read, a series of seven blessings is recited, and at the end of the ceremony, the groom stomps on a glass that will shatter beneath his foot. The bride's veil is removed, and the couple proceeds from under the "chuppah" to great rejoicing from the guests.

From even such a quick and cursory overview of the rituals associated with the wedding ceremony, we see a consistent focus on the dynamics of concealment and revelation with which God created, and creates, the universe. The separation of the bride and the groom for the week prior to the wedding mirrors the division that God has created

---

[122] See Chapter four, section "Halleluy-ah"

within His unity in order for the creation to be formed. The "kabbalat panim/meeting of the faces" of the bride and the groom at the "badeken" is the beginning of the reunification that is not only the goal of each marriage, but of the creation as a whole. The veil with which the groom covers his bride at the "badeken" ceremony parallels not only the veil with which Moses covered the "horns of light" that projected from his face, but also the veil of this physical universe with which God has shrouded His own face and buried it within our flesh. With the veil, the groom acknowledges that it is not the surface or physical beauty of his bride that he embraces, but the spiritual core that is deep within her. The two then proceed to the "chuppah" where the canopy above them alludes not only to the home that they will build together, but also to the reality that they dwell beneath a cloak that God has spread over them, and that the holiness of their union lies beneath it. They encircle one another - she with seven revolutions around him, and he with a single ring around her finger - both representing the fact that they are enveloped and contained. He then shatters a glass, which commemorates the destruction of the temple in Jerusalem but may also allude to the shattering of the barriers that divide them and conceal their Godly core. Her veil is then lifted, and they go forward together from under the "chuppah" as a married couple.

In summary, we find that the dominant and repeated images at the wedding are faces, coverings, circles and breakage (the plate after the reading of the "tena'im," and the glass at the end of the "chuppah" ceremony). The marriage will later be consummated with the act of intercourse, which once again enacts this process of encircling and covering, penetrating, opening, and revealing. Intimacy is fusion. The woman opens to the man and draws him inside. They reconnect after having been separated before birth. Together, they are able to then touch the divine. The ultimate outcome of this process is procreation, in which the process of God's creative project is mimicked and the miracle of new life results from the act of enclosing and concealment.

Death/Completion

The soul, as we have discussed, finishes its investment in the body at the "bar/bat mitzvah," and then reunites with its other half at marriage. For the remainder of its time in this body, it will be working to answer God's question "ayecha/where are you," and to fulfill its task of "bara Elokim es hashamayim v'es haaretz," revealing God within this realm of hiddenness. The time it is allotted to do so will depend on a variety of factors, and it will remain here, ideally, until its mission is accomplished. While birth, according to Torah, is the moment that God has determined that the world requires this particular soul's service, death is the moment that its service in this particular incarnation is complete. This does not mean that the soul's journey is over. The soul does not, and cannot, die; it only detaches from the casing in which it was temporarily infused. It will now continue its process either in the spiritual realms, or it may require additional incarnations in this physical world in order to finish the task that it is called upon to perform here.

Death, according to Torah, is nothing to fear. We fear death because it is unknown and because it seems to be the end. But it is not the end. It is the culmination of one progression and the beginning of another. We tend to view death as a punishment, a consequence for misdeeds. It is commonly seen as the threat that God holds over us to keep us subservient, and the vengeance He administers when we step too far out of line. But where does this conception come from? Why do we imagine God as this temperamental, hostile force? This is certainly not the view of Torah, which declares:

אֵין דָּבָר רַע יוֹרֵד מִלְמַעְלָה:
Ein davar ra yored mi'lemaala.
No evil descends from above.
(Breishis Rabba 51:3)

כִּי לְעוֹלָם חַסְדּוֹ:
Ki l'olam chasdo.
His kindness is eternal.
(Psalms 136:1)

עוֹלָם חֶסֶד יִבָּנֶה:

Olam chesed yibaneh.

The world is built on lovingkindness.

(Psalms 89:3)

God, as we have seen, does execute judgment in His creation, and there are indeed consequences for improper action within the framework of this world. But the notion of a punitive, vengeful God, and the perception of death as nothing more than a penalty for disobedience, are only products of a superficial and unsophisticated reading of the Torah's text which is inconsistent with its inner spirit and essence.

The first time death is mentioned in Torah is in the second chapter of Genesis soon after the creation of Adam and Eve. They are still in the garden of Eden, and God informs them of the prohibition of eating from the fruit of the tree of knowledge of good and evil:

וַיְצַו יְ-הֹוָה אֱ-לֹהִים עַל-הָאָדָם לֵאמֹר מִכֹּל עֵץ-הַגָּן אָכֹל
תֹּאכֵל: וּמֵעֵץ הַדַּעַת טוֹב וָרָע לֹא תֹאכַל מִמֶּנּוּ כִּי בְּיוֹם
אֲכָלְךָ מִמֶּנּוּ מוֹת תָּמוּת:

Vayitzav A- donai Elokim al-ha'adam leimor Mikol etz-ha-gan ochel tochal. U'me'etz ha'daas tov v'rah lo tochal mi-menu ki b'yom achalcha mimenu mos tamus.

And the Lord God commanded man, saying, "Of every tree of the garden you may freely eat. But of the Tree of Knowledge of good and evil you shall not eat of it, for on the day that you eat thereof, you shall surely die."

(Genesis 2:16-17)

On the simple level, this can be read as a warning and a statement of punishment: if you eat the fruit, I will penalize you with death. Alternatively, it can be read as a statement of fact: if you eat the fruit, you will surely die *at some point*. In other words, you will be susceptible to death if you eat the fruit, whereas if you do not eat the fruit, death cannot affect you. With either reading, God forbids the eating of the fruit; but in the first interpretation, death is utilized as a threatened retribution, and in the second interpretation, death is offered as an explanation for the prohibition. Why were Adam and Eve liable to death following the eating of the fruit? In the simple reading, it seems to be because they were sinners who were now deserving of execution. But if so, why were they not executed upon eating the fruit and merely exiled instead? The "threat" indicates that they would die "on the day that you eat thereof." But they did not die on that day, and as a matter of fact they lived for nearly a millennium afterwards. Therefore, we can understand that what God is conveying to them in this verse is that through the consumption of the fruit they would become, on that very day, *liable to death*. Somehow the act of eating the fruit altered their nature in such a manner that death was now a possibility for them at some time in the future. In other words, it's not that Adam and Eve *should* die because they ate the fruit, but rather that they *could* die because they ate the fruit. How and why did the fruit create this new dynamic?

The tree of the knowledge of good and evil represents dichotomy - good AND evil - and eating its fruit internalized duality within humanity. It brought us down into the world where there is differentiation - good and evil, light and darkness, life and death. Had we not eaten the fruit, we would have remained in the Edenic realm beyond all of these dialectics and oppositions. Eden was an intermediate space between the heavens and the earth. It is a way station between the ultimate reality of God's complete unity, and this world of division, concealment and multiplicity. Adam and Eve existed in Eden as "others," distinct and individualized from God, but they were not conscious of their otherness and individuality until they ate the fruit. They were not conscious of themselves at all - therefore they were not aware of their nakedness - but immediately afterwards they were self-conscious and ashamed. Ingesting the fruit introduced the existence of a self within them. When one is united with God, s/he is infinite and cannot die. But as soon as one exists independently, then s/he is finite and susceptible to death. This is what it means to be "mortal," the root of which is "mort," which is Latin for "death."

As we have discussed repeatedly, a realm of Godliness beyond all duality is not what God intended for this world. This was what existed before the creation, and therefore, if this was His desire, then there would have been no need for the creation at all. On the contrary, He wanted us to live within a world of darkness in order to enlighten it. In such a finite and superficial dimension, death is not a punishment, it is a simple reality. In fact, it is an act of mercy without which one might be consigned to darkness for eternity. After Adam ate the fruit, God removed him from the garden "lest he stretch forth his hand and take also from the Tree of Life and eat and live forever." Living forever within the framework of duality is not desirable, and not what God wants for us. Existence within this realm that is known as "olam hasheker/world of falseness" is only to be temporary. What would truly be a punishment would be to condemn us to this darkness forever. Death is actually a release, a liberation from the confines of good and evil, and a re-entry into the "olam ha'emes/world of truth" where one can once again experience God's oneness.

If this is so, then perhaps life itself is a punishment. Perhaps one could imagine that s/he would be better off ending her/his life as soon as possible in order to avoid the illusion of separation and thereby exist within the more ultimate truth of unity with God and all. Indeed, the Chassidic masters explain that the soul does in fact yearn to be free of this world so that it can return to the place from which it came. In this sense, they explain the expression from Proverbs:

נֵר י-הוָה נִשְׁמַת אָדָם:

Ner Hashem nishmas Adam.
The soul of man is the candle of God.
(Proverbs 20:27)

The human soul is like the flame of a candle. If we observe a flame, we see that it is always reaching upward no matter what direction the candle is oriented, and it is never still but always flickering. This flicker represents its constant striving to leap from off the wick that holds it, in order to reunite with the source of fire above. So too, the mystics teach, the soul is constantly flickering upward, yearning to free itself from the 'wick' of the body and to reunite with the source of all souls in the heavens. Nevertheless, it knows it has a job to do here in this world. It was placed into the body in order to discover itself and its creator and to illuminate the darkness. Therefore, though it longs for the realm of light from which it came, it simultaneously recognizes the reason and necessity for its being here. With this, we can understand the saying of the sage Rabbi Elazar Hakapor:

עַל כָּרְחֲךָ אַתָּה חַי, וְעַל כָּרְחֲךָ אַתָּה מֵת:

Al karchacha atta chai, v'al karchacha atta meis.

Against your will you live, and against your will you die.

(Pirkei Avos 4:22)

The soul does not want to come down to this world of darkness and concealment where it will be confined and deluded. However, once it is here and it becomes enwrapped in the body, it becomes entangled in the life of the flesh and doesn't want to leave. On a deeper level, it doesn't want to leave because it knows it has a job to do here, and it is so devoted to God that it does not want to abandon its post until the job is complete.

All of this will enable us to understand a strange verse in the prayers of Rosh Hashana, which is the Jewish new year and is also known as "Yom hadin/the Day of Judgment." The new year is not simply celebrated as the beginning of a new cycle and a time of renewal and resolution; it is a time of deep introspection when one considers her/his conduct throughout the past year and refocuses her/himself on the purpose for which s/he was created. It is a time of contemplation and evaluation for God as well, and on the first day of each new year, He reconsiders His creation and decides how He will conduct it going forward. The prayers of the day therefore focus on "teshuvah," returning to a consciousness of who we are and why we are here. We recognize our failings throughout the past year, and aware of God's great love and mercy, we ask for another opportunity to do better. We request life and sustenance and all of the things that will make the coming year more successful than the past. God is then said to inscribe each of us in the book of life, writing precisely what will happen to us in the year ahead. In one of the central prayers of the day, the following is recited:

זָכְרֵנוּ לְחַיִּים מֶלֶךְ חָפֵץ בַּחַיִּים וְכָתְבֵנוּ בְּסֵפֶר הַחַיִּים **לְמַעַנְךָ** אֱ-לֹהִים חַיִּים:

*Zochreinu l'chayim, melech chafeitz bachayim, v'chatveinu l'sefer hachayim, **l'maancha** E-lohim chayim.*

Remember us for life, King Who desires life, and inscribe us in the book of life **for Your sake** God of life.

What do we mean to say that one is asking for life for God's sake? To be honest, is it not that one begs for life because s/he loves life and fears death? To suggest that the prayer is for God's benefit seems to be disingenuous. However, at this holiest time of the year, one is speaking from the deepest level of her/his soul. When one accesses her/his "pnimyus" and finds the "Pnei Hashem" within, s/he knows that s/he is completely one with God, that s/he is simply a piece of Him hidden within the illusion of plurality. What one desires then is only to do God's will, to make Him revealed in the darkness. Therefore, one asks for life not because s/he desires it for her/his sake, but rather for God's sake; in order that s/he can complete the task that God assigned her/him. With such consciousness, one is not worried about death. One doesn't beg to be signed in the book of life because s/he fears the alternative. One requests more time to do her/his work "l'maancha Elokim chayim," for the sake of "Elokim chayim," the aspect of God that desires life.

For our own sake, death seems to be an elevation. It is an end to the groping in the darkness that life in this world represents. Yet we do not request death. Ironically, it is with self-sacrifice that we request life. 'Please allow me to stay here,' we ask, 'in spite of the darkness and confusion and struggle that I face here daily, because I know that you want me here. Though I seem to be distanced from You here, and I flicker upward constantly because I would much prefer to exist in a realm where there is no apparent separation between us, yet because I love You, I will remain attached to the wick as long as You require my service here.' We therefore remain in this world, and we work daily to reveal the reality that God is here just as He is above. As a matter of fact, the mystics teach that God is here even more than He is above. For though He is not seen here, it is specifically through performing His will in the darkness that we can connect to Him most completely. The self-sacrifice with which we remain in the dark is a profound manifestation of the Godliness that is hidden within us even if we are not aware of it. This enables us to understand a fascinating statement of the sages:

יָפָה שָׁעָה אַחַת בִּתְשׁוּבָה וּמַעֲשִׂים טוֹבִים בָּעוֹלָם הַזֶּה, מִכָּל חַיֵּי הָעוֹלָם הַבָּא: וְיָפָה שָׁעָה אַחַת שֶׁל קוֹרַת רוּחַ בָּעוֹלָם הַבָּא, מִכָּל חַיֵּי הָעוֹלָם הַזֶּה:

Yaffa shaah achas b'teshuvah u'maasim tovim ba'olam hazeh mikol chayei ha'olam haba. V'yaffa shaah achas shel koras ruach ba'olam haba mikol chayei ha'olam hazeh.

A single moment of repentance and good deeds in this world is greater than all of the World to Come. And a single moment of bliss in the World to Come is greater than all of the present world.

(Pirkei Avos 4:17)

How is it possible that a single moment of labor in this world exceeds all of the heavenly realms? This is answered by the second part of the phrase which tells us that the bliss of the world to come is far greater than any bliss in this world. This heavenly bliss results from an apprehension of our connection to God, and because we cannot see this connection in this world, we are unable to experience anything comparable to such bliss here. And it is precisely because we cannot experience that bliss in this world that our service here is so precious to God that even one moment of it is greater than all of the world to come. Not only does He deeply appreciate our blind and selfless service, but it is precisely this selflessness which reveals Him in the darkness. In spite of our ego and the passions of the flesh which incline us toward self-gratification, we nevertheless transcend our personal desires and thereby expose our Godly essence when we commit ourselves to the truth and purpose that is hidden deep within us.

From this brief exploration and comparison of the roles and functions of life and death, we can appreciate that death is not a punishment. It is rather a completion of the soul's work in this particular body and a transition from this "olam/world" of "helam/hiddenness" back to a realm where the truth of God's unity is apparent. This is not to say that death cannot also be a consequence for deviant action in this world. Clearly this is the case in a variety of circumstances when one transgresses severely and is sentenced by Torah law to the death penalty. Yet even in such an event, we can understand this not simply as a penalty, but as a removal of the soul from the situation in which it will continue to be led astray by its inability to see its truth. The soul is taken from this world not because it is evil, but because it has been unable to penetrate the physical veil in which it is garbed and to thereby express its essential Godliness. It is therefore extracted from the darkness that has overwhelmed it in order to be reunited with the light from which it originates and of which it is comprised.

While most souls are not liable to such drastic measures, the vast majority do not complete within one lifetime the revelation and transformation that we have been assigned. As such, death comes as a respite and a completion of this particular phase in this particular incarnation. The soul reunites with its source to refresh its connection before it is sent back again to continue the work that is incumbent upon all souls throughout history. Eventually, through our collective work across the millennia, this world will be transformed from darkness to light, from concealment to revelation. At this point, we will no longer require death in order for our unity with God to be manifest.

Funeral

Now that we have a better understanding of Torah's conception of death, we can explore the rituals that Torah prescribes to mark this final phase of the life-cycle. As we saw with the rituals of "bris milah," "upsherin," "bar/bat mitzvah," and the wedding, we will find that the funeral rites include very specific practices that focus us on the lifelong process of opening and the revelation of our innermost core. Several of the observances of the funeral bear striking resemblance to the rituals that we have described previously, and this is a reflection of the constancy of these themes of inward exploration and disclosure that underpin every stage and aspect of our existence. In particular, the procedures and ceremonies of the funeral resemble those of the wedding. From this we will see that death is, in many ways, another form of marriage.

Just as the male and female halves of the soul were separated at birth and then reunited at marriage, so too our soul is severed from its revealed union with God when it is sent down into this world at birth, and then it is reunited with its source when it leaves the body at death. As we have discussed at length, there can be no true separation from God as He is one and there is nothing other than Him. It is the mission of the soul to confirm this ultimate reality while it is within the body. But on the revealed plane, birth represents distance and division, and death releases the soul from its perceived detachment and therefore resembles the reunification of souls at the wedding. For this reason, it will not be surprising that one of the Hebrew scriptural terms for death, "כְּלוֹת הַנֶּפֶשׁ/ klot hanefesh," which literally means "expiry of the soul," shares the same root as the word for bride, כַּלָּה/kallah. The root itself, "כַּל," means "all." The linguistic correspondence of these terms reveals their conceptual connectedness. Just as at marriage, the husband and wife fuse to become one and cease to be the individuals that they were previously, so too at death, one ceases to be the distinct individual that s/he had been while confined to the body, and s/he returns to the inter-inclusion ("הִתְכַּלְלוּת/hitkallelut" in Hebrew) within all. Each of the life-cycle events, as we have seen, represents a stage of progression in our process of moving from individuality to oneness.

Like the wedding, the end of life ceremony is divided into parts. The first ritual after death is called "tahara," which literally means "purification." The second phase is called "levaya," which means both "escorting" and "joining." The "tahara" is the ritual washing of the body, and the "levaya" is the formal funeral service. Following the service, the body is buried and the process is complete. These three phases parallel the phases of the wedding that we discussed earlier. Prior to the wedding, both the bride and the groom customarily immerse in a "mikvah," a ritual bath. This bathing is not a cleansing of the body, but a purification of the soul in preparation for its coming unification. Similarly, the ritual washing of the body after death is not a matter of hygiene, but a spiritual cleansing that readies the soul for its transition. Prior to the burial, the soul is still attached to the body though it is no longer contained within it. It is in an intermediate stage where it is no longer incarnate, but it cannot yet proceed on its journey back to its incorporation in its source. For this reason, the funeral and burial are conducted as soon as possible after death. After the body is washed, it is wrapped in a shroud. It is not dressed in finery, and nothing is to be placed into the casket other than the body and the shroud in which it is wrapped. The casket is to be made of simple wood with no metal. This will enable it to decompose more quickly. Just as the soul reunites with its source, so too the body is to reunite with the earth - ashes to ashes, dust to dust.

While the washing of the "tahara" service resembles the immersion in the "mikvah" prior to the wedding, the subsequent shrouding of the body parallels both the veiling of the bride at the "badeken" and the covering of the couple at the "chuppah." Once again, the theme of covering and enwrapping is central. This is then compounded when the shrouded body is placed into the wooden casket prior to the "levaya" ceremony. At this point there is a body, which itself was a cloak for the soul, wrapped in the secondary layer of cloth, which is then housed in the casket, another layer of containment. As we know, the purpose of enclothement and concealment of the soul within the body was for a subsequent revelation in which the extraneous layers would be pierced, the barriers would be broken, and the inner essence would manifest. It would then be able to permeate and transform its surroundings. At the wedding, this was symbolized by the breaking of the plate, the shattering of the glass, the removal of the bride's veil, and the couple's emergence from under the "chuppah." Similarly, at the funeral, the formal ceremony begins with a ritual called "kriah/tearing," in which the immediate family of the departed soul rips their clothing near the area of their heart. On one level, this represents the fact that their loved one has been torn from them and they are left with a hole in their heart which their loved one used to fill. In the context of our discussion, however, this tearing alludes to the rupturing and removal of the layers that obscure what is underneath. The soul is now ready to be freed and unencumbered from the veil of the body so that it can rejoin its source.

This phase of the funeral which begins with the "kriah" is therefore called "levaya," which, as we have mentioned, means not only "escorting," because we escort the soul as it begins the next stage of its journey, but also "joining," because the soul is now able to reconnect to the unity from which it had been sundered. The breakdown of the barriers and the shedding of the concealing layers will continue with the burial. Just as the married couple embraces intimately and thereby unites after the wedding, so too the body penetrates into the ground in order to decompose and become nullified and incorporated into its source. The soul remerges with its origins in the spiritual realm.

There are further parallels between the wedding and the funeral, like the seven days of celebration known as the "sheva brachos" which follows the wedding, and the seven days of mourning known as "shiva" which follows the burial. Similarly, there is the special status of the bride and groom for one year after the wedding known as "shana rishona/first year" and the year long period of "aveilus/mourning" after the burial in which the mourner recites the "kaddish" prayer and is restricted from certain activities. All of these similarities reflect the thematic correspondence in these transitional phases of the soul. The customs and rituals that Torah has assigned to them enable us to remain focused on the essential concepts of inner discovery and Godly reunion that define every phase of our existence.

Chapter 9: DAILY PRACTICE

Prayer

From the previous chapter's overview of the observances of the major lifecycle events, we have begun to see how Torah's practice focuses us on the theme and process of opening that will enable us to find and reveal the face of God within. Now that we have surveyed Torah practice on the macro scale from birth to death, we are ready to focus in on a more granular level and examine the rituals that Torah provides to assist us in penetrating and manifesting our core on a more regular basis. As we have mentioned, the calendrical cycle is replete with observances and commemorations that redirect our consciousness from the outside world to our inner reality, and we will address Torah's yearly, monthly, and weekly practice shortly. Before doing so, we will first explore the daily rituals that keep us aware of our inherent Godliness and assist us in removing the crust that grows over us every moment.

The Torah establishes numerous mitzvah observances throughout the course of each day, and each of these, when performed with their proper "kavana/intention," is an integral component of our liberation practice. This is to say that they will focus our attention on the reality of God's unity, and will therefore free us from the darkness that conceals our inherent Godliness. While this is the underlying goal of all mitzvos, there is one mitzvah that is particularly attuned to this redirection of consciousness, and that is prayer.

Prayer is arguably the single most important part of the process that will enable us to find the face of God. It is no coincidence then that the day begins with prayer, and that one is to pray multiple times throughout the course of each day. However, as we have mentioned several times already, the concept and intention of prayer is often misunderstood, and therefore the potent opportunities that this vital practice provides us are frequently underestimated and unexploited. We have already explored several specific prayers at various points throughout this book. We have delved into some of the meditative experiences of prayer in chapter seven specifically, and we have thereby provided somewhat of an introduction to the transformative power of Torah prayer already. But as we discuss prayer as an integral facet of our daily practice, it will be worthwhile now to analyze the origins and nuances of the Torah's conception of prayer, and to further parse out both its ultimate purpose and potential.

As we have discussed previously,[123] the Hebrew word that is commonly translated as "prayer" is "תְּפִילָה/tefilla." However, this is an imprecise and problematic translation of the term. The English word "prayer" implies requesting or pleading, and as the Lubavitcher Rebbe points out,[124] the more exact phrase in Hebrew for this concept is "בַּקָשָׁה/bakasha," which connotes asking or appealing for some need or desire. The word "tefilla," the Rebbe explains, is more accurately rendered as "bonding" or "attaching." As Torah has become filtered through a westernized "Judeo-Christian" sensibility throughout the period of exile, many Torah concepts have been subjected to a cultural lens that subtly alters them from their authentic and original implications. This is not to say that there is not a place and time for "prayer" in the context of "tefilla" - indeed we are commanded to request our needs and desires from God and to know that everything we have and want will always

---

[123] See chapter three, section "Inward Bound" and elsewhere

[124] *Likkutei Sichos*, Vol. 5, Shabbat Shuva

come through Him. The explicit requests and supplications in the prayer liturgy make this obvious. However, we must understand that while "prayer" is an aspect of "tefilla," it is not its exclusive or central purpose or theme.

The ultimate aim and point of "tefilla" is to delve inward and reconnect with that which is hidden beneath the surface. We can see this from the citation in Torah that is generally understood to be the source for the notion of prayer.

אָנֹכִי מְצַוֶּה אֶתְכֶם הַיּוֹם לְאַהֲבָה אֶת־יְ-הֹוָה אֱ-לֹהֵיכֶם
וּלְעָבְדוֹ בְּכָל־לְבַבְכֶם וּבְכָל־נַפְשְׁכֶם:

*Anochi metzvah eschem hayom l'ahava es A-donai E-lohe-
ichem u'l'avdo b'chol levavchem u'v'chol nafshechem.*
I command you this day to love the Lord your God and
to serve Him with all your heart and with all your soul.
(Deuteronomy 11:13)

The classical commentator Rashi indicates that the "service of the heart" that is referred to here is what is defined as "tefilla/prayer." From this we see that prayer is a form of "service" rather than a form of entreaty. "Service" clearly implies doing something for another - in this case God - as opposed to asking for something from Him. Furthermore, this service is "of the *heart*," which connotes a turning inward to that which is deep inside of us. From its Torah origin then we see that prayer was not primarily intended as a daily appeal. Rather, it is a stepping away from our daily grind in order to contemplate our reality and condition, and to refocus our consciousness on that which is subliminal and essential.

As for the mechanics of prayer, if we search in the Torah for the directive to pray three times daily, we won't find it. Nowhere in the Five Books of Moses does it indicate when or how one should perform this "service of the heart." The prayer liturgy that is memorialized in the Hebrew "siddur/prayer-book," and which forms the basis of the Jewish prayer services, is not found in Torah. It was compiled by the "anshei knesset hagadolah/men of the great assembly" in the fourth century BCE, roughly one thousand years after the Torah was given on Mount Sinai. It is comprised of a selection of citations from the Torah, the book of Psalms, and other scriptural sources, as well as supplications that were written by the sages themselves. Prior to this formalization of the service, Jews "prayed" with their own words and on their own schedule.

So when did it become standard practice to pray three times a day? It is taught in the Talmud[125] that the Patriarchs - Abraham, Isaac, and Jacob - introduced the thrice daily structure, each of them establishing one of the times to pray: Abraham in the morning, Isaac in the afternoon, and Jacob in the evening. Yet what they said during those times was not standardized, nor was it mandated to pray with a "minyan" or quorum of ten supplicants. In Psalms, king David, who lived in the ninth century BCE (seven centuries after the Patriarchs and four centuries after the giving of the Torah) indicates that he prayed three times daily:

עֶרֶב וָבֹקֶר וְצָהֳרַיִם אָשִׂיחָה וְאֶהֱמֶה וַיִּשְׁמַע קוֹלִי:

Erev va'voker v'tzaharayim asicha v'ehemeh va'yishma koli.
Evening and morning and noon I speak and moan and
He hears my voice.
(Psalms 55:18)

In the book of Daniel, four centuries after David, it is written:

וְזִמְנִין תְּלָתָה בְיוֹמָא הוּא בָּרֵךְ עַל־בִּרְכוֹהִי וּמְצַלֵּא וּמוֹדֵא
קֳדָם אֱלָהֵהּ כָּל־קֳבֵל דִּי־הֲוָא עָבֵד מִן־קַדְמַת דְּנָה:

*V'zimnin tlasa b'yoma hu bareich al birchohi u'mitzalei u'-
modei kadam E-lahei kol kaveil di-hava aveid min kadmas
d'nah.*
Three times a day (Daniel) kneeled on his knees and
prayed and offered thanks before his God just as he had
done prior to this.
(Daniel 6:11)

We find, therefore, that the custom to pray three times throughout the day was established, at least for those who were particularly devout, for quite some time before it became formalized.

But what were those who were "praying" before the liturgy was standardized doing, and how exactly did they do it? Regarding Abra-

---

[125] Berachot 26b

ham, it says he "עָמַד/amad/stood" before the Lord.[126] Regarding Isaac, we are told that he "לָשׂוּחַ/lasuach/conversed" with God.[127] As for Jacob, he "וַיִּפְגַּע/vayifga/encountered" God.[128] David "spoke and moaned," and Daniel "kneeled" and "offered thanks." The use of all of these various terms indicates that there was no one, definitive practice. What was consistent was merely that they allotted time to withdraw from their work and worldly matters in order to seclude themselves with God. Does the Torah offer us any further guidance on what prayer essentially is and how precisely we are to go about it?

<hr/>

Origins Of Prayer

There are two primary components of daily service which were ordained in the Torah a millennium before the liturgy was established by the Great Assembly. The first is the commandment to recite the Shema every morning and evening:

שְׁמַע יִשְׂרָאֵל יְ-הֹוָה אֱ-לֹהֵינוּ יְ-הֹוָה אֶחָד: וְאָהַבְתָּ אֵת יְ-הֹוָה אֱ-לֹהֶיךָ בְּכָל־לְבָבְךָ וּבְכָל־נַפְשְׁךָ וּבְכָל־מְאֹדֶךָ: וְהָיוּ הַדְּבָרִים הָאֵלֶּה אֲשֶׁר אָנֹכִי מְצַוְּךָ הַיּוֹם עַל־לְבָבֶךָ: וְשִׁנַּנְתָּם לְבָנֶיךָ וְדִבַּרְתָּ בָּם בְּשִׁבְתְּךָ בְּבֵיתֶךָ וּבְלֶכְתְּךָ בַדֶּרֶךְ **וּבְשָׁכְבְּךָ וּבְקוּמֶךָ:**

*Shema Yisroel A-donai E-loheinu A-donai echad. V'ahavta es A-donai E-lohecha b'chol levavcha u'v'chol nafeshecha u'v'chol meodecha. V'hayu hadevarim ha'eileh asher Anochi mitzavcha hayom al levavecha. V'shinantem levanecha v'dibarta bam b'shivtecha b'veisecha u'v'lechtecha vaderech **u'v'shachbecha u'v'kumecha.***

Hear O Israel, The Lord is our God; the Lord is one. And you shall love the Lord, your God, with all your

<hr/>

[126] Genesis 19:27

[127] Genesis 24:63

[128] Genesis 28:11

heart and with all your soul, and with all your means. And these words, which I command you this day, shall be upon your heart. And you shall teach them to your sons and speak of them when you sit in your house, and when you walk on the way, and **when you lie down and when you rise up**.

(Deuteronomy 6:4-7)

The last words of these verses instruct us to speak the words of the Shema "when you lie down and when you rise up." From here the sages deduced that the Shema must be pronounced at the beginning and the end of each day. In terms of reciting specific verses on a daily basis, this is the extent of what the Torah mandates. As such, we find that the recital of the Shema is the crux and origin of daily prayer. Regardless of what else they may or may not have said or done, we know that those who were devoted to serving God through the Torah's instructions would recite the Shema morning and evening. If they did nothing else, through the pronouncement of the Shema they would satisfy their recital requirement. In order to understand the essence of prayer, then, we must appreciate the meaning and intention of the Shema. We have begun to explore this prayer earlier in chapter one,[129] and we will examine it further in the following section.

The second commandment from the Torah that dictates a particular form of daily service is the offering of "karbonos / sacrifices" on the altar in the Tabernacle in the desert and the Temple in Jerusalem.

וְאָמַרְתָּ לָהֶם זֶה הָאִשֶּׁה אֲשֶׁר תַּקְרִיבוּ לַי-הֹוָה כְּבָשִׂים בְּנֵי־שָׁנָה תְמִימִם שְׁנַיִם לַיּוֹם עֹלָה תָמִיד: אֶת-הַכֶּבֶשׂ אֶחָד תַּעֲשֶׂה בַבֹּקֶר וְאֵת הַכֶּבֶשׂ הַשֵּׁנִי תַּעֲשֶׂה בֵּין הָעַרְבָּיִם:

V'amarta lahem zeh ha'isha asher takrivu l'A-donai kevasim bnei shana temimim shnayim layom olah tamid. **Es hakeves echad taaseh baboker v'es hakeves hasheini taaseh bein ha'arbayim.**

And you shall say to them: This is the fire offering which you shall offer to the Lord: two unblemished lambs in their first year each day as a continual burnt offering. The **one lamb you shall offer up in the morn-**

---

129 Section "The Only One"

ing, and the other lamb you shall offer up in the afternoon.

(Numbers 28:3-4)

Sacrifices were offered by individuals from the time of Adam, as
we see in the fourth chapter of Genesis when Adam's sons Cain and Abel
each bring offerings to God. However, the command to bring daily offerings - one in the morning and one in the afternoon - was not instituted
until the construction of the "mishkan/tabernacle" in the desert in the
first year after the Exodus from Egypt. From this time onward, the
priests would offer sacrifices each day on behalf of the entire nation. This
practice lasted until the destruction of the Temple in Jerusalem. It was
then that the sages of the Great Assembly established the formalized
prayer service in order to substitute for the sacrifices which could no
longer be offered. The daily prayers thus took the place of the physical
offerings, as it is stated by Rabbi Yehoshua ben Levi in the the Talmud:

תְּפִלּוֹת כְּנֶגֶד תְּמִידִין תִּקְנוּם:
Tefillos k'neged temidin tiknum.
The prayers were established corresponding to the dai-
ly offerings.

(Talmud, Berachos 26b)

The prophet Hoshea stated the same idea more poetically:

וּנְשַׁלְּמָה פָרִים שְׂפָתֵינוּ:
U'n'shalma parim sifaseinu.
Let us render [for] bulls [the offering of] our lips.
(Hoshea 14:3)

The words of prayer would fulfill the intention and responsibility that had previously been effectuated by the sacrifices. But what is the
relationship between prayers and sacrifices? How do words that we utter
substitute for animals that were slaughtered and burned? In order to
draw this correlation, we must understand the meaning and purpose of
sacrifices in general. How did the animal offerings demonstrate our devotion to God, and why was this very graphic and bloody act such a focal aspect of our divine service?

Uncovering And Uniting

As we have seen, the two primary components of daily service in the Torah are the recitation of the Shema and the performance of "karbonos/sacrifices." If we analyze the liturgy that is memorialized in Jewish prayer books today, we will find that these continue to serve as the backbone of the daily devotional service. "Shacharis," the morning prayer, includes four primary elements:

1) **karbonos/sacrifices**
2) Pesukei d'zimra/Verses of Praise
3) **Shema**
4) Amida/the silent standing prayer.

The two main components of "Mincha," the afternoon prayer, are:

1) **Karbonos/sacrfices**
2) Amida/the silent standing prayer.

And "Maariv," the evening service consists of:

1) **Shema**
2) Amida/the silent standing prayer.

While other elements have been added - namely the "Verses of Praise" in the morning service and the "silent standing prayer" in all three daily services - if we want to understand the essence of Torah prayer and how it serves as an integral element of our daily liberation practice, we can do so by first paring it down to its original components, and then exploring the need for the sages' additions.

As we mentioned, the original and exclusive commandment in the Torah regarding the daily repetition of a citation from scripture is the recital of the Shema. What is it about this particular verse that is so significant that of the nearly 6,000 verses in the five books of Moses, God selected this one to be the subject of our daily focus and concentration?

In chapter one,[130] we touched on the centrality of the Shema prayer in Torah practice and on the profound depths of meaning that are contained within this seemingly simple verse:

שְׁמַע יִשְׂרָאֵל יְ-הֹוָה אֱ-לֹהֵינוּ יְ-הֹוָה אֶחָד:

Shema Yisrael A-donai E-loheinu A-donai echad.
Hear O Israel, the Lord or God, the Lord is One.
(Deuteronomy 6:4)

At first glance, and on the simplest level of its interpretation, the verse is a statement of monotheism. At the time of the giving of the Torah, the idea of One God was revolutionary in an environment of paganism and polytheism. Yet, as we discussed, while monotheism was a tremendous innovation in the ancient world, the ultimate contribution of this verse was even more profound. On its deeper level, the verse is a declaration not only of God's sole rulership, but of His unique and sole existence. What the verse tells us is not merely that there is one God, but that God is One and there is nothing other.

Simply stated, this awareness of God's complete oneness, and our fusion and inclusion in this unity, is the point and goal of all prayer. To go a step further, this is not merely the objective of prayer, but, as we have discussed throughout this book, the recognition and revelation of God's absolute oneness is the aim and intention of everything we do. We have repeatedly explained that the purpose of our existence is summarized in both the very first verse of Torah, "Breishis bara Elokim es hashamayim v'es ha'aretz/the primary thing is to reveal God in the heavens and the earth," and the very first commandment that God assigned to the first Jew, Abraham, "lech lecha/go to (find) yourself." Internalizing and manifesting God's oneness discharges both of these tasks. Finding and exposing the "Pnei Hashem" within us is the fulfillment of the commandment "Lecha lecha" - in finding God's face within us, we discover who and what we truly are. Identifying and disclosing that same "Pnei Hashem" in the root and core of all things is the fulfillment of "Breishis bara Elokim" - for we have revealed the Godliness that permeates and comprises every aspect of creation. We can understand, therefore, why the Torah commands us to focus on the Shema at the be-

---

130 Section "The Only One"

ginning and end of every day. It is a concise statement of the elemental truth that we have been created to discover and to disseminate.

From this fundamental component of the daily service, we can now comprehend what prayer is supposed to be. It is the time that we pause from our engagement in the physical world in order to contemplate the deeper nature of our existence and to reconnect to our source. We do so (at least) three times daily because the nature of our "olam/ world" is "helam/hiddenness," and without frequent breaks and reminders, we are easily lost in the darkness. The truth of God's unity is quickly obscured and forgotten. Creating us in a realm where His oneness would intentionally be concealed, God thus commanded us to close our eyes multiple times each day in order to shut out the distraction and dissimulation of the sensate world so that we are able to reconnect with the invisible truth within.

The daily recitation of Shema is therefore one of the key components of the practice that Torah provides us in order to help us find the "Pnei Hashem" in our "pnimyus." But in order to reach our inner depths, we must be able to discard or penetrate the many layers of the physical world that cover and conceal them. This is precisely the "kavana/intention" of the service of "karbonos/sacrifices." The word "קָרְבַּן/karbon/ sacrifice" is derived from the root "קרב/karov," which means "close." The implication is that we become close to God by offering Him sacrifices. But how is it that one becomes closer to the divine by slaughtering and burning an animal?

As we mentioned briefly in chapter seven,[131] the inner meaning of the sacrifices was the consumption of the physical flesh and the eradication of the animal casing that conceals the spirit within. It is the "animal" aspect of ourselves that covers and constrains our spiritual essence. As we also touched on in the same chapter, and as we developed further in chapter eight,[132] the Alter Rebbe characterizes life as a constant battle between our "nefesh Elokis/Godly soul" and our "nefesh habehamis/ animal soul," like two rival armies vying for control over one city. When the animal soul is strengthened, the Godly soul is suppressed, and when the animal soul is weakened, the Godly soul is able to assert and express

---

[131] Section "Fearlessness"

[132] Section "Shearing and Shining"

itself. We must therefore reduce the vitality of the animal within us so that our Godly essence is able to radiate. Ultimately, the goal is not to destroy the animal, but to subdue it and utilize its strength in the service of the spirit. In this sense, the sages taught:

רַב־תְּבוּאוֹת בְּכֹחַ שׁוֹר:

Rav tevuos b'koach shor.
There is much gain in the power of the ox.
(Proverbs 14:4)

When we are able to control the animal and enlist its strength and speed, we can accomplish far more labor and cover greater distances. However, in this physical realm where brute strength often dominates and where the spirit is frequently overpowered, in order for the animal to be mastered and harnessed, it must first be 'slaughtered' and 'cooked.' In other words, it must be broken and refined. As the vast majority of the Temple sacrifices were consumed as food, this concept of utilizing the strength of the animal for divine service was tangible and explicit. While the animal's spirit was liberated from its corporeal casing and thereby reunited with its source, its flesh was consumed by the priests and those who brought the offering, and thereby its energy was incorporated into the bodies of those who would utilize it to continue their mission of revealing God in His creation.

This physical sublimation, whereby the brute strength of the animal would be elevated through the labor of the human, was paralleled on the spiritual level as well. When one offered her/his actual livestock and adopted its energy through consuming its meat, s/he simultaneously intended the metaphysical offering of her/his animal soul for the service of the Godly soul. The "kavana/intention" was to devote not only the strength of the body, but also the passions of the animalistic inclinations, to the pursuit of her/his divine purpose and task. Recognizing that God had implanted the soul into a corporeal form for a reason, one would resolve daily to utilize the body and all of its capacities to further the mission which s/he had been assigned.

When the Temple was destroyed and the ritual of animal offerings was discontinued, this spiritual "kavana/intention" of the sacrifices persisted even without its physical counterpart. In the prayer service today, "karbonos/sacrifices" is the first of the four segments of the morning service. One recites the chapters from scripture that describe the sacrifices in the Temple, and s/he reads sections from the Talmud that discuss the laws of how and where the offerings were processed. In so doing, we "render [for] bulls [the offering of] our lips," substituting our words for our livestock. Though the physical experience may be dramatically different, the intention is not. The actual animals were always a material manifestation of the animal soul. Though we no longer slaughter livestock and place them on the fire of the altar, we continue to offer the animal within us, breaking its control over us and harnessing its strength for the service of our deeper essence.

This symbolism is apparent even in the Torah's original commandment of the material sacrifices. In the opening verse of the book of Leviticus where the sacrifices are introduced, God spoke to Moses, saying:

אָדָם כִּי־יַקְרִיב מִכֶּם קָרְבָּן לַי-הֹוָה מִן־הַבְּהֵמָה מִן־הַבָּקָר
וּמִן־הַצֹּאן תַּקְרִיבוּ אֶת־קָרְבַּנְכֶם:

Adam ki yakriv mikem karbon l'A-donai min habehema min habakar u'min hatzon takrivu es karbonchem.

When one sacrifices from [among] you a sacrifice to the Lord; from animals, from cattle or from the flock you shall bring your sacrifice.

(Leviticus 1:2)

The sages question the order of the verse, noting the strange arrangement of its opening words. They are simply interpreted to mean 'when one of you sacrifices a sacrifice...'. However, if this were the true intent of the verse, then the word "מִכֶּם/mikem/of you," should have been placed after the first word "Adam/one," thereby reading "one of you." In its current placement, "mikem" instead modifies "ki yakriv/who sacrifices." Therefore the opening of the verse more literally translates as "when one sacrifices of you a sacrifice" - in other words, when one brings a sacrifice, it is "of you." It is part of yourself that must be offered.

As we have seen previously with other examples of Torah's wording, the order is precise, and the variant interpretations represent the "pshat/simple reading" of the verse and its "sod/secret meaning." On the simple level, the verse is introducing the laws of sacrifice, and

begins by laying out the scenario, "when one of you brings a sacrifice...."
But on its deeper level, this very first verse on the subject of sacrifices is
informing us of the mystic "kavana/intention" underlying all offerings:
whether it is the physical offerings in the Temple or "the offering of our
lips" that will substitute for bulls after the Temple has been destroyed,
the true offering is "mikem/of you." It is the animal aspect of ourselves
that must be slaughtered and consumed so that its energy can be harnessed and so that the "Pnei Hashem" which our flesh conceals can be
liberated and expressed.

The Most Important Verse

From the two aspects of our daily devotional service that were
commanded directly in Torah, Shema and "karbonos/sacrifices," we
have come to understand the essential aim and intention of prayer. The
focal point of our service is Shema, the recognition and manifestation of
God's absolute and exclusive unity; and the mechanism through which
we can achieve this epiphany of the Shema is "karbonos/sacrifices," the
removal of the fleshy coverings that block and conceal the face of God
within us.

In the preface to the Midrash "Ein Yaakov,"[133] there is a fascinating conversation amongst the sages regarding which verse in the Torah is
the most important. Four verses are suggested by various rabbis, and
among them are the two that we have been discussing. The sage Ben
Zoma opines that it is the Shema:

שְׁמַע יִשְׂרָאֵל יְ-הֹוָה אֱ-לֹהֵינוּ יְ-הֹוָה אֶחָד:
Shema Yisrael A-donai E-loheinu A-donai echad.
Hear O Israel, the Lord or God, the Lord is One.
(Deuteronomy 6:4)

---

[133] One of the primary works of biblical interpretation and commentary from the
Talmud, compiled by Rabbi Yaakov ibn Habib and his son Rabbi Levi ibn Habib
in the 16th century.

The sage Shimon Ben Pazi asserts that the most important verse in Torah is the one that establishes the daily sacrifices:

אֶת־הַכֶּבֶשׂ אֶחָד תַּעֲשֶׂה בַבֹּקֶר וְאֵת הַכֶּבֶשׂ הַשֵּׁנִי תַּעֲשֶׂה בֵּין הָעַרְבָּיִם:

Es hakeves echad taaseh baboker v'es hakeves hasheini taaseh bein ha'arbayim.

One lamb you shall offer up in the morning, and the other lamb you shall offer up in the afternoon.

(Numbers 28:4)

Based on our previous analysis, it would seem that Ben Zoma is correct, and the answer would be the Shema. What greater insight does the Torah provide than the secret of God's absolute oneness? However, the sages rule in favor of Shimon Ben Pazi and conclude that the most important verse in all of Torah is the the verse from the book of Numbers that legislates the daily offerings. This seems odd, particularly in light of our assertion that the enlightenment of the Shema is the ultimate aim, and "karbonos/sacrifices" are simply the means by which we peel back the veils to reveal this precious insight.

The sages' selection is even more puzzling when we consider the other two options that were offered as contenders. The sage Ben Nanas suggested the verse "v'ahavta l'reaicha kamocha/love your fellow as yourself," the import of which we have discussed at length in chapter seven.[134] The sage Ben Azai proposed the verse "b'yom b'roh E-lohim adam b'dmus E-lohim asa oso/on the day that God created man, in the likeness of God He created him."[135] We have mentioned in chapter five[136] how profoundly significant it is for us to know that we are created in God's image. Both of these verses would also seem to be better candidates for the Torah's most important verse than the seemingly mundane and procedural verse about the daily sacrifices. Yet it is the latter which the sages ultimately selected.

---

[134] Section "Radiating Love"

[135] Genesis 5:1

[136] Section "Human Nature"

Various answers have been offered to justify the sages' conclusion. Some have suggested that the verse's focus on daily service stresses the value of consistency and selfless devotion, both of which are crucial for the fulfillment of our mission. Others submit that the verse reveals how precious our small mortal service is to the infinite God. While these explanations have tremendous merit, we can also understand the sages' selection as an indication of something even deeper. That is the extraordinary significance of "karbonos/sacrifices" in the very meaning and purpose of our creation. This will come as a surprise to many who consider the sacrificial service to be a primitive and barbarous rite which has no place in our modern spiritual consciousness. But when we grasp the profound inner dynamics that the sacrifices represent, then we can appreciate the sages' choice, and we will see that "karbonos/sacrifices" are the crux of what we have been created to do. Our very mission in this world is the removal of the animal and physical coverings that conceal the truth of God's singularity. He created the world as a veil for His unity, and He created each of us to remove the veil and to thereby reveal Him beneath the surface of everything.

We can now understand why the daily prayer service begins with the recital of "karbonos/sacrifices." While many either skim or even skip this segment of the service completely, the daily "reenactment" of the sacrifices with genuine "kavana/intention" creates immense impact within us and within the world around us. As we awaken in the morning, the very first thing we do in our initial moments of consciousness is pronounce the words "modeh ani lefanecha." As we discussed at length in chapter four,[137] the deeper meaning of this verse is an awareness of the pure Godliness that is hidden within us. "I acknowledge Your face," and I admit that it is within me though it is not visible. Our goal throughout the day will be to progress from "modeh/acknowledgement" of something that we cannot see, to "baruch/revelation" of this truth, bringing it to a clear and manifest reality. Therefore, we immediately set out to remove the layers that conceal it. In order to do so, we begin the morning service with the recital of the sacrifices.

As we read of the animals being consumed in the fire of the altar, we imagine placing our own animal - our very body and material self - on the fire and burning away the crust that covers and eclipses our God-

---

137 Section "From Knowing to Showing"

ly core. We allow the flames to burn off the outer husk, the fleshy garments that have become sullied through our engagement in the dirt and grime of our physical engagements. Simultaneously, we inhale deeply and draw in the fire so that it can move through our interior and incinerate all of the muck and mold that has grown within us from our egoistic thoughts and emotions. As we allow our cloak to smolder on the fire of the altar, we draw the fire inward and burn away the micro-lesions that have invaded our innermost spiritual organs. With every inhale we send this cleansing fire through our system, and with every exhale we breathe out a dark mist laden with soot and dross. Finally, we can breathe freely and fully, our airways clear and our essence clean. We are unshackled and unburdened from the heavy outer carapace, and we have cleansed the inner fungus that has obscured the face of God within our deepest recesses. Our "pnimiyus" can radiate and shine with no blockage and our skin has become translucent. The fire has consumed our "עוֹר/ohr/skin" (ohr spelled with an "ע/ayin"), and reveals our "אוֹר/ohr/light" (ohr spelled with an "א/aleph"). Just as God originally clothed Adam and Eve in a "כָּתְנוֹת אוֹר/kasnos ohr/coat of light" which was then transformed to a "כָּתְנוֹת עוֹר/kasnos ohr/coat of flesh" after the eating of the apple, we now reverse that process by burning away the coat of flesh and revealing the coat of light which is beneath it.[138] Like Adam and Eve before the apple, our skin no longer conceals our essence and depths, but rather it transmits them.

It is important to reiterate that the goal is not to destroy the body in the fire, but to refine and elevate it. Throughout this process of "performing" the "karbonos/sacrifices," we have decided that in the coming day we will harness and utilize our animal rather than allowing it to control us. We have taken our animal to the altar, and claimed its vitality rather than subjecting ourself to its strength. We allow the flames to burn away the crust, but our body does not expire or dissolve. Rather, cleansed of its filth, it reveals itself as incandescent. It is not simply transparent, allowing that which is beneath it to be revealed, but it is radiant and resplendent. It is 'magnificent' in the sense that it 'magnifies' the gleam of the light that glows within it.

---

[138] See chapter six, section "Skin and Light"

It is a mistake to believe that we must nullify the body/self in order to liberate the soul/infinite that is trapped within. The truth is that the infinite has implanted itself within the self for a good reason: because the self, shorn of its selfishness, can amplify it. How is it possible to amplify the infinite? By revealing it in the finite, and thereby conveying it somewhere where it could not possibly exist. This is the miracle and paradox of our existence. The infinite soul is contained by a finite body, and then through that body it is expressed within a realm of finitude and limitation. To nullify the body would simply be a reversion to the spiritual unity that existed before the creation. If the goal were simply to get back to where we began, then we may as well have not been at all. On the contrary, the aim is to transmute the self. In this way, it is not merely that the body/self will no longer be cloaking the infinite soul; and not only that it will now allow the soul to pass through unobstructed; but it will come to project and augment the infinite soul by rendering the invisible visible and the impossible possible.

This is the power of "karbonos/sacrifices." And this is the meditation that accompanies the recitation of the sacrificial service each morning and afternoon. We begin the day by extracting ourselves from the bounds imposed by our gross materialism and the self-centrism that it engenders. We resolve that in the day ahead we will allow our "pnimyus/inner core" to be manifest and to irradiate our surroundings. By afternoon, we must recite "karbonos" again. Our dealings with the world throughout the day have already encumbered and encrusted us anew. There is yet another animal for us to offer up on the altar. And so it goes daily. We constantly work to burn away the shell that delimits us, and to refine the body that conveys and communicates us. In so doing, we are ever moving *closer* to God by removing the aspect of ourself and of the universe that keeps us distant from Him. This explains why sacrifices are called "karbonos" from the root "karov" meaning "close." And yet as close as we come, our job is never complete. As long as we exist in a physical body (at least until the messianic age), there will always be a barrier that interposes between us and our source, and we will always be required to offer ourselves daily and to thereby draw ever closer and thus allow the face of God to beam through us. We thus understand why the sages have determined that the verse "one lamb you shall offer up in the morning, and the other lamb you shall offer up in the afternoon" is the most important verse in Torah. The daily removal of our animal crust - and by extension the physical covering that conceals God throughout the creation - is precisely what the Torah was given us in order to do.

***

More Darkness, More Light

Now that we have explored the origins and foundations of prayer, we are left with a question. If the two components of Shema and "karbonos/sacrifices" are the essence of the Torah's conception of daily prayer, then why does the liturgy today include more than these two original elements? As we mentioned previously, the morning prayer is comprised of four sections: 1) "karbonos/sacrifices," 2) "Pesukei d'zim-ra/verses of praise," 3) Shema, and 4) "Amida/silent standing prayer." The afternoon prayer includes both 1) "karbonos/sacrifices" and 2) "Ami-da/silent standing prayer." And the evening prayer includes both 1) She-ma and 2) "Amida/silent standing prayer." Why are these additional sections necessary, and why is the silent standing prayer included in all three daily services?

The Alter Rebbe explains that while the Shema is the primary focus of prayer, the other elements of the daily service were instituted in order to help us to experience the Shema properly. While the command-ment of the Shema is literally to speak the words "Shema Yisrael A-donai E-loheinu A-donai echad/Hear O Israel, the Lord our God, the Lord is One" - as it says, "vedibarta bam/you shall speak them" - the goal is that this recitation will bring us to a profound state of love and awe as a result of the revolutionary insight that the words express. If we have merely vocalized the verse, but the words have not elicited in us a pow-erful emotional response, then while we may have discharged the legal responsibility of the commandment to say the Shema, we have certainly not exploited its powerful spiritual potential. This, the Alter Rebbe ex-plains, is why the verse of the Shema is followed immediately by the subsequent verse:

וְאָהַבְתָּ אֵת יְ-הוָה אֱ-לֹהֶיךָ בְּכָל-לְבָבְךָ וּבְכָל-נַפְשְׁךָ וּבְכָל-מְאֹדֶךָ:

254

> *V'ahavta es A-donai E-lohecha b'chol levavcha u'v'chol*
> *nafeshecha u'v'chol meodecha.*
> And you shall love the Lord your God with all of your
> heart, and all of your soul, and all of your might.
> (Deuteronomy 6:5)

While this can be read as a directive which is requiring us to love God, it can also be read, and is better understood, as a statement of fact and a natural outcome. In such a reading, God is not commanding us to love Him - after all, how can you dictate someone's emotions. He is informing us that we will necessarily love Him when we recite the previous verse (Shema) properly. When one internalizes the truth of God's complete unity which is expressed in the words of the Shema, then s/he will inevitably experience an overwhelming sense of love. Why is this so? Because love is connection. It is the sense of being utterly bound up and united. And with the declaration of God's singularity, we realize (or remember) that we are completely one with Him. We cannot help but be stirringly moved by this remembrance of what God is and what we ultimately are.

Nevertheless, it is quite possible, and quite common in fact, that our articulation of this earth-shattering truth every morning and evening will not inspire in us such a powerful emotional response. This is an indication that we have not fulfilled the recitation of the Shema ideally, and we have not achieved the absolute oneness that the verse expresses. As the nature of our "world/olam" is "hiddenness/helam," it therefore buries our essence under a multitude of coverings. The Hebrew word for nature, "עֶבַע/teva," shares the root of the word "טוּבַע/tuba," which means "sunken." This is because we become so habituated to our daily routines within the natural/physical world that our senses become muffled and dulled as if we are under water. In other words, the repetitious nature of our existence desensitizes us to the miracles that occur around us constantly. Our heart is encrusted, and it must be circumcised constantly (see chapter eight, section "Bris Milah") in order to peel away its wrappings and allow it to express the deep emotions that dwell within it.

Therefore, the mere recitation of the Shema will not necessarily suffice to arouse in us the tremendous love and connection that it is intended to stimulate. While this may have been sufficient for the patriarchs and matriarchs and for our ancestors to whom the Torah was given, one thousand years later the sages of the Great Assembly determined that additional elements should be added to the daily service in order to assist us in evoking the proper astonishment and rapture. Our ancestors who left Egypt and traveled through the desert were witness to constant miracles and explicit expressions of God's presence. In the succeeding generations, throughout the times of the tabernacle and then the Temple in Jerusalem, fire descended from heaven onto the altar to consume the sacrifices, and the people were thus visually exposed to God's immanence regularly. But when the temple was destroyed and the conspicuous miracles ceased, it became more challenging to maintain a connection to the divine. Rather than seeing manifestations of God with one's fleshy eyes, one would have to close her/his eyes and remind her/himself of God's omnipresence with her/his inner vision. As the generations continue on and the time of revelation becomes ever more distant, it grows increasingly difficult to arouse in oneself a recollection of the divine truth and the love and awe that it provokes. For this reason, prayer becomes an ever more vital part of our daily practice. And as it requires more labor for us to connect with God's oneness and to arouse the resulting love from within us, therefore additions have been made to the daily service in order to help us uncover and expose our Godly core.

The first addition is the "Pesukei D'Zimra/Verses of Praise" section of the morning service that we recite between the reading of "karbonos" and the recitation of the Shema. This collection of psalms, other scriptural citations, and prayers composed by the men of the Great Assembly, is intended to assist us in building up to the epiphany of the Shema, as the Alter Rebbe writes:

ועל דבר זה תקנו גם כן כל כל סדר התפלה קודם קריאת
שמע, כדי שיקבל עליב בקריאת שמע ואהבת באמת.

V'al davar zeh tiknu gam kein kol seder hatefilla kodem krias shema, kdei she'yikabeil alav b'krias Shema v'ahavta b'emes.

And for this was also established all of the order of prayers before the reading of Shema, in order that one should truly receive love upon himself in the reading of the Shema.

(Torah Or, parsha Ki Tissa, p.85:3)

In this sense, we can understand why prayer is traditionally referred to as a ladder in Torah tradition. The image originates in the
dream of Jacob when he slept on the mountain that would later house
the Temple. He dreamt of a ladder that rested on the ground and climbed
into the heavens with angels ascending and descending.[139] The Zohar
interprets the dream to be a reference to the service of prayer which connects the heavens and the earth and enables us to climb out of our mundane existence to experience deeper and more ethereal levels of reality.
The Midrash[140] specifies that Jacob's ladder had four rungs, and that
these correspond to the four sections of the morning prayer. From this
we see that each component of the service is a preparation for the elevation that will come after it.

The first rung is "karbonos/sacrifices," removing the coarse animal covering that contains and conceals us, as we have discussed at
length in the previous sections. Once we have done so, we can climb to
the next rung, "Pesukei D'zimra/Verses of Praise," in which we begin to
focus on the Godliness that exists beneath the surface. The word "Zimra"
derives from the root "zemer," which literally means "song," and several
parts of this section are traditionally sung aloud. A chassidic proverb
teaches that while words are the pen of the mind, song is the quill of the
soul. This section of prayer gives voice to the soul so that it can express
and assert itself. The root "zemer" also means "to prune" or cut. As we
recite these verses of song, we are also continuing to cut through the external coverings that remain even after we have offered our animal in the
service of "karbonos/sacrifices." Like an onion, there are layers upon
layers that veil our inner essence, and as quickly and diligently as we
prune them away, they grow back and enwrap us once again. Therefore,
our focus on this second rung of the prayer service is two-fold and is expressed in the dual meaning of its name pesukei d'**zimra**: we are **cutting**
away the external as we **sing** to give expression to the internal.

Singing brings us not only to our own "pnimyus/inwardness,"
but also to the "Pnei Hashem/Face of God" that is hidden within our

---

[139] Genesis 28:12

[140] Megaleh Amukot 1

"pnimyus." We have mentioned this in chapter two[141] with the citation of the verse from Psalms:

עִבְדוּ אֶת־יְ-הֹוָה בְּשִׂמְחָה בֹּאוּ לְפָנָיו בִּרְנָנָה:

*Ivdu es A-donai b'simcha, bo'u **lefanav** b'renana.*
Serve God with joy, come **before Him** with singing.
(Psalms 100:2)

As we have seen many times already, the word "lefanav" is simply translated as "before Him" or 'in His presence,' but it literally means "to His face." Through our singing, therefore, we are trying to find and reveal the "Pnei Hashem." This intention is expressed at the very outset of this section in the initial verses of the "Hodu" prayer which (in the Chassidic and Sephardic traditions) serves as the opening of the section of "Pesukei D'zimra": "Yismach leiv m'vakshei Hashem/Happy of heart is the one who seeks God" and "bakshu panav tamid/seek His face always."[142] Our goal in the first section, "karbonos/sacrifices," was to clear away the external barriers that block our entry inward. Our intention on this second rung of the ladder is to delve far beneath the surface and to plumb our depths in search of the Godliness that has been buried and forgotten through our engagement in the material world.

This theme of opening and discovery is underscored by another verse that we already devoted extensive attention to in chapter six. One of the focal points of this second section, "Pesukei D'Zimra," is the "Ashrei" prayer and its verse "poseach es yadecha, u'masbea l'chol chai ratzon/You open Your hand and satisfy every living thing's desire."[143] As we discussed at length, this verse expresses one of the fundamental thrusts of our entire divine service: opening the structures and strictures of this finite realm in order to access the infinite reality that lies within and beyond them. We ask God to "poseach/open" His "yud," which represents the rational and orderly conduct with which He directs this finite realm. We can then reach and activate His "ratzon/will," which is

---

[141] Section "Singing in the Dark"

[142] See chapter two, "The Joy of the Search" for more on these verses

[143] Psalms 145:16

supra-rational and beyond all judgment and strict justice.[144] We simultaneously work to "poseach/open" the "yid/Jew," to penetrate all of our own limitations and constrictions. In opening ourselves in this way, we can allow God's infinite bounty both to flow into us and to radiate forth from our core.[145] Here again, we see that the theme of this second rung is infiltration and illumination.

From "Ashrei," the section of "Pesukei D'Zimra" moves on to a series of five psalms which are the five concluding chapters of the book of Psalms (chapters 146-150). Each of these Psalms begins and ends with the word "halleluy-ah." This term has great significance in Torah, and we explored it in detail in chapter four.[146] It is a compound of two words, "הַלְלוּ/hallelu," which means "praise," and "יָ-הּ/Y-ah," which is a name of God that represents His hidden essence. The simplest understanding of the word is therefore "praise God." However, as we pointed out, "hallel/praise" of God is difficult to understand. Why does the infinite God want or need our praise? When we analyze the deeper meaning of the term "hallel," we see that it comes from the root "hil" which means to light or ignite, as in the verse from the book of Job "BeHILo nero alai roshi/He lit His candle over my head."[147] "Halleluy-ah" therefore is an act of lighting up "יָ-הּ/Y-ah," or illuminating the Godliness that is hidden within us. It is fanning the spark within our innermost core so that it glows more brightly and is therefore easier for us to find. This is the primary objective of this second rung of the ladder. We are working to make the Godliness within us more apparent and accessible so that when we reach the third rung, Shema, we are more easily able to experience God's oneness.

After these five "halleluy-ah" psalms, the "Pesukei D'zimra" section continues with the reading of the story of the splitting of the Red Sea.[148] This is one of the most renowned narratives in the Torah. As the fledgling nation left the bonds of slavery in Egypt, Pharaoh and his army

---

144 See chapter six, section "Yadecha"

145 See chapter six, section "Yidecha"

146 Section "Halleluy-ah"

147 Job 29:3

148 Exodus 14:30-15:18

pursued them and trapped them at the sea. God then split the waters so that the people could pass through on dry land. When the Egyptian army followed into the sea-bed, the waters crashed down onto them and drowned them. The liberated slaves emerged unscathed, and sang a joyous song of gratitude which would become known as the "Shir shel yam/song of the sea."

While this was one of the greatest and most illustrious miracles of all time, we might wonder why this story is read daily in our morning prayers. On the simple level, the recitation of the most renowned song from the Torah, the *"Song* of the Sea," is a fitting selection for this section of "Verses of Song." However, on a deeper level, the mystics explain how this story fits into the process of opening and revelation that we are to engage in as we begin each new day (and which is specifically the function of this second rung of the prayer ladder). The sea represents the hidden world. Unlike the land, where the surface teems with a vast array of life, the surface of the oceans conceals the incredible diversity that dwells beneath it. The splitting of the sea therefore symbolizes the opening of the external covering so that one can explore and expose the depths beneath. This represents the ultimate deliverance from slavery, because one cannot truly be free until s/he is liberated from the veils and barriers that hide and constrict her/his ultimate truth. If we are not aware of our Godliness, then we will forever believe that we are "only human." But when we will peel back the surface and recognize our infinite nature and potential, then we will never again be enslaved or suppressed.

On an even more Kabbalistic level, the Alter Rebbe explains[149] that the spiritual idea of the "yam/sea" represents the barrier between the upper realm where God is completely revealed, and the lower realms where He has hidden Himself in order to allow for the ability of otherness to exist. As we have discussed previously, if God's oneness were fully manifest, then it would be impossible for anything other to be, just as there can be no individual flames in the orb of the sun. He therefore "contracted" Himself, so to speak, in order to create a place of darkness where His light was not apparent. He then clothed tiny fragments or sparks of Himself within "kelipos/shells" so that they would consider themselves distinct and individual. Between this area of darkness and

---

[149] *Likkutei Torah*, maamar Sheishes Yamim

the infinite light that is beyond it, there is a protective layer that deflects the light so that it does not penetrate the darkness. If the infinite light were able to penetrate into the darkness, it would obliterate it completely. Therefore, this barrier between the two realms is what maintains and assures the existence of our world. The barrier is called "yam/sea." On the day when the sea was split, God allowed that barrier to be opened so that His infinite light could pour into the darkness and enable His people to "see" all that had been hidden from them until then.[150] This was their ultimate liberation, and the death of the Egyptian army in the sea represented the inability of anyone to enslave them any further now that they understood their inherent Godliness and God's absolute unity.

The sages instituted the reading of the story of the splitting of the sea each morning in "Pesukei D'zimra" because our intention is to open within us the barrier that divides between our limited world and our infinite reality. As we do so, we conclude this second section of the service, and we are ready to climb to the third rung of the ladder where we will fully experience the ecstatic epiphany of the recitation of the Shema.

Bringing It Down

We have discussed the third rung at some length. However, in truth we could devote this entire book to an analysis of the Shema (in fact there are a number of Chassidic and Kabbalistic works that do just that), and we would still be unable to plumb all of its depths. Our goal here has been to expound on the basic fundamentals of Torah prayer and to demonstrate how it serves as a primary component of the daily practice that enables us to find the hidden face of God. Therefore, we will not delve much further into the Shema beyond what we have explained already in the previous sections and in the very first chapter.[151] We will simply reiterate that it expresses the central tenet of the Torah, which is

---

[150] We will discuss this subject in more depth in chapter ten, section "Splitting Open."

[151] See chapter one, section "The Only One"

the unequivocal declaration of God's absolute unity. The awareness of this ultimate reality is the goal of our daily meditation, coupled with the love and awe that it inspires. Yet there is a fourth rung on the ladder of prayer, indicating that the intellectual consciousness and the emotional arousal which the Shema stimulates are not the end of the process or the summit of our aspirations.

After the recital of the Shema in both the morning and the evening, we rise and recite the "Amida," the silent standing prayer. In the afternoon prayer, we also recite the "Amida" after the reading of "karbonos." This is therefore not only the highest rung of the four-tiered ladder in the morning service, it is also the only element of prayer which we perform in all three of the day's services. Though the "Amida" was not mentioned in the Torah itself, it was instituted by the sages of the Great Assembly because it fulfills the ultimate function of prayer which was in danger of being lost after the destruction of the temple. Just as "Pesukei D'zimra" was added before the Shema in order to assist us in reaching the immense epiphany of the declaration of God's absolute oneness (as we explained in the previous section), so was the "Amida" added after the Shema in order to then enable us to direct the profound energy of that experience into the action that it was intended to effectuate.

The goal of Torah is not simply to alter our consciousness or elevate us to an experience of spiritual bliss. Rather, it offers us enlightenment and rapture specifically in order for us to then change and fix the world. We climb the ladder not simply in order to rise above the creation, but rather in order to intermittently reconnect with the divine so that we can then descend and reveal God within the darkness and confinement of the physical realm. This task and responsibility was understood by our early forebears. The patriarchs and matriarchs and the early generations of their progeny recognized that through the recitation of the Shema, their job was not merely to transcend the world, but to then transform it by introducing this radical knowledge of God's oneness into their surroundings. This is expressed within the recitation of the Shema itself. As we discussed in the previous section, the first verse of the Shema is followed by the verse "v'havta es A-donai E-lohecha / And you shall love the Lord your God...."[152] Love is not simply an emotion, but also a desire. It is not merely a feeling of something, but it is a longing for

---

[152] Deuteronomy 6:5

something. As the Alter Rebbe points out,[153] the word "אַהֲבָה/ahava/ love" is etymologically related to the word "תאב/taev/desire." When we love another, we are not only united with her/him, but we also long to do for her/him, or to give to her/him. As such, the result of the stunning revelation of God's oneness is not only adoration and awe, but also an intense yearning to give to Him, to respond with some reciprocity to His incredible generosity to us. What is it that we can possibly give to the infinite God? The spreading of the awareness of His presence throughout the darkness of His creation.

The early generations understood what it meant to be a "light unto the nations" in this way. But after the destruction of the temple, as the nation was exiled and its light was dimmed, it became not only more difficult to connect with one's inner glow, but also to radiate it. Therefore, the "Amida" was established in order to memorialize the task of illumination that was intended to be the outcome and summit of our daily prayer. How does the "Amida" fulfill this function? The silent standing prayer is a series of nineteen (originally eighteen) blessings, each of which concludes with the phrase "Baruch Atta A-donai/blessed are You God," followed by a phrase that summarizes the content of that particular blessing. On a simple level, these blessings can be understood as entreaties, ranging from requests for wisdom, to forgiveness, to redemption, to health, prosperity, etc. However, the Alter Rebbe explains the more mystic and essential "kavana/intentionality" that underlies the entire "Amida" prayer:

שעיקר המכוון בתפלה הוא, שמבקשים שיהיה אור אין סוף ב"ה שלמעלה מהשתלשלות "ברוך" ונמשך למטה בבחינת ההשתלשלות.

She'ikar ha'mchavin b'tefilla hu, she'mvakshim she'yihyeh ohr ein sof baruch hu she'lemaaleh me'hishtalshelus "baruch" v'n-imshach lemata b'bechinas ha'hishtalshelus.

The main intention in prayer is, that we request that the infinite light of God that is above the creation should be brought down and drawn down below into the aspect of the creation.

(Likkutei Torah, Parshas Balak, Lo hibit)

---

[153] *Likkutei Torah*, Parshas Naso, Koh T'varchu Bnei Yisrael

This intention of drawing Godliness down into the world is the inner meaning of the word "Baruch/Blessed," as we discussed in chapter four.[154] There we indicated that the root of "Baruch," בּ-ר-ך, means to "draw down," as in the word "מַבְרִיךְ/mavrich." This term is utilized in the Talmud in the phrase *"hamavrich es hagefen,"* meaning to "draw down a vine" in order to plant it in the ground so that it grows a new plant.[155] The root is also found in the word "בְּרֵיכָה", which means "pool," a place where water has descended and settled. When we say "Baruch Atta A-donai/Blessed are You God," we are thus intending that God should be brought down and revealed within the depths of this world. More specifically, the kabbalists teach that "Atta/You" refers to a level of God that is so high that it is beyond any name, and "A-donai" is the name of God that symbolizes His emergence into this realm.[156] Therefore, "Baruch Atta A-donai" is a formula in which we are verbalizing our intention to "baruch/bring down" the transcendent level of "Atta" into the level of "A-donai" which connects Godliness to the creation.

It should be noted that when we say "bring down," we are not referring to an actual spatial dynamic. Similarly, when the Alter Rebbe discusses the light of God that is "above the creation," he does not mean to describe God's location in a physical or geographic sense. Spatial terms like "above," "below," "beyond," "within," "up," and "down" in this context refer, rather, to the extent of revelation or concealment in regards to our consciousness. When we say that something is above or beyond the world, we mean that it is not apparent. When we draw Godliness down into the world, it means that we are revealing it within our own consciousness and making it more accessible to the consciousness of those around us. God is not actually "removed," "distant," or "detached" from any part of the creation. On the contrary, there is no part of the universe that is not completely and exclusively God, as we have already established in our understanding of the Shema. Yet He has "con-

---

[154] Section "Blessed Are You"

[155] Sotah 43a

[156] See chapter six, section "Yudecha" for a detailed analysis of how the name Yud-Hei-Vav-Hei, which we pronounce as A-donai, depicts the process of the creation of the world.

tracted Himself," so to speak, in order to allow for the existence of other-ness. Therefore, because He is not seen or recognized, we describe Him as being "above" or "beyond" us, and our task is to "bring Him down." Doing so does not actually "bring" or transport Him to a place where He was not already; it rather reveals His presence in a place where it was previously unnoticed.

It is also crucial to understand that when we say "heights" or "heavens," we are not referring to a realm that is literally above us or in the sky. When we "climb" the ladder of prayer, we are "delving inward" as much as we are ascending upward. We are moving toward ever greater depths within us as we are scaling ever greater heights beyond us. As we have discussed in many places throughout this book, what we are seeking ultimately is the "Pnei Hashem," the face of God which is hidden "beneath" all of the layers of concealment in which He has em-bedded and hidden Himself. This "PaNiM/face of God" is to be found in the "PNiMyus/inner core" of everything. This is what we are acknowl-edging with the exclamation of the Shema, and this is what we are trying to expose with the "Amida" and each of its nineteen expressions of "Baruch Atta A-donai." While "baruch" means "bring down," its true connotation is bringing OUT and making manifest something that was previously inconspicuous.

This said, we can now appreciate the "Amida" as a series of rep-etitions of this phrase "Baruch Atta A-donai." Each of the nineteen bless-ings which are concluded by this phrase represents the "bringing down" or revealing of Godliness through various aspects of our existence. After we have reached the awareness of God's unity in the Shema, we now pronounce these nineteen blessings in order to take this "lofty" wisdom "down" into the "lowest" realms (or we can alternatively say, in order to take this "deep" wisdom "out" into the "most superficial" realms). With this, we can understand why the "Amida" is considered a fourth rung on the ladder, even "higher" than the third rung of the Shema. If we are now conveying what we gathered on the third rung "downward," then why is this described as another ascent in level rather than a descent or return? The answer is because the height of our service is not elevation but dissemination. We are paradoxically most high when we descend most low. We are closest to God when we bring Him into the world in which He seems to be absent. Therefore, although the Amida is a process of bringing down, it is a tremendous elevation and the pinnacle of our prayer service.

This idea of elevation through descent is one of the hallmarks of Torah and one of the most precious insights that distinguishes it from other forms of spiritual wisdom. While other wisdom systems have taught that the pursuit of Godliness and personal development will lead one to transcend the material and retreat from the exigencies of the physical world, Torah teaches that the apex of self-actualization is complete involvement with the world. While other disciplines offer mountain-top temples and retreat centers that remove one from the daily grind in order to encounter the divine, Torah tells us that Godliness is found nowhere more than where you are. While priests, monks, and leaders of various spiritual systems practice celibacy, asceticism, and various forms of abstinence, Torah ordains that all, including the most holy leaders and teachers, must seek marriage, intimacy, procreation, and full engagement in bodily affairs.

Gluttony is surely forbidden, and numerous Torah practices are intended to train us to control our bodily drives and passions rather than allowing them to control us. But the Torah life is not one of denial and divorcement from the physical. On the contrary, every day is a process of removal and then return. The mystics refer to this as "ratzo v'shov/running and returning." Our soul is like a flame that flickers upward, constantly reaching toward the heavens, but holding fast to the wick and remaining below to shine its light in the darkness of this world. Our prayer service represents this flickering and this "running and returning." We pray three times daily to temporarily remove ourselves from the world and reconnect to our core, but we end each of those services with the "Amida," reciting "Baruch Atta A-donai" nineteen times in order to come back into the world and bring with us the Godliness that we have encountered in the heights and depths of our soul.

We are able to accomplish this by making ourselves completely open to the Godliness that exists within us and allowing it to flow through us. At the very beginning of the "Amida," before we even begin the first of the nineteen blessings, we recite the verse:

אֲ-דֹנָי שְׂפָתַי תִּפְתָּח וּפִי יַגִּיד תְּהִלָּתֶךָ:

A-donai sifasai tiftach ufi yagid tehillasecha.

Lord open my lips and let me declare Your praise.
(Psalms 51:17)

We have discussed this verse earlier in chapter seven,[157] where we explained that we are asking God to allow us to be a vessel through which He can express Himself. We are acknowledging, after the recitation of the Shema, that we are nothing but an instrument through which God can play His divine music. We then allow our lips to be opened, and the blessings of the "Amida" spill forth, channeling the light from the "Pnei Hashem" that is in our "pnimyus" out into the environment that surrounds us.

Meditation

There is so much more to say about Torah prayer. But what we have hopefully conveyed in this very brief introductory section on the subject is that a) the function of prayer is far more about introspection and revelation than supplication, and b) this daily practice is a central component of our lifelong liberation process. While the prayer service does include requests to God for sustenance, health, and other physical needs, these serve primarily as an external layer and a point of entry into our relationship with the divine. As a child (or an adult who is new to Torah practice and is therefore still "young" in her/his level of connection and understanding), we are taught to pray for our needs three times daily in order to remind ourselves that there is something greater than us, and we are not ultimately in control. As we mature in our conception of ourselves and our world, we begin to recognize that what we ultimately require and desire from God is assistance in penetrating the veneer of our existence so that we can perceive our essential nature. As such, we come to see that *the four-tiered ladder of prayer can best be understood as a directed meditation* which conducts us on a (thrice) daily journey from concealment to revelation.

---

[157] Section "Radiating Love"

Prior to prayer, we are engrossed, consumed, and submerged in the facade of our material circumstances. Our individual concerns and travails have engulfed us and blinded us to our universality. As we begin to pray, we peel away the particularities and expose the underlying divine. We unplug ourselves from the web of sensate stimuli that barrage us and adhere us to the surface. We descend inward beneath the veil, and we climb upward above the fray. The words of our prayer are an extended mantra, the rhythm and repetition of which enable us to transcend the cacophony of our busy lives. The stream of scriptural passages that we recite supplants the constant stream of self-referential thoughts from our psyche that keep us grounded and stuck. We begin to sing, and the melody carries us deeper and higher. As we reach "Shema Yisrael…", it is a whispered crescendo, and we bask in the reunification with everything that we had considered foreign and other. In this ecstatic state of communion and intimacy, we are not nullified, but unified. This Oneness does not render us meaningless, it makes us sacred. Our task is not to get out of the way, but to prepare the way, and ultimately to be the way in which God is expressed where He was previously concealed. In this, God not only loves us, not only desires us, not only requires us, but God is us![158] This connotes that we are purely, simply, and gloriously the Godliness that manifests through us.

This is the height of the awareness and mindfulness that we seek to attain and then convey through the meditative journey of prayer. On the first rung of "karbonos," we pare away the gross physicality that inevitably encrusts us through our involvement in the world. On the second rung of "Pesukei D'zimra," we then fan the flame of the fire of God that crouches in our core in order to make it more visible and accessible. On the third rung of "Shema," we recognize that the light of the divine fire within us is the ultimate truth and reality of all things. And on the fourth rung of the "Amidah," we then bring that awareness and enlightenment down and out into expression and revelation. By the time we have completed our prayer, we are luminescent and serene. The world cannot bother us, deter us, or contain us. We are infinite, we see God in everything, and we are ready to express God in all that we touch and do.

---

[158] Do not confuse 'God is me' with 'I am God.' You are not God, you are an expression of God, who is the One and Only being. The difference is subtle, but important.

Torah - From Prayer To Study

Having climbed the ladder of prayer, we are ready to go forward into the new day from the very lofty level that we have described in the previous section. Our intention for the day ahead is clear - in everything we do, we are to be like a torch that dispels the darkness for all those with whom we come in contact. However, the clarity with which we leave the house of prayer is ephemeral and incredibly hard to maintain. The "helam/hiddenness" of our "olam/world" is so thick and dark that the moment we abandon our focus, we are liable to tumble from the ladder and lose consciousness of our inherent Godliness. Though we have just devoted considerable time and effort to peeling away the crust that conceals our core, it grows on us again so quickly that we are once again disoriented and enshrouded in darkness as soon as we involve ourselves in worldly pursuits.

It is as if we live in a dark cave deep beneath the earth's surface, and every morning upon awakening we make an arduous journey through a network of ascending tunnels to reach the surface where a fire constantly burns. There, we light a torch from the fire and then descend again through the tunnels to our cave in order to provide light for ourself and our tribe. But on the way back down, the torch is extinguished. When we reach the cave, we are once again cloaked in darkness. However, we immediately become engrossed in our daily concerns, and therefore we forget that there is an alternative to this blind existence.

Even if we had succeeded in reaching the greatest insights of God's complete oneness in Shema, and we had subsequently focused our intention on bringing that oneness down into the world through the recitation of the "Amidah," we can (and the vast majority of us generally do) leave the house of prayer no different and no more enlightened than we were when we arrived. The Alter Rebbe addresses this tendency to immediately lose our focus after prayer:

כִּי הִנֵּה אָנוּ רוֹאִים בְּחוּשׁ שֶׁאַחַר תְּפִלַּת שְׁמוֹנָה עֶשְׂרֵה חוֹזֵר לִהְיוֹת כְּבָרִאשׁוֹנָה.

Ki hinei anu roim bchush sheacharei tefillas shemona esrei chozer l'hiyos k'barishona.

For we see clearly that after the amida prayer one returns to be as s/he was previously.

(Likkutei Torah, U'shaavtem mayim b'sasson, ch. 4)

Why does this happen? How is it that we can work so diligently to uncover our core, but in a mere moment, it is once again hidden from us? This is because "eretz ocheles yoshveha/the land consumes its inhabitants."[159] This phrase was uttered in the desert one year after the nation had been liberated from Egypt. The people had received the Torah on Mount Sinai, and God now instructed them to enter the land of Canaan. But the nation was reluctant to leave the desert. They sent twelve spies to assess the land, and when the spies returned, they advised the nation to remain in the desert, saying that "the land consumes its inhabitants." On the simple level, their implication was that it was a treacherous land which was inhabited by fearful giants who would destroy them. But on a deeper level, the chassidic masters explain that it was not their physical wellbeing that concerned the people, but rather their spiritual welfare. In the desert, they were fed by manna that fell from the heavens, and they drank from a well that miraculously followed them as they traveled. Their clothes grew on their bodies and they were cleansed by the clouds of glory. They were not encumbered with physical pursuits or bodily needs. Upon entering the land, however, these miracles would cease, and they would be required to work the ground and provide for their daily needs. This material involvement with the land would "consume" them, and they would be unable to devote themselves fully to the meditation and study of Torah which enabled them to maintain their closeness to God.

This is indeed the nature of the world we inhabit, and the concern is valid. Our physical trappings and our material engagements do distract us from our essence and our purpose. Nevertheless, God did not intend for us to inhabit the desert. He did not create us so that we would

---

[159] Numbers, 13:32

live a sequestered and miraculous existence, removed from the challenges of the world. On the contrary, He wants us to enter the land in
spite of its tendency to consume us. There, within the strivings and
struggles of daily existence, He wants us to make Him apparent. If God
resides only in the rarefied and supernatural realms, then He is not infinite at all. It is our task to reveal Him even in the most mundane depths
where He is least obvious and accessible. How can we do so? Only by
being simultaneously within the world and beyond the world. We must
engage material existence without being enslaved and blinded by it.

The first step to achieving this precarious balancing act is prayer,
as we have just discussed. We establish regular times each day to step
out of the world in order to maintain our awareness of its transience and
its inability to hold us. But this is only a first step. Meditation and consciousness are not sufficient to contend with the darkness and urgency of
the material world. Prayer is like a retreat to the calm and quietude of the
desert. But if we are to leave the desert and return to the din of "civilization," then we will need to infuse our elevated consciousness into something worldly and tangible so that it will not remain relegated to the celestial heights. The Alter Rebbe tells us precisely how to do so:

אַךְ לִהְיוֹת בְּחִינָה וּמַדְרֵיגָה זוֹ קְבוּעָה וּנְטוּעָה בְּלֵב הָאָדָם כָּל
הַיוֹם שֶׁלֹא יָמוֹט מִזֶה ... הָעֵצָה הָאֲמִיתִית הוּא עֵסֶק הַתּוֹרָה
וְהִלְכוֹתֶיהָ.

*Ach l'hiyos bechina u'madrega zu kevua u'netua b'leiv
haadam kol hayom shelo yimot mizeh … ha'eitza ha'amitis hu
esek haTorah v'hilchoseha.*

But in order that this lofty level should be fixed and implanted in the heart of the person the entire day so that
s/he shouldn't lose it … the true counsel is to labor in
Torah and its laws.

(ibid)

This guidance is found not only in the esoteric writings of Chassidus, but also in the exoteric teachings of the Code of Jewish Law, which
states "from the house of the prayer to the house of study."[160] The implication is that the study of Torah immediately after prayer ensures that

---

[160] Shulchan Aruch, Orach Chaim 155:1

we will not lose the insights that we had worked so diligently to uncover in our meditative service. How does Torah study do so?

In order to answer this vital question, we must comprehend what Torah study is. Like prayer, which, as we explained in the beginning of this chapter, is commonly misunderstood, so too the study of Torah is often misconstrued. This is because Torah is frequently characterized too narrowly as a book of legality and morality. Indeed, Torah is a book of law and ethics, but it is also far more than that. To limit Torah to its legal and ethical code is tremendously reductionist. It is like referring to the sea as a gathering of water, or the galaxy as a series of stars. There is so much more to the sea than water, and so much more to the galaxy than stars. And there is so much more to Torah than law and ethics. Yet there are those who commit their entire lives to the study of Torah, but they never launch beyond the orbit of its rules, and they never paddle beyond the surf of its procedural disputations to reach its true depths and expanse. To be clear, the contemplation and analysis of the Torah's systems of judicial and societal legislation is a holy and imperative endeavor. Furthermore, one could spend every day of his life probing the intricacies of the Torah's legal arguments, and still never exhaust the wealth of wisdom and insight that is contained within them. However, if one delves no deeper than the Torah's revealed and intellectual plane, then s/he will know only the iceberg's tip, and not the vast majority of its mass that remains concealed beneath the water's surface.

Torah is not a book, it is a relationship. It is not merely a legal code, it is a marriage between each of us and God. It is not merely a volume of guidance, it is a map of both our soul and of the universe. It is a microscope that penetrates the nucleus of every nucleus, and a telescope that pierces the farthest reaches of the heavens. Torah is a cipher that encodes the spiritual within the physical. It converts infinity into every grain of matter, and it trains our eye to detect the celestial in even the most base and mundane creation.

There are those who study Torah endlessly and feverishly in order to amass knowledge, understanding and wisdom. But the goal of Torah is not knowledge, understanding and wisdom as we commonly conceive of them. All of these terms (in their English connotation) imply an acquisition of something that the learner did not previously possess. They confer upon her/him an increase in comprehension and capability.

In this conception of Torah as wisdom, one may selflessly pursue its study in order to become more deeply versed and fluent so that s/he can pursue God's ways and teach them to others. Less altruistically, one may study it in order to achieve a higher level or status. Either way, Torah is seen as something that one must acquire in order to grow and rise. Study, therefore, becomes a type of commerce or livelihood - the more I invest in study, the more I earn in knowledge, and the more reward I will be granted for my efforts. There is a truth to this calculus, in that Torah does yield wisdom and does elicit reward. But that is only the surface of Torah, and not its deepest intent or potential. The knowledge, understanding, and wisdom that we ultimately seek through Torah study is not an acquisition, but rather a surrender. We study Torah not in order to *gain something*, but rather in order to *lose everything* that prevents us from channelling and transmitting God's wisdom and will.

We can see this through the Hebrew terms for knowledge, understanding, and wisdom. "Knowledge" in Hebrew is "דעת/daas." To "know" something in the Hebrew or "biblical" sense is to fuse with it completely, as in the Torah's expression of Adam's relationship with his wife:

וְהָאָדָם **יָדַע** אֶת־חַוָּה אִשְׁתּוֹ וַתַּהַר וַתֵּלֶד אֶת־קַיִן:

*V'haadam **yada** es Chava ishto vatahar vateled es Kayin.*
And the man Adam **knew** Chava his wife and she became pregnant and gave birth to Cain.
(Genesis 3:1)

It was through Adam "knowing" his wife that she became pregnant. Knowledge is intimacy because to truly know something means to unite with it in order to experience it fully. Similarly, "understanding" in Hebrew is "בינה/binah," which the mystics explain to be a compound of two words, "בן/ben/son" and "י-ה/Y-H/God." The deepest understanding is the awareness that we are God's offspring, born of Him and carriers of His "genes" or image. "Wisdom" is "חכמה/chochmah" in Hebrew, which, as we discussed in chapter seven,[161] is comprised of the two words, "כח/koach/power" and "מה/mah/what." True wisdom is "the power of what," the ability to ask 'what am I,' and to know that I am nothing but an expression of Godliness. We therefore find that each of these terms describes a relationship. Through Torah study, we fuse and unite with God. We recognize that we are His seed that He implants in the material world. The wisdom, understanding, and knowledge that we seek through Torah is not something that makes us greater or more substantial, but on the contrary, it nullifies us, unifies us with God's infinity, and enables us to be a clear and open vessel through which He can be revealed in His creation.

With this new characterization of Torah study, we can better understand the sages' directive that one should proceed daily "from the house of prayer to the house of study." We can also comprehend the Alter Rebbe's guidance that it is through Torah study that one will be capable of holding on to the clarity of purpose that s/he attained by ascending the ladder of prayer. The study of Torah, we now see, is not simply a process of learning and gaining information, it is a method of drawing the depths of God's essence into manifestation. As we saw earlier in this chapter,[162] this was precisely the goal of the fourth rung of the ladder of prayer, the recitation of the "Amidah," the silent standing prayer. With its nineteen blessings ending in "Baruch atta A-donai," the intention of the "Amidah" is to take the insight of God's absolute oneness that we gained in the Shema and to convey it downward into the material realm. Torah study is therefore not a distinct activity, but rather a continuation of the same process. Yet Torah provides a mechanism through which the abstract ideation and meditation of prayer can be captured and directed before it dissipates and floats off into the atmosphere.

The connection to the divine that we achieve through prayer is on the level of the soul, a level so lofty and spiritual that is difficult to hold onto. It is like smoke, or vapor, completely invisible and intangible. A somewhat more accessible level is the plane of the intellect. Ideas are still beyond the reach of the physical senses, but we can "grasp" an idea with our brain, which is both the seat of the intellect and a physical organ. Through Torah, God enables us to utilize the intellect to take soul concepts, which are completely ethereal and therefore ephemeral, and garb them in something graspable. By going "from the house of prayer to the house of study," we transform the spiritual heights that we reached in our prayers into something that we can integrate and carry

---

[162] Section "Bringing It Down"

with us throughout the entire day. Torah's laws and narratives concern the physical world, connecting the infinite to the finite and enabling us to tether the heavens to the ground. We can thereby create a bridge that unifies the previously distinct aspects of our being.

It is important to remind ourselves here that Torah is comprised of many different levels, as we discussed in chapter six.[163] There we identified the levels of "sod/secrets" of Torah, which pertains to the deeper, mystical significance of every word and verse, and "pshat/simple meaning," which is the way the Torah applies to our physical reality. These levels can also be referred to as "nistar," which literally means "hidden" and refers to the Kabbala and the arcane mysteries of the universe, and "nigleh," which means "revealed" and refers to the legal dimensions of Torah and the way it applies to societal and inter-relational dynamics. While study of "nistar" is an integral part of our liberation practice in that it exposes us to the depths that exist beneath the surface, the Torah study that we are discussing here, and which the Alter Rebbe prescribes after prayer, is specifically "nigleh." We see this from the Alter Rebbe's wording, "the Torah and *its laws*." It is the exoteric and the legal aspects of Torah that convey the esoteric heights down into the physical creation and thereby enable us to transform our lives and the world.

In other words, in order for us to liberate ourselves from the "helam/hiddenness" of this "olam/world," it is not simply through study and contemplation of the Torah's secrets. Rather it is specifically by bringing the deep mystic truths of creation down into the mundane material realm that we can free ourselves from our existential captivity. We do this through the study and practice of the Torah's legal code. That said, it is also crucial that we don't allow ourselves to become so mired in the Torah's legality and practicality that we lose sight of its transcendence. In this regard, the Baal Shem Tov taught that one should pause every hour in the midst of Torah study in order to connect and cleave to God. For this, the Baal Shem Tov was criticized by many Torah sages who argued that this interruption was "bittul Torah," an unnecessary "nullification of Torah study." They demanded that one should rather devote every possible moment to increasing one's Torah knowledge. The Baal Shem Tov responded that the ultimate aim of Torah study is connecting to God, and that if one fails to pause and consider the nature of

---

her/his relationship and unity with God, then while s/he may be amassing a tremendous amount of information, s/he is missing the entire point.

With this fusion of both the transcendent and practical dimensions of Torah, we can now understand how Torah study is another integral component of our daily liberation practice. The study of Torah is essential not only in order to know God's laws and ethics, and not only in order to live a life of meaning and spiritual growth. Torah, as we've seen, is the mechanism through which we can convert and condense our spiritual reality into an intellectual blueprint. What began as a flash of inspiration is now brought down into a detailed system and plan of action. What was formerly just an idea of divine unity is now a methodology through which that unity can be made manifest. Beyond some abstract notion of being freed from the many veils that cover and conceal our essence, we now have a very tangible and systematic approach to implementing our liberation.

But we don't stop here. Now that we have translated our divine consciousness into a blueprint, it is time to move to the next step and render our ideas and intentions into action. This continuation of the process is accomplished through the performance of daily mitzvos.

Mitzvos - From Study To Action

We began our day with prayer in order to climb above our physical reality and remind ourselves of our Godly essence and our divine purpose. From the house of prayer, we went directly to the house of study in order to take the profound insights that we gained through our meditation and capture them in a systematic intellectual framework so that they don't drift back into the ethers and leave us groping in the dark. From the house of study, we now set out into the world of action in order to implement our plan and fulfill our task of revealing God in the depths of His creation. We do this through every aspect of our engagement with the physical world. Most of this engagement is regulated by various mitzvos in order to provide us the opportunity to bring Godliness directly into the most mundane and ordinary aspects of existence. If we wonder why there are so many mitzvos and why they apply to so many details of our lives, this is precisely the reason.

Like prayer and Torah study, which, as we have explained, are commonly misunderstood, mitzvos are similarly subject to frequent misinterpretation and limitation. Simply perceived as laws or rules to keep us in line or to test and gauge our devotion and obedience, mitzvos are in fact much more. While the 613 mitzvos of the Torah do in fact legislate our interaction and behavior, they were established by God not simply in order to delimit our lives or to enforce His rulership. They are intended to provide us a means by which we can fuse heaven and earth by introducing Godly intentionality into base materiality. As we mentioned previously, the word "mitzvah" derives from the root "tzav," which means "command," but it is also etymologically related to the Aramaic "tzavsa," which means "bond." By performing mitzvos, we are not merely fulfilling God's commandments, but we are also creating bonds through which we connect and unite this lowly world with its ultimate divine source and reality. The mitzvos are therefore not a burden that God foisted upon us in order to control and subjugate us. They are rather a gift that He bestowed on us in order to enable us to unite with Him in intimacy and actuality.

Thus, as we complete our daily regimen of prayer and Torah study through which we have focused our consciousness and intellect on the task of revealing God's unity throughout the day ahead, we then move into the workday world to activate and actualize that intention. Work itself is a mitzvah, as we are commanded to earn a livelihood with which we can sustain ourselves and our family. Additionally, we are commanded to donate at least ten percent of our earnings to those in need. Therefore, our labor enables us to fulfill the mitzvah of "tzedaka/charity," which the sages equate to all of the other mitzvos combined. Furthermore, our interactions in the marketplace - whether it is the actual marketplace of goods and services or the marketplace of ideas, depending on what type of work we do - will provide us innumerable other mitzvah opportunities. These can range from the detailed regulations on fair business practices to the ethics of proper speech and interpersonal relations. Throughout the course of an average day, every one of us will perform numerous mitzvos, each of them providing us the opportunity to infuse our environment with another spark of Godly light. The mystics describe every aspect of this world as a kernel of God that is encased in a shell, known as "kelipah" in Hebrew. When we engage that portion of the world properly, we crack the shell and reveal the divine light that was hidden within it. When we are provided with a mitzvah opportunity and we neglect it, however, we leave the "kelipah/shell" intact, and we render the Godliness within it undetected and untapped.

What we begin to recognize then is that the daily order that the Torah prescribes is a progression that lifts us out of the world and then lowers us back into it. As we had mentioned earlier in this chapter,[164] this is the constant fluctuation of "ratzo v'shov/running and returning," like a flame that flickers upward toward its source, but holds fast to its wick in the lower realms. It does so in order to serve its purpose of providing light in the darkness. Similarly, when we return below through Torah study and then mitzvos, we carry with us that light which we had gathered above through climbing the ladder of prayer. But as we descend, we must convert what we are conveying into a form in which it can be contained and utilized. In prayer, we reached up and grabbed the spiritual. With our soul's "hand," so to speak, we grasped something that is beyond the world. Through Torah study, we then utilized the fingers of our mind, so to speak, and brought it down into the intellect, which is still amorphous, but is at least related to the world. Finally, through mitzvos, we transfer it onto our fleshy and physical hand, infusing it into action, and literally marrying the Godly with the material.

We might compare this to a common chemical process by which a substance is condensed from a vapor to a liquid and then a solid. In prayer, we are dealing with divine breath (which speaks through our mouths, as we discussed above regarding the verse "God open my lips and let me declare Your praise"). With Torah, which is commonly compared to life-giving waters, we have brought God's whisper down into a more tangible and relatable form. But like liquid, it is still shapeless and unembodied. And so we move on to mitzvos, and through them we convert this liquid into a palpable and malleable solid with which we can influence and perfect our world.

Modeh To Baruch

This progression from the ethereal to the tangible reflects a process that we have discussed multiple times throughout this book: the transition from "modeh" to "baruch." As we have explained, "modeh" is acknowledgement of something we admit but cannot see, and "baruch" is revelation to the extent that we can clearly see what was previously only acknowledged.[165] We begin each day with the statement "**modeh** ani lefanecha/I acknowledge Your face," reminding ourselves that God's "panim/face" is our ultimate reality and admitting to its presence within our "pnimyus/innermost dimension" even though we cannot perceive it. Our task, today and everyday, will be to move from this situation of "modeh" to a state of "baruch" in which the existence of God's face within the core of all things is clearly manifest. Thus, as we begin our prayer with "modeh ani," we then climb the four-tiered ladder of the morning service and consummate it with the "Amida" and its nineteen blessings of "**baruch** atta A-donai." As we finish praying, we have clearly internalized this intention to draw Godliness down into actuality. However, it is not until we move into the realm of mitzvos that we are able to actually do so. How do mitzvos accomplish this?

We have discussed in the previous section how mitzvos translate the Godly into the material, but we must still wonder whether the face of God is any more "baruch/revealed" through the performance of mitzvos than it was previously? In order to answer this question, we must determine what it means for God's face to be manifest or revealed. What is it that we are actually praying for when we say "baruch atta A-donai" and intending that You, God, should be "baruch/brought down" into the world?

We touched on this idea earlier, when we first introduced the deeper connotation of the word "baruch" in chapter four.[166] There, we explained that the ultimate goal of "bringing God down" is to enable the truth of His oneness to emerge from its obscurity and to become overt. Progressing from "modeh" to "baruch" is moving from "knowing" to "showing," from being aware of something intellectually to making it

---

[165] See chapter 4, section "From Knowing to Showing"

[166] Section "Blessed Are You"

obvious and universally apparent. But what, precisely, does this mean? Is it a sensory experience whereby every sentient creation will be capable of literally seeing God's presence in the physical world? Or is it a matter of consciousness, an inner vision through which all will know of God's oneness in spite of the seeming multiplicity that appears to our audiovisual senses?

This question gets to the very essence of our life's purpose and task. If, as we have asserted repeatedly, our mission is laid out in the opening verse of Torah - "Breishis bara E-lohim es hashamayim v'es ha'aretz/the primary thing is to reveal God in the Heavens and the earth" - then in order to fulfill this duty, it is imperative for us to understand what this "revelation" means. If being "ohr l'goyim/a light unto the nations" connotes, as we established in the very first chapter, that our charge is to share with all the people of the world the message that God is hidden beneath every aspect of the veil of creation, then is it enough for us to simply shout this message from the rooftops? Or is there some resulting transformation of the nature of existence that is required for us to know that we have properly discharged our assignment? Clearly, the implication of "revelation" seems to be more than the simple introduction or publication of an idea. We must first understand what it is to "reveal God in the heavens and the earth," and only thereafter can we explore the issue of how to go about doing so.

According to Torah, there were times in history when Godliness was seen explicitly within the physical phenomena of the material world. The plagues in Egypt, the splitting of the sea during the Exodus, and the events at Mount Sinai are all examples of miraculous conduct where the natural order was altered to reveal God's mastery and supremacy. So clear was God's existence and presence during these supernatural events that the people were able to declare:

זֶה אֵ-לִי וְאַנְוֵהוּ:
Zeh E-li v'anvehu.
This is my God and I will enshrine Him.
(Exodus 15:2)

On this verse, Rashi comments:

בִּכְבוֹדוֹ נִגְלָה עֲלֵיהֶם וְהָיוּ מַרְאִין אוֹתוֹ בְּאֶצְבַּע, רָאֲתָה
שִׁפְחָה עַל הַיָּם מַה שֶׁלֹּא רָאוּ נְבִיאִים:

B'kvodo nigleh aleihem v'hayu marin oso b'etzbah, raasa shifchah al hayam mah shelo ra'u neviim.

He revealed Himself in His glory to them, and they pointed at Him with their finger. By the sea, [even] a maidservant perceived what prophets did not perceive.
(Rashi, Exodus 15:2)

It is the word "זֶה/zeh/this," from the phrase "*this* is my God," that informs Rashi's commentary on this verse. In various places in Torah, we find both the words "זֶה/zeh/this" and "כֹּה/koh/*like* this." The latter term, "koh," implies an idea, or something that is envisioned or understood but not clearly seen. "Zeh," on the contrary, connotes clarity of vision and palpability. The use of this term informs Rashi that God was so conspicuous and present at the splitting of the sea that every individual there could point to Him and say 'there He is.' As a matter of fact, the degree of vision was so remarkable at that moment that Rashi asserts that even those with the least spiritual perception could then see more than the loftiest prophets could ordinarily see. Prophets generally spoke in the language of "koh/like this." Other than Moses, prophets usually received their prophecy in dreams while they slept. Only when they were divorced from the fetters and distractions of the material world could they attune to their inner vision and receive the word of God. Yet there were extraordinary moments, like the splitting of sea, when prophetic vision was granted to all.

From here we see that the actual vision of God was extremely rare, not only to the average person, but even to those with prophetic powers. There was, however, a place and a time when Godliness could be seen plainly and regularly. In the tabernacle in the desert, and subsequently in the Temple in Jerusalem, fire descended from heaven daily to consume the sacrifices on the altar.

וַתֵּצֵא אֵשׁ מִלִּפְנֵי יְ-הֹוָה וַתֹּאכַל עַל-הַמִּזְבֵּחַ אֶת-הָעֹלָה
וְאֶת-הַחֲלָבִים וַיַּרְא כָּל-הָעָם וַיָּרֹנּוּ וַיִּפְּלוּ עַל-פְּנֵיהֶם:

Va'teitze aish milifnei A-donai va'tochal al hamizbe'ach es ha'olah v'es hachalavim vayar kol ha'am vayaronu va'yiplu al p'neihem.

And fire went forth from before the Lord and consumed the burnt offering and the fats upon the altar, and all the people saw, sang praises, and fell upon their faces.

(Leviticus 9:24)

Throughout the nearly 900 years (2449-3338 on the Hebrew calendar, or1312 BCE to 423 BCE) that sacrifices were offered in the tabernacle and the first temple, God's presence was thus visible through the form of fire descending from heaven.[167] However, other than brief periods of miraculous conduct like the Exodus from Egypt and the ensuing forty years in the desert, and other than very specific locations (the site of tabernacle and then the Temple in Jerusalem) millennia ago, throughout the vast majority of human history, and in the vast majority of places throughout the earth, God's presence has not been physically discernible. Are we to conclude, then, that throughout the ages, the mission of revealing God and being a light unto the nations has not been fulfilled? Can we suggest that even the most devout and accomplished Torah sages throughout history have failed to accomplish their mission? Is our duty discharged only if and when the world witnesses miracles akin to the splitting of the sea when each of us can point and say "zeh E-li/this is my God"?

To complicate matters even further, we find that even the witnessing of miracles is not the "revelation of God in His creation" that we are tasked to manifest. This is evident from a verse that Moses speaks to the nation soon before his death:

וַיִּקְרָא מֹשֶׁה אֶל־כָּל־יִשְׂרָאֵל וַיֹּאמֶר אֲלֵהֶם אַתֶּם רְאִיתֶם אֵת כָּל־אֲשֶׁר עָשָׂה יְ-הֹוָה לְעֵינֵיכֶם בְּאֶרֶץ מִצְרַיִם לְפַרְעֹה וּלְכָל־עֲבָדָיו וּלְכָל־אַרְצוֹ: הַמַּסּוֹת הַגְּדֹלֹת אֲשֶׁר רָאוּ עֵינֶיךָ הָאֹתֹת וְהַמֹּפְתִים הַגְּדֹלִים הָהֵם: וְלֹא־נָתַן יְ-הֹוָה לָכֶם לֵב לָדַעַת וְעֵינַיִם לִרְאוֹת וְאָזְנַיִם לִשְׁמֹעַ עַד הַיּוֹם הַזֶּה:

Vayikra Moshe el Kol Yisrael vayomer aleihem, atem r'isem es kol asher asa A-donai l'einechem b'eretz Mitzrayim l'paroh u'l'chol avadav u'l'chol artzo. Hamassos hagedolos asher ra'u

---

[167] There is an argument amongst the sages whether fire descended from heaven during the period of the second temple as well. See Talmud Yoma 21b

einecha, ha'osos v'hamofsim hagedolim haheim. V'lo nassan A-donai lachem leiv ladaas v'einayim liros v'aznayim lish-moa ad hayom hazeh.

And Moses called to all of Israel and said to them, "You have seen all that the Lord did before your very eyes in the land of Egypt, to Pharaoh, to all his servants, and to all his land; the great trials which your very eyes beheld and those great signs and wonders. Yet until this day, the Lord has not given you a heart to know, eyes to see and ears to hear."

(Deuteronomy 29:1-3)

Here Moses informs us that the miracles that the nation witnessed in Egypt and during the Exodus did not represent true vision. In spite of the perception of these signs and wonders, the people still did not possess "a heart to know, eyes to see, and ears to hear." Indeed, Pharaoh witnessed the miraculous plagues and still refused to admit God's existence or submit to His dominion. If even these types of supernatural occurrences were not sufficient to produce the irrefutable revelation of God that we are working toward, then what is? In what way can we be granted a knowing heart, seeing eyes, and hearing ears if even such spectacular miracles will not do the trick? And if God's miracles do not suffice to make Him revealed in His creation, then how are we mere mortals expected to do so?

Revelation

What we learn from Moses' statement is that there is vision, and then there is VISION. There is revelation, and then there is a deeper and more essential type of revelation that is not a function of our fleshy eyes or our sensate perception. Physical sight is external, but the revelation that we're instructed to effect is far more profound, permanent, and indisputable. We are all familiar with the common saying that "seeing is believing," but the reality is that our eyes are deceptive and are not the optimal mechanism for our ability to know and verify the ultimate truth. In fact, as we have discussed repeatedly already, in this "olam/world" of "helam/hiddenness," what our eyes see is generally not an indicator of the most authentic reality, but rather a concealment of it. How, then, are we to effect the revelation of the imperceptible divine truth?

Torah teaches us that the way we are to do so is by translating mystic consciousness into routine action through the performance of mitzvos. We see this in the following Talmudic citation:

אדם נותן פרוטה לעני זוכה ומקבל פני שכינה שנאמר
אני בצדק אחזה פני (תהלים יז, טו):

Adam nosein prutah l'ani zocheh u'mekabeil **Pnei Shechina**,
shene'emar "ani b'tzedek echezeh **panecha**."

When a person gives a prutah (coin) to a poor person, he merits to receive the Divine Presence, as it is stated in Psalms 17:15: "I will behold Your face through charity."

(Talmud, Bava Basra 10a)

Here we find that it is specifically through the very simple and physical action of giving "tzedaka/charity"[168] that God's presence is revealed in the world. What's more, this is accomplished not through any prodigious act of lavish generosity, but even through the donation of a single coin. It is noteworthy that in both the Talmudic text, and in the verse that the text quotes from Psalms, it is specifically the "face of God" that is referenced: "panecha/Your face" in the verse from Psalms, and "Pnei Shechina" in the Talmudic text, which has been translated as "Divine Presence," but which literally means "the face of the Shechina."[169] Remarkably, the "Pnei Hashem/face of God," which we have been searching for all along, and which it is our ultimate task to manifest throughout the creation, is accessed and displayed through an act as seemingly ordinary as providing a mere coin to someone who needs it. How can such a simple act effect such a profound revelation?

---

[168] In many places in Chassidus, the sages state that tzedaka represents all of the mitzvos.

[169] "Shechina" is from the root "shochein" which means "to dwell," and is a term for God that refers specifically to His indwelling presence, as opposed to His transcendent essence.

What is it about a small and ostensibly inconsequential action that is so much more consequential and impactful than deep and extensive meditation or profound intellectual cognition? The answer is that **a mitzvah deed is the will of God materialized**. As such, it is the bridge that fuses the highest and lowest worlds. Before the act, there may be an abundance of consciousness and understanding, but there is no physical confirmation. There is theory and belief - "modeh" - but there is no transference and activation - "baruch." God is an idea prior to the act of the mitzvah, but once the mitzvah is performed, God is present and apparent. A physical/animal being, by "nature" has every reason to be self-serving and self-preserving, and no reason to be self-effacing or altruistic. When such a being chooses, through the performance of a mitzvah, to subvert its innate instincts in service and devotion to something beyond itself, this is the appearance of a Godly aspect of that being that was previously concealed beneath its flesh.

This is not to say that animals cannot be "kind" or generous to their young, to other members of their group, or even to other species from time to time. Nor is it to say that there are no acts of kindness in the world other than when one performs a specific mitzvah. Much debate has been focused on the question of altruism and the notion that all kindness is ultimately self-serving. Even devotion and obedience can be characterized as self-interest if it is done primarily for the sake of reward or for the sense of pride and self-satisfaction that it brings. But the idea of a mitzvah is that it expresses one's inherent inclination to transcend the selfish nature that is characteristic of the body, and thereby reveals the Godly nature that is housed within it.

In this sense, we can understand the deeper meaning of the previous citation from the Talmud, as well as the verse from Psalms that it quotes. On the simple level, the implication of the teaching seems to be that the revelation of God's face is an outcome or reward for the act of charity that one has performed: "When a person gives a prutah (coin) to a poor person, he merits to receive the Divine Presence" - first one donates a coin, and then the Divine Presence appears to her/him. *Because* one acts generously, *therefore* s/he is granted a vision of God. However, on a more profound level, we can understand that this revelation of God's face is not a result or reward of right action, but rather, on the contrary, the right action is a revelation and expression of the face of God that has been concealed within the one who acts. "I will behold Your face through charity" - in other words, "Your face" is always there, but I can only "behold" it "through charity." The Talmud is thus informing us not merely that one deserves and receives a vision of God as compensation for her/his mitzvah, but that the mitzvah is a result and a manifestation of the fact that the face of God is already invested within her/him.

Tellingly, while the common English translation of the citation is that "when a person gives a prutah to a poor person, *he merits **to** receive* the Divine Presence," the Hebrew/Aramaic original, "זוכה ומקבל/zocheh *u'*mekabel," does not literally say "he merits *to* receive," but rather "he merits **and** receives." The word "zocheh," translated as "he merits," is from the root "זך/zach," which means "pure" and also "transparent." As such, we can interpret the teaching to mean that when one gives a coin to a poor person, s/he becomes pure or transparent and thereby "receives" or manifests the face of God that has been concealed within her/him. It is not that God is suddenly revealed to the person from above or outside of her/him on account of the good deed. It is rather that through the Godly deed, the Godliness within her/him is now given expression and enabled to shine outward. The person has become "zach/transparent" as a result of the nullification of her/his ego, which is represented by the corporeality and individuality of the body. Once the body and its hungers for self-gratification are transcended, the soul that is beneath it is able to be seen and expressed.

The verse quoted from Psalms can be similarly understood. On the simple level, "I will behold Your face through charity" can imply a causality, such that the perception of God's face will be an outcome of one's performance of charity. But as we have discussed, it can also indicate that the charitable act itself *is* the revelation of God's previously obscured face. This latter, and deeper, interpretation is even more consistent with the verse's actual language. Unlike the Talmud's wording which does suggest, on the simple level at least, that the human action "merits" the divine response, there is no explicit causality or conditionality to this verse's language. Though we have been conditioned to believe that divine revelation is a reward for subjugation and obedience, this is not the Torah's perspective. Our relationship with God is not commerce, a system of earning benefits for our compliance. It is rather a dynamic of absolute love and availability, in which He is simply waiting for us to allow

Him to be experienced. The verse is therefore not a statement of consequence or incentive, it is rather a statement of simple fact. God is always operating through me, but when I am charitable, I will be able to see this reality clearly. It does not say that I will be *granted* a vision of God or *rewarded* with a vision of God, but simply that I will behold Him. There is nothing new or additional that I need to acquire or earn; He is already here, and I simply need to create the condition in which I can perceive His presence.

As a matter of fact, the word "אחזה/echezeh," which is translated as "behold" from the verb "לחזות/lachazot/to look at," is also a form of the word "לאחוז/le'echoz," which means "to grasp." Read this way, the verse can be rendered "through charity will I *grasp* Your face." As we have explained previously, our progression from prayer to Torah study and then to mitzvos is a process of bringing Godliness down from an abstract and intangible state into a concrete and material form that we can grasp or hold onto in this physical realm. Our verse instructs us how to do so. If we desire to make the face of God palpable and apprehensible, we can do so through the performance of "tzedaka/charity" and all of the mitzvos which are represented by this term.

The Alter Rebbe expresses this remarkable revelation of God's face through the performance of mitzvos in his work *Tanya* as follows.

חִיְּיבוּ רַבּוֹתֵינוּ־זִכְרוֹנָם־לִבְרָכָה לָקוּם וְלַעֲמוֹד מִפְּנֵי כָּל עוֹסֵק בְּמִצְוָה, אַף אִם הוּא בּוּר וְעַם הָאָרֶץ, וְהַיְינוּ, מִפְּנֵי ה' הַשּׁוֹכֵן וּמִתְלַבֵּשׁ בְּנַפְשׁוֹ בְּשָׁעָה זוֹ.

Chiyvu Razal lakum v'laamod mipnei kol osek bamitzvah, af im hu bor v'am haaretz, v'haaynu mipnei Hashem hashochein u'mislabeish b'nafsho b'shaah zu.

The sages made it obligatory to rise and stand before anyone who is engaged in a mitzvah, even if he is a boor and uncultured person, that is to say before the face of Hashem that dwells and is garbed in his soul at this time.

(Tanya, chapter 46)

While the face of God is vested within each of us at all times, it is only when one is engaged in the fulfillment of a mitzvah that the Sages ordained that others must rise and stand in her/his presence. And this show of respect must be paid to anyone who performs a mitzvah, regardless of whether s/he is a communal leader or a social outcast.[170] This is because the mitzvah act - each and every mitzvah act - makes the "Pnei Hashem" so apparent that it is as if one is in the presence of God Himself. Significantly, this does not apply to Torah study, as we learn in the Talmud:

אָמַר רַבִּי יוֹסֵי בַּר אָבִין בּוֹא וּרְאֵה כַּמָּה חֲבִיבָה מִצְוָה בִּשְׁעָתָה שֶׁהֲרֵי מִפְּנֵיהֶם עוֹמְדִים מִפְּנֵי תַּלְמִידֵי חֲכָמִים אֵין עוֹמְדִים.

Amar Rebbi Yosei bar Avin bo u'reeh kamah chaviva mitzvah b'shaata she'harei mipneihem omdim mipnei talmidei chachamim ain omdim.

Rabbi Yosei bar Avin says: Come and see how beloved is a mitzvah performed in its proper time, as they stood before those who were fulfilling a mitzvah, whereas they did not stand before Torah scholars.

(Talmud, Kiddushin 33a)

One might think that such respect would be more appropriate for scholars and leaders, as opposed to ordinary people whose simple act could have been performed by anybody. However, this standing before those engaged in even a simple mitzvah act displays how it is specifically through the practical performance of deed in the world of action (as opposed to spirit or intellect) that God is revealed in the world.

Mission Accomplished

We can now address our questions regarding our assigned mission and the seeming challenges of its fulfillment. How are we to satisfy the monumental task of "bara Elokim es hashamayim v'es haaretz/revealing God throughout His creation," particularly if the miracles that

---

[170] This does not apply to all mitzvos today, but was applicable during the time of the Temple when one performed the mitzvah of bringing the First Fruits or other similar rituals. See Kiddushin 33a

God performed Himself throughout history did not do the trick? How are we to be "ohr l'goyim/a light to the nations" if the world does not believe that it is in the dark and is not interested in the illumination that we offer? While we have come to an understanding of what it means to make God manifest through the performance of mitzvos, does this suffice to effect the revelation that we have been assigned? Have we, and all who have come before us, failed if the world remains steeped in darkness as it is today? And if the very nature of this "olam/world" is "helam/concealment," then how can anything we do really make a difference?

What we have learned throughout this chapter is that Torah provides us a daily practice that includes prayer, study, and mitzvos. Prayer focuses us on the reality of God's oneness; Torah study provides us an intellectual system to capture that enlightenment in an earthly framework; and then mitzvos enable us to concretize that spiritual reality and give it a body in which it can be enacted, activated, and actualized. While any one of those mitzvos may not produce the effect of revealing God universally, what we must come to appreciate is that every mitzvah adds up in a composite. This means that through the aggregate of all of the mitzvos that have been, and are being, performed throughout history, we are each contributing to the process of making God revealed in His creation. While each of us is charged with the task of revealing God and being "ohr l'goyim/light to the nations," none of us is responsible for completing the task ourselves, as it is taught in *The Ethics of the Fathers*:

לֹא עָלֶיךָ הַמְּלָאכָה לִגְמוֹר, וְלֹא אַתָּה בֶן חוֹרִין לְהִבָּטֵל מִמֶּנָּה:

Lo Alecha hamelacha ligmor, v'lo atta ben chorin l'hibatel mimena.

It is not incumbent upon you to finish the task, but neither are you free to absolve yourself from it.

(Pirkei Avos 2:16)

It is not through earth-shattering miracles like the splitting of the sea or the descent of fire from the heavens onto the altar that we fulfill our duty. If God chooses, He will once again make Himself visible in these ways, but this has nothing to do with the task of manifestation that He has assigned to us. It is not through a visual experience of God that

He becomes known and revealed. It is, rather, through the consciousness of His complete oneness, which means His presence in everything that we already see and experience. Therefore, the *subversion* of the natural world is not what He aspires to, but rather the *suffusion* of it. The question is not whether God is miraculous and other-worldly, but whether He exists within the ordinary, natural, and mundane. Our task is therefore to reveal him there, within the minutiae of daily life.

The ultimate goal is that the awareness of His omnipresence will so permeate the collective consciousness that it will not only be plainly apparent, but furthermore it will be undeniable and universally accepted. This is the meaning of the prayer that we recite during the High holidays:

וְיֵדַע כָּל פָּעוּל כִּי אַתָּה פְעַלְתּוֹ.

V'yeida kol pa'ul ki atta pi'alto.

And all that You have created should know that You created them.

(Festival Amida for Rosh Hashana)

At the start of the new year, we focus our attention on our primary task in the time ahead. We ask God for the ability to make Him known throughout His creation. We furthermore pray:

וְיֵעָשׂוּ כֻלָּם **אֲגֻדָּה אֶחָת** לַעֲשׂוֹת רְצוֹנְךָ בְּלֵבָב שָׁלֵם.

*V'yeaisu kulam **aguda echas** la'asos ratzonecha b'leivav shalem.*

All should form **one group** to do Your will with a complete heart.

(Festival Amida for Rosh Hashana and Yom Kippur)

Here, we can read "aguda echas" not only as "one group," but also as "a group of oneness." Our deepest prayer and intention on these holiest days of the year is that all of God's creations should come together in the recognition that He is one, and therefore all is one. This consciousness will eventually be accomplished through the combination of all of the work that we have been doing throughout the ages. Each mitzvah we do is the cracking of another shell and the revelation of another spark of light. Eventually enough light will be liberated and illuminated so that the darkness will finally be transformed.

We thus see that the daily rituals and the minute daily actions that Torah assigns are not simply regulations that govern our behavior, or even cultural traditions that provide us a rich and unique ethnic character. Ultimately, daily prayer, daily Torah study, and daily mitzvos are essential components of the intricate liberation practice that God has granted us in order to help us each and every day (and each and every moment of the day) to peel away the veneer and find His face within. Just as we discovered in the previous chapter that Torah's life-cycle observances all express the theme of uncovering and uniting, so we see this same process and motif in the course of every day, and on an even more granular level, in each individual mitzvah that we engage in throughout the day. In the next chapter, we will go on to explore how these themes are reflected in the weekly, monthly, and annual observances of the calendrical cycle and the many holidays or "yomim tovim" that Torah establishes for us to celebrate throughout the year.

Chapter 10: HOLY DAYS AND HOLIDAYS

Cycle, Lines, And Spirals

W e have been on a journey. We began with the question of "where are you," establishing that by virtue of our creation in a world of darkness, we are inevitably lost and in need of being found (chapters 1 and 2). We then set out to find ourself, determining that the direction of the search must be inward because our "panim," our face and essence, is hidden within our "pnimyus," our inner core. We established that it is not only our face that we will find there, but also "Pnei Hashem," the face of God. For "Anochi nosein lifneichem," He has placed His deepest self in our deepest recesses (chapters 3 and 4). As we proceeded on our inbound expedition, we addressed a second question, "how are you," exploring the notion of our hidden potential and our ability to feel great if and when we do discover the greatness that is at our core (chapter 5). From there, we moved on to examine the veils and blockages that keep us from tapping this infinite potential (chapter 6), as well as the tremendous spiritual heights and depths that can be achieved if we manage to penetrate these barriers (chapter 7).

Having determined that there is great incentive to persevere in our search in spite of its difficulties, we then asked a third question, "how can you" - how can we succeed in this search in spite of all of the pitfalls and obstacles that impede our progress. We then asserted that we have been granted not only a map, but also an intricate regimen of exercises or practices that will enable us to see through the darkness and peel away the veils that obscure each of the openings through which we must progressively pass. Torah's rituals and observances are a liberation practice that empower us to move ever further inward. We have explored how this is so in Torah's life-cycle rituals (chapter 8) and in its daily service (chapter 9). We will now go on to survey the very detailed set of calendrical occasions that assist us in our journey throughout the course of the year.

We have spoken about the life cycle, and the daily cycle. In this chapter, we are going to discuss the weekly, monthly, and annual cycles. To begin, we might wonder why there are so many cycles in Torah and in life generally. Why is our experience so cyclical, as opposed to being more linear? Why do the processes of the natural world and of our inner world move in circles, such that we keep revisiting the same seasons, experiences, themes and challenges rather than moving from one thing to the next without coming around again periodically to the same things that we already experienced so frequently in the past? Doesn't a cycle suggest a more regressive and stagnant situation rather than a line which would seem more progressive and evolutionary?

Furthermore, it is worth asking why we mark the passage of time in the cyclic segments that we do. How were these particular periods of time (weeks, months, years) selected and agreed upon, and what do they represent? Are the markers of our lives merely arbitrary, or do they reveal some deeper meaning and purpose? Do they trap us in an inevitable hamster wheel in which we are constantly spinning and going nowhere? Or do they provide us some opportunity to transcend the rat race and free ourselves from the existential dilemma of our small and seemingly inconsequential place in the grander scheme?

Often, we speak of a "timeline" or an "arc of history," but Torah's conception of time is not a line or an arc. It is rather a spiral. What is a spiral? It is not a circle or a line. It is a series of circles that are connected and rising. This is the model of our existence according to Torah. Each year is another full cycle which brings us back to the place where we were previously, but in an increasingly higher space. We will develop this concept more fully in the coming section on the yearly holidays. But before we get to the annual cycle, we must first explore the smaller cycles that exist within its framework. Like the moon which rotates as it revolves around the earth, which is simultaneously rotating on its axis as it revolves around the sun, in our experience of time we are also making constant smaller cycles as we move through the course of larger cycles. Each day we pirouette through the circuit of day and night as we meanwhile dance a larger circle for seven days to complete a week, roughly four of which take us around the course of the month, after twelve of which we have completed the lap of the entire year. It's almost dizzying to think of all of this simultaneous spinning, and twirling, and revolving. What is the significance of this constant gyration, and how does it enable us to elevate ourselves so that we are rising in a spiral rather than merely spinning our wheels and reeling in a circle?

Revolution vs. Evolution

The cyclical character of reality is reflected in nature itself as a series of loops that play themselves out constantly around us and within us. One of the most obvious cycles that we experience is the progression of the seasons. As we move from winter, to spring, to summer, to fall, and then back around again, the temperatures rise and fall, the plants bloom and then wither, and the world expands and contracts, giving and withholding in a fairly predictable alternation of growth and then rest. Throughout this process, a number of other cycles are operating at greater or lesser degrees of perceptibility: there is the constant sequence of evaporation and condensation of the water cycle; the invisible carbon cycle which balances carbon dioxide and oxygen allowing us to breathe and sustain a viable atmosphere; the circle of life in which increasingly complex predators consume lower levels on the food chain and then die and decompose to feed the soil which nourishes plant life which subsequently nourishes their prey; and a variety of other organic and chemical circuits that sustain life as we know it. Meanwhile, within each of us, food is consumed, nutrients are integrated and waste is excreted, blood courses throughout our body, and our breath cycles in and out.

On a more macro level, our solar system is a complex matrix of spinning and revolving bodies, and the segments of time that we count are primarily determined by this interplanetary motion. As we know, the year marks the revolution of the earth around the sun, the month marks the revolution of the moon around the earth, and the day marks the rotation of the earth around its axis. But why? If we were to assume that the nature of reality is either accidental or just "the way it is," then we might simply conclude that early humans observed the natural order and synchronized their systems to the phenomena around them. The cycle of seasons takes roughly 365 days, so we'll call that a year. The moon's phases repeat themselves approximately every 29 days, so we'll call that a month. The sun rises every 24 hours, so we'll call that a day. However, if we begin from the standpoint of a divine consciousness that arranged those cycles to exist as they do, then we will not be satisfied to simply observe cycles and conform to them. Rather, we must wonder why the cycles exist as they do. Why did God create the universe in such a way that everything revolves? And why do our lives "revolve" around these revolutions? Why do we count our time by them? Is this simply "natural" or convenient, or is there something more profound to be gleaned from all this cyclic motion?

To answer these questions, we must try to understand what the circle represents. As we mentioned in the introduction to this chapter, it is possible to conceive of a circle as regressive as opposed to progressive. Rather than moving forward, one is constantly moving back around to where s/he has already been. Harnessed and restrained to a point in the middle of the circle, one can never move farther away and is therefore condemned to constantly travel the same worn path over and over again. However, there is a very different way to understand a circle, and we can see this in the term "revolution." When we discuss a revolution in thought, we are referring to something so new and innovative that it is was previously unthinkable. Whereas an 'evolution' is simply a new step in the direction that one has been moving, a 'revolution' is completely beyond and different from what came before it. What is the cause of this radical novelty? It is the fact that one has re-volved rather than e-volved. Instead of simply moving forward, one has managed to leap far above and beyond where s/he was before by virtue of the fact that s/he has first moved back around to where s/he had previously been.

As we know, a revolution is not only a circular movement around an axis, or just an innovation in thought, but it is also an act of revolt. When one revolts, s/he is turning back rather than blindly moving forward. It is a reconsideration that follows the realization that one is not moving in the proper direction. We come back to where we were and understand that we must do this differently. In this sense, we can fully evolve only when we revolve. Of course, there could be a type of gradual evolution that need not follow this cyclic trajectory. One could theoretically begin in one place and move constantly away from it horizontally with a slight vertical ascent. But the mechanism for true evolution in the spiritual sense is a scenario in which one moves away from, and then back toward, her/his starting point. Through the experience that s/he gains along the way, when s/he returns to the same place or situation that s/he had previously experienced, s/he is now able to deal with the same circumstances differently. This is authentic growth. If one were to never re-experience the same conditions that caused her/him trouble or challenges previously, then s/he would never be able to demonstrate actual advancement. Fleeing from a problem or a weakness is not a veritable sign of change or growth. Rather, we can only demonstrate genuine progress when we face the same circumstances that caused us to fail or transgress previously, and this time we prevail or resist temptation.

This revisitation of previous circumstances with a completely different reaction and outcome is the ultimate level of "תְּשׁוּבָה/ teshuvah," as Rambam[171] explains in his laws of "teshuvah":

אֵי זוֹ הִיא תְּשׁוּבָה גְּמוּרָה. זֶה שֶׁבָּא לְיָדוֹ דָּבָר שֶׁעָבַר בּוֹ וְאֶפְשָׁר בְּיָדוֹ לַעֲשׂוֹתוֹ וּפֵרֵשׁ וְלֹא עָשָׂה מִפְּנֵי הַתְּשׁוּבָה. לֹא מִיִּרְאָה וְלֹא מִכִּשָּׁלוֹן כֹּחַ. כֵּיצַד. הֲרֵי שֶׁבָּא עַל אִשָּׁה בַּעֲבֵרָה וּלְאַחַר זְמַן נִתְיַחֵד עִמָּה וְהוּא עוֹמֵד בְּאַהֲבָתוֹ בָּהּ וּבְכֹחַ גּוּפוֹ

171 Rabbi Moses ben Maimon, also known as Maimonides. Twelfth century sage who authored several of the most influential works of Torah philosophy, and codified all of Torah law in his master work "Mishneh Torah." Also a physician who served the king of Egypt. 1135-1204

וּבַמְּדִינָה שֶׁעָבַר בָּהּ וּפָרַשׁ וְלֹא עָבַר זֶהוּ בַּעַל תְּשׁוּבָה גְּמוּרָה.

Ei zo hi teshuvah gemurah? Zeh she'bah l'yado davar she'avar bo v'efshar b'yado la'asoso u'peirash v'lo asa mipnei ha'teshuvah. Lo mi'yirah v'lo mi'kishlon koach. Keitzad? Harei she'bah al ishah ba'aveirah u'l'achar zman nis'yacheid imah v'hu omed b'ahavaso bah u'b'koach gufo u'va'medina she'avar bah u'fareish v'lo avar zehu baal teshuvah gemura.

What is complete teshuvah? A person who confronts the same situation in which he sinned, when he has the potential to do it [again], and, nevertheless, abstains and does not commit it because of his teshuvah alone and not because of fear or a lack of strength. For example, a person engaged in illicit sexual relations with a woman. Afterwards, they met in privacy, in the same country, while his love for her and physical power still persisted, and nevertheless, he abstained and did not transgress. This is a complete Baal-Teshuvah.

(Mishneh Torah, Hilchos Teshuvah, 2:1)

"Teshuvah," as we discussed previously,[172] is the Torah's term for spiritual advancement, and though it is commonly translated as "repentance," it literally means "return." When one has "fallen" or "strayed" from the proper path, Torah does not mandate that s/he should work to become something different from what s/he has been, but rather that s/he should "return," moving back to where s/he originally was. This act of returning seems to be a strange description or prescription for advancement. How is that we move forward by going backward?

We do so because it is only by delving inward that we can rise upward. In moving inward, we access the inherent Godliness ("Pnei Hashem") within us which we had not previously detected. The act of turning back, or circling back, to where one previously was is thus the impetus for "revolutionary" growth. We see this in the teaching of the Sages (also quoted in chapter five) that "in the place where the "baal teshuvah" (one who does "teshuvah") stands, the "tzaddik" (perfectly righteous) does not stand."[173] While the "tzaddik" can progress gradual-

---

[172] See chapter five, section "Being and Becoming"

[173] Brachot 34b

ly and continually, s/he cannot make the unbounded revolutionary progress that is effected through the backward and cyclical motion of the "baal teshuvah." This wisdom is embedded in the universe all around us through the cycles that we experience constantly. Our movement through time - reflected particularly in the weekly, monthly, and annual circuits of the calendar year - attunes us to the efficacy of turning back and delving in.

<hr>

Seven

We have seen that time is measured in cycles, and that it is the cyclical nature of time that forces us to pause our forward momentum to regularly move backward for the sake of rising upward. If we were always moving onward, we would neglect the vital movement inward. It is the motion of the cycle that allows us to rise in an ever growing spiral. This spiral is therefore the shape that is traced by the process of constant "teshuvah." We move outward to engage with the world, and then we return inward in order to reconnect with our essence which has inevitably become obscured by the darkness of the world we have ventured into. This alternating "ratzo/running" and "shov/returning" is like a candle's flame[174] - it reaches upward while simultaneously maintaining its connection below and fulfilling its responsibility to illuminate the shadows. We are perpetually moving out, back, and up, like a coil that is ever ascending as it loops around and back.

This progression is precisely the trajectory of the weekly cycle. We involve ourselves with worldly pursuits for six days, and then withdraw from the workday world and focus on our spiritual reality on the sabbath. It is no coincidence, then, that the word "תשובה/teshuvah/return" shares the root of both the words "שבוע/shavuah," which means "week," as well "שבת/shabbat/sabbath," which is the end of the weekly cycle. The terms "shavuah" and "shabbat" are also related to the word "שבע/sheva," which is the number "seven." A shavuah is a period of seven days, and shabbat is the seventh day. But why is a week comprised

<hr>

[174] See chapter nine, section "Bringing It Down"

of seven days, and what is the relationship of the number seven to the concept of "shav/return" (so much so that even the English name of the number, "**seven**," is related to this Hebrew root ב-שׁ (sh-v) as well)?

Of the segments of time that we have introduced, the weekly cycle is the only one that does not pertain explicitly to a revolution or rotation that we can visually detect in the natural world. As mentioned, the duration of the day, month, and year are all determined by astronomic phenomena: twenty-four hours is the amount of time it takes the earth to rotate completely on its axis, thirty days (approximately) is the amount of time it takes the moon to circle the earth, and 365 and a quarter days is the amount of time it takes the earth to orbit around the sun. What does seven days represent, and how did the week come to be seven days and not five or ten days or any other random number?

If one would suggest that there was a need for a measure of time larger than a day but smaller than a month, those who established the calendar could have chosen three weeks of ten days per month, or five weeks of six days, or six weeks of five. How did we land on four weeks of seven? Some suggest that the seven day week was established by the Babylonians based on their perception of seven bodies in the sky: the sun, the moon, and the five planets that are visible to the naked eye.[175] Others suggest that the month was broken down into four segments to correspond to the four phases of the moon: the new moon, the waxing half moon, the full moon, and the waning half moon. What is consistent about these theories is that they are based on an agnostic premise which supposes that our established systems are based on human observation of the natural world. They do not account for a divine logic that has established the functioning of the world that we observe, and therefore, rather than asking why nature operates the way it does, they simply ask how we have responded and adapted to the design-less dynamics of nature. Attempting to understand a system of four weeks per month, they theorize correspondence to four phases of the moon - though the moon

---

[175] We can see this correspondence to the heavenly bodies in the Roman/Romance names of the week: Sunday obviously corresponds to the sun, Monday corresponds to the moon, Tuesday is Mardi in French, corresponding to Mars, Wednesday is Mercredi in French, corresponding to Mercury, Thursday is Jeudi in French, corresponding to Jupiter, Friday is Vendredi in French, corresponding to Venus, and Saturday corresponds to Saturn.

in fact undergoes eight phases.[176] Attempting to explain seven days per week, they identify five planets and the sun and the moon - though there are more than five planets in the solar system and a number of stars that appear as boldly or brightly to the naked eye as the planets that were included.

Rather than trying to back into a theory that makes the numbers work, when we begin with the Torah and explore the Godly perspective that it records, we find that the number seven is a profound and prominent factor throughout the universe and throughout both the exoteric and esoteric scriptural texts. Some examples of sevens in the natural world include: seven continents and seven seas, seven colors of the spectrum of light (ROYGBIV), seven notes in the major scale (do, re, mi, fa, so, la, ti), and seven rows or periods of the periodic table. Regarding the human body, we find that there are seven openings in the head (two eyes, two ears, two nostrils, and the mouth), and seven primary portions of the body (head, torso, two arms, two legs, and the sexual organ).

Some of the many groupings of seven in Torah include: seven days of creation; seven "middos" or emotional attributes; seven heavens; seven millennia; seven years of the agricultural cycle; seven branches of the menorah in the Temple; seven species of Israel (wheat, barley, grapes, pomegranates, figs, olives, and dates); seven days of purification for spiritual impurity; seven shepherds (Abraham, Isaac, Jacob, Moses, Aaron, Joseph, David); seven female prophets mentioned in Talmud (Sarah, Miriam, Deborah, Hannah, Avigail, Chuldah, and Esther); seven wedding blessings and seven times the bride circles the groom; seven days of the wedding celebration (sheva brachos); seven days of mourning after death (shiva); seven days of the holidays of Passover and Sukkos (in the Torah and in Israel today, though outside Israel eight days are celebrated); seven primary Jewish holidays (Rosh Hashana, Yom Kippur, Sukkos, Chanukkah, Purim, Passover, and Shavuos); seven gates of the Temple in Jerusalem; seven words of the opening verse of Torah; seven Noachide commandments; and seven years for a servant to gain freedom.

Seven is not the only significant and frequently repeated number in Torah, but it is the most prominent and commonly referenced. The

---

[176] In addition to the new moon, the waxing half moon, the full moon, and the waning half moon, there are also the waxing crescent and the waxing gibbous, and the waning gibbous and waning crescent.

Midrash even goes so far as to inform us of the number seven's importance by stating:

כָּל הַשְּׁבִיעִין חֲבִיבִין.

Kol ha'shviin chavivin.
All sevenths are precious.
(Vayikra Rabba 29:11)

The Midrash then goes on to list several sets of sevens, followed by verses from scripture that extol the virtue of the seventh in each list: in generations, the seventh generation from Adam was the generation of Chanoch, and "Chanoch walked with God" (Genesis 5:25); in the succession of forefathers, all were holy, but the seventh was Moses, and "Moses ascended to God" (Exodus 19:3) to receive the Torah on Mount Sinai; in the order of sons, David was the premier son of Yishai and therefore became the king of the nation, and "David was the seventh" (I Chronicles 2:15); in the order of kings, Asa was the seventh, and "Asa called out to the Lord" (II Chronicles 14:10); in years, debts are forgiven and fields are set aside from agriculture every seven years, "but in the seventh you shall let it rest and lie fallow" (Exodus 23.11); in days, the seventh is the holy sabbath, "And God blessed the seventh day" (Genesis 2:3); in months, the seventh is the time of the high holidays, "In the seventh month on the first day" (Leviticus 23:24).

What we realize from all of these distinguished sevens, is that it is not that those things that are precious happen to be seventh, but rather that those things that are seventh are specifically beloved. Why is this? What is it about seven that is so special and holy? The easy answer would be to indicate that God created the world in seven days, and therefore seven became a holy number. But why did He choose seven as the number of creation and of purity and of preeminence? In other words, is seven holy because God chose it, or did He choose it because it is holy?

To answer this question, we will return to the Hebrew word for seven, "שבע/sheva." As we mentioned previously, "sheva" shares a root with the word "שב/shav," which means return. But we can glean an additional insight from the fact that the Hebrew "שבע" can alternatively be read as "sovah," which means satiated, full, or complete.[177] Indeed, the concept of "שב/shav/return" and "שבע/sovah/complete" are conceptually consistent because a circle or cycle is *complete* when one *returns* to where s/he began. In this sense, a "שבוע/shavua/week," which shares the root of both "שב/shav/return" and "שבע/sovah/complete," is a complete cycle through which one has gone forth from the holiness of one sabbath into the frenzied obscurity of the work week, and then returns on the next sabbath to the holy point at which s/he began. "שבת/shabbat" is the same letters as "תשב/tashev," which means "return," because it is on every shabbat that we step out of the workday world to return to our source and remember what we truly are and why we have been placed in this darkness. Interestingly, the traditional greeting on shabbat is "שבת שלום/shabbat shalom," which simply translated means "peaceful sabbath." But on a deeper level, understanding "שלום/shalom" not merely as "peace," but also in its sense of "שלם/shalem/complete" (as we discussed in chapter 7, section "Peace"), what we are wishing one another when we say "shabbat shalom" is that on this shabbat, we should experience the "שלמות/shleimus/wholeness" and "שבע/sovah/completeness" that comes with the culmination of our "שבוע/shavua/week."

We have thus come to understand that the number seven, "sheva," represents "sovah/completeness" and "shav/return," but we have not yet explained why. We have explained that the reason that "all sevens are precious" is because seven represents wholeness and the introspection of coming back to one's source, but why is it specifically the number seven that symbolizes these characteristics? Once again, is there something about this figure specifically that connotes wholeness and therefore God made the week seven days, or is it only because God chose to make the week seven days that we consider this number to be complete?

The answer is that the number seven is inherently whole, and we can see this in both the physical and mystic realms. On the spiritual plane, seven is the number of the "middos," or the emotional attributes that exist within a person and within the universe as a whole. Kabbala

---

[177] Depending on the vowels, Hebrew words are pronounced differently and take on variant meanings; שֶׁבַע is sheva/seven, while שָׂבָע is sovah/complete.

refers to ten "sefirot" that comprise the various divine energies that created and sustain the universe. The term "sefirot" literally means "spheres"
or "countings," but it is generally translated as "emanations," and it
refers to the ways that God manifests and expresses Himself in order to
form the creation. These same ten attributes are found in microcosm
within each person as well, and when we say that humanity is formed in
the "image of God," we mean that just as God has these ten attributes, so
too do each of us. These "sefirot," or attributes, are broken down into
two categories: the "mochin/intellectual attributes," and the "middos/
emotional attributes." There are three "mochin/intellectual attributes"
(which we have discussed briefly already in chapter nine, section
"Torah"). They are:

1.   Chochmah/wisdom
2.   Binah/understanding
3.   Daas/knowledge

And there are seven "middos/emotional attributes." They are:

1.   Chesed/kindness
2.   Gevurah/restraint
3.   Tiferes/compassion
4.   Netzach/victory
5.   Hod/humility
6.   Yesod/bonding
7.   Malchus/sovereignty

It is beyond the scope of this book to go into a detailed analysis
of the sefirot,[178] but what is relevant to our current discussion is the fact
that seven represents the complete complement of the "middos." Translated simplistically as "emotional attributes," what these seven "middos"
really refer to are the ways in which we interact with the world. While
the the three "mochin/intellectual attributes" concern cognition and
ideation, the "middos" concern action and relation. While "chochmah,"
"binah," and "daas" are located within the head, the "middos" represent
the body and the mechanisms through which we interface with creation.

---

[178] See "Mystical Concepts in Chassidism" by J. Emmanuel Schochet for a thorough introduction to these concepts.

"Chesed/kindness" is the right arm, "gevurah/restraint" is the left arm, "tiferes/compassion" is the torso, "netzach/victory" is the right leg, "hod/humility" is the left leg, "yesod/bonding" is the sexual organ, and "malchus/sovereignty" is the mouth. Seven therefore represents completion because it is the whole spiritual body, so to speak. The physical body mirrors this spiritual form, as do the many series of sevens that we have listed previously, including, of course, the seven days of the week. In other words, the reason that all of these sets of seven exist in both the natural world and the Torah is because seven is the spiritual schematic format of creation.

Of course if this is so, then we should be able to see this in physical space as well. And indeed we do. Spatially, we commonly refer to six directions: right, left, front, back, up and down. However, there is a seventh space, and that is the center, the point or region from which all of these other six directions project and to which they refer. We can better understand this by considering a cube:

How many sides or faces does a cube have? At first glance, we would say six, pointing to the right side, the left side, the front side, the back side, the up side, and the down side. But what about the "in" side? In counting only its external faces, we are ignoring the space within the cube, without which there is no cube at all. The "in" side is the cube's "pnimyus," or inner face. It is this seventh dimension that connects and establishes all of its external dimensions.

While we are on the subject of geometry, it is also significant to note that if one draws a circle, one can then fit exactly six circles of the inner circle's same size around its circumference. Like the cube, there is the one at the center, and then the six that surround it.

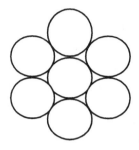 

Interestingly, and not coincidentally, the "Magen David/Star of David" is also comprised of a center field with six fields projecting from it. All of these configurations of seven correspond to the seven "middos." Just as the spirit has seven attributes, so too does our material world. The fact that seven represents wholeness and completion, therefore, is not simply a coincidence or an arbitrary occurrence, but rather it is the reality of both our spiritual and physical makeup. We move in weekly cycles of seven days because God created the world in seven days, but why did God create the world in seven days? Because the cycle of seven is the complete tour and aggregate of both our external and interior realities.

Shabbat

The renowned sixteenth century Kabbalist Yehudah Loew, known as the Maharal of Prague, explained this intersection of time and space and spirit in his work *Gevurot Hashem*:

כאשר תעיין ותמצא שהגשם יש לו חלופי ו' צדדין, והם:
המעלה והמטה, ימין ושמאל, פנים ואחור. וכל שש צדדין
אלו מתיחסים אל הגשמית בעבור שכל צד יש לו רחוק,
וזהו גדר הגשם. אמנם יש בו שביעי, והוא האמצעי, שאינו
נוטה לשום צד. ומפני שאינו מתיחס לשום צד, דומה
לדבר שהוא בלתי גשמי, שאין לו רוחק. ולפיכך יש גם כן
לזמן, המתיחס ומשתתף עם הגשם, ששה ימים, והם ימי

חול, אבל השביעי קדוש. ונמצא כי שבעה ימי שבוע הם
דומים לגשם הפשוט, שיש לו ששה קצות והאמצעי
שבניהם. זהו ענין ששת ימי חול והשביעי הוא קדש.

*Ka'asher t'ayen v'timtza she'hageshem yesh lo chilufei vav
tzedadin, v'heim: ha'maalah v'hamatah, yamin u'smol, panim
v'achor. V'kol shesh tzedadin eilu mis'yachasim el hagashmis
baavor she'kol tzad yesh lo rachok, v'zehu geder ha'geshem.
Amnam yesh bo shevii, v'hu he'emtzai, she'aino noteh l'shum
tzad. U'mipnei she'aino mis'yachas l'shum tzad, domeh l'davar
she'hu bilti gashmi, she'ain lo rochek. U'lifikach yesh gam kein
l'zman, ha'mis'yachas u'mishtateph im hageshem, shisha
yamim, v'heim yimei chol, aval he'shevii kadosh. V'nimtza ki
shivah yimei shavuah heim domim l'geshem, hapashut, sh'yesh
lo shisha ketzavot b'ha'emtzai she'beinehem. Zehu inyan
shishat yimei chol v'hashvii hu kodesh.*

When one observes, he will find that physicality has six
alternative sides, and they are: above and below, right
and left, front and back. And all six of these sides are
connected to physicality in that each side has dimension, and this is the category of physicality. However,
there is also a seventh, and that is the center, which
does not spread to any side. And because it is not related to any side, it seems to be something that is without
physicality, because it doesn't have dimension. And
therefore, there is also with time, which is connected
and partnered with physicality, six days, and they are
the days of the week, but the seventh is holy / separate.
And we find that because the seven day week is similar
to space, simply speaking, that there are six edges and
the center of them. This is the concept of six days of the
week and the seventh day which is holy.

(Gevurot Hashem 46:3)

The seventh day, we see, is to the six workdays of the week what
the "in side" of the cube is to its six outer surfaces. It is the foundation on
which everything else rests. In this sense, it is interesting that "שַׁבָּת /
shabbat / the sabbath" is known as the "day of rest," because in multiple
senses, everything rests on it. Not only is the sabbath a day of rest in the
sense of respite and renewal, it is also the day on which all of the other
days rely and depend. Just as there would be no outer aspect and quali-

ties to the cube (or any physical substance for that matter) without the internal space which it garbs and envelops, so too there would be no week and no time in general if not for the sabbath on which it is based and established. Just as the "pnimyus" is the essence and raison d'etre of the physical world that surrounds it, so too shabbat is the core and soul of the six days which it precedes and completes.

The word "שַׁבָּת/shabbat" is related not only to the words "שבע/sheva/seven" and "שב/shav/return" as we have discussed already, but also and primarily to the term "שֶׁבֶת/sheves," which means "to rest" or "to sit." Just as God completed the work of creation in six days and then rested on the the seventh, similarly He commanded us to perform all of our work in six days and then to rest on the sabbath. But what does it mean that God rested? Does God grow weary and need to take a break to refresh Himself? Furthermore, why do we say that there are "seven days of creation" when in fact the universe was completed in six days? The seventh day was not a day of creation but rather a day of rest subsequent to the completion of creation. The wording in the verse in Genesis that describes the seventh day leaves us even further confused:

וַיְכַל אֱ-לֹהִים בַּיּוֹם הַשְּׁבִיעִי מְלַאכְתּוֹ אֲשֶׁר עָשָׂה וַיִּשְׁבֹּת בַּיּוֹם הַשְּׁבִיעִי מִכָּל־מְלַאכְתּוֹ אֲשֶׁר עָשָׂה.

Va'yichal E-lohim bayom ha'shvii melachto aher asa va'yish-bot bayom ha'shvii mikol melachto asher asa.

And God completed on the seventh day His work that He did, and He abstained on the seventh day from all His work that He did.

(Genesis 2:2)

The first phrase of the verse indicates that God "completed" His work on the seventh day. Yet the second half of the verse says that He "abstained" from work on the seventh day. Which is it? "Completing" the work on the seventh day implies that there was some finishing touch that needed to be performed then. Whereas "abstaining" from work implies that the work had already been finished by the end of the sixth day, and there was nothing left to do. The sages resolve this anomaly with the suggestion that the creation was completed in six days except for one element. It was lacking something essential, without which it was not only incomplete, but completely lacking. This final and vital creation was introduced on the seventh day. On this day, God created rest itself. Just as the seventh "side" of the cube, the inside, is the cube's most vital and important side without which the cube does not exist, but it is simultaneously not truly a "side" at all, similarly the creation of rest on the seventh day is both the most significant creation for the sake of which all other creation was created, and simultaneously it is no creation at all but rather the absence and discontinuance of creation.

What is "rest" according to Torah, and why is it so important? God does not need to rest from His labor. He is infinite and does not become exhausted or expended. He created a day of rest not for Himself, but for His creations. In the simple sense, this rest is a cessation of labor for the sake of recovery, leisure, and recreation. But the rest of shabbat is not merely passive and inactive. From all of the related terms and concepts we have discussed so far, we can deduce that it is rather a return to one's center. It is a delving beyond the surface to reach the "in side" or the inner face that has been covered and concealed as we move throughout the cycle of the week and perform our labor along the six exterior sectors of space and time. Shabbat is a time of great pleasure and satisfaction, but this is not simply because we are liberated from the daily grind and its many pressures and responsibilities. When we truly appreciate the depth and intentionality of shabbat, the relief and release that it brings are far more profound and intensely rewarding.

This will be understood through the parallel of the two seemingly conflicting verbs in the verse cited above, "completed" and "abstained." In the Hebrew original, the two terms are "וַיְכַל/ va'yichal" and "וַיִּשְׁבֹּת/va'yishbot." The latter term should be recognizable - its root is "שבת/shabbat," and this is where the idea of rest on the seventh day is first introduced. The first term may be familiar as well, as we have discussed it previously in both chapter seven[179] and chapter eight.[180] Its root is "כל," which means both "all" and "to complete." While we have initially considered the terms "וַיְכַל/va'yichal" and "וַיִּשְׁבֹּת/va'yishbot" to be divergent and conflicting, in a deeper sense we will find that their juxtaposition in the verse is intended to demonstrate their correlation and to deepen our understanding of each through the connotation of the other.

---

[179] Section "Bittul"

[180] Section "Funeral"

True "rest/שבת," we will come to see, comes only with the appreciation that everything is "complete/כל." One can only fully "יִּשְׁבֹּת/rest" and make a proper sabbath when s/he feels that "יְכַל/s/he has completed" all of the work that needs to be done. In this sense, the sages teach that the moment shabbat begins, one is to consider it as though there is nothing that remains unfinished or incomplete. One is not merely pausing from work that will need to be continued next week, but rather all worldly concerns and burdens have ceased and one is completely at peace. This is consummate rest, and this is the level of bliss and freedom that we are intended to achieve every shabbat.

But how is such an attitude possible? How is one expected to experience such complete rest when the stressors and responsibilities of the work week do not truly vanish simply because the seventh day arrives? This is precisely what the Torah's wording is teaching us. As we mentioned above, the word "יְכַל" means not only "complete," but also "all." True completion is the state of being unified with all and everything. To complete something is not only to finish it, but furthermore to make it whole. Understood this way, the verse above would be rendered, "And God *made whole* on the seventh day His work that He did." In other words, He completed the cycle. Throughout the first six days, He moved outward, so to speak, creating multiplicity and darkness. But on the seventh day, He closed the circle, moving back to the essence and reunifying everything that had seemed disparate and diverse. This is the consummation that shabbat brings.

"כל," as we noted in chapters seven and eight, is also the root of the word "כִּלָיוֹן/kilayon/annihilation," as well as "כְּלוֹת/klot/expiry," which is commonly used in chassidic philosophy to refer to "כְּלוֹת הַנֶּפֶשׁ/klot hanefesh," the expiry of the soul. It is similarly the root of "כַּלָה/kallah/bride," and we explained the correlation of "bride" and "expiry" to be an expression of the union of souls that occurs at both marriage and at death. When a man and woman marry, their souls not only "complete" one another, but they "expire" into one another, ceasing to be the isolated individuals that each of them seemed to have been before. Similarly, when one dies, the soul leaves the confines of the body and reunites with all of the other souls that had also seemed to have been temporarily separated and distinct. On shabbat, this is our consciousness - our soul returns to its source and reunites with everything. Therefore, in the service that we recite to welcome shabbat, we recite not only the verse cited above "va'yi**chal** E-lohim bayom ha'shvii melachto asher asa/and God *completed* on the seventh day His work that He had done," but the center point and highlight of the service is the singing of the "Lecha Dodi" prayer, the beginning and refrain of which is:

לְכָה דוֹדִי לִקְרַאת **כַּלָּה** פְּנֵי שַׁבָּת נְקַבְּלָה:

*Lecha dodi likrat **kallah** pnei Shabbat nikabala.*
Come, my beloved, to meet the **bride**, let us greet the face of Shabbat.

Here we see that shabbat is referred to as the "kallah/bride." Our intention as we sing this mystic prayer is not only that we are welcoming the sabbath as if it is our most beloved friend and partner, but furthermore that we are "כלה/expiring" in reunion with all of existence. We are ceasing to be individual, and we are returning to the reality that we are one with everything. We have completed the cycle of the previous week, and we have accomplished all that we were able to in that time. In the awareness of God's complete oneness and our inclusion in that unity, we let go of regrets for what could have, should have, and would have been, and we release all concern for what may or may not be in the week ahead. At this moment, just as God has completed His work at the end of the sixth day, so too I have completed my work, and I am now able to fully rest.

As a matter of fact, I am not only able to rest in this way, but I am commanded to do so. The mitzvah to rest on shabbat is not only a directive to cease all work. On a deeper level, it is an obligation to relinquish all of our tension and material concerns and to experience the "shalom/peace" and "shleimus/completeness" that the unity of shabbat brings. As we have discussed several times already, "mitzvah" is not only a "commandment" as derived from the root "tzav/command," but it is a "connection" deriving from the root "tzavsa/bond." We can therefore understand how there can be a mitzvah to experience this lofty sense of rest. While it may be unreasonable to *command* someone to relinquish all of her/his worries and to thereby experience the feeling that everything is complete, when one fully connects to God and His absolute oneness through the "tzavsa/bond" that the mitzvah creates, then her/his worries will vaporize and s/he will experience the true rest that is available to us every seven days.

We can now appreciate how shabbat is one of the primary and most powerful components of our liberation practice. To return to our broader discussion, we have been exploring how each of the Torah's rituals and observances provides us an opportunity and a methodology through which we can cast off the veils that conceal our "pnimyus" and reveal the "Pnei Hashem" that is at our core. The weekly cycle, culminating in shabbat, creates a rhythm for our lives which reminds us that every day is part of a system that leads us out into the darkness, and then back into the light. On shabbat, we "שב/shav/return" to our essence, turning back inward after we have ventured outward throughout the past six days. We "שבת/shevet/rest" from our occupation and engagement with the world in order to reconnect to the ultimate truth of what we are and why we are here. Freed from the busyness and preoccupation of our labor, we leave the facade of multiplicity behind and embrace the shabbat "כלה/kallah/bride," fusing with her and expiring into the oneness of "כל/kol/all."

Just as we have come to understand prayer as the pausing from our daily grind to reorient ourselves inward three times each day, so we now recognize shabbat as the time we allot every seven days to pause and refocus for an entire twenty-four hours on our divine reality. Yet while we devote extra time to prayer, meditation, and Torah study on shabbat, we do not divorce ourselves from the physical world. On the contrary, it is a mitzvah to feast on both Friday night and Saturday, to wear fine clothes and to utilize our finest china, silver, and linens. Furthermore, marital intimacy is especially encouraged on shabbat. This is because there is such a revelation of God's unity on this seventh dimension of time and space that the spiritual and physical are no longer contrary. Shabbat is "a foretaste of the world to come" in which Godliness will be completely revealed in every aspect of creation. Once we have reached the seventh face of the cube, the inner face, we have found the "Pnei Hashem" and recognized that it is the core and essence of all things. This seventh day is therefore a glimmer of the seventh millennium, the messianic era, when our work of "bara Elokim/revealing God" will be complete. We will then be able to truly rest and bask in the brilliant light of Godliness that dispels the darkness and pervades the universe.

———◆———

Rosh Chodesh

While the weekly cycle and shabbat are extraordinarily powerful and significant components of Torah's liberation practice, the monthly cycle is also a major focal point in Torah law and tradition which provides a profound mechanism for inward progress and discovery. Unlike the secular Gregorian calendar which is based on the solar cycle, the Hebrew calendar is based on the rhythm of the moon and the succession of the months. The new moon is marked in secular society with little notice or fanfare, but "Rosh Chodesh," literally the "head of the month," is a quasi-holiday in Torah which is distinguished by various special rites and observances. It is not a day of rest like shabbat and the high holidays on which work is forbidden, but it is more sacred than typical weekdays. Like shabbat and holidays, there is an additional prayer service on Rosh Chodesh, called the "musaf/additional" service, which corresponds to the additional sacrificial offering that was made in the temple on holy days. Furthermore, the "Hallel/Thanksgiving" prayer is recited on Rosh Chodesh, a series of psalms which mark calendrical events that are miraculous or deserving of special gratitude.

Aside of these additional observances on Rosh Chodesh, its eminence is indicated by the fact that it is the first formal mitzvah that is delivered in Torah. It is not commanded until the twelfth chapter of Exodus, the second book of the Torah, but Rashi refers to it in his very first commentary on the very first verse of Genesis, Torah's opening book. On the introductory words, "In the Beginning," Rashi comments:

אָמַר רַבִּי יִצְחָק לֹא הָיָה צָרִיךְ לְהַתְחִיל אֶת הַתּוֹרָה אֶלָּא,
מֵהַחֹדֶשׁ הַזֶּה לָכֶם, שֶׁהִיא מִצְוָה רִאשׁוֹנָה שֶׁנִּצְטַוּוּ בָּה
יִשְׂרָאֵל, וּמַה טַּעַם פָּתַח בִּבְרֵאשִׁית?
*Amar Rebbi Yitzchak lo haya tzarich l'hatchil es HaTorah ela
(Shemos 12:2) me'hachodesh hazeh lachem, she'hi mitzvah*

rishona she'nitztavu bah yisrael, u'mah taam patach
b'Breishis?
Said Rabbi Isaac: It was not necessary to begin the
Torah except from "This month shall be to you (the
head of the months)," (Exodus 12:2) which is the first
commandment that the Israelites were commanded.
Now for what reason did He commence with "In the
beginning?"
(Rashi on Genesis 1:1)

Rashi is stating here that the Torah could have begun with the
twelfth chapter of the book of Exodus, where this first commandment -
to sanctify the moon and establish the lunar calendar - was delivered. If
the Torah is to be understood merely as a book of laws, then why, Rashi
asks, does God choose to begin with the story of the creation rather than
simply jumping right in with the first commandment. Rashi will go on to
respond that Torah is more than merely a book of laws, and it begins
where it does in order to establish God's "ownership," so to speak, of the
universe. This explains why an entire book and a half of the Torah precede the delivery of the first formal mitzvah, but it does not provide any
insight into why the mitzvah of the new moon is the first to be commanded.

This first commandment was communicated to the fledgeling
Israelite nation on the eve of their Exodus from Egypt, just days before
they marched out of slavery and began their journey in the desert. Two
questions must therefore be addressed: 1) why this commandment, and
2) why now? In other words, why is this precept the first one that is
communicated to the nation, and what is its relevance to the liberation
from bondage? Wouldn't we assume that there are other commandments -
like the prohibitions of idolatry, murder, theft or the other ten commandments - that would seem to be more primary and urgent than the
establishment of the months? And as the vast majority of the mitzvos,
including the ten commandments as well as the rest of the full complement of the Torah's 613 mitzvos, would be given on Mount Sinai in just a
matter of weeks, then why did this mitzvah need to be given several
weeks early when the nation had not yet left Egypt?

We can understand that the formulation of a calendar is important
for an incipient nation. Any schedule of rites, observances, and holidays

will require a framework and structure. Therefore, marking the beginning of the year and determining the measure-ment and ordering of time would certainly be one of the initial tasks undertaken by a new people setting out to establish their own identity and independence. However, it is difficult to imagine that this would be the very first initiative implemented. Furthermore, it is hard to understand why it would be so crucial a task that it would be discussed and formulated even prior to the people's independence from its oppressors. Wouldn't we expect to focus on liberation first, and only afterwards to begin to plan the society that will be built once the imminent threat of the enemy is resolved? Or even if the confidence in the coming deliverance was so great that there was to be no delay in planning for the future, wouldn't we expect that there would be more pressing issues to be addressed initially; issues like the leadership structure, the tenets of belief, or the fundamental laws that were to be enacted?

From the primacy of this mitzvah and the precise moment in history in which it was delivered we can glean two things: 1) that the establishment of the new moon and the observance of Rosh Chodesh contains a fundamental lesson that needed to precede all of the other mitzvos, and 2) that it is particularly relevant to the concept of liberation itself. The mitzvah was given on the verge of the Exodus, rather than just afterward at Mount Sinai like the other mitzvos, because it was a part of the process of leaving Egypt and it offered vital instruction on how to achieve true emancipation. Yet if we read the verse itself, it is difficult at first glance to perceive the vital guidance that it contains:

הַחֹדֶשׁ הַזֶּה לָכֶם רֹאשׁ חֳדָשִׁים רִאשׁוֹן הוּא לָכֶם לְחָדְשֵׁי הַשָּׁנָה:

Hachodesh hazeh lachem rosh chadashim rishon hu lachem l'chadshei hashana.

This month shall be to you the head of the months; to you it shall be the first of the months of the year.

(Exodus 12:2)

Read plainly, the words seem to simply instruct us which month is to be the first of the year. However, upon further analysis, we will find that the verse is teaching us something far more profound. We will note that the redundancy of the verse is perplexing. It seems to repeat itself unnecessarily, yet it is a basic tenet of Torah study that there are no extraneous words or insignificant repetitions. Therefore the verse cannot merely be telling us twice over that "this month," the month in which the Exodus occurred (the Hebrew month of Nissan), is to be the first month of the year. Rashi explains the seeming redundancy as follows:

הַחֹדֶשׁ הַזֶּה. הֶרְאָהוּ לְבָנָה בְּחִדּוּשָׁהּ וְאָמַר לוֹ כְּשֶׁהַיָּרֵחַ
מִתְחַדֵּשׁ יִהְיֶה לְךָ רֹאשׁ חֹדֶשׁ. וְאֵין מִקְרָא יוֹצֵא מִידֵי פְשׁוּטוֹ,
עַל חֹדֶשׁ נִיסָן אָמַר לוֹ, זֶה יִהְיֶה רֹאשׁ לְסֵדֶר מִנְיַן הֶחֳדָשִׁים
שֶׁיְּהֵא אִיָּר קָרוּי שֵׁנִי, סִיוָן שְׁלִישִׁי:

Hachodesh hazeh: herahu levana b'chidush v'amar lo k'she'hayareach mis'chadesh yihyeh lecha rosh chodesh. V'ein mikra yotzei midei peshuto, al Chodesh Nissan amar lo, zeh yihyeh rosh l'seder minyan hachadashim she'yhei Iyar karui sheini, Sivan shlishi.

"This month:" He [God] showed him [Moses] the moon in its renewal and said to him, "When the moon renews itself, you will have a new month." Nevertheless, a biblical verse does not lose its simple meaning. Concerning the month of Nissan, He said to him, "This shall be the first of the order of the number of the months, so Iyar shall be called the second [month], and Sivan the third [month]."

(Rashi on Exodus 12:2)

The second phrase of the verse, Rashi expounds, does indeed indicate that the current month of Nissan, in which this conversation and the ensuing Exodus occurred, will be first month of the year. However, the first phrase of the verse is telling us something different. Rashi quotes the first words of the verse - "hachodesh hazeh" - and explains that while they can be translated as "this month," that is not their only translation. "Hachodesh" means not only "month" but also "renewal," from the word "chadash/new." Therefore, "hachodesh hazeh" should be understand not simply as "this month," but as "this renewal." God showed Moses the "renewal" of the moon in the sky as it was just beginning to appear as a mere sliver after it had disappeared completely in its final phase of the previous cycle, and He informed him that this is the sign of the beginning of the month. In other words, what God was instructing

Moses here was not simply how to order the months of the year, but also how to determine when a month begins.

———————

Celebrating Absence

When does a month begin? In the secular calendar, the month's commencement is unrelated to the moon. While the term "month" is derived from "moon," it is only the length of the month that is related to the lunar cycle, and the months of the solar-based Gregorian calendar are simply twelve random divisions of roughly thirty days that have no connection to the moon's phasing. The first of any given Gregorian month, therefore, may fall at any time during the moon's progression and will fall at a different point in the lunar cycle each year. The months of the Hebrew calendar, on the contrary, are strictly coordinated to the moon's movement and appearance. But how do we know at which phase of the moon to begin the month's counting?

Unlike our discussion of the seven day week above, we don't have to think too deeply about the duration of a month or how this time period of twenty-nine or thirty days was determined. This is because the moon cycles visibly above us in a fairly regular interval. Yet we have to consider how one decides the start and end point of that cycle. Theoretically, any point on a perfect circle could be its beginning. As a cycle revolves and repeats itself indefinitely, there may be multiple places that could serve as its starting point. However, in most cycles, there are points that would more obviously be identified as the commencement and/or conclusion. In our case, in the phasing of the moon, it is unlikely that anyone would assume that the appearance of a fraction of the moon - either a crescent, gibbous, or quarter moon - would reflect the start of the cycle. But a case could certainly be made that the cycle should begin and end when the moon is full rather than when it is visibly absent.

As it has been established, the Hebrew month begins when the moon is just beginning to appear in a mere sliver, and ends when it is no longer discernible at all. The first of the month is the day after the moon has become invisible. The moon then waxes, or grows, each day until it reaches its fullness at the midpoint of the month (the 15th day), and then wanes throughout the next two weeks until it once again vanishes completely. On the monthly day of celebration, Rosh Chodesh, the moon is thus barely visible at all. Would it not make at least as much sense to begin and end the monthly cycle with the full moon? In such a scenario, Rosh Chodesh would be observed when the moon is whole and glorious in the sky; the moon would then diminish for two weeks until it becomes imperceptible, and then it would grow again for the following two weeks so that the month would culminate with the moon's plenary wholeness.

To forestall this latter proposition, God instructs Moses "hachodesh hazeh lachem rosh chadashim" - the *renewal* of the moon will be the beginning of your months. You will not begin counting the cycle from wholeness or fullness, we are told, but from emptiness. Why? This may seem like an obvious choice to us now, because this is what we are accustomed to, and it is the way it has always been done. But assume, for a moment, that we arrived on this planet with no prior knowledge or experience, and we were tasked with establishing a calendar and marking the passage of time. We would observe the moon's 29.5 day cycle and deem it a fitting period of measurement. We would then have to decide whether to begin the counting of the cycle from when the moon is fully visible, or when it is not visible at all. A reasonable debate would ensue with valid arguments for each option.

There would be those who would suggest that the celebration of the moon would be most apt when the it reaches its apex. Let us begin each month by rejoicing in the moon's full glory, and let the month end again with this ascendance and completion. Others would counter that the beginning of the month should commence with the moon's "birth," like all things that begin small and grow. Just as we begin with nothing and we increase in size, strength, knowledge, and possessions; just as we eventually reach the apex of our growth in adulthood, and then begin to decline in old age until we are once again nothingness, reabsorbed in the dust from which we were formed; so too we should track the moon's cycle from nothingness to nothingness, paralleling the cycle of life from birth to maturity to decline and then death.

Both positions are compelling and have their respective merits. In a democracy, the issue would theoretically be debated and then put to a vote. But according to Torah, humans did not consider and then decide how the month was to be counted. There was no debate and no vote. Rather, God informed Moses that the month will begin and end with the moon's absence rather than its fullness. And our task therefore is not to determine when the month commences, but rather to understand why God chose for it to begin when it does. We can do so by exploring the celebratory quality of the quasi-holiday of Rosh Chodesh. As we mentioned at the outset of this section, the beginning of the month is not merely another trivial date, as it is on the secular Gregorian calendar, but it is marked by the recitation of Hallel (the additional prayers of thanksgiving) and the musaf service, which is otherwise performed only on sabbath and holidays. Why is the inauguration of the month a cause for this type of additional gratitude and festivity?

The classic answer is that we are celebrating the concept of restoration and rejuvenation. In spite of all of the challenges and persecutions that we suffer historically and personally, we always manage to rebound and rise again from the flames. It is no coincidence that the Jewish people chart their history by the moon, for just as the moon wanes over and over again, it thereafter waxes repeatedly, regaining its former stature. Similarly, just as the Jewish nation has been persecuted and oppressed by every empire throughout history, they have eventually survived and rebuilt and flourished. Not only does the moon control the ocean tides, but the rising and falling of the moon itself mirrors the tides of Jewish history. Yet if we want to celebrate renewal, then would it not have made more sense to begin with fullness, to chart the inevitable decline that comes with life's challenges, and then to build back up to the full expression of gleaming potential? Why must the cycle begin and end with nothingness and oblivion? Doesn't this progression seem more defeating than triumphant? Isn't the initial gain subsumed in the eventual loss? What are we truly celebrating in this cyclic process of temporary increase and inevitable subsequent decline?

It would seem that one would be more inclined to celebrate not when s/he has hit rock bottom and just begins to return from the brink, but rather when, after having fallen precipitously, s/he successfully returns to the full heights of where s/he had been prior to the descent. Therefore, in terms of the celebratory nature of Rosh Chodesh, it could once again be argued that it would be more fitting to begin and end the month with the moon's fullness rather than its absence. This notion is compounded by the fact that in half of the months of the year, we observe two days of Rosh Chodesh, including both the first day of the new month as well as the last day of the previous month.[181] Therefore, in practice, half of the year we are celebrating not only on the day when a sliver of the new moon just begins to appear, but also on the day when the previous moon vanishes completely. Why did God choose this dynamic of celebrating absence rather than plenitude?

He did so to inform us that culmination in Torah is not fullness, but rather emptiness. We celebrate nullification rather than acquisition and amplitude. We recognize that it is the elimination of self and substance that renders us complete. The lesson of Rosh Chodesh is thus not only renewal, but also removal. In order to be truly whole, we must become completely empty. We must peel away all of the veils and garments that cover and conceal the "Pnei Hashem/face of God" that is at our core. Like the moon, we begin with nothing, we grow and acquire everything we can, and we then realize that our true destiny and ultimate fulfillment is "bittul/self-nullification," giving everything away and becoming nothing once again.[182] Our greatest accomplishment is the admission and revelation that we are nothing but everything - in our nothingness, we are united with all.

With this, we can now answer our previous questions regarding a) the primacy of this commandment, and b) the necessity of delivering it prior to the Exodus from Egypt. The ten commandments were deemed to be so fundamental that they were communicated prior to the hundreds of other mitzvos that were taught by Moses to the people after he had descended from Mount Sinai. If so, the mitzvah of Rosh Chodesh, which was conveyed even prior to those fundamental ten commandments, must contain a lesson/message that exceeds everything that it precedes. Even the first two mitzvos - "I am the Lord Your God" and "You shall have no other gods but me," which all of the people heard directly from God Himself, and which, the sages teach, include within them the root of all of the other mitzvos - were in some way secondary and subordinate

---

[181] Five months of the Hebrew calendar are thirty days, five months are twenty-nine days, and two months fluctuate between twenty-nine and thirty days. Whenever a month is thirty days, Rosh Chodesh is celebrated on both the first of the new month and the last of the previous month.

[182] See chapter seven, section "Bittul"

to this commandment to declare and celebrate the new moon. Why? What is so urgent and elemental about this teaching?

What the new moon teaches, as we have established, is the absolute necessity and priority of "bittul." This self-nullification is both the prerequisite for all progress, and the objective of all development. Like the moon, we begin with modesty and simplicity. As we grow in "chochmah/wisdom," we develop ever great "koach mah/the power of what," which is the ability to understand our nothingness and the humility and surrender that this wisdom breeds.[183] Without this mitzvah of the new moon, there is no way to receive any of the other mitzvos properly. If one is already full, then s/he can receive nothing new. The Talmud explains this simply as follows:

כְּלִי רֵיקָן מַחֲזִיק, מָלֵא אֵינוֹ מַחֲזִיק:
Kli reikan machazik, malei Eino machazik.
An empty vessel can hold, a full one cannot hold.
(Talmlud Brachot 40a)

The mitzvah of the new moon was delivered prior to Mount Sinai to convey to Moses and his people that in order to receive the Torah and its incredible wealth of divine wisdom, they would first need to empty themselves of everything that they previously contained. Like the complete abnegation of the moon, they must nullify themselves in preparation for the immense growth and fullness to come. This "bittul/ self-nullification" is the requisite precursor for everything to come.

But could this message not have been delivered in the desert as they approached Mount Sinai? Why was it necessary to command this first mitzvah and convey this principal teaching in Egypt before their freedom had even been gained? The fact that it preceded not only the giving of the Torah, not only the splitting the of Sea, but even the actual departure from the house of bondage, indicates that it contains some additional lesson that is particularly relevant and instructive for the process of liberation. That lesson is that it was precisely through this "bittul," symbolized by the new moon, that the liberation from slavery would be accomplished. A full vessel cannot hold, but it can be held. It is heavy

---

183 Chochmah/Wisdom as "the power of what" or humility is discussed in chapter seven, section "Bittul."

and slow and easy to restrain and manipulate. Fullness would not only inhibit the people from receiving, it would also weigh them down and tether them in place. An empty vessel, on the contrary, is not only open to receive, but it is far more difficult to grasp and hold down. It is free not only of contents, but of constraints. Like the moon in its absolute emptiness, once the people emptied themselves *of* themselves, they would no longer be detected, delimited, or detained. With true "bittul/self-nullification," one can no longer be held. As we explained earlier in chapter seven,[184] "im ain ani li, mi li," if there is no me, then no one can harm me or catch me.

We can now understand the integral role that Rosh Chodesh plays in Torah's liberation practice. The Exodus from Egypt represented freedom from a physical captor. But as we have alluded to multiple times throughout this book (and as we will discuss more fully in the upcoming section on the holiday of Passover), we have been captive and confined throughout our entire history. Not only on account of the long exile and the frequent persecutions that have spanned the bulk of our history, but more generally on account of the darkness that characterizes our very existence in this "olam" of "helam," our essence has been hidden away and constrained. As we have discussed at length, the liberation and revelation of the "Pnei Hashem" within our innermost core is the very purpose and mission of our being. The cycle of the moon and the celebration of its abnegation reminds us that we begin undifferentiated and unadorned, and that we will reach our objective and culmination only by removing all of our outward trappings and returning to our singular, unadulterated essence.

Once again, we find that the Torah's systems and rituals are far more than mere customs or legal strictures designed to control our behavior and gauge our obedience. They are guides and practices by which we can discover and manifest the divinity that is our ultimate root and reality. God introduced the commandment of the new moon to enable us to go out of the exile in Egypt, and through the mindful observance of this mitzvah each month, we can liberate ourselves from our current exile and allow the light of God's face to shine brightly from within us even on the darkest night.

---

[184] Section "Bittul"

Shana

We have discussed the life cycle (in chapter eight), the daily cycle (in chapter nine), and now the weekly cycle and the monthly cycle. We have explored the ways that their rituals and observances assist us in our lifelong task of shedding our coverings and discovering the face of God within us. We will now complete this discussion with an analysis of the annual cycle and the festivals that we celebrate throughout the year. The direction of our journey, as we have established already, is inward. However, in this chapter, it has taken us around the earth and around the moon, and it will now take us around the sun.

The yearly cycle, known as "shana/year" in Hebrew, is, as we know, the time that it takes the earth to orbit the sun. While the Hebrew calendar is generally lunar, it is also reconciled to the progression of the solar system. This reconciliation of the lunar and solar circuits involves a complicated structure of leap-years in which an additional month is added seven times every nineteen years. In order to eliminate this type of complexity, the Gregorian calendar abandoned any connection to the moon and was established as a strictly solar order - as we mentioned previously, the months in the Gregorian system are not tethered to the phases of the moon at all. However, the Hebrew calendar maintains its connection to the moon for all of the reasons discussed in the previous section. Yet simultaneously, the Torah mandates that the annual festivals occur in their proper seasons, and therefore it is also imperative for the calendar to remain consistent with the solar cycle. In other words, because the Torah dictates that "you shall observe the festival of matzos (Passover) … in the spring",[185] therefore the calendar must assure that the month of Nissan, in which Passover is celebrated, is always in the spring. If the Hebrew calendar were strictly lunar, with no mechanism of correction to calibrate it to the sun, then because twelve lunar months of 29.5 days equals only 354 days, and the cycle of the sun is 365 days, each successive year would see an additional 11 day disparity. Within a matter of just a few years, Nissan would no longer fall in the spring, and

---

[185] Exodus 34:18

Passover would no longer be celebrated in its designated time. This is the case with the strictly lunar Muslim calendar, in which holidays shift across various seasons throughout the years.

Such a shifting of seasons is untenable according to Torah, because the holidays are intrinsically connected to the time of year in which they initially occurred. This is because holidays in Torah are not simply commemorations of previous events, but rather they are actual reoccurrences of those events in the spiritual planes. The mystics teach that when we revisit a date on the calendar, we are not merely remembering what happened on this day in the past, but we are actually re-experiencing the same energy and the same divine influence that occurred at that time. Holidays and holy days in Torah are not simply celebrations of historic occasions, they are channels through which the spiritual power of those moments are made manifest and accessible again. This is the inner meaning of the verse from the Book of Esther:

וְהַיָּמִים הָאֵלֶּה נִזְכָּרִים **וְנַעֲשִׂים** בְּכָל־דּוֹר וָדוֹר:

*V'hayamim ha'eileh nizkarim **v'naasim** b'chol dor vador.*

And these days shall be remembered **and done** throughout every generation.

(Megillas Esther 9:28)

We can easily understand what it means that these days will be "remembered" in every generation. But what is the implication of the addition of the word "v'naasim/and done" in this verse? It teaches us that on the holiday of Purim, we are not merely commemorating the salvation that happened in Shushan 2400 years ago, but rather that God is now, every year on the fourteenth of the month of Adar, "doing" it again. In other words, He is sharing this miraculous power of deliverance with us now just as He did then. This is true not only of Purim, but of all the holidays. Therefore our task in celebrating them is to make ourselves sensitive to the particular divine efflux that each holiday represents, and to bring it down into our consciousness and reality.

This is the concept of the spiral of time that we introduced briefly at the beginning of this chapter. Torah's conception of time is not a line or an arc, but rather a spiral. What this means is that we are not moving linearly away from the events of our past, but we are continually returning to them, yet always at a slightly higher level. This idea is encapsulated in the very word for year itself, "שנה/shana." The root "ש-נ/

sh-n" means both "repeat" (as in the words "שני/sheini/second" and "משנה/mishneh/review") as well as "change" (as in the words "לשנות/leshanot/to change" and "שינוי/shinui/difference"). In the movement of the spiral, one is constantly repeating and retracing the circular trajectory that s/he traveled previously, but because s/he is at a somewhat more elevated station each time around, the experience is simultaneously new and different.

This, as we discussed previously in the section entitled "Revolution vs. Evolution," is how we grow. We continue to revisit scenarios and energies from our past, but each time we do, we have an opportunity to correct any previous errors and/or deficiencies. Based on the experience and insight we have gained along the way, thanks in no small part to our prior missteps, we are now able to understand more deeply and internalize ever more of the wisdom and guidance that the experience was intended to offer us. If time were to move in a line, and we were constantly encountering change (the **shinui** of shana) without simultaneously facing the repetition (the "mi**shn**eh" of shana) of the past, then we would never know if we were truly progressing or if we were simply plowing onward with no sense of direction, intention, or advancement. In the Torah's sense of time, and in the sense of "shana" as both change *and* repetition, we are moving always toward a goal. That goal is an ever deeper penetration of the mysteries of our existence. The spiral therefore takes us constantly both higher and deeper. In repeatedly revisiting our past, we bore ever closer to the core and essence which was hidden from us last time around. "Shana/year" by "shana/year," we progress level by level, removing layer after layer until we will reach and uncover that which has been awaiting us all along. Each "shana" is thus another cycle of simultaneous repetition and change that brings us to a slightly more graduated place at the end of it than we were at the beginning. Life, which is a collection of all of our years, is therefore the helix that is formed by the series of these "shana" cycles that continually move us closer to our source.

Flow

As we have established, Torah's holidays are times when the energies that emerged on that date at some point in the early history of the universe are once again manifest and accessible. They are opportunities to seize upon the flow of Godliness that was particularly conferred to us at that time. To comprehend this more clearly, it will be useful to establish what we mean by the "flow of Godliness" or divine energy. Does Godliness "flow"? Are there different flows, and therefore different types and qualities of Godliness? Are we only able to access these various emanations at certain times and under particular circumstances? This would seem to contradict Torah's fundamental principle of God's consummate oneness. If He is truly one, then is He not available everywhere at all times? How can He "flow" from one place to another if He is already in both places? And how can we suggest that His flow is more accessible at one time than another if He is eternal and beyond the construct of time?

First, we must distinguish between God and Godly flow. God is one, and yet, as we established in the opening chapters, He has intentionally hidden His unity and created multiplicity. This plurality simultaneously exists within the framework of the creation and does not exist within the ultimate reality of God's exclusive oneness. From our human perspective, and within the architecture of our limited being, there are aspects of creation that are Godly and others that are not. Ultimately what this means is that there are times and places in which God is revealed and times and places in which He is concealed. Of course there is truly nothing in which God is not present, but there are those things in and through which His presence is not recognized. Therefore, while God is indeed in all places, times, and things equally, we can say that the flow of Godliness into certain parts of the creation is not as apparent. Thus it is more difficult to access and manifest that Godliness and thereby demonstrate that this particular time, place, or thing is as Godly as everything else.

To elaborate, as we discussed in chapter two,[186] God's first act in the creation of this world was the formulation of darkness. He did so by

---

[186] Section "Good Nature"

"removing" Himself, so to speak, from the space that the world would inhabit in order that otherness could exist here. This "tzimtzum/contraction," the mystics explain, resulted in the dark "chalal/void" in which the universe would be created. Though He was in truth no less present in this "void" than He had been prior to the "tzimtzum/contraction," He made Himself and His light undetectable and seemingly absent. After this, in order to create the universe and all of its multifarious beings, He infused a portion of His light into this darkness. This beam of Godly light that was injected into the darkness is referred to as the "kav/ray," and it is the divine flow through which the universe is constructed.

While the "pshat/simple reading" of Torah's opening chapters suggests that the creation of the universe was a seven day procedure that occurred nearly six thousand years ago, Kabbala and Chassidus explain that creation was not a historic event, but rather that it is a recurrent and constant process. The "kav/ray" of Godly energy is perpetually flowing into the creation to vitalize it. God did not fashion the creation and then step away from it, allowing it to endure as an independent entity. This would imply some sort of separation from Him. As we have discussed several times now, God continuously conducts the universe in the way of "hashgacha protis/divine providence," whereby every occurrence is not only overseen by Him, but is precisely effected by Him. As there is nothing distinct from God, therefore He is recreating the world and everything in it at every moment.

The Alter Rebbe, in his treatise *Shaar Hayichud V'haemuna*,[187] explains that we tend to conceive of God's work anthropomorphically, equating it with the labor of a human being. When a human fashions something, whether it is a vessel, a building, or a work of art, s/he takes some existing material and molds it into the new form that s/he desires. But this is merely converting one configuration of substance to another. It is thus referred to as the formation of "yesh mi'yesh/something from something." God, on the contrary, does not simply transform one material into another, but rather He creates "yesh me'ayin/something from nothing," bringing about a new and unprecedented existence. In the construction of an item from some other pre-existing item, there is no need for the craftsman to maintain her/his connection to the new fabrication. As it was extant and stable prior to her/his involvement, so will it re-

---

[187] The second section of the Alter Rebbe's masterwork, *Tanya*.

main extant and stable when s/he leaves it and moves on to something else. In the creation of something from nothing, however, which is only in God's capability, the Creator cannot simply leave His creation to be on its own. He must imbue Himself in that thing in order for it to have on-going permanence. As He is one with each and every thing He has created, He cannot simply leave it behind - He must reside in it constantly. This, according to the Baal Shem Tov, is the inner meaning of the verse from Psalms:

לְעוֹלָם יְ-הֹוָה דְּבָרְךָ נִצָּב בַּשָּׁמָיִם:

L'olam A-donai divarcha nitzav bashamayim.
Forever O Lord Your word stands firm in the heavens.
(Psalms 119:89)

God's "word" is the divine speech and breath that He infuses into each creation in order to bring it into being. As we see in the opening chapter of Genesis, the phrase "and God *said* let there be..." prefaces each day's creation. The mystics teach that this indicates that it is through His spoken word that the world is born. These words and letters cannot dissipate into the ether like human speech after they are spoken, because they form the soul or spirit that remains fixed within the object that they have materialized. In order for the being to persist, the word must persist. And in order for the word to persist, it must be continually spoken. This is the Godly flow that vitalizes each aspect of the creation that would otherwise cease to exist without it.

We can now answer our question about God's omnipresence and how it is possible for something that is already everywhere to flow from one place to another. It is not that the flow of Godliness implies that God was not previously within the space or events that His energy now flows into. Rather, it is that without this influx of particular creative energy, there would be only God's infinite and undifferentiated presence there and no physical or worldly features. In other words, while God exists in the space without this Godly flow, there would be nothing visible from the perspective of the creations. The Godly flow is what creates and sustains the material world in all of its plurality.

To put all this in the more technical terms which are employed by Torah's esoteric teachings, there are various forms of God's light and influence. These include:

- "Or Ein Sof/infinite light," which is the aspect of God that exists everywhere in the higher and lower realms equally;

- "Or Makkif/Encompassing light," also known as "Sovev Kol Almin/surrounding all worlds," which is the flow of God that descends into the created universe but hovers over each creation equally because it is too lofty and powerful to dwell within the limited vessels of physicality;

- "Or Pnimi/Indwelling light," also known as "Memale Kol Almin/filling all worlds," which is a more condensed divine light that is capable of penetrating and vitalizing each individual creation according to its particular character.

The existence of God everywhere is the level of "Or Ein Sof/infinite light." The Godly flow that forms and animates creation as we see and know it is "Or Pnimi/indwelling light" or "Memale Kol Almin/filling all worlds." "Or Makif/encompassing light" or "Sovev Kol Almin/surrounding all worlds" is an intermediary level of divine energy that both transcends the creation and yet influences it. At the level of "Or Ein Sof," God is omnipresent and undifferentiated and does not exist any more at one time or place than any other. At the lower levels of "Or Makif/Sovev Kol Almin" and "Or Pnimi/Memale Kol Almin," God can be said to "flow" into the creation at different times and in varying degrees.

There is obviously far more to say on this subject, but more than this brief introduction is beyond the scope of our discussion, and it may be more confusing than helpful for those unfamiliar with these Kabbalistic concepts. What is relevant here is that while God is always present beneath the surface of all things, there is a creative divine energy that is perpetually flowing into the universe in order to enable it to persist within the framework of this perceptible material world. Yet while this general Godly flow is always streaming into the world and into each and every creation, there have been moments in history that God determined to be ripe for the introduction and/or increase of particular energies or capabilities. At these times, the normal and habitual conduct of the world is temporarily interrupted in order that there should be a supernatural influx of additional Godly energies.

In other words, while the regular "natural" functioning of the world is generally conducted through the "indwelling" level of Godly energy (Or Pnimi/Memale), there have been occasions when God has decided to overload the system, so to speak, by flooding the world with a higher level of His light than it can ordinarily accommodate. At these moments, when the flow of "encompassing light" (Or Makkif/Sovev) is intensified, the "natural" bounds of the universe break, and therefore "supernatural" or miraculous events occur. These are the miraculous events that the Torah records and which it commands us to memorialize as annual holidays on the anniversary of their occurrence. What makes them truly "holy days" is that they expose us to heights (or depths) of Godliness that we cannot ordinarily access without tremendous effort and refinement. Just as the additional divine energies became manifest and accessible when they were first introduced, so are they once again radiated into the creation each year when we return to that same position on the spiral of time. If we can attune ourselves to that schedule of flow and take advantage of the times when the doors of heaven are open, so to speak, then we will be able to avail ourselves of the especial opportunities for growth and revelation that they represent.

Musaf - The Fourth Level

We have explored the general concept of the Torah's annual cycle and the opportunity that its holidays afford us to grasp additional Godly energies that are not as readily available to us on other days of the year. Now we can begin to examine each of these holidays more specifically and the particular energies that they offer us respectively. While there are numerous holidays throughout the Hebrew year, all of which are worthy of detailed discussion, we will focus on those that are specifically mentioned in the Torah. This includes the three pilgrimage festivals of Passover, Shavuos, and Sukkos, as well as Rosh Hashana and Yom Kippur.

Before we delve into the specific particularities of these occasions, it will be worthwhile to note that there is an additional observance that is common to all of these holy days which is reflective of the increased opportunity that they offer us to access the depths of our being.

In addition to the distinct observances of each holiday, on each of them we add an extra prayer service, called "musaf." As we mentioned above in our discussion of Rosh Chodesh, the "musaf" service parallels the additional offering that was brought on the Temple altar on the sabbath and special holy days. On an ordinary day, we pray the three formal services of "shacharis/morning prayer," "mincha/afternoon prayer," and "maariv/evening prayer." On shabbat, Rosh Chodesh, and festivals, we add this fourth service, "musaf/additional prayer." As we discussed in chapter nine (section "Prayer"), each of these prayer services corresponds to the offerings that were brought on the altar in the Temple in Jerusalem.[188] Yet beyond their relationship to the procedures in the Temple, there is a more mystical reason that there are three prayer services in a typical day and four on the sabbath and holidays. This has to do with the various levels of the soul and their accessibility at these varying times.

As we have mentioned more than once, there are five distinct levels of the soul: "nefesh," "ruach," "neshama," "chaya," and "yechida." Of these, the first three - "nefesh," "ruach," and "neshama" - are contained, so to speak, within the body. The fourth level, "chaya," is too lofty and expansive to "fit" into the confines of the limited physical human form, so it hovers over the person, connected to the body but not contained within it. The fifth level, "yechida," is an aspect of the soul that is so "vast" that it cannot even descend into this world. Of course, we are not speaking of its size in terms of physical dimension, but rather its ability to be accommodated by the limited spiritual capacity of the creation. "Yechida" means "singular" or "united," and this level of our soul is so united with God's absolute oneness that its presence within the confines of space and time would obliterate all of the divisions and distinctions of this finite realm.

The three daily services correspond to the three levels of the soul that are housed within us, and which we therefore have access to on a daily basis. While the fourth level, "chaya," is close, hovering above us, it is generally just beyond our reach. It influences us subtly, but we cannot grasp it and harness its power of spiritual vision and clarity. However, there are special occasions when we are able to access this fourth level,

---

[188] Though there were only two daily offerings in the Temple, the service of the afternoon offering stretched into the evening, and therefore an evening prayer service was instituted as well.

and on those days, we therefore offered a "musaf/additional" sacrifice in the Temple when it stood, and we recite a fourth prayer service accordingly to this day. What this informs us is that what distinguishes the holy days of shabbat, Rosh Chodesh, and the festivals from the other days of the year is that we have the ability, on these days, to reach and incorporate an aspect of our being that is more elevated, powerful, and spiritually attuned than those soul levels with which we ordinarily engage the world. With this added dimension of spiritual perception and potential, we are assisted at these times in our purpose and mission of finding and revealing God's face in our core and in the core of all things.

It is as if, on these sacred occasions, we are provided an extra flashlight that enables us to more effectively penetrate and dispel the darkness around us. Or as if some of the many veils that obscure the proper route to our innermost destination are lifted during these periods, and our progress is thereby facilitated and expedited. God provides us these special occasions to assist us on our journey and to alleviate some of the burden that we carry throughout the ordinary days of the year. The question, of course, is whether we will be conscious of the supplemental power and vision that we are granted at these times; or whether we will be insensitive to these energies and therefore let these days pass like every other. If we are not sensitive to the power of these holy days, we thereby forfeit the opportunity for advancement and enlightenment that they provide us.

It is the fourth level of our soul, then, that affects us on these special occasions. If you are wondering at this point if there are any times throughout the year that we can access the fifth level of our soul, there is, in fact, one day on the calendar when we pray five services, and we will get to that shortly.

When Does The Year Begin?

We are now ready to explore the festivals more specifically. It should be noted that an entire book, and even many books, could be devoted to each of the holidays, and indeed many books have been written on each. Our discussion of these occasions will serve only as a brief introduction and will focus specifically on our topic of their role in our liberation practice. As we have already demonstrated in regard to the Torah's lifecycle events as well as its daily, weekly, and monthly rituals, all of the observances that the Torah assigns are methods and mechanisms through which we can peel away the layers of concealment that cover the face of God within us. The annual festivals are no exception. In fact, they can be understood essentially (as we will explain) as moments of pause throughout the year to redirect our attention to this work of uncovering and revealing for which we have been created.

It will be helpful to recognize the Torah's festivals not as a series of individual occasions, but rather as a sequence of events that build on one another to create a program for development and inner discovery throughout the year. To do so, we must determine where to begin. As we discussed previously in regards to the monthly cycle, it is not always easy to detect the starting point of a circle, as all of its points are identical. The Hebrew calendar makes this even more complicated, as it identifies multiple beginnings to the year. There are actually four "new years" designated by the Torah:

אַרְבָּעָה רָאשֵׁי שָׁנִים הֵם. בְּאֶחָד בְּנִיסָן רֹאשׁ הַשָּׁנָה לַמְּלָכִים
וְלָרְגָלִים. בְּאֶחָד בֶּאֱלוּל רֹאשׁ הַשָּׁנָה לְמַעְשַׂר בְּהֵמָה. רַבִּי
אֶלְעָזָר וְרַבִּי שִׁמְעוֹן אוֹמְרִים, בְּאֶחָד בְּתִשְׁרֵי. בְּאֶחָד בְּתִשְׁרֵי
רֹאשׁ הַשָּׁנָה לַשָּׁנִים וְלַשְּׁמִטִּין וְלַיּוֹבְלוֹת, לַנְּטִיעָה וְלַיְרָקוֹת.
בְּאֶחָד בִּשְׁבָט, רֹאשׁ הַשָּׁנָה לָאִילָן, כְּדִבְרֵי בֵית שַׁמַּאי. בֵּית
הִלֵּל אוֹמְרִים, בַּחֲמִשָּׁה עָשָׂר בּוֹ:

Arbaa rashei shanim heim. B'echad b'Nissan rosh hashana la'melachim v'la'regalim. B'echad b'Elul rosh hashana l'maasar beheima. Rabbi Elazar v'rabbi Shimon omrim, b'echad b'Tishrei. B'echad b'Tishrei, Rosh hashana la'shanim v'la'shmittin v'la'yovlos, la'netiah v'layerakos. B'echad b'-Shevat, rosh hashana la'ilan, k'divrei Beis Shammai. Beis Hillel omrim, ba'chamisha asar bo.

There are four new years: The first of Nissan is the new year for kings and for festivals. The first of Elul is the new year for the tithe of beasts. Rabbi Elazar and Rabbi Shimon say: the first of Tishri. The first of Tishri is the new year for years, for shmita and jubilee years, for planting and for [tithe of] vegetables. The first of Shevat

is the new year for trees, according to the words of Bet Shammai. Bet Hillel says: on the fifteenth of that month.
(Mishnah, Rosh Hashana 1:1)

The Mishnah here identifies four different starting points for the annual cycle. This is somewhat confusing, but it is only truly confounding if we conceive of time as linear. When we understand time as cyclical, however, or as a spiral as we have discussed at length, then these multiple starts are less perplexing. Because a circle has no beginning and no end, there can be multiple points of embarkation. The question becomes what it is that we are tracking. If it is the cycle of trees, then we begin on the day (in Israel) after the winter season ends and the new fruits begin to grow. If it is the cycle of vegetable tithes, then we begin on the day that is designated for the new season of planting crops. If it is the cycle of years, then we begin with the anniversary of creation. Yet what remains strange is that the cycle of festivals does not correspond with the cycle of years. The first of the month of Nissan is the new year for festivals, but the first of the month of Tishrei, exactly six months later, is the new year for years. If the world was created in Tishrei,[189] then wouldn't it make sense to celebrate the cycle of festivals from that day as well? What is even more perplexing is that the month of Tishrei is referred to in Torah as the seventh month.

בַּחֹדֶשׁ הַשְּׁבִיעִי בְּאֶחָד לַחֹדֶשׁ יִהְיֶה לָכֶם שַׁבָּתוֹן זִכְרוֹן תְּרוּעָה מִקְרָא־קֹדֶשׁ:

Bachodesh ha'shvii b'echad la'chodesh yihyeh lachem shabbaton zichron teruah mikrah kodesh.

In the seventh month, on the first of the month, it shall be a Sabbath for you, a remembrance of the shofar blast a holy occasion.
(Leviticus 23:24)

---

[189] The first day of creation was actually six days earlier than the first day of Tishrei, on the twenty-fifth of Elul. The first of Tishrei, which we celebrate as the beginning of time, was actually the sixth day of creation, the day on which Adam and Eve were created. God established this day as Rosh Hashana because humanity is the primary goal and purpose of the creation.

This is a reference to the holiday of Rosh Hashana, which commemorates the creation of the universe on the first of Tishrei. If this date was indeed the beginning of creation, then why is it called the seventh month?

The sages explain that while there are four "new years" in Torah, two of them pertain particularly to human history and experience. The first is the beginning of humanity in general, which occurred on the first of Tishrei. The second is the birth of the Hebrew nation, which began in the month of Nissan with the Exodus from Egypt, and culminated forty days later with the giving of the Torah on Mount Sinai. Both of these beginnings were monumental, and each of them is marked and celebrated with a succession of profound holidays. Rosh Hashana, Yom Kippur, and Sukkos occur in Tishrei, and Passover falls in Nissan followed by Shavuos seven weeks later. However, the "new beginning" that occurred with the birth of the nation at the Exodus from Egypt was an even more significant start, in many ways, than the creation of the universe two and a half millennia earlier. This is because the creation of the world was only a setup, so to speak, for the giving of the Torah. The Torah was the tool with which the creation would be completed and perfected. Tishrei, the chassidic masters explain, was the origin of the natural conduct of the world. Nissan was the origin of the miraculous conduct that would enable us to transcend the world's inherent limitations and reveal the infinite within the finite. Therefore, Torah counts Nissan as the first month, and Tishrei is counted as the seventh.

This will enable us to address a classic question posed by the sages regarding the wording of the first of the Ten Commandments:

אָנֹכִי יְ-הֹוָה אֱ-לֹהֶיךָ אֲשֶׁר הוֹצֵאתִיךָ מֵאֶרֶץ מִצְרַיִם מִבֵּית עֲבָדִים:

Anochi A-donai E-lohecha asher hotzeisicha me'eretz Mitzrayim mi'beis avadim.

I am the Lord your God who took you out of the land of Egypt from the house of bondage.

(Exodus 20:2)

Why, in this opening statement to the nation at Mount Sinai does God introduce Himself, so to speak, as the One who took us out of Egypt? Wouldn't it have been more "impressive" for Him to mention His creation of the universe? Should He not have said something like 'I am the Lord your God who fashioned you from nothingness and created every single aspect of the world that you inhabit'? Granted, the people had just experienced the miracles of the ten plagues and the splitting of the sea which effectuated their liberation from generations of slavery. Yet isn't the formation of the cosmos an even greater display of God's omnipotence than the Exodus?

To answer this question, the mystics explain that while the creation was ineffably great, it did not reflect God's ultimate intent. God would introduce Himself in the opening of the ten commandments as the One who took us out of Egypt because there is something about this act of liberation that expresses His being and essence even more than His creation of the universe does. While Tishrei would forever commemorate the "what" of creation, Nissan would commemorate the "why." What is this underlying "why," and what is it that is so fundamental about the Passover story that even as we continue to count the years from the date of the original creation in Tishrei, the time of the Exodus would become the starting point from which the cycle of the months and festivals of the year would from now on be counted?

Passover

Passover is the anniversary of the Exodus from Egypt. In its most basic sense, it marks the birth of the Hebrew nation subsequent to their emancipation from generations of forced servitude and crushing labor. But there must be something more to this holiday than the commemoration and celebration of independence. Freedom and self-determination are certainly worthy of festivity and remembrance, but the extent to which the Exodus is hallowed and centralized in Torah practice indicates that it is more than a simple independence day, like America's Fourth of July or the modern state of Israel's Yom Ha'Atzmaut. As we mentioned above, the Exodus is so integral to God's plan for creation that of all the ways He could have introduced Himself in the first of the ten commandments, with the very first words that He utters to the nation from Mount Sinai He chooses to identify Himself as the force behind this liberation: "I am the Lord your God who took you out of the land of Egypt from the house of bondage" (Exodus 20:2). Furthermore, as also discussed above, from the time of the Exodus onward, the cycle of the year is shifted to begin from this momentous occasion. In case these are not enough to indicate the intense significance of this event, we are commanded to remember and mention the Exodus every single day:

לְמַעַן תִּזְכֹּר אֶת־יוֹם צֵאתְךָ מֵאֶרֶץ מִצְרַיִם כֹּל יְמֵי חַיֶּיךָ:

L'maan tizkor es-yom tzeischa me'eretz Mitzrayim kol yimai chayecha.

You shall remember the day when you went out of the land of Egypt all the days of your life.

(Exodus 16:3)

This verse is recited as the first of the "six remembrances" that must be recalled daily and are therefore enumerated at the conclusion of the morning prayer. Additionally, the Exodus is mentioned in the culminating verse of the Shema prayer every morning and evening:

אֲנִי יְ-הֹוָה אֱ-לֹהֵיכֶם אֲשֶׁר הוֹצֵאתִי אֶתְכֶם מֵאֶרֶץ מִצְרַיִם
לִהְיוֹת לָכֶם לֵא-לֹהִים אֲנִי יְ-הֹוָה אֱ-לֹהֵיכֶם:

Ani A-donai E-loheichem asher hotzeisi eschem me'eretz Mitzrayim l'hiyos lachem l'E-lohim Ani A-donai E-loheichem.

I am the Lord, your God, Who took you out of the land of Egypt to be your God; I am the Lord, your God.

(Numbers 15:41)

As we detailed in chapter nine,[190] the Shema prayer and its declaration of God's complete oneness is the focus and apex of our daily meditation. What is the relevance of the Exodus to this fundamental statement of divine unity? We don't connect any of the other holidays or historic events to the Shema. We don't mention the many other miraculous deliverances and salvations throughout our history every day, let alone multiple times every day. What is so important about leaving Egypt that it becomes not just the occasion of one of Torah's primary hol-

---

190 Section "Uncovering and Uniting"

idays, but also arguably the most predominant trope and theme in Torah practice and literature?

To answer these question, we must reiterate that Torah's holidays are not merely commemorations of historic events, but they are the recurrence each year of the same divine energy that flowed into the creation on that date. They mark and represent, therefore, not merely experiences that we wish to remember and celebrate, but concepts and forces that have been encapsulated and materialized in the physical historic circumstances that the holiday memorializes. While this is true of all of the Torah's holidays, it is particularly emphasized regarding Passover. The idea and energy that the Exodus represents is liberation, and the sages of the Talmud decreed that it is not sufficient for us to celebrate on Passover the fact that our ancestors were liberated from slavery millennia ago. Rather, each of us must consider it as if we ourselves have left Egypt personally and presently:

בְּכָל דּוֹר וָדוֹר חַיָּב אָדָם לִרְאוֹת אֶת עַצְמוֹ כְּאִלּוּ הוּא יָצָא מִמִּצְרַיִם, שֶׁנֶּאֱמַר וְהִגַּדְתָּ לְבִנְךָ בַּיּוֹם הַהוּא לֵאמֹר, בַּעֲבוּר זֶה עָשָׂה ה' לִי בְּצֵאתִי מִמִּצְרָיִם.

B'chol dor va'dor chayav adam liros es atzmo k'elu hu yatza miMitzrayim, shene'emar (Shemos 13:8), v'higadta l'bincha bayom ha'hu leimor, baavor zeh asa Hashem li b'tzeisi miMitrzayim.

In every generation a man is obligated to regard himself as though he personally had gone forth from Egypt, because it is said, "And you shall tell your son on that day, saying: It is because of that which the Lord did for me when I came forth out of Egypt" (Exodus 13:8).
(Mishna Pesachim 10:5)

The verse from the book of Exodus that is quoted in this mishna - "And you shall tell your son on that day…" - is the source for the mitzvah to tell the story of the salvation from Egypt to our children every year at the Passover seder. In recounting the story, we are to tell our children of the miraculous deliverance that God "did for _me_ when _I_ came forth" from Egypt. This, of course, raises the question of whether each of us did in fact go out of Egypt. In one sense, this can be understood as a reference to the experience of our soul in a past incarnation. It is taught that there are only 600,000 root souls from which all Jewish souls throughout history originated,[191] and each of those root souls was represented by the 600,000 Israelite men that left Egypt at the time of the Exodus. Therefore, each of us was there and "personally (went) forth from Egypt," as the mishna suggests. However, the rabbis teach that the Exodus that each of us participates in was not merely this historical event that occurred three and a half millennia ago. Rather it recurs, as the mishnah states "in every generation." The mystics take this even further, insisting that the Exodus takes place not only in every generation, and not only every year on the holiday of Passover, but veritably every day! In quoting this Mishnah in *Tanya*, the Alter Rebbe makes two astounding additions:

בְּכָל דּוֹר וָדוֹר **וּבְכָל יוֹם וָיוֹם** חַיָּיב אָדָם לִרְאוֹת עַצְמוֹ כְּאִילוּ הוּא יָצָא **הַיּוֹם** מִמִּצְרָיִם.

*B'chol dor va'dor **u'b'chol yom va'yom** chayav adam liros atzmo k'elu hu yatza **hayom** miMitzrayim.*

In every generation **and every day** a man is obligated to regard himself as though he personally had gone forth **that day** from Egypt.

(Tanya, Likkutei Amarim ch. 47)

The Alter Rebbe here insists that every one of us must consider it as if s/he is leaving Egypt every single day. What could this possibly mean? We are not in Egypt, so how can we go forth from there? Sadly, slavery still exists in some parts of the world, and in terms of illicit human trafficking, it continues even in the most modern and civilized societies around the globe. Yet the vast majority of us have never known slavery, and therefore it is difficult to understand how we are to regard ourselves as though we are personally being emancipated each day. This is even more of a conundrum when we recognize that "*chayav* Adam liros atzmo/a person is **obligated** to view himself" this way. How are we to fulfill this "obligation" daily? The Alter therefore clarifies what this daily liberation means:

וְהִיא יְצִיאַת נֶפֶשׁ הָאֱ-לֹהִית מִמַּאֲסַר הַגּוּף.

---

[191] See Arizal, *Shaar HaGilgulim*, chapter 11

> *V'hi yetzias nefesh ha'E-lohis mi'maasar haguf.*
> This refers to the release of the divine soul from the
> confinement of the body.
> (ibid)

The Exodus is the release of our spirit from its imprisonment in, and servitude to, the body and the constraints of the material word more generally. This is the captivity that we are all subject to constantly. By virtue of the nature of this "olam/world" of "helam/concealment,"our essence is obscured and suppressed by the animal crust in which it is contained, as we have detailed. The Exodus from Egypt, therefore, is not only an episode in our ancestral timeline, it is a metaphor for our perpetual reality. The slave is our soul, Pharaoh and his taskmasters are the forces that inhibit us from expressing our infinite Godliness, and Egypt is the environment of darkness and unconsciousness that shrouds and entraps us. The Exodus from Egypt is therefore such a focal and daily theme because it is precisely the discovery and revelation of our innermost essence that, as we have been discussing throughout this book, is our primary mission and purpose.

The Sages teach that the the Hebrew name for Egypt, "מִצְרַיִם/ Mitzrayim," is related to the word "מֵיצָרִים/meitzarim," which means "straits" or "limitations." Egypt, therefore, is representative of all boundaries and shackles in our life, and "yetzias Mitzrayim/going out of Egypt" is a daily process of "yetzias meitzarim/going out of limitation." We must work constantly to go beyond those things that consign and confine us to the flawed and finite beings that we believe ourselves to be. Passover is thus a celebration of our divine potential and our ability to transcend all of the bounds that have been holding us back from expressing our infinite essence. Yet if one is to truly regard her/himself, as the Alter Rebbe obligates, as if s/he is leaving Egypt *every day*, then what is the particular significance of the holiday of Passover? If transcending our limitations is a daily practice and requirement - if, in other words, we are to "bakshu panav tamid/seek His face within us constantly"[192] - then what is it about Passover that is so holy and extraordinary?

The answer is that while we are perpetually engaging in the work of going beyond our limitations and discovering the light that is

---

[192] See chapter two, section "The Joy of the Search"

hidden behind the darkness, on Passover God granted us special assistance and potential to do so. On these seven days (eight days outside of Israel), He infused into this world an extra capacity for liberation and transcendence. Therefore, on the recurrence of these dates every year, we once again revisit the point on the spiral of time in which these additional energies are radiated into the creation. We thus have the ability at this time to once again take advantage of this supplemental divine power to fulfill our task of finding God's face within our core. While we are working to go out from our "meitzarim/limitations" every day, our "kavana/ intention" on Passover is to devote even greater effort and mindfulness than usual to this process because we know that this is a particularly fortuitous time for liberation. Simultaneously, we are trying to gather as much as we can of the additional power that is accessible on these holy days, so that we can utilize it to continue to strive for liberation after the holiday is over and throughout the year ahead.

To provide an analogy, it is as if we have been imprisoned and devising an escape plan all year long, and we find out that on a certain date, our allies on the outside will sabotage the transformer that provides power to the electric fence that surrounds the camp. There will remain guards to overcome, and the fence and walls will yet need to be scaled and surmounted, so escape will therefore still not be easy or guaranteed. But the electric fence has always been our most imposing obstacle, and knowing the time that it will be disabled provides us our best chance of breaking free. It will take our captors a week to restore power, and therefore, during these seven days, we will seize the opportunity to fight for our freedom even more ferociously than we have throughout the rest of the year. If we are not aware that the fence has been deactivated at this time, then we will not take advantage of the additional assistance that we have been granted. If we do seize the moment, we are not guaranteed success, but through our increased efforts and engagement with our captors, we will learn something about their strategies and fortifications. This will assist us in our ongoing struggle for escape throughout the rest of the year even after the power to the fence is restored.

Splitting Open

We have established that the Exodus represents liberation from limitations. On a simple level, this concept of emancipation is applicable to all of our personal constraints and shortcomings. We mention the Exodus daily because each day is an opportunity for growth and development as we endeavor to constantly improve and surpass today the obstacles that hindered us yesterday. On a deeper level, the limitations that we strive to transcend are more universal than personal. Leaving Egypt in this sense is not merely about becoming a better or more actualized person, but about going beyond the artificial boundaries of this world completely. At this level, we mention the Exodus daily because we are working every day to escape the confines of this material reality and to reveal the divine unity that is hidden beneath it. This is why the subject of the Exodus is appended to the recital of the Shema. When we meditate on the ultimate reality of God's oneness, we liberate ourselves from any and all of the worldly boundaries and restrictions that have previously held us and concealed our unlimited Godly essence.

We have explained that while we are working toward this transcendence daily, Passover is a particularly auspicious time for this liberation. This is because God infuses, every year on these days, additional energy into the world that both strengthens our ability to escape and weakens the power of the world to confound and confine us. Yet an important question remains: does God not want us to be in this metaphorical "Mitzrayim/Egypt"? Aren't the "meitzarim/limitations" in which we are bound also His creation and His intention? If He wanted us to be "free," then wouldn't we be free already?

If, as we have asserted repeatedly, everything is "hashgacha protis/divine providence," such that every occurrence is precisely as God determines and desires it to be, then it would seem that we are meant to be lost in the "helam/darkness" of this "olam/world." And it would seem that we will not be able to be released from our current captivity within the material world until He determines it is time, no matter how much or little energy we devote to our liberation. Why, then, should we be working so hard to free ourselves? And why does He keep teasing us, every year on Passover, and every day at the mention of the Exodus, with the notion that we can and should transcend our bounds this very moment? To make our question more concrete, why did God subject us to the slavery of Egypt if He wanted us to be free? And if He wants us to be free now, then why does He allow us to continue to languish in the darkness of exile?

In order to answer these questions, we must explore the underlying spiritual dynamics that the events of the Passover story represent. In chapter nine,[193] we mentioned the mystical significance of the splitting of the sea, which was the culmination of the Passover story that had begun seven days earlier. The first day of Passover is the fifteenth day of the month of Nissan, the date that the slaves departed Egypt proper. The end of the holiday is a week later, which is the day of the splitting and crossing of the sea. As the narrative goes, Moses had been commanded by God to order Pharaoh to let the people go, Pharaoh refused, and God afflicted Egypt with ten plagues. After the tenth plague, Pharaoh relented, and Moses and the Israelite nation marched out of Egypt toward the desert. Three days later, Pharaoh regretted his decision and chased after his former slaves with his entire army. He caught up to them on the sixth day on the banks of the Red Sea, and the following morning God made the waters split. The Israelites fled into the seabed and the army followed. When the slaves emerged from the seabed, God allowed the waters to crash down onto the pursuing army, drowning them and completing the process of liberation.

As we explained in our discussion of the "Song of the Sea"[194] (which we recite in our prayer service every morning), the "yam/sea" represents the barrier between the world of concealment and the realm of infinite revelation. There is a need for a sturdy boundary between these two realms, because limitation cannot exist in the presence of infinity. In other words, if the infinite light from the highest worlds was able to seep into the lower realm, the darkness would be obliterated, and all of the creations that rely on the concealment of God's infinity in order to exist as independent beings would cease to be. The splitting of the sea signifies an opening of that boundary in order to allow into this lower world a glimmer of the infinite Godly light that had previously been carefully prohibited from penetrating into the darkness. Passover is

---

193 Section "More Darkness, More Light"

194 See chapter 9, section "More Darkness, More Light."

therefore a reversal of the dynamic of concealment that God had established at the very beginning of creation. What is the reason for this sudden tear in the fabric of creation? Why did God decide at this moment that the "olam/world" of "helam/concealment" needed an infusion of some of the light that He had hidden from it until now? Furthermore, if this splitting of the sea is the moment of ultimate liberation, then what is the significance of the first day of Passover seven days earlier, and why is this first day the primary occasion of feasting and celebration?

God created darkness and concealed Himself in order to allow for the possibility of otherness, as we have explored at length.[195] The very creation of the world, then, was the establishment of "meitzarim/ limitations," because without limitations, there would be only God's oneness, and nothing else could exist. In His desire for beings who He could give to and nurture, God therefore hid His infinity and constructed a realm of apparent limits. These confines were created in love, so that we seemingly individual and independent creatures could come to be. We lost sight, however, of the fact that the boundaries erected around us were only a framework for our existence. We forgot that there was a source and force of our being that was not truly constrained by the limitations, and that these limits were created only to allow us to perceive ourselves as distinct. We thus became lost and captive within the construct that was made to serve and support us. We became attached to the world and mired in it, forgetting that we were the very reason for its origin. This is what it means to be enslaved.

As time wore on, we became ever more blind to the nature of our ultimate reality. From the realm of "meitzarim/limitations" into which we were born, we eventually descended to the land of "Mitzrayim," a state of complete unconsciousness and bondage. It is one thing to be a soul that is housed in, and therefore constrained by, a body. It is quite another thing to identify completely with the body and forget that we are the soul that resides within it. At this point, we have become enmeshed, entranced, and enslaved by the material world. We believe in our powerlessness and in the ability of a mortal ruler like Pharaoh to control us. We have ceased to believe in our ability to be free. In such a circumstance of utter degradation and myopia, God determines that it is now time to res-

---

195 See chapter two, section "Good Nature"

cue us and to take us out of Egypt in order to remind us of who and what we ultimately are.

He does so by breaking the system, so to speak. The Hebrew word for Passover is "פֶּסַח/Pesach," which literally means "to skip" or "leap over." In the Passover story, the "pshat," or simple significance, of this term is that the angel of death "skipped over" the houses of the Israelites during the tenth plague, and he killed the first born only in the homes that did not have blood painted on the doorpost. Yet on a more mystical level, what was "leapt over" on this date were the boundaries of the orderly, limited conduct of the world. As we explained above in the section "Flow," this world is ordinarily governed by "Memale Kol Almin," a Godly light that is contracted to the extent that it is able to "fit" into the confines of the material world. This flow creates borders and systems. It crystalizes and vitalizes the creation without overpowering it. Yet at the time of the Exodus, God decided that the structure of the universe needed to be ruptured temporarily in order to remind His creations that they were not truly bound within it. He therefore "leapt over" the habitual and "natural" conduct of the creation by infusing a higher level flow, the light of "Sovev Kol Almin." This Godly light, which literally means "surrounds all worlds," is too powerful to be contained by the narrow framework of the creation, and therefore hovers, so to speak, above and around it. By directing this inordinate light into the world, God breaks the "meitzarim/limitations" of "Mitzrayim/Egypt" and allows the erstwhile slaves to leap over the constraints that have imprisoned them.

This then, is what occurred in the spiritual realms on Passover. On the first day of the holiday, which fell on the fifteenth of the month of Nissan, God overloaded the system, so to speak, with the infusion of an energy that it could not contain and incorporate. This resulted in a breach in the walls of reality that enabled the enslaved people to break free from their powerful captors. Yet this was not the end of the process. The infusion of "Sovev Kol Almin" enabled the people to leave "Mitzrayim/Egypt," but it did not destroy "Mitzrayim" or the "metizarim/limitations" that it represents. Pharaoh and his forces soon pursued the nation into the desert. Though the people had left Egypt, Egypt still existed within them, so to speak, and therefore would follow them wherever they went.

As the mystics point out, there is slavery to an external master, and then there is an internal slavery whereby one may be physically free but remains psychically and spiritually bound. Such is the situation of most of us today. Though we are controlled by no whip-wielding taskmaster, we are shackled by the limits that we place on ourselves and the restrictions that we believe about our existence. It is as if Pharaoh and his army chase and threaten us even though we are ostensibly free. In order to be liberated from this type of servitude, it is not enough to leave Egypt, but the Egypt within us must be destroyed. This is accomplished by the splitting of the sea, through which "Or Ein Sof/infinite light," an even greater efflux of Godly light than "Sovev Kol Almin," is admitted into the world when the screen that divides between the realms of finitude and infinity is torn open. Such a profusion of God's infinite light flooded into the world at that moment that the forces of "Mitzrayim/meitzarim" were overwhelmed and eliminated.

This, however, was not a permanent change to the creation. Soon after the sea split, its waters crashed down and once again covered the seabed. The boundary was sealed as it had previously been, and the "natural" conduct of the universe resumed. God's intention was not to obliterate the finite world that He had established, but only to rupture its boundaries temporarily in order to provide His creations a glimpse of their transcendent essence and potential. For those precious moments that the veil was opened, the people were able to apprehend the "pnimyus/inwardness" of all things - they could see the "Pnei Hashem/face of God" that dwells in their core and the core of all of reality. With this vision and insight, the worldly forces that had dominated and crushed them instantly melted away. Afterwards, having armed His children with this new understanding of their sublime nature, God drew the veil over His face once again and restored the finite dynamics of the universe so that His relationship with His creation could continue.

While the extreme darkness and captivity of "Mitzrayim/Egypt" had been destroyed, the regular "meitzarim/limitations" of the world would persist. Throughout history from then on, the "helam/concealment" of this "olam/world" would cause us to forget that the limitations are created for our benefit so that we can exist. We would lose sight and awareness of the "Pnei Hashem" within our "pnimyus." Therefore, we would speak of the Exodus daily in order to remind ourselves of our liberty. And each year on the anniversary of these events, we would once again be granted the ability to re-experience them on the spiritual plane, and thereby to maintain or connection to our ultimate divine reality.

New Beginning

We can now answer all of our previous questions on this subject:

Why did God decide it was now time to reverse the process of concealment that He had initiated 2500 years earlier with the creation of the universe? Why do we celebrate the first day of Passover more outwardly than the seventh day even though a higher degree of revelation occurred on the seventh day? Why, from the time of the Exodus, did the calendar shift so that thereafter the year was counted from Nissan, the time of the Exodus, rather than Tishrei, the time of the creation?

In the very first chapter of this book,[196] we explained the set up that God established for His creation. He would begin with darkness, and only afterwards would He introduce His light. Only if God concealed His oneness completely would it be possible for the world's inhabitants to consider themselves "other" and thereby serve as recipients of God's love and generosity. The first phase of the universe would therefore be a period of increasing darkness and obscuration in order to bring the creations to a sense of absolute independence and individuality. While the first beings, Adam and Eve, spoke openly with their Creator, and the first generations of their descendants knew God and received occasional communications from Him, as the centuries wore on, knowledge of, and apparent connection to, God became increasingly remote. Within ten generations, the people of earth had become oblivious to their Source.

וַיַּרְא אֱ-לֹהִים אֶת־הָאָרֶץ וְהִנֵּה **נִשְׁחָתָה** כִּי־**הִשְׁחִית** כָּל־בָּשָׂר אֶת־דַּרְכּוֹ עַל־הָאָרֶץ:

*Va'yar E-lohim es ha'aretz v'hinei **nishchasa** ki **hishchis** kol basar es Darko al ha'aretz.*

---

[196] Section "Intentional Error"

God saw the earth, and behold it had become **corrupted**, for all flesh had **corrupted** its way on the earth. (Genesis 6:12)

Interestingly, the word for "corrupted" that is used twice in this verse, "נִשְׁחָתָה/nishchasa" and "הִשְׁחִית/hishchis," both come from the infinitive "לְהַשְׁחִית," which also means "to deface." After ten generations of increasing concealment, the earth had become "de*faced*" - it had fallen into corruption because it had completely lost sight of its face, the "Pnei Hashem" that is its underlying essence and reality. Yet there was one man who was righteous in this generation. "Noah found favor in the eyes of the Lord"[197] because he had not forgotten God. Thus he and his family were saved when the rest of the earth's inhabitants were wiped out in the flood.

Yet within a matter of another ten generations, the multitudes that had derived from Noah's progeny had also abandoned their Creator and rebelled against Him with the tower of Babel. Abraham was born in this twentieth generation, and now that God's children had forgotten Him entirely, the set up was complete and it was time for God to begin to reveal Himself. Now that the darkness was so thick that those who dwelled within it did not even realize that it was dark - the concealment itself was concealed from them - the time had come to begin to reintroduce them to light. Abraham began the process, and five hundred years later, the nation that had developed from his descendants would be freed from Egypt and provided an unobstructed glimpse of God's infinite light when the sea split open for them. "Mitzrayim/Egypt" was the result of two and a half millennia of increasing darkness. The Exodus was the moment that God determined that the first phase - the establishment of utter concealment - was concluded and the time for the second act of the story - the liberation from darkness and the revelation of Godliness in the world - had come.

He began this second phase, as we mentioned above, with an infusion of energy into the system that it could not contain. The structure was thereby breached, and his children "leapt over" the boundaries that had constrained them. Their erstwhile masters chased after them into the desert, and in order to eliminate the threat of recapture and further en-

---

[197] Genesis 6:8

slavement - from both outside of them and within them - God split open on the seventh day the boundary between this finite world and the realm of infinite divine revelation. While this splitting of the sea at the end of Passover reflects an even greater manifestation of God's infinite light than the influx of energy which breached the limits of "Mitzrayim" on the first day, we conduct the seder at the outset of the holiday because this was the beginning of the process of "leaping over" and our ongoing project of liberation. The light that we can access on the seventh day is extraordinarily lofty and precious, but it is so sublime and inscrutable that it is beyond the senses of all but the most mystic seers. The Alter Rebbe referred to "Shvii shel Pesach/the seventh day of Passover" as the happiest day of the year because of the intense Godliness that is accessible then. Yet the seventh day is not as widely observed as the first day because few are cognizant of the supremely rarefied light that streams into the creation at this time.[198]

With all this, we can now understand why the yearly cycle shifts at this moment and thereafter begins with Passover, and why the Exodus is such a prevalent theme in Torah practice. The "leaping over" of boundaries and "tearing open" of coverings that Passover represents are precisely the processes of exploration and revelation that we have been discussing throughout this book and pursuing throughout our journey. Our very purpose and mission (as laid out in the verses "Breishis bara Elokim/the primary thing is to reveal God" and "lech lecha/go to you") is to pull back the veil and penetrate all barriers that impede our inward progress in order to reveal the "Pnei Hashem" that is hidden within our "pnimyus." "Breishis bara Elokim" describes the creation of the universe, and therefore came two and half millennia prior to the Exodus. And "lech lecha" was the first communication that is recorded between God and Abraham and therefore came four centuries prior to the Exodus. However, it wasn't until the nation of slaves left Egypt that these directives became not only possible, but became the formalized mission statement of an entire nation, and through them, the entire world.

History until the Exodus from Egypt was a gradual increase of concealment and limitation. The Exodus was a new beginning, a com-

---

[198] Some chassidim have the practice of remaining awake throughout the seventh night of Passover to study Torah and prepare themselves for the vast spiritual revelation of the splitting of the sea that occurs at dawn.

plete innovation in the direction of the universe. While the first phase of history was a process of burying, from the time of the Exodus onward, we have been gradually excavating and digging out. The counting of the months shifts from Tishrei to Nissan because the entire focus of our existence shifts at this moment.

We can see this shift toward the "panim/pnimyus" in the language that Moses uses to describe these events. In recounting the story of the Exodus shortly before his death in the book of Deuteronomy, Moses states:

וַיּוֹצִאֲךָ **בְּפָנָיו** בְּכֹחוֹ הַגָּדֹל מִמִּצְרָיִם:

Vayotziacha b'fanav b'kocho hagadol miMitzrayim.
And He (God) took you out of Egypt **before Him** with His great strength.
(Deuteronomy 4:37)

As we have seen many times already, the word "בְּפָנָיו/b'fanav" is simply translated as "before Him," which can mean either 'in His presence' or 'in front of Him.' Rashi thus comments that on the simple level, the verse is telling us that the manner in which God delivered us from Egypt was like a father who leads His son but allows the son to walk "in front of him." Yet we know by now that "panav" literally means "His face," and that therefore if we read the verse literally, it can also be translated "and He took you out **in** His face..." or "He took you out **with** His face...." On a deeper level, Moses is therefore informing us *how* God liberated us (and liberates us today) from all boundary and limitation. He did/does so by revealing "panav/His face" and by inviting us into the realm of His infinite reality.

Leaving Egypt is the beginning of the process of going out from the concealment of this world and going into His face, which is the recognition that He is the "pnimyus/essence" of everything. This is the journey that we have been on throughout this book, and indeed it is the journey that we are on every day and every moment of our lives. While this journey ultimately began at the very outset of the creation, it was not revealed to us as our mission and purpose until we went forth from Egypt. Passover marks the beginning of the cycle of the holidays, as well as the new beginning of the counting of the months, because it is the inception of the journey to the face and essence of our existence that we have been engaged in ever since.

Sefiras Haomer

As we mentioned previously, the Torah's festivals are a sequence of events rather than a series of unrelated occasions. From the beginning of the yearly cycle to its end, we are engaged in a progressive process of growth and discovery that carries us ever closer to our goal. Though the process may not be completed in a single yearly cycle, each revolution around the course of the holidays brings us gradually higher/deeper so that we begin again the following year slightly more advanced along the spiral of time. The beginning of the process, as we have identified, is Passover's liberation from utter darkness and constriction. Released from our chains on the first day of Passover, the starting gate is raised and we set out on our way. This is an unprecedented moment and a powerful new beginning. Yet liberation is only a beginning, not an end in itself. Where are we to go now, and what are we to do with this new freedom? Have we been released from slavery merely to wander in the desert, untethered and aimless? If not, then God must provide us some direction. Seven days after the Exodus, He does so. The sea splits, and we are granted a glimpse of our goal and destination. We perceive a glimmer of the heavenly light that we are seeking and that we are destined to eventually reveal. But this vision is fleeting. It vanishes as soon as the sea waters once again cover the seabed. We will need a more enduring guide, something that we can hold on to and carry with us, something which will inform us precisely where to go and how to find what we are after.

Seven weeks after the Exodus, God provides us precisely this type of map when He delivers the Torah on Mount Sinai. The occasion of this remarkable gift is what we celebrate, and re-experience, on the next holiday, Shavuos. The connection between Passover and Shavuos is thus clear - the Exodus is the inception of the journey, and the giving of the Torah is the moment that we receive the instructions and directions for the journey that we began seven weeks earlier. In case this inherent interrelation is not perfectly clear, it is emphasized by the fact that unlike all of the other holidays chronicled in Torah, Shavuos is not identified by a specific date, but the time of its observance is indicated only in relation to the holiday of Passover:

עַד מִמָּחֳרַת הַשַּׁבָּת הַשְּׁבִיעִת תִּסְפְּרוּ חֲמִשִּׁים יוֹם ...
וּקְרָאתֶם בְּעֶצֶם הַיּוֹם הַזֶּה מִקְרָא־קֹדֶשׁ יִהְיֶה לָכֶם:

Ad mimacharas hashabbat ha'shviis tispiru chamishim yom ... u'krasem b'etzem hayom hazeh mikrah kodesh yihyeh lachem.

You shall count fifty days (from Passover) until the day after the seventh week ... and you shall proclaim on that very day: It shall be a holy convocation unto you.
(Leviticus 23:16-21

While Shavuos falls on the sixth day of the third month of Sivan, its date is identified in the text of the Torah only as the fiftieth day from the day following the Exodus. Furthermore, the holiday's name, "שָׁבֻעֹת/ Shavuos," means simply "weeks" and has nothing specifically to do with the content of the occasion, i.e. the giving of the Torah). The name refers only to the duration of time that elapses from Passover. It would not be unreasonable to expect that the holiday that celebrates the Torah's bestowal would be called something that indicates the amazing transmission of divine insight that occurred on that day. Indeed, in later rabbinic sources and in our prayers, the day is referred to as "zman matan Toraseinu/the time of the giving of our Torah." Yet somewhat anti-climactically, in the Torah itself, the occasion is named simply "Weeks." From this, we see that while Shavuos is one of the three holy pilgrimage festivals (Passover, Shavuos, and Sukkos), and while it marks one of the most profound events in the entire history of the creation, it is characterized by Torah itself primarily as an element of the process of liberation and revelation that began seven weeks prior. The implication is that while Torah is the very will and wisdom of God encapsulated, it is not an end in itself. Rather, it is a means to the ultimate end, which is the complete Godly revelation that will be accomplished at our journey's destination only with the Torah's guidance.

We will address the holiday of Shavuos more specifically in the following section, but first we must understand the relevance of these seven "weeks" that precede it. Why was the Torah not given immediately upon the nation's emancipation from Egypt? If Torah is the map for the journey ahead, then why does God wait so long to supply it? Wouldn't it make more sense to identify the destination and the route, and then send the nation on its way? Why must there be a delay at all, and if there must be a delay, why must it be seven weeks specifically?

The answer is that the freed slaves were not ready or able to integrate the Torah's intense revelation of Godliness immediately upon their liberation from Egypt. The miracles of the ten plagues and the unprecedented opening of the heavens at the crossing of the sea were temporary interruptions of the natural order. Their function, as we have discussed, was to break the bounds of the material world in order to release the people from the limits to which they had become enslaved. Yet unlike these miracles, the goal of the giving of the Torah would be to infuse the highest levels of Godliness into the lowest levels of the creation in a way that would not cause the framework of the world to breach or break. This would require a vessel so precious and inscrutable that it could contain both the infinite and finite, both the miraculous and the mundane. The level of Godly light infused in the Torah would be even more brilliant and potent than that which was revealed at both the initial Exodus and the splitting of the sea seven days later. Yet it would need to descend into the creation in a way that would not overwhelm its circuitry and obliterate its structure. In order to receive such a holy and powerful implement, the people would need to be purified and prepared. Therefore, a seven week period intervened between the day of emancipation (the first day of Passover) and the day of the Torah's revelation (Shavuos). This period is know as "sefiras haomer/the counting of the omer."

The "Omer" is the name of a special offering of barley that was burned on the altar in the Temple on the second day of Passover. Because the forty-nine day count begins on this day, it is associated with, and named for, the offering that was brought then. But what we count during this period of the "the counting of the omer" are the days that separate between Passover and Shavuos. On the simplest level, this counting displays our great anticipation and excitement for the extraordinary revelation that is to come. It is as if one awaits a momentous occasion and crosses off the days on her/his calendar as the date approaches. Yet in such a case, one would generally engage in a count*down*, beginning with the number of days until the awaited time and each successive day counting the fewer number of days that remain. The counting of the omer, however, is a progressive count - on the first day we say "today is one day of the omer," and on the following day we say "today is the second day of the omer," counting upward until the day before Shavuos when we say "today is forty-nine days, which is seven weeks of the omer." We might assume that this formula is simply a stylistic preference, and that one might choose to either count up our count down as s/he sees fit. However, the counting of the omer is a formal mitzvah, and the precise order of its recital is recorded explicitly in the prayerbook. We count in ascending order, recording the number of days and weeks that have passed from the time of our release from bondage.

This order of ascent (as opposed to counting down in a way of descent) is significant because it represents our rise from the depths of Egypt to the heights of Mount Sinai. Torah refers to Egypt as "ervas ha'aretz/the nakedness of the earth"[199] because it was the most debauched and impure nation in the world. From the time that Jacob transplanted his family to Egypt, his descendants had spent two hundred ten years in this debased environment, and it inevitably influenced them. In describing the Egyptians' treatment of the Israelites, the Passover Haggadah states:

וַיָּרֵעוּ אֹתָנוּ הַמִּצְרִים.

Va'yareiu osanu haMitzrim.

And the Egyptians treated us badly.

The simple interpretation of the verse is that the Egyptians mistreated the slaves. However, the Lubavitcher Rebbe points out that this translation is not grammatically precise. The proper Hebrew for such a translation would be "וַיָּרֵעוּ לָנוּ הַמִּצְרִים/Va'yareiu *lanu* haMitzrim" - the word "lanu" means "to us" and would be the appropriate object of the verb "va'yareiu/treated badly." The word that the verse employs however, "אֹתָנוּ/osanu," is in the causative form. Therefore the verse more precisely means not that the Egyptians did something *to* us, but rather that they *caused* us to do something. The literal translation is "the Egyptians bad-ed us," or in other words, they caused us to be bad. What was so

---

199 Exodus 42:9

destructive and devious about Pharaoh and his people was not that they abused and afflicted the bodies of the Hebrew slaves, but rather that they sought to corrupt their souls. "Mitzrayim," as we have pointed out, is an idiom of "meitzarim/limitations," and the goal of the "Mitzrim/Egyptians" was to restrain and conceal the light of Godliness so completely that it would be utterly forgotten and extinguished. In this aim, they were very nearly successful, as the Haggadah avows:

וְאִלּוּ לֹא הוֹצִיא הַקָּדוֹשׁ בָּרוּךְ הוּא אֶת אֲבוֹתֵינוּ מִמִּצְרַיִם, הֲרֵי אָנוּ וּבָנֵינוּ וּבְנֵי בָנֵינוּ מְשֻׁעְבָּדִים הָיִינוּ לְפַרְעֹה בְּמִצְרָיִם.

V'ilu lo hotzi Hakadosh Baruch Hu es avoseinu miMitzrayim, harei anu u'vanenu u'vnei vanenu m'shubadim hayyinu l'Pharo b'Mitzrayim.

Had the Holy One, blessed be He, not taken our ancestors out of Egypt, then we, our children, and our grandchildren, would still be enslaved to Pharaoh in Egypt.

In regard to this declaration, the Chassidic masters teach that if our ancestors had remained even one more moment in Egypt, we would have been enslaved there forever. This is because we had descended to such a dark and debased level that we were at risk of losing all connection to our source and core. The Zohar teaches that there are fifty levels of impurity, and by the time of the Exodus, the children of Israel had fallen all the way to the forty-ninth level.[200] Had they remained another moment, they would have been dragged down to the fiftieth level from which there is no return.

With this, we can now understand why there were precisely forty-nine days between Passover and Shavuos. Each of those days correspond to one of the levels of impurity to which we had sunken and from which we needed to free ourselves. We can also understand why we count in ascending order rather than descending order - because our task throughout those seven weeks was to climb step by step out of the depths. Only after pulling ourselves up and out of the grips of impurity

---

[200] Zohar Chadash, Yisro 39a

would we be capable of receiving the holy Torah and the intense degree of Godliness that it contained.[201]

But what does it mean to be submerged in impurity? And how does one elevate her/himself from these depths? These questions are not merely theoretical. If, as we have asserted repeatedly, the events and energies of the calendrical cycle reemerge and reoccur annually, then just as each year we are liberated from Egypt, so too each year we are enslaved anew. Therefore, we are required, every year between Passover and Shavuos, to lift ourselves day by day from level to level until we are once again ready and worthy to receive the Torah. What is this annual ascension, and how are we to go about it? We will find our answer in the language that the Torah employs to command the daily counting of the omer.

וּסְפַרְתֶּם לָכֶם מִמָּחֳרַת הַשַּׁבָּת מִיּוֹם הֲבִיאֲכֶם אֶת־עֹמֶר
הַתְּנוּפָה שֶׁבַע שַׁבָּתוֹת תְּמִימֹת תִּהְיֶינָה:

U'sfartem Lachem mimacharas hashabbas miyom heviachem es omer hatenufah sheva shabbasos temimos tihyenah.

And you shall count for yourselves, from the day after the day of rest, from the day you bring the omer as a wave offering, they shall be seven complete weeks.

(Leviticus 23:15)

The Rabbis note that the second word in this verse seems to be extraneous. "U'sfartem lachem" is simply translated "you shall count for yourselves." Yet if this second word, "lachem/for yourselves," were removed, the verse would still be instructing us to count the seven weeks. What, therefore, is the necessity of this term "for yourselves"? Every word in Torah is precise, and therefore there must be a significance to this seemingly excess word. On the level of "pshat," the halachic sages derived from the inclusion of this term that the mitzvah of counting the

---

[201] The Zohar teaches that there are also "nun shaarei binah/fifty gates of wisdom" corresponding to the fifty levels of impurity. Throughout the journey from Egypt to Mount Sinai, God provides us the ability to actually climb two levels each day - with every step we rise out of impurity, He elevates us correspondingly on the ladder of wisdom, so that by the end of the seven weeks, we have not only ascended from the negative 49th level to level zero, but we have actually ascended to the 49th gate of wisdom. This is what enables Moses, on the fiftieth day, to ascend Mount Sinai and retrieve the Torah which encapsulates all fifty levels of wisdom.

omer is required of every individual. As opposed to other mitzvos which could be performed on behalf of the community by the communal leader, the counting of the omer must be done "lachem/for yourselves." This indicates that each member of the community is required to count the forty nine days personally.

Beyond this legal ramification of the verse's wording, the Chassidic masters identified a deeper and more mystic insight. "Lachem" literally means "to yourself," and therefore what the verse is teaching us, according to the mystics, is that the counting of the omer is the process whereby one can reach "to yourself" and find the self that has been lost. How does counting days accomplish this?

Impurity, the mystics explain, is not a matter of uncleanness, defilement, or wickedness as it is commonly misunderstood. It is, rather, a state of concealment, alienation, and distance. Godliness, as we have stressed throughout this book, is the root and core of everyone and everything. The further obscured the Godliness is in something, the greater is the level of its 'impurity.' The more something's inherent and essential Godliness is revealed, the more it is pure, unadulterated, and unencumbered. We see, therefore, that the descent into the 49 levels of impurity in Egypt represented a progressive eclipsing of our core and essence. Through our backbreaking labor in the realm of "meitzarim/limitations," we gradually sank ever deeper into the quicksand of the slave mentality. The light of our infinite and indomitable soul grew increasingly dim and remote as it was covered in a growing crust of material hardship and spiritual oppression. On Passover, God broke our chains, but for the next seven weeks, it would be our task to chisel away at the forty-nine layers of crust in order to uncover the Godly light that was hidden beneath.

This, the Chassidic masters teach, is the secret of the verse's very particular language. "Lachem," as we explained, means "to you" and indicates that the goal of these preparatory days and weeks is to identify and excavate our hidden self. But this idea is further conveyed in the first word of the verse, "u'sfartem/you shall count." The Alter Rebbe points out that the root of this verb, "ספר/sapir," means not only "to count," but also "shining" or "luminescent." The English word "sapphire" is derived from the Hebrew "even sapir," which is a sapphire stone, or a stone that shines. "U'sfartem lachem" thus means "you shall make *you* shine." In other words, through the process of "sefiras haomer/counting the omer," we reveal the brilliant light that is hidden in our deepest self. We do so not simply by "counting" each of the forty-nine days (the simply meaning of "u'sfartem"), but by "illuminating" each day (the term's deeper interpretation). To illuminate each day means that on every one of the forty-nine days, we are working on another "layer" of our personality. We are transforming it from something that is opaque, and therefore conceals what is beneath it, to something that is translucent, and therefore reveals and projects its core.

In this sense, forty-nine is no arbitrary number. It represents not only forty-nine levels of impurity, but also forty-nine aspects of the soul. As we discussed earlier in this chapter,[202] the soul is comprised of seven "middos" or emotional attributes. Each of the seven weeks between Passover and Shavuos represents another one of these attributes. Therefore, throughout each week, we are focusing on transforming that particular quality from the impurity that it had acquired in Egypt to the purity that it reflects in its unencumbered essence. For example, the first emotional attribute, "chesed/lovingkindness," can be either "pure" when it is expressed in charity, or "impure" when it is expressed in a lust for illicit carnal pleasure. Similarly, the emotional attribute of "gevurah/restraint," can be either "pure" when it is expressed in a resistance to gluttony or self-indulgence, or "impure" when it is expressed in an unwillingness to assist those in need. In Egypt, each of our seven emotional attributes had become corrupt, and therefore we required seven weeks to return them to their original and essential purity.

Of course, each of the seven weeks is comprised of seven days, and this is because each of the seven attributes is "inter-included" in each other so that there are seven aspects of each attribute. "Chesed/lovingkindness," for example, can be broken down into seven component parts:

1. Chesed she'b'chesed/lovingkindness of lovingkindness
2. Gevurah she'b'chesed/restraint of lovingkindness
3. Tiferes she'b'chesed/compassion of lovingkindness
4. Netzach she'b'chesed/fortitude of lovingkindness
5. Hod she'b'chesed/humility of lovingkindness

[202] Section "Seven"

358

6. Yesod she'b'chesed/bonding of lovingkindness
7. Malchus she'b'chesed/ Royalty of lovingkindness

Each of these parts can be either impure (i.e. concealing our God-ly essence) or pure (revealing the "Pnei Hashem" within us). "Chesed she'b'chesed/lovingkindness of lovingkindness" is unrestrained giving or permissiveness, which can be impure/negative if it pertains to un-healthy attraction or desire, or pure/positive if is related to altruistic pursuits. "Gevurah she'b'chesed/restraint of lovingkindness" is the ex-tent to which one measures and limits her/his unbridled giving, which can be pure/positive if one's generosity is excessive and therefore harm-ful to another - for example if one allows her/his child to eat as much candy as s/he would like - or impure/negative if one restrains her/his love and care for another because s/he believes that the recipient is not sufficiently deserving. In order to rectify and purify the attribute of "Chesed/lovingkindness" in general, we need to modulate each of its finer points. Therefore, we have seven days of each of the seven weeks to refine every aspect of our character, or in other words, to "sfartem/illu-minate" each component of "lachem/yourself."

By the end of these forty-nine days, we have removed ourselves from the forty-nine levels of impurity that obscure the "Pnei Hashem" within us. We have transformed our "middos/attributes" from concealing veils of "עוֹר/ohr/flesh" to translucent garments of "אוֹר/ohr/light",[203] and we are now ready and able to receive the Torah. Once again, we see that each element of our practice is a part of the process of removing cover-ings and revealing the Godly essence that is hidden within us.

Shavuos

The period from Passover to Shavuos is, as we have discussed, a continuum that begins with liberation, continues with purification/preparation, and concludes with revelation. Our journey from darkness and concealment to light and discovery begins with the Exodus. We then

---

[203] See chapter six, section "Skin and Light"

devote the subsequent seven weeks to making ourselves fit receptacles for the immense revelation that we are to receive on Mount Sinai. Once we have succeeded in shaking off the husk and shackles that tethered us to the "meitzarim/limitations" of the Egyptian view of ourselves and the world, we are now ready for Torah. But what is Torah? In order to understand Shavuos, we must know what is it that we received on this fiftieth day after the Exodus, and what is it that we receive anew every year on the sixth day of the month of Sivan.

If Torah is simply a book of laws, stories, and wisdom, then it is difficult to understand how its reception is repeated annually. But as we have mentioned on several occasions already throughout this book, Torah is far more than this. In chapter nine,[204] we explained that Torah is more of a relationship than a book. It is the marriage contract, so to speak, between each of us and God. Shavuos is therefore characterized as our wedding day, and indeed in Midrash it is said that God held Mount Sinai above us like a "chuppah/marrige canopy" when he gave us the Torah, and the Torah itself is compared to the "ketubah/marital contract" that a husband presents to his bride upon their marriage. As we discussed in the section on marriage in chapter eight, the wedding is not simply the connection of two distinct individuals. It is, rather, the reuniting of two parts of a single entity which had temporarily seemed to be separate. Shavuos is therefore this moment when we become fully aware of our complete unity with God. And each year, on the date of our original "wedding," it is not simply our anniversary in the sense of a commemoration of our nuptials, it is not even merely a renewal of our vows, but it is the actual recurrence of the matrimony every year. We are not only reenacting our wedding day annually, we are literally getting married once again.

To drive this point home, imagine if a couple on their wedding anniversary determined that the absolute fusion of their souls had not yet been realized or consummated, and therefore their wedding would need to be repeated so that they could once again commit to one another completely and exclusively. It's not that they had been unfaithful with extramarital affairs, or even that their relationship had been on the rocks. But in recognition of the extent to which their consciousness had not been perfectly aligned, the extent to which they had each occasionally

---

[204] Section "Torah - From Prayer to Study"

felt themselves to be individual and distinct, they recognized the opportunity - and indeed the urgency - to be wed even more authentically than they had been until now. They therefore rent a hall, convene their loved ones, and perform the entire wedding as they had done previously. What is it that brings them to this realization and this desire for a deeper commitment? It is the energetic flow into the universe on this day of the same transcendent energy that was introduced and infused on their first wedding day.

On the first Shavuos, fifty days after the Exodus, God had imbued us with a level of His light that we had not known since the creation. Just as the groom lifts the bridal veil to reveal the bride's formerly hidden face, God disrobed us, so to speak, removing all of the veils that conceal us, and exposed the naked truth of our Godly essence. At that point, our union was not the fusion of two distinct beings, but the fading of the illusion that we were ever anything other than one. Every year on Shavuos, this energy once again flows into the universe. The canopy is once again suspended above us, the "ketubah" is once again prepared and delivered, the vows are once again declared and enacted, and the heavens once again open as God lifts the bridal veil to reveal our hidden face.

With this analogy of the wedding, which includes the "kabbalas panim / receiving faces"[205] and the removal of the bridal veil, we can gain an even deeper appreciation of our discussion in chapter four[206] of the verse from Deuteronomy in which Moses describes the events of Mount Sinai:

פָּנִים בְּפָנִים דִּבֶּר יְ-הֹוָה עִמָּכֶם בָּהָר:

Panim b'panim dibber A-donai imachem bahar.
Face to face God spoke to you at the mountain.
(Deuteronomy 5:4)

In our analysis there, we noted the unusual phraseology of the words "panim B'panim," literally meaning "face IN face," rather than the more common and expected phrase "face TO face." On this, the Alter

---

205 See chapter eight, section "Wedding"

206 Section "Face to Face"

Rebbe commented that the Sinai experience was the moment that God implanted His face into our face.

והנה כתיב "פנים בפנים דבר הוי' עמכם." כי בשעת קבלת התורה נמשך לכל אחד ואחד מישראל בחינת הוי' בבחינת 'פנים' שלהם בכל ניצוץ נשמותיהם. וזהו ענין קבלת הדיבור "אנכי ה' א-לקיך", פירוש שיהיה בחינת שם הוי' מאיר ומתגלה בך.

V'hinei kasiv "Panim b'panim dibber Havaya imachem" ki b'shaas kabbalas haTorah nimshach l'kol echad v'echad m'yis-rael bechinas Havaya b'bechinas panim shelahem b'kol nitzutz nishmoseihem. V'zehu inyan kabbalas hadibbur Anochi Hashem Elokecha, peirush she'yihyeh bechinas Shem Havaya me'ir u'misgaleh b'cha.

And behold it is written "Face to face A-donai spoke with you" because at the time of the receiving of the Torah there was drawn down into every single individual of Israel the aspect of A-donai into the aspect of their 'face' in every spark of their neshama. And this is the concept of receiving the statement "I am the Lord your God," the explanation of which is that the aspect of the name A-donai should shine and be revealed within you.

(Likkutei Torah, Parshas Reeh)

The Alter Rebbe explains here that the expression "panim B'pan-im/face IN face" connotes that with the giving of the Torah, God actually insinuated Himself into our core. This is also the deeper meaning of the opening words of the first of the Ten commandments, "I am the Lord your God," which the Alter Rebbe also quotes here and which was the first communication that God delivered on Mount Sinai. As we discussed in chapter four,[207] these words "Anochi A-donai E-lokecha/I am the Lord your God" are not simply a statement of introduction, but they also de-scribe the process by which the highest level of Godliness penetrates our deepest recesses. The level of God that is completely beyond the world, "Anochi/I," descended into the level that creates and conducts the world, "A-donai/the Lord," and then descended even further into the

---

[207] Section "The First Commandment"

level of Godliness that is contained within the world and within each of us, "E-lohecha/your God." What this establishes, therefore, is that Shavuos is not only the commemoration of divine communication and revelation, it is the time when God provides us the ability to explicitly recognize His presence within our innermost core, and thereby to understand what we truly and ultimately are.

What we can appreciate with all the aforementioned, is that the journey to our "panim/face" and "pnimyus/inner core" which we have been engaged in throughout this book is parallel to the national journey that is chronicled in the Torah. Passover was the moment that we broke free from the illusion that we are limited and constrained. Shavuos was the moment, soon after our awakening, that we were granted the ability to see all the way into our deepest depths. But like the splitting of the sea, which rent the heavens and provided us merely a glimmer of the divine glory before it closed once again, so too the revelation at Sinai on Shavuos was temporary and fleeting. The difference, however, is that a remnant of the Sinai experience remained with us even after the miracles of the moment ceased. Moses remained on the mountain for forty days in order to commune with God and create an artifact that would encapsulate the Sinai experience in words and practice. Within the Torah, the light of God's face is miraculously contained. Through it, we are able to penetrate the "helam/concealment" of this "olam/world" and once again meet with God "panim b'panim/face to face" just as we did on Shavuos. This experience is available to us at all times if we can plumb the Torah's depths. It is for this reason that every morning when we recite the blessings over the Torah, we use the present tense:

בָּרוּךְ אַתָּה יְ-הֹוָה **נוֹתֵן** הַתּוֹרָה.

*Baruch attah A-donai **nosein** haTorah.*

Blessed are You, God, Who **gives** the Torah.

We do not say "who *gave* the Torah," but rather "who *gives*" it currently and constantly. As we have been describing throughout the past several chapters, Torah presents us a detailed practice that enables us to open ourselves and penetrate to our essence daily, weekly, monthly, annually, and throughout our life cycle. A verse from the book of Ruth states this succinctly, informing us clearly what it is that we received at Mount Sinai.

וְזֹאת לְפָנִים בְּיִשְׂרָאֵל:

V'zos lifanim b'Yisroel.
And this was the custom before (previously) in Israel.
(Ruth 4:7)

In its simple translation, the verse states that "this was the custom before (previously) in Israel." It then goes on to describe the procedure by which one marries, or refuses to marry, the wife of a deceased relative. But the Talmud[208] teaches that the word "v'zos" is also a reference to Torah, as the sages derive from the expression in Deuteronomy "v'zos hatorah/and this is the Torah."[209] Applying this alternate meaning of "v'zos" as Torah, and reading the subsequent word "lifanim" literally as "to the face" rather than "before," the verse can be read "Torah is to the face in Israel." In other words, Torah is the map which leads us to the "Pnei Hashem" and "pnimyus" within each of us. With this Godly guide, we are ready to travel to the promised land, equipped with the wisdom and tactics that will enable us to not only remain free ourselves, but to fulfill our function as a "light unto the nations" to free all of those who are lost, chained, and groping in the dark.

Rosh Hashana

The next holiday in the annual cycle is Rosh Hashana, which literally means "the head of the year." It is odd that this holiday, which is commonly understood as the Jewish New Year, comes not at the beginning of the cycle, but in its middle. Rosh Hashana is the first day of Tishrei, which, as we discussed earlier, is referred to by Torah as the seventh month. How can Rosh Hashana be both the "head of the year" and the beginning of the seventh month? As we previously explained, this is

---

[208] Avoda Zara 2b

[209] Deuteronomy 4:44

because there are multiple new years in Torah. Rosh Hashana, on the first of Tishrei, marks the genesis of humanity on the sixth day of creation, and therefore the first day of the counting of years from the beginning of recorded time. The calendar therefore begins with Tishrei, and the number of the calendar year changes at this time. The cycle of the festivals, however, begins in Nissan because the festival cycle charts our spiritual evolution beginning with the Exodus.

Understood simply and individually, Rosh Hashana is a time of renewal when we are introspective about the year behind us and we make resolutions for the year ahead. In this unsophisticated sense, it is not so different from the secular New Year of January first. On a deeper level, Rosh Hashana is recognized as the day that God once again creates the universe. The original creative energy that launched a world of multiplicity from a realm of God's singular unity is once again introduced into the universe as God decides to continue the project for another year. We respond to this re-creation with incredible humility and gratitude and with a recommitment to fulfill the purpose for which we were conceived. In addition to the name Rosh Hashana, the holiday is also referred to as "Yom Hazikaron/the day of remembrance" and "Yom Hadin/the day of judgement" because on this day God "remembers" and "judges" our conduct throughout the past year in order to determine whether to provide us another opportunity to serve Him in the year ahead. Simultaneously, we engage in deep introspection to remember and evaluate our past actions in order to determine how we can do better in a new year if we are given the chance.

To comprehend Rosh Hashana on an even more profound level, we can explore its place in the annual festival cycle and examine how it fits into the process of liberation and revelation that we have been describing until now. So far, we began with emancipation from slavery on Passover, we climbed out of the depths of impurity and up to the heights of Mount Sinai, and there we were exposed on Shavuos to our deepest essence and the deepest secret of our existence: that we are absolutely one with God. We may have thought that this moment of revelation and unification would have been the climax and culmination of our journey. But in fact, it was only the beginning. The Torah was given to us not so that we could dwell on the mountaintop in enlightened bliss, but rather so that we would descend with it into the darkness of the world in order to transform concealment into manifestation.

Understanding this duty, the "plan" was that the Israelite nation would proceed from Mount Sinai with the Torah and then march directly to "the promised land." This promised land was not merely a geographic place, but also a concept and a time. It represents the messianic era, and it is taught that if Moses had led the people into Canaan with the Torah eleven days after their departure from Sinai as intended, this would have ushered in the time of peace and light and knowledge of God that will permeate the creation in the messianic future. But something went "wrong." On the border of Canaan, the nation hesitated. Rather than trusting God and proceeding directly into the promised land, they decided to send spies to determine whether the land was habitable and conquerable. We have discussed this issue in chapter nine,[210] explaining that the people were reluctant to abandon the divine space of the desert and enter the earthly realm of labor and distraction where "the land consumes its inhabitants." They understood that toil in the earth would be exhausting and soul-deadening, and that one would become so preoccupied with earning a livelihood that s/he would have no time to focus on God and the Torah He had given. What they did not understand is that this was precisely God's desire and design. Our task would be to bring Him and His light into the darkness and thereby make it shine. Yet this would not be easy, and indeed it has not been easy.

On the historic national level, it was only eleven days after the departure from the foot of Mount Sinai that the nation - who had just witnessed not only the ten plagues of Egypt, not only the splitting of the sea, but also the unprecedented Godly revelation of Mount Sinai - lost its way in the desert and was therefore condemned to wander for forty years. On a more personal level, it is not hard to imagine how each of us, throughout history, manages to lose our way each year soon after we have re-experienced the revelation of Mount Sinai on the holiday of Shavuos. As we leave Sinai behind, we continue to wander in the desert of uncertainty and the darkness of this concealing reality. We come to settle and dwell in a habitable land with security, comfort, and even luxury, yet we must still toil in the "fields" of livelihood and communal interaction. Though we may no longer be enslaved to Egyptian taskmas-

---

[210] Section "Torah - From Prayer to Study"

ters, we become indentured to our work and preoccupied with our status and our possessions. It is not long before we are consumed by the land and by our labor, and the clarity and unity that we had glimpsed at Mount Sinai is lost and forgotten.

Once again, none of this is unforeseen by God, and it is, on the contrary, all part of the divine plan. We become consumed by the land not because we are at fault, but rather because it is only by implanting ourselves completely in the earth that we can decompose, sprout, and grow. Like a seed, we must first be broken down in the soil in order to reveal the essence of life and growth that is contained within us. Therefore, after it is revealed to us on Shavuos that God has embedded Himself in our core - "Anochi nosein lifneichem / I have placed Anochi within you" - we then enter the land of Canaan in order to cultivate the earth. We become farmers and builders. We sow the soil, implanting ourselves in our environment and disseminating the Torah that we were given in the desert. We rid the land of idolatry, we purify the atmosphere, we plant fields and orchards. We are working to recreate the garden that was lost by our first ancestors when they ate the apple and thereby lost contact with their interior.

However, eventually this toil in the fields becomes numbing and mindless. We lose our way because that is the nature of the "helam / concealment" of this "olam / world." We become dizzied and disoriented with the cycle of the seasons. We become "tubu / drowned" in "teva / nature."[211] We have forgotten why we are working and to Whom we are employed. It is not simply grain that we have come here to implant and grow, but it is rather faith and knowledge of God that is our true crop. Agriculture is simply the allegory for our mission, but we have become lost in the labor and forgotten the metaphor. We went into the fields to make them blossom, but our feet have become stuck in the mud as we have become mired in the mundane and abandoned our divine origin and our divine task. We have dozed off, and without mindfulness or consciousness, we continue to go through the motions, but we fail to yield the intended fruits of our labor.

It is in the context of this forgetfulness and unconsciousness that Rosh Hashana occurs several months after we have left Mount Sinai and

---

211 See chapter nine, section "More Darkness, More Light," where we discuss the identical root of these two terms.

immersed ourselves in the land. While Passover rescues us from slavery, Rosh Hashana rouses us from sleep. At Passover, the task is to break free, but at Rosh Hashana, the task is to wake up. Therefore, the primary ritual observance on Rosh Hashana is the blowing of the "shofar/ram's horn," which, amongst other connotations, represents a clarion call to reawaken and redirect one's consciousness to that which is of primary importance.

Shofar

Nowhere in the Five books of Moses is the holiday of Rosh Hashana referred to with this name by which it is commonly known today. The term originated in the Talmudic period, a millennium and a half after the Torah was received. In the Talmud, an entire tractate is called by the name Rosh Hashana and is devoted to exploring the laws of this seminal holiday. In the Torah itself, the holiday is referred to two times, neither of which mention this name:

בַּחֹדֶשׁ הַשְּׁבִיעִי בְּאֶחָד לַחֹדֶשׁ יִהְיֶה לָכֶם שַׁבָּתוֹן זִכְרוֹן תְּרוּעָה מִקְרָא־קֹדֶשׁ:

Bachodesh hashevii b'echad lachodesh yihyeh lachem shabbaton zichron teruah mikrah kodesh.

In the seventh month, on the first of the month, it shall be a Sabbath for you, **a remembrance of the shofar blast**, a holy occasion.

(Leviticus 23:24)

וּבַחֹדֶשׁ הַשְּׁבִיעִי בְּאֶחָד לַחֹדֶשׁ מִקְרָא־קֹדֶשׁ יִהְיֶה לָכֶם כָּל־מְלֶאכֶת עֲבֹדָה לֹא תַעֲשׂוּ יוֹם תְּרוּעָה יִהְיֶה לָכֶם:

U'bachodesh hashevii b'echad lachodesh mikrah kodesh yihyeh lachem kol meleches avoday lo taasu **yom teruah** yihyeh lachem.

And in the seventh month, on the first day, there shall be a holy convocation for you; you shall not perform any mundane work. It shall be **a day of shofar sounding** for you.

(Numbers 29:1)

In both of these cases, the day is identified with the sounding of the shofar, the festival's central ritual. Prior to coming to be known by its current name, the holiday was referred to simply as "Yom Teruah/the day of shofar sounding." This name expresses its simple essence. In order to understand Rosh Hashana, we must therefore explore the significance of the shofar.

The shofar is a ram's horn that has been hollowed to create a rudimentary instrument that emits a trumpet-like blare. It is sounded over one hundred times throughout the holiday's prayer service, and the sages provide a variety of explanations for this practice. Historically, the shofar recalls one of the most striking and pivotal moments in the biblical narrative - the binding of Isaac. In a test of his faith and obedience, Abraham is commanded by God to sacrifice his beloved son. Without hesitation, Abraham binds Isaac on the altar and raises the knife to slay him. At the last moment, God calls to him and tells him not to harm his child. Instead he offers a ram that has become caught in the thicket behind him. Ever since, the ram's horn has been a symbol of complete devotion and self-sacrifice.

Explaining the unique loyalty of this act, the Lubavitcher Rebbe points out that Abraham was not the first or the last to make the ultimate sacrifice for a cause he believed in. Yet what distinguished Abraham's devotion was that while there have been many examples of martyrdom throughout history, they are always in service and furtherance of a cause or movement. One will give her/his life or will sacrifice everything that s/he holds dear in order that this act of self-transcendence will serve as an example to others and will therefore ultimately galvanize the movement. In Abraham's case, on the contrary, the sacrifice of Isaac would serve no such purpose because God had informed him that it was specifically through Isaac that the Hebrew nation would be born and built. In offering his son on the altar, therefore, Abraham would not only be sacrificing his own flesh and blood, but he would be putting an end to everything he had worked for throughout his life. Nevertheless, Abraham did not hesitate, nor did he question for a moment the seeming senselessness of God's request. He nullified himself completely and immediately to God's will, and it is this consummate allegiance that the shofar represents. In blowing the shofar on Rosh Hashana, we are reminding ourselves of this quality of selflessness and zealousness that has been passed down to us as an inheritance from our ancestors, and we are recommitting ourselves to serving our Creator in this unconditional way.

Another interpretation of the shofar's significance is the sounding of the royal horns to announce the arrival or coronation of the king. Rosh Hashana is the day on which God is declared king once again for the year ahead. On this day, we are instructed:

וְאִמְרוּ לְפָנַי בְּרֹאשׁ הַשָּׁנָה מַלְכִיּוֹת זִכְרוֹנוֹת וְשׁוֹפָרוֹת. מַלְכִיּוֹת - כְּדֵי **שֶׁתַּמְלִיכוּנִי עֲלֵיכֶם**, זִכְרוֹנוֹת - כְּדֵי שֶׁיַּעֲלֶה זִכְרוֹנְיְכֶם לְפָנַי לְטוֹבָה וּבַמֶּה - בְּשׁוֹפָר.

*Imru lefanai be-Rosh Hashana malchiyot, zichronot ve-shofrot. Malchiyot kedai **she-tamlichuni aleichem**, zichhronot kedai she-yavo lefanai zichroneichem le-tovah u-ba-meh? Be-shofar.*

Recite before me on Rosh Hashana (verses that reference) kingship, remembrance, and shofar. Verses of kingship in order **that you should make me king over you**, verses of remembrance in order that there should come before me remembrance of you for good, and how (should this be accomplished)? With the shofar.

(Talmud, Rosh Hashana 16a)

Several questions arise on this subject of God's coronation: What does it mean to coronate God as king - is there something that being "king" signifies that being "God" does not? And if God desires to be king, then why does He need us to declare Him so - isn't He in control whether or not we recognize His rulership? How is this coronation effected by blowing a ram's horn? Why must this coronation be repeated annually - why is the term of kingship only one year? Why is Rosh Hashana the day that this coronation annually takes place?

The notion of kingship creates a relationship that is more personal and tangible than the dynamic of God and His creations alone. "God" is an abstract and mystifying concept. It is beyond our comprehension, and if we cannot comprehend something, then we cannot relate to it fully. It is true that God is beyond our mortal framework in this way, yet it is simultaneously true that He lowers Himself, so to speak, in order that we can interact with Him. This, as we have discussed multiple times already, accounts for the various names by which God is known. Regarding the two most common names to which He is referred in scripture, "A-donai" connotes God as He exists beyond the structure of this world, and "E-lohim" connotes God as He exists within the worldly bounds that He has created. If we examine the basic formula of Torah blessings, we find that both of these names are invoked:

בָּרוּךְ אַתָּה יְ-הֹוָה אֱ-לֹהֵינוּ מֶלֶךְ הָעוֹלָם...

*Baruch atta **A-donai, E-loheinu** melech haolam....*

Blessed are You **God our Lord** King of the world....

Immediately following these names, the term "melech haolam/king of the world" is inserted. From this we see that kingship is the next step in the progression that conveys Godliness downward into our realm and consciousness. From a remote and unfathomable being - "atta/You," a level so high that it is even beyond any name - God descends through "A-donai" and "E-loheinu," until He eventually becomes "melech haolam/king of the world," a form and level that is at least somewhat identifiable, graspable and sympathetic. God thus asks us to make Him king in order for us to bring Him down into our everyday lives. This makes Him relevant and not so far beyond us that we have no hope of relating to Him or detecting Him in our daily interactions.

Additionally, the relationship to a king is distinctly different from the relationship to God in that (ideally at least) a monarch is chosen by His subjects. Whereas God is God regardless of the will of His creations, a king is only king if his subjects pledge their allegiance to him. Of course, history has had more than its share of monarchs who imposed and enforced their rule on the populace. But Torah draws a clear distinction between "memshala/rulership" and "melucha/kingship." A "moshel/ruler" is one who subjugates his subjects by force, whereas a "melech/king" is one to whom the people have voluntarily pledged their devotion and service. The sages express this concept in the phrase:

אֵין מֶלֶךְ בְּלֹא עָם.

Ein melech b'lo am.

There is no king without a people.

(Rabbeinu Bachaye on Bereishis 38:30)

The simple implication here is that one cannot be a ruler if there is no one to rule. But on a more subtle level, it indicates that if the "am/ people" do not agree that this person should reign, then while he may impose his will over them by force and serve as a dictator or tyrant, no matter how powerful he may be, he is no "melech/king" at all.

The chassidic masters glean an even deeper lesson from this statement "ein melech b'lo am/there is no king without a people." The word "עַם/am" means "nation" or "people," but vowelized differently, it can also be read "עִם/im" which means "with." Rendered as such, the statement would read "there is no king if there is no 'with'." In other words, there can be no king if there is no one "with" him - no one to whom he is close or similar or related. In this sense, it is understood that we cannot possibly make God our king if we are not similar to Him. A person can own many sheep or horses, and s/he can control them completely, but s/he cannot be a monarch over them. One cannot be king over trees or rocks. He can own many physical possessions, but this ownership does not render him a sovereign. In order to be king over something, the king and his subjects must be of the same species or kind. The implication, then, of God's commandment for us to "tamlichuni ale-ichem/make Me king over you" is that we are inherently like Him and therefore we are capable of being His subjects. Only because we are God-ly beings can we make God our king. Only by revealing our inherent Godliness can we fulfill His directive to coronate Him.[212] How do we reveal our inherent Godliness? We will answer that question shortly in the following section.

From all of the above, we appreciate that God desires to be king in order to deepen His relationship with us. Furthermore, though He is a ruler with or without our consent or support, He gives us the ability to choose Him because He desires our participation in the relationship rather than our passive submission. Why is it that we must make this choice every year, and why on Rosh Hashana specifically?

As we have explained already, Torah time is a spiral, which means that every year when we come around again to a particular date, the same energies that occurred on that day previously are revisited and reactivated. It was on the very first Rosh Hashana - the first day of the

---

[212] *Likkutei Torah*, Atem Nitzavim Hayom, ch. 5

very first month of Tishrei - that God originally became our king. That day, the sixth day of creation, was the day that Adam was created. The Zohar[213] records that upon Adam's creation, all of the animals of the world recognized his preeminence and bowed to him to declare him their ruler. But Adam refused their fealty and instead directed them to kneel to the true king, saying (in a phrase that would later be recorded in Psalms 95:6), "come let us bow down together and worship the One Who created us all."

On each anniversary of this first coronation, spiritual history repeats itself. We are given the opportunity once again to direct the attention of all of God's creations to Him and to invite them to recognize and accept His kingship. In so doing, we literally determine the fate of the entire universe. If we sincerely invite God to be our king for another year, recognizing our relationship to Him and committing ourselves to working to reveal Him throughout His creation in the year ahead, then He once again recreates the world and thereby provides us the opportunity to do so. If, however, He is forgotten by His creations and we have devoted ourselves instead to false gods, earthly kings, and self-serving agendas, then He may determine that there is no reason to sustain the creation any further.

It is taught in Kabbala[214] and explained in *Tanya*[215] that at the start of every Rosh Hashana, God withdraws Himself from the creation. The world is recreated every moment by His breath and His word,[216] and at sundown on the eve of the first of Tishrei, God inhales deeply and holds His breath, so to speak, so that through that night the universe stands in a state of suspended animation. At this time, God is deciding whether to exhale and reinvest His "ruach/breath" into the creation for another year. We flock into synagogues at this time and fervently pray for Him to breathe life into us and into everything yet again. Our prayer is not "please give me life, and wealth, and health because I am afraid of Your punishment and greedy for Your blessings." It is "please provide

---

[213] Zohar 1, 221b

[214] Sefer Etz Chaim

[215] Iggeres HaKodesh, Epistle 14

[216] See section "Flow" earlier in this chapter

me another opportunity to make You manifest within me and through-out Your creation."

We anxiously hold our breath, so to speak, as He is withholding His. The anticipation builds as we await His decision. After the morning service, the moment of truth finally arrives at the time of the blowing of the shofar. The congregation stands in awe and trepidation. And finally the blast of the shofar rips through the silence. With it, God's life-giving energy once again flows into the universe. The breath that is blown through the ram's horn symbolizes God's breath returning to vitalize us for another year. "Tamilchuni aleichem/make me king over you," God tells us; "ba'meh, b'shofar/how do we accomplish this? With the shofar." What is it about this blowing of a ram's horn that convinces God to once again recreate us and the world in which we dwell?

The Voice Of The Soul

In the simple sense, the blowing of the shofar is understood as an announcement of the king's coronation or arrival. But on a deeper level, as we have seen, the shofar is not only a herald, but also the very mechanism through which the coronation is accomplished. This is indi-cated by the Talmud's words, "ba'meh, b'shofar/ how? with the shofar." We therefore find that there is something about this act of blowing and the sound that it generates which effectuates God's kingship and the continued existence of the creation that this kingship achieves. How does the shofar accomplish this?

The Baal Shem Tov tells a story of a King who sends his son out from the palace on a journey into the world to learn of its ways and to expand his appreciation of the kingdom. The prince sets off, accompa-nied by servants and supplied with much finery and wealth from the king's storehouses so that he will lack nothing on his travels and will be able to maintain his high standard of living along the way. But as he goes, the prince is captivated by all of the enticements that the world has to offer. He overindulges his desires and squanders his riches in order to satisfy his ever-growing appetites. Time passes, and eventually the prince finds himself far away from the land of his father, a place where the King's name is not known. He stays there so long that he eventually forgets his native language. He sells his servants and princely possessions to sustain and entertain himself, and finally, he finds himself destitute, alone, and far from home.

At this point, he remembers his Father and the palace where he was raised, and he sets out to return there. It is a long and arduous journey, but finally he arrives at the palace gates. The guards there don't recognize him, because he has long ago traded away his fine clothes and appears now in pauper's rags. Though he explains to them that he is the prince, the son of the King, they understand nothing he says, because he has forgotten the dialect of the kingdom and he speaks in a strange foreign tongue. Unable to gain entry, and pining for his Father's warm embrace, the prince sinks to the ground and lets out a loud sob from the depths of his heart. Deep inside the palace, the King hears the sound, and immediately recognizes it as the voice of his son. He hurries to the gates and throws them open. He brings the prince into his innermost chamber and there embraces his long lost child.

This, the Baal Shem Tov teaches, is the story of each of us at Rosh Hashana. The King is God, the prince represents every one of God's children, and the sob through which the king recognizes and embraces his child is the call of the shofar. There are no words that can gain us access to the palace. There is nothing we can say or do that will convince the guards to readmit us after we have wandered so far away, squandered all of our precious garments and possessions, and relinquished all signs of our royal lineage. The only thing that will reunite us with the King is His complete and unconditional love for us. And all we need to do to elicit that love is let Him know that we have returned and we are here. The King in the Baal Shem Tov's allegory does not chastise His child for having gone astray. He does not berate him for his indiscretion and irresponsibility. He does not shame him for having wasted his time or for losing his fortune. This is my beloved child, he exults, and he immediately welcomes him and rejoices in his return. As for the prince, there are no words to his cry. No logic or eloquence. He offers no excuses or explanations. He makes no promises or resolutions. He simply cries out, broken, and broken open. It is this simple, formless, artless sound that tears through all barriers and reunites father and child.

In chapter nine,[217] we alluded to a chassidic aphorism which states that words are the pen of the mind and music is the quill of the soul. Human beings communicate in a variety of ways - language, gestures and expressions, art and music, to name just a few. Language enables us to succinctly and concretely transmit our thought and ideas, but there are limits to language and there are many different languages. Even if one were to be fluent in every tongue, there are still many things that words cannot convey. Music has been described as a universal language which can carry us to levels beyond words and express things that words cannot. Yet even music has its limitations. There are only so many notes and only so many ways to arrange and perform them. Furthermore, there are those who are adept at music and sensitive to its nuances and those who are not. But there is something that is even more universal and which is understood by all, no matter where they are from, how much or little they know, and how trained or insensitive their ear. And that is the wordless cry from the depths of the soul. What makes this mode of communication universal is its simplicity and invariability. It pertains and translates to all of us because it resonates within all of us. That is because it emanates from the place within us that is the very same no matter who we are: the "Pnei Hashem" that is our essence and core.

The word "shofar" comes from the root "שפר/shefer" which means beauty or grace or even eloquence. This seems strange at first glance, because the sound that the shofar produces could hardly be described as beautiful or graceful in any traditional sense. It is certainly not dulcet or pleasing to the ear. "Eloquence" generally connotes an ability to express oneself with verbal mastery or with deep insight and meaning. Again, this seems to be in contrast with the crude and unsophisticated sound that the shofar blares. Yet what the relationship of the word shofar to its root "shefer" comes to teach us is that true and ultimate beauty is a far more inward concept. It is an eloquence that cannot be expressed with words because it is completely beyond reason and differentiation. It is a sound that emanates from deep within the recesses of our core. It can be heard whenever one genuinely cries from her/his depths, but it resounds even more emphatically when we place a special instrument to our lips and invite it to come forth and announce itself. This instrument is the shofar.

---

217 Section "More Darkness, More Light"

The shofar is the mouthpiece that gives the soul a voice, and allows it to cry out for all to hear. The sound of the shofar is the intonation of the "Pnei Hashem" that is buried deep within us. We place the ram's horn to our lips to allow our "pnimyus" to be heard. The Tanya teaches (quoting the Zohar) that:

כְּמוֹ שֶׁכָּתוּב בַּזֹּהַר, מַאן דְּנָפַח מִתּוֹכֵיהּ נָפַח, פֵּירוּשׁ מִתּוֹכִיּוּתוֹ וּמִפְּנִימִיּוּתוֹ.

K'mo she'kasuv b'Zohar, mon d'nafach mitochia nafach, peirush, mi'tochiuso u'mi'pnimyuso.

As it is written in Zohar, 'He who blows, blows from within him,' that is to say, from his inwardness and his innermost being.

(Tanya, chapter 2)

Ordinarily when we blow through our lips, there is little sound. But when the shofar is at our lips, this innermost breath reverberates and blares. The shofar is the megaphone that enables us to clearly hear the voice of the "Pnei Hashem" that is constantly whispering from within us. Once a year, we provide it this mystic amplifier and allow it to declare, "here I am, deep inside you! You've been looking elsewhere, outside and around you. But I'm right here, where I have always been, animating you, whispering to you, awaiting you."

Rosh Hashana is the day that God initially placed a piece of Himself into a physical body. On that first day in the garden of Eden, Adam and Eve knew precisely what they were. Their skin was translucent and they could plainly see the "Pnei Hashem/face of God" in their "pnimyus/innermost core." On that same day, they ate the fruit and their ultimate reality was concealed from them. But every year on that occasion, their descendants are reminded. The soul calls out to us through the shofar, and we remember what we are and why we are here. As we mentioned previously, Rosh Hashana is also known by the names "Yom Hazikaron/the day of remembrance" and "Yom HaDin/the day of judgment." Many understand this to indicate that it is our actions and conduct throughout the past year which are "remembered" by the "heavenly court" on this day so that we can be evaluated and "judged" in order to determine our verdict for the year ahead. But on a deeper level, it is we ourselves who are made to remember on this "day of Remembrance."

What is remembered is not our failings and our superficial gesticulations in this realm of darkness and concealment. Rather, we are given the opportunity to remember our true essence and our innermost nature which has been hidden from us all this time.

As for the "day of judgment," the Alter Rebbe teaches that the judgment on this day is not simply who will live and who will die, who will be rich and who will be poor, who will have peace and who will suffer (as we read in the climactic "Unetana tokef" prayer on Rosh Hashana). The deeper and more essential judgment of the day, according to the Alter Rebbe, is the extent to which one will be granted the ability to see God within her/him and within the world in the coming year:

אך הנה כתיב משפט לא-לקי יעקב, שיש משפט למעלה מי יזכה להיות במדרגה זו להיות גילוי א-להותו עליו ושיתקשר נפשו בקשר אמיץ וחזק בה'.

Ach hinei kasiv "mishpat l'E-lokei Yaacov," she'yesh mishpat l'maala mi yizcheh l'hiyos ba'madreiga zu l'hiyos gilui E-lohuso alav v'she'yishkasher nafsho b'kesher amitz v'chazak b'Hashem.

Behold it is written "a judgment for the God of Jacob," meaning that there is a judgment above concerning who will merit to be at such a level that Godliness will be revealed to him, and that his soul will be bound in a strong and mighty bond with God.

(Likkutei Torah, Atem Nitzavim, sec. 5)

Here the Alter Rebbe quotes a phrase from Psalms, "mishpat l'E-lokei Yaacov," and explains its "sod," or mystic secret. The full verse that he cites is:

תִּקְעוּ בַחֹדֶשׁ שׁוֹפָר בַּכֶּסֶה לְיוֹם חַגֵּנוּ: כִּי חֹק לְיִשְׂרָאֵל הוּא **מִשְׁפָּט לֵאלֹהֵי יַעֲקֹב.**

*Tiku b'chodesh shofar ba'keseh l'yom chagenu. Ki chok l'Yisroel hu, **mishpat l'E-lohei Yaacov.***

Sound the shofar on the New Moon, on the appointed time for the day of our festival. For it is a statute for Israel, **the judgment of the God of Jacob.**

(Psalms 81:4-5)

The verse speaks of the holiday of Rosh Hashana, indicating on the simple level that it is the time for divine judgment and the blowing of the shofar. Yet the Alter Rebbe translates the phrase "mishpat l'E-lohei Yaacov" slightly differently. Its "pshat/simple meaning" is "the judgment of the God of Jacob," implying that it is the occasion when the God of Jacob will judge the people. However, the Alter Rebbe renders it "the *judgment of Godliness* for Jacob." He thus explains that what is ultimately judged and determined on Rosh Hashana is the extent to which Godliness will be revealed to a person (i.e. the descendants of Jacob) in the coming year. Will her/his essence continue to be concealed from her/him, or will s/he finally be granted the vision to see the Godliness at the root and core of everything? In this sense, the question for each of us on Rosh Hashana is not "what will happen *to* me in the year ahead," but rather "what ME will happen in the year ahead?" Will it be the true me - my divine essence - or the version of me that acts in strange and often unproductive and self-defeating ways because it is lost, scared, and confused?

How is this judgment determined? How does God assess how much or little we should be able to perceive Him in the coming year? If we have been working to find His face throughout the past year - as we say every morning "bakshu panav tamid/seek His face constantly" - then we will merit to see His face and express it in the year ahead. If we did not work diligently to find it, then it may remain concealed from us. If it is revealed, then the year ahead will be "good;" and if it is hidden from us, then we will remain in the dark as we have been until now.

Yet even if we have neglected this duty every day throughout the past year - even if we have not taken advantage of all the practices that Torah provides us to assist us in removing the coverings that conceal our "pnimyus" on a daily, weekly, monthly, annually, and lifelong basis (as detailed in the past three chapters) - still the blowing of the shofar on Rosh Hashana has the power to shake us from our slumber and awaken us to the voice that calls from within us. We are instructed to engage in the work of "teshuvah/return" every day and every moment of every day, casting off our veils and returning to our divine essence. But even if we have have paid no attention to the whisper from within us, the blast of the shofar is a roar that we cannot ignore. It shatters the surface of our superficial lives and draws us inward to our deepest depths.

When we hear and heed this inner voice, there is no longer a decision to be made whether or not God will be our king. When we reveal this ultimate reality, God *is* our king automatically and unquestionably. It is not a choice, it is simply making this essential state of being manifest. "Tamlichuni aleichem/Make Me king over you," does not mean to appoint God as king or even to convince Him to be your king. It means to bring out the "you" over whom God has always been, and always will be, king. We accomplish this by blowing the shofar - by reaching down deep within us and exhaling what is in there so that it now breaks through all of the coverings that conceal it. When we do so, we are "inscribed in the book of life" for tremendous blessings in the year ahead. This is not because we are suddenly guiltless or flawless or more worthy now than we were in the past year or the many years behind us. We will be blessed with the further revelation of goodness and Godliness as a result of the fact that we have finally come to see a glimmer of the divinity that has been within us all along. Enthused and inspired with the realization of our Godly nature, we will bound into the new year with a powerful sense of meaning, purpose, and dignity. Encouraged by the glimpse of our essence and goal, we will proceed on our journey with increasing confidence and ardor, overcoming all barriers that stand in our way. God will furnish us with the strength and the resources we need to reveal Him throughout His creation, and we will work even harder in the time ahead to access and manifest the "Pnei Hashem" and to transform and eradicate the darkness that has kept it hidden until now.

Elul

Before moving on to the remaining holidays of Yom Kippur and Sukkos which follow Rosh Hashana in quick succession, it is important to note that the profound revelations of Rosh Hashana and the high holiday season do not just come upon us suddenly and without preparation. The sages have described the shofar as a wake up call - as Rambam writes "Sleepers, wake up from your slumber! Examine your ways and repent and remember your Creator"[218] - yet it is not a sudden reveille that jolts us without warning. As a matter of fact, there is a custom to blow the shofar every day (other than shabbat) throughout the month of Elul which precedes Tisrei. Thirty days prior to Rosh Hashana, we begin to rouse ourselves from our dormancy in preparation for the upcoming Days of Awe (as the holidays of Rosh Hashana, Yom Kippur, and Sukkos are collectively known).

In addition to the daily blowing of the shofar throughout the month of Elul, there is also the custom to recite chapter twenty-seven of Psalms twice daily, in the morning and afternoon (or evening) services. We have referenced this psalm already in this book, all the way back in chapter three[219] where we cited its eighth verse:

לְךָ אָמַר לִבִּי בַּקְּשׁוּ פָנָי אֶת־פָּנֶיךָ יְ-הֹוָה אֲבַקֵּשׁ:

Lecha amar libi, bakshu panai, es panecha A-donai avakeish.
On Your behalf, my heart says, 'Seek My face.' Your face,
O Lord, I will seek.

(Psalms 27:8)

Reciting this Psalm twice daily throughout the month leading up to Rosh Hashana, we focus ourselves on the ultimate task of this holy time: seeking the face that has been hidden from us. As we have mentioned already, we repeat the verse "bakshu panav tamid / seek His face constantly" at the beginning of the morning service every single day of the year, thus indicating that the search for God's face is supposed to be a daily, and even constant, undertaking. Nevertheless, as the year draws to a close and the new year approaches, we recognize that we have been remiss in this duty, and we have not sought it as aggressively and earnestly as we could have and should have. We have become distracted by our worldly involvements, and we have let nearly another complete year slip by without fulfilling our most fundamental task. Yet there is still time. A month remains before the world is to be reevaluated and recreated. We blow the shofar every morning of this final month to re-

---

[218] Mishneh Torah, Hilchos Teshuvah 3:4

[219] Section "The Face Within You"

mind ourselves of the urgency of the waning weeks and days of the year. With each shofar blast, we begin to awaken, to remember, to be drawn inward toward the source of that breath and voice within us. With each recital of the verse "seek my face, Your face O Lord I seek," we reinforce our intention and mission.

However, as we discussed in chapter three, the verse is unclear regarding whose face it is that we are seeking. First we are instructed by our own heart to "Seek My face," implying that it is one's own face that is to be sought. But the verse then concludes "Your face, O Lord, I will seek," seemingly indicating that it is God's face that we are trying to find. This intentional ambiguity informs us that it is both our face and God's face that we are seeking, because ultimately, they are one and the same. Repeating and reemphasizing this concept twice daily throughout the entire month of Elul, we arrive at Rosh Hashana with a clarity of purpose. When the great shofar blows on the morning of the first of Tishrei, we are primed and prepared to let the voice of the one and unique divine soul resound throughout us and throughout the creation.

The work that we do in Elul is not only a preparation for Rosh Hashana, however. As holy and lofty as Rosh Hashana is, it is not the pinnacle of the year. The holiest day on the Hebrew calendar comes ten days later, on the holiday of Yom Kippur. As such, the thirty day period from the first of Elul to Rosh Hashana is only a preparatory phase in the larger forty day period that culminates on Yom Kippur. This forty day span marks a very significant time in Torah history. Forty day intervals are fairly common in Torah: during the flood in the times of Noah, it rained for forty days and forty nights; when the nation sent spies from the desert into Canaan, the spies surveyed the land for forty days; after Moses ascended to Mount Sinai at the giving of the Torah, he remained on the mountain for forty days; and after the nation sinned with the golden calf and Moses descended and shattered the tablets, he ascended the mountain once again and pleaded for forty days and nights for God to have mercy on the people; Moses descended at the end of this second forty day period to let the people know that God agreed to forgive them, and then he ascended a third time and remained atop the mountain for a third period of forty days.

Thus, there were three consecutive periods of forty days that Moses communed with God on Mount Sinai. If we apply these three forty day periods of Moses' mountain ascents to the calendar, we find that he climbed the mountain on the seventh of Sivan (the day after Shavuos) and descended forty days later on the 17th of Tammuz, when he smashed the tablets. He climbed the mountain again on the 19th of Tammuz, prayed for forgiveness for 40 days, and then descended on the 29th of Av to inform the people of God's willingness to show clemency. He then climbed the mountain once again on the first day of the month of Elul and remained there for the third forty day interval. These last forty days ended on the tenth of Tishrei, when Moses descended from Mount Sinai with a second set of tablets, a sign that God had granted the nation complete forgiveness. This tenth day of Tishrei was the first Yom Kippur, and every year on this date, this energy of divine compassion and reunification flows into the creation anew.

Yom Kippur

Each of the holidays, as we have discussed so far, is a part of a process and progression that replays itself annually. When the year begins on the first of Nissan, we are slaves in Egypt, completely subordinated to the confines of the world and unaware of our divine essence and potential. Passover comes two weeks later to liberate us from this slavery and instruct us that we have the power within us to transcend all limitation and boundaries. We work to internalize this new awareness throughout the seven weeks of sefiras haomer, and then on Shavuos we experience an unprecedented meeting with God in which He informs us that He has literally implanted Himself within us, "Anochi nosein lifneichem hayom/Today I place Anochi within you." In fact, He has been within us from the moment of our creation, but He is now providing us His Torah which will enable us to make the world aware of this essential fact. We descend from the lofty heights of Mount Sinai and transport this holy awareness from the desert into the land where we are to implant it in the soil and let it blossom and manifest. But we become consumed by our labor in the fields, and we lose the Godly consciousness that we had come to disseminate. To rouse us from our slumber, Rosh Hashana arrives with the blowing of the shofar that calls to us from our "pnimyus" and reminds us of our underlying Godliness. We meditate on this revolutionary truth for a period of ten days, which are known as the "aseres ymei teshuvah/ten days of return," and then we observe Yom Kippur, the most sacred and awesome day of the year.

On this day, God forgave us for the egregious sin of creating and worshipping the golden calf only months after the Exodus from Egypt and weeks after the giving of the Torah on Mount Sinai. And on this day every year since, God forgives us for all of our missteps and shortcomings that have accrued since the previous Yom Kippur. But why is this day considered the holiest of the year? Forgiveness is divine, but why is the day that we are pardoned and absolved more hallowed than Passover, the day that we were liberated from slavery, or Shavuos, the day that we received the Torah, or Rosh Hashana, the day that God decides to recreate the universe for another year? In order to understand this, we must explore the concept of forgiveness in Torah - what does it truly mean, and how is it ultimately accomplished?

Yom Kippur is a day of forgiveness, but it is not "the day of forgiveness." The word "forgiveness" in Hebrew is "סְלִיחָה/selicha" or "מְחִילָה/mechila." The holiday is not known as Yom Selicha or Yom Mechila, but Yom *Kippur*. "כְּפּוּר/Kippur" is from the term "כַּפָּרָה/kapara," which means "atonement," and thus Yom Kippur is "the day of atonement." What is "atonement," and how does it differ from "forgiveness"?

In English, we conceive of "atonement" as the process through which we gain "forgiveness." We "atone" for our sins, and we are subsequently pardoned. This, however, is not the authentic understanding of the Hebrew "kapara," nor is it, for that matter, the original connotation of the English term "atonement." Though "atonement" has indeed become virtually synonymous with "repentance" in English, the word itself reveals its original definition. Etymologically, "atonement" is a compound word deriving from "at onement." It is the state of being 'at one,' and not the process by which one arrives at that state. Similarly, "kapara" is not synonymous with "teshuvah." "Teshuvah" is the act of return or repentance, while "kapara" is the state of absolution or reunification that is achieved after "teshuvah" has been performed.

Contrary to popular opinion, therefore, Yom Kippur is not primarily the time that one is to engage in repentance. If it were, it would have been called "Yom Teshuvah/the day of repentance." In fact, as mentioned above, there are "ten days of teshuvah," the "aseres ymei teshu-vah" from Rosh Hashana until Yom Kippur. Yom Kippur is the tenth of these days, and as such there is certainly an element of repentance in the prayers and service of the day. However, there is an additional element on this day that distinguishes it from the other nine days of "teshuvah." That is that on this day, subsequent to the "teshuvah" we have performed, we attain the level of "kapara/atonement." If one waits until Yom Kippur to engage in sincere soul searching and repentance, then s/he has waited far too long. And if one spends the entire day of Yom Kippur thinking about all the things that s/he has done wrong throughout the past year, then s/he is missing the point of this day almost completely. Sincere soul-searching and rectification are activities that one should engage in prior to Yom Kippur - at least throughout the ten days of repentance, preferably from the first day of Elul, and ideally on a daily basis - so that by the time of Yom Kippur, nothing remains to stand in the way of the "at one-ment" that is effected by the day.

We have thus established that the "kapara/atonement" of Yom Kippur is different from the "teshuvah/repentance" that precipitates it. Yet to fully comprehend the profundity of Yom Kippur, we must consider a fascinating debate of the sages. In the Talmud, the rabbis question what it is about the day of Yom Kippur that brings us to the level of atonement at which we are completely forgiven and our past misdeeds are expunged. The simple answer would be that we are absolved on account of the repentance that we have already performed. Because we have worked diligently throughout the "ten days of teshuvah" (and throughout the forty days from the first of Elul) to examine our conduct and to make amends for all of our errors and transgressions, therefore our efforts are rewarded, and our past sins are excused. Yet what about one who has not engaged in this introspection and correction? What if the month of Elul came and went without any awareness or redirection? What if the shofar on Rosh Hashana did not inspire any awakening? What if the "ten days of teshuvah" passed without any "teshuvah" at all? What about one who is so far from her/his roots that s/he is not even conscious of the fact that it is the high holidays? Does Yom Kippur effect atonement for one who has made absolutely no effort her/himself?

The sages debate this question, and Rabbi Yehudah HaNassi concludes that Yom Kippur grants atonement whether one engages in "teshuvah" or not.

רבי אומר על כל עבירות שבתורה בין עשה תשובה בין
לא עשה תשובה יום הכפורים מכפר.

Rebbi omer al kol aveiros she'b'Torah bein asah teshuvah bein lo asah teshuvah Yom hakippurim mechaper.

Rebbi (Yehuda HaNasi) says: For all transgressions that are stated in the Torah, whether one repented, or whether one did not repent, Yom Kippur atones.

(Talmud, Shavuos 13a)

Rabbi Yehudah HaNassi goes on to qualify this ruling by pointing out that Yom Kippur does not atone for one who transgresses the laws of Yom Kippur itself, for nullifying the covenant of circumcision, or for leading people astray by intentionally misinterpreting Torah. Yet in general, aside of these three offenses, he contends that the day itself brings atonement regardless of the individual's efforts. The other sages do not concur that atonement is granted across the board without repentance, and in spite of Rabbi Yehudah HaNassi's opinion, the "halachic/legal" ruling is that repentance is necessary. However, all agree that there is a quality to the day of Yom Kippur itself that brings one to a level of atonement that "teshuvah" itself cannot effect. We see this in the accepted ruling regarding certain more severe transgressions:

תְּשׁוּבָה תּוֹלָה וְיוֹם הַכִּפּוּרִים מְכַפֵּר.

Teshuvah tola v'yom hakippurim mechaper.

Repentance suspends (delays punishment) and Yom Kippur atones.

(Talmud, Yoma 86a)

This indicates that certain transgressions are absolved immediately when "teshuvah" is performed, but other more serious transgressions cannot be expiated simply through "teshuvah." Therefore, the performance of "teshuvah" delays the consequences for the transgression until the day of Yom Kippur, and on Yom Kippur the transgression is expunged. The sages derive this ruling from the Torah verse itself which states:

כִּי־בַיּוֹם הַזֶּה יְכַפֵּר עֲלֵיכֶם לְטַהֵר אֶתְכֶם **מִכֹּל חַטֹּאתֵיכֶם**
לִפְנֵי יְ-הֹוָה תִּטְהָרוּ:

*Ki bayom hazeh yechaper aleichem l'taher eschem **mikol chatoseichem** lifnei A-donai titharu.*

For on this day (Yom Kippur) He shall effect atonement for you to cleanse you. Before the Lord, you shall be cleansed from **all your sins**.

(Leviticus 16:30)

We see here that *all* of one's sins are eradicated on Yom Kippur, regardless of their severity. Furthermore, the verse establishes that atonement is something that is done to or for a person, not something that s/he does her/himself. How is it that the day of Yom Kippur itself brings one to the state of "at one-ment"?

To answer this, we must dig deeper in order to distinguish more clearly between forgiveness, "selicha/mechila" in Hebrew, and "atonement/kapara." Both of these concepts connote a state of rapprochement and reunion that follows a former fracture and separation. Yet there is a question of degree which differentiates between the two terms. One can be *forgiven*, yet there can still be a certain distance that remains. "At one-ment," however, indicates that any division and individuation has been eliminated completely. In its Hebrew root, "כפר/kapar" means "to cleanse" or "to scour." "Kapara" in its ultimate sense means that one has not only been excused for her/his past actions, but s/he has been cleansed of them completely so that no remnant or blemish of them continues to exist.

The difference can be explained with the allegory of a king and one of his trusted ministers. The minister has broken a law of the kingdom, and therefore he has incurred the king's wrath. Fearful of punishment, the minister begs the king's forgiveness, and successfully convinces the king that his remorse is genuine and his transgression will not be repeated. The king forgives him and restores him to his post. However, the next time there is an important job to be done, the king hesitates to assign it to this minister, cognizant of his past failing. In such a case, forgiveness has been granted, and the minister is subject to no punishment or retribution. Nevertheless, the relationship with the king has been blemished, and there remains a certain subtle distance between them. This is "selicha/mechila" or forgiveness. With "kapara," on the other hand, there is no memory whatsoever of the minister's error. It is not simply that the king mercifully forgives him. Rather it is as if either time has been reversed so that the event never happened, or the memory banks have been wiped and though the incident may have occurred, no one is conscious of it in any way at this point. The relationship between the king and his minister is completely untarnished, and when the next opportunity to serve the king arises, the minister is afforded the honor without any hesitation. This is what "kapara" ultimately means - the past has been scoured and cleared entirely, and no guilt or blame remains.

This "kapara," or complete cleansing, is what occurs on Yom Kippur. Each of us is restored on this day to a level of absolute purity and innocence. It is not simply that we are forgiven for our past misdeeds, but it is as though we never transgressed at all. We are not innocent because our guilt has been excused or pardoned, but because there is no guilt that needs to be expunged. It is not merely that we are given another chance, but it is as if we are an altogether new or different being that never failed or erred initially. How is this rewriting of history accomplished?

Neila - The Fifth Level

Earlier in this chapter, in the section entitled "Musaf - The Fourth Level," we explained that each of the holidays contains and achieves a level that is higher than the ordinary weekday. There, we discussed that on regular weekdays - this includes days that are not either the sabbath, holidays, or Rosh Chodesh - there are three prayer services: the "maariv/evening," "shacharis/morning," and "mincha/afternoon" prayers. These three services correspond to the three levels of the soul - "nefesh," "ruach," and "neshama" - that are housed within the body. The fourth level of the soul, "chaya," is too lofty and expansive to be contained within the confines of the body, so it hovers just above our head, so to speak. On shabbat, Rosh Chodesh, and yomim tovim (holidays), a fourth prayer service - "musaf" - is added to our daily regimen. This is because we are able to access the fourth level of our soul on account of the added spiritual energy that is invested into the world on these days.

There is also a fifth level of the soul, and it is called "yechida." It so "vast" that it cannot come down into this physical plane at all. We place the word "vast" in quotations because it is not, of course, physical size that we are discussing. Rather, it is the spiritual quality of the soul level which distinguishes its ability to manifest itself within the limited physical realm. The lower three levels of the soul are condensed enough to be able to express themselves within the body. The level of "chaya" is 'above' the body, but attached to it - meaning that it is generally beyond the framework of day to day interaction, but it can be accessed and manifest on occasions when one is inspired to act in a way that transcends her/his normal human inclinations. The level of "yechida," however, is completely outside the schema of this world.

"Yechida" means "singular" or "unique," and it represents a level that is completely unified with God's ultimate unity. Its inability to express itself in this world is a function of the "helam/concealment" that the "olam/world" was created to effect. As we have discussed on a number of occasions already, if God's true oneness were to be revealed, then no individuality or otherness could exist. The "yechida" is the innermost aspect of our soul which is an expression of this simple oneness. It is the very "Pnei Hashem/face of God" itself.

There is only one day a year on which we recite five prayer services, and that is Yom Kippur. In addition to the "maariv," "shacharis," "musaf" and "mincha" services that we perform on other holidays, we also add a service called "נְעִילָה/Neila" which is performed subsequent to the afternoon service just before the day of Yom Kippur draws to an end. The word "נְעִילָה/neila" means "closing," and the service is so named because it is at this time, when the holy day wanes, that the gates of the heavenly palace are closing. Throughout the "ten days of teshuvah," each of us has been granted special access to the the highest realms, which we alluded to with the metaphor of the king's palace. In the Baal Shem Tov's parable of the king and his child who had strayed and then returned, the shofar on Rosh Hashana represented the prince's cry, and in response to that call, the king ran to the palace gates, opened them, and ushered his long lost child inside. God is the king, and each of us is

His child, and throughout the "ten days of teshuvah," the King leads us further and further into the palace until, on Yom Kippur, we reach His innermost chamber. It is a place where no one can ordinarily enter. Yet because of His great love for us, and because we have wandered so far, the King brings us inside, and we are able to share a closeness with Him that is unique to this holy day. The simple understanding of the "closing" of "neila" is that the gates are drawing shut, and we have only a short time left to be in the palace. But the chassidic masters explain that the doors of the innermost chamber are closing not to shut us out, but rather to enclose us inside where we are finally alone with the King in this exalted state of intimacy.

This fifth service of "Neila" is added on Yom Kippur because this is the one day a year that the energy of the fifth level of our soul, "yechida," is manifested in the world. The rest of the year, our oneness with God is concealed so that we can continue to function as independent entities in a realm of multiplicity. Yet, as we have discussed throughout this chapter, there are designated times throughout the year that the veil is lifted and we are reminded of the ultimate reality of God's unity. On Yom Kippur we are exposed to this unity in a way that transcends all of the other holy days. While every sabbath, Rosh Chodesh, and holiday lifts us out of our mundane reality to enable us to glimpse our existence from a higher vantage, Yom Kippur transports us to a different dimension completely. While the other holy days provide us a glimpse beyond the veil, Yom Kippur removes the veil entirely and affords us not only a glimpse, but full exposure and accessibility.

This is why our conduct on Yom Kippur is so different from the other sacred occasions. Whereas it is a mitzvah to feast on the sabbath and the other festivals, on Yom Kippur we fast completely. Additionally, we refrain from marital relations, from wearing leather shoes, and from washing and anointing our bodies on Yom Kippur. On the simple level, these acts of abstinence are viewed as methods of self-mortification to chastise ourselves for the wrongs we have performed throughout the past year. But on a deeper and more essential level, we separate from the physical world on Yom Kippur not as a means of penance, but rather as an expression of our inherent Godliness. On this day, with the manifestation of our "yechida," it is revealed that we are truly beyond the world.

With this consciousness, refraining from food and physical engagements is not a challenge, but it is a natural expression of our most authentic self.

The effect of the "yechida's" exposure on Yom Kippur is not merely that we are elevated to a lofty and transcendent dimension, but rather it fuses and unifies all dimensions and thereby alters the nature of the entire creation as we know it. On other holy days, we transcend the world, but then we return to it when the period of additional holiness concludes. We may have changed from the experience of elevation, but the world remains the same. On Yom Kippur, on the contrary, the very nature of the universe has been transformed because its essence and core has been exposed. In that experience of primordial revelation, everything superficial and extraneous fades away. It is as if the creation has come in contact with a light so hot and so bright that it instantly incinerates whatever is not essential and infinite itself.

As we have mentioned previously,[220] Kabbala explains that all matter is a fragment of divine light encapsulated in a "kelipah" or shell. On Yom Kippur, when the source of all light is able to radiate freely into the creation, every "kelipah/shell" is burned away and only the light remains. This is how our histories are rewritten. It is not merely that our soiled garments and misdeeds are overlooked or even cast aside. Rather, they are consumed. Or perhaps more accurately, they are *subsumed*. What we discover on Yom Kippur is that even the blemishes themselves are Godly, and therefore they are not blemishes at all. If there is nothing that is not Godliness, then there can be no soiled garments. There can be nothing that ultimately conceals God because even the veils themselves are only layers of Godliness with which He has temporarily disguised His face. With this awareness, all otherness vanishes and only God remains. This is true "at onement," and this is the "kapara/atonement" that Yom Kippur accomplishes. It is the holiest day of the year because it is the day when the "Pnei Hashem" that we have been seeking every other day of the year is finally revealed.

We can now understand the teaching of Rabbi Yehudah HaNassi that whether or not one engages in introspection and correction on Yom Kippur, throughout the high holidays, or any time throughout the year, the day itself effects atonement. Though the other sages rule that "teshuvah" is required, they concur that Yom Kippur itself effects a cleansing

---

[220] See chapter nine, section "Mitzvos - From Study to Action"

which "teshuvah" alone cannot achieve. Therefore, while "teshuvah" suspends punishment for more severe transgressions until Yom Kippur, the energy of Yom Kippur eradicates the transgressions so that no penalty is necessary. What is it about the day itself that effects atonement? It is the fact that the level of "yechida" is revealed at this time, and therefore regardless of one's actions, s/he is purified from her/his core.

But why on this day in particular is the "yechida" revealed?

As we explained in the section entitled "Flow" above, Torah time is a spiral, and on each day of the calendar we are revisiting the same point on the cycle that we experienced last year and all previous years on this same date (but on a higher level). Certain dates have an especially powerful flow of particular divine energies based on the events that occurred on that day in the past, and on those days we are given the opportunity to access that power or potential more than other days. On the tenth of Tishrei, in the year 2448 from creation (1313 BCE), six months after the Exodus and three months after the sin of the golden calf, Moses completed his third period of forty days on the mountain, and God then exposed the universe to its deepest essence. This was in order to expunge any and all blemish that was caused by the worship of the calf, and to enable the new nation to begin again with a completely clean slate. This date thereafter became known as Yom Kippur, the day of "at one-ment." Every year on the tenth of Tishrei, when we come back around on the spiral of time to that same position, we are once again cleansed completely as the universe re-experiences the reset and reunion that is enacted through this influx of the deepest divine energy.

Sukkos

We have reached the "destination" of our journey, but our journey is not over. We have been seeking God's face, the "Pnei Hashem," at the innermost depths of our "pnimyus," and we have found it. Whether by virtue of our desire and perseverance, or simply on account of God's tremendous love for us regardless of our efforts, our "yechida" has been revealed on Yom Kippur, and everything else has, for the moment at least, faded away. However, Yom Kippur is not the end of the process, even if it is the holiest day of the year. The progression of the festivals continues with the week long holiday of Sukkos which begins five days after Yom Kippur on the fifteenth of Tishrei. And of course, as it is a cycle, the festival progression will begin again anew even after it is complete. We must address the question of why the journey starts over after it has seemingly ended; or in other words, why we remain in the dark even after we have "seen the light." But before we do so, we must complete the cycle and explore the final festival of Sukkos. What more is there once the culmination of Yom Kippur has occurred?

Each of the three pilgrimage festivals - Passover, Shavuos, and Sukkos[221] - is also referred to by another moniker which describes its theme. Passover is called "zman cheiruseinu/the time of our liberation." Shavuos is called "zman matan Toraseinu/the time of the giving of the Torah." Both of these terms succinctly illustrate the events that the respective holidays memorialize, and knowing these names will enable us to appreciate the essence of these festivals. We would therefore expect the same to be the case with the holiday of Sukkos. The alternate name for this final festival is "zman simchaseinu/the time of our joy." Unlike the specificity of the first two cases, this term tells us nothing of the historic events that the holiday commemorates. That is because Sukkos is not the occasion of any particular incident or episode, but rather it is the aftermath of the events that come before it. Though there is great "simcha/joy" on all of the holidays, Sukkos is the only one which is specifically identified as "the time of our joy." It is the week-long period when we celebrate the entire progression which has culminated on Yom Kippur.

The name "Sukkos" means "booths," and it refers to the temporary structures that the Israelites built for themselves as shelters in the desert. Alternatively, the "shelter" that is commemorated is the divine "clouds of glory" that surrounded the nation as they moved through the desert and protected them from the elements and other threats. In gratitude for this divine protection, and in remembrance of the fact that God is the only truly reliable shelter, Sukkos is observed annually by the construction of temporary "booths" outside the home in which one dwells as much possible throughout the seven days of the holiday. On the sim-

---

[221] These three holidays are referred to as "pilgrimage festivals" because it was customary to make a pilgrimage to the Temple in Jerusalem on these occasions.

plest level, the "simcha/joy" that we experience at this "zman simcha-seinu/time of our joy" is the awareness of the care and love with which God guides us and protects us as we move through the "desert" of this uncertain and hazardous world. Yet this does not explain the specific time at which Sukkos occurs. The nation "dwelled in booths" for forty years as they wandered in the desert. If Sukkos were merely a commemoration of our shelter and protection during this period, then it could seemingly be celebrated at any time throughout the year. Why does it fall directly in the wake of Yom Kippur? Because it is then that we can experience the greatest joy of the entire annual cycle, and because simcha is the ultimate outcome of the cycle, as we will explain.

As mentioned above,[222] each festival marks the introduction into the universe of a particular divine energy that is especially available and accessible at that time. At the time of Passover, God infuses into the world a uniquely powerful capacity for liberation. If we are sensitive to it and we reach for it, we can access during the days of Passover a particularly potent ability to transcend any limitations that have bound us and hindered us throughout the past year. On each Shavuos, God once again gives us the Torah, and we can therefore access especial divine energies that will enable us to reach ever greater levels of Torah understanding and insight. On Rosh Hashana, we are able to hear the voice of our soul, and if we work vigorously to gather and incorporate the extraordinary potential of this day, we will be more capable of detecting the innermost depths of our being even when the shofar is not blowing in the days and months to come. On Yom Kippur, we are exposed to our "yechidah," and though it is once again hidden after the holiday ends, our receptivity to it on Yom Kippur will allow us to be mindful of it even when it is not manifest.

What, then, is the special divine power that flows into the creation on the holiday of Sukkos? It is the power of "simcha/joy." Throughout the days of Sukkos, there is an influx into the universe of joy that is unlike any other time of the year. If we access this energy, then we can bring tremendous happiness into the year ahead. Sukkos is thus referred to as "zman simchaseinu/the time of our joy" not only because we are joyous at this time, but furthermore because we can access and stockpile happiness throughout these days to carry with us into our fu-

[222] In the section entitled "Flow" earlier in this chapter

ture. But in order to do so, we must understand what we are looking for. What is simcha/joy? And why, again, is it specifically on the fifteenth of Tishrei that the time of simcha begins?

Simcha

In order to understand the holiday of Sukkos fully, and thereby to appreciate why it has been designated as the completion of the annual festival cycle, we must explore the concept of "simcha" and plumb the depths of the idea of happiness or joy. What is genuine happiness, and what is it that truly brings us joy in life? If we answer these questions haphazardly, then we can spend all of our days seeking happiness and fulfillment, but never find it because we have no idea what it is. Torah provides us a potent clue by designating the end of the high holidays as the one time of the year to bear the title of "the time of our joy." By connecting this consummate level of simcha to the aftermath of the "ten days of teshuvah" and the climax of Yom Kippur, we are informed that joy is the result of the process that we undergo during these holy days. What is it about this process that induces such great joy?

There is a palpable feeling of happiness that follows Yom Kippur. If we were to ask people what they are happy about at this time, we would receive a range of answers. On a simple level, the joy may be a sense of relief and release after the last ten days (or forty days, if we properly begin the process at the beginning of Elul) of intense introspection and evaluation. These preceding days are known as "days of awe," and joy is a natural response when this heavy and intense period concludes. Joy can certainly result from a release of pressure and tension, but we would not therefore extrapolate that the key to happiness is a lack of seriousness or fervor. We might recognize this type of relaxation and relief as an element of joy, or perhaps a factor that can contribute to happiness, but lasting joy is clearly not merely the absence of earnestness and self-discipline. As a matter of fact, though we may fantasize about lives of leisure without responsibility, this will often lead to boredom and self-reproach as one eventually feels idle and purposeless.

On a somewhat deeper level, the joy subsequent to the days of awe may result from a sense of renewal, forgiveness, and acquittal. We have all been less than perfect throughout the past year, and there was therefore a pending charge against us in the heavenly court. Throughout these days of judgment, we have been awaiting our verdict with anxiety and trepidation. On Yom Kippur, we were pardoned, and we can finally let out a sigh of relief and breathe freely again. This is certainly a positive feeling, but is it happiness? Is happiness simply the absence of concern? Or is this not, as we saw in the previous instance, more a sense of relief than a sense of true joy?

Perhaps our joy is a function of our appreciation and gratitude for the fact that we are governed and judged by such a merciful king or God. Gratitude is absolutely one of the paths to wisdom and one of the ways to cultivate joy. But if our happiness is predicated on the realization that our king has chosen to be merciful rather than vengeful, then though we may be grateful for the moment, can we ever truly be happy? Do we not need to begin worrying that next year He won't be so merciful? Is there ever true joy if we are always, at least in the recesses of our mind, concerned about how we will be judged tomorrow?

On an even higher level, our happiness may be the result not of anything that God has done to or for us, but on account of our consciousness of what *we* can do for *Him*. We rejoice at this time because we know that God is rejoicing at this time. In this sense, the expression "zman simchaseinu" is in the plural - the time of OUR joy - because there is joy both here below and up above. Why is God happy at this time? Because His children have returned to Him. Like the prince in the Baal Shem Tov's story, we were far away, and we have come back to the palace where we belong. What greater joy is there for the king than to have his long-lost child back under his roof and within his loving embrace? We are ecstatic not only because we have been welcomed back without reproach, but because we see the ecstasy that our return has brought to our beloved father and king. This type of joy is lofty and rare - it is focused not on what we receive, but on what we give, and therefore it is a joy that one can experience even when things are not going precisely as s/he might like. Yet even this type of joy is limited. It is predicated on a binary, and thus inherently finite, dynamic. There is me, and there is God, and though my pleasure in focusing on His pleasure is certainly more elevated than when I am focusing on my pleasure alone, it is still a function of division and distinction. There is still a distance between us and the infinite God by virtue of the fact that we conceive of ourselves as an other.

The true joy of "zman simchaseinu" is not a matter, as in our first case above, of the removal of some previous negative emotion. We are not happy simply because we have withstood or survived something unpleasant, the completion or absence of which now renders us less anxious or uncomfortable. It is beyond the elevated level of gratitude, as in our second case, as it is a much deeper state of being that is not subject to the fluctuation of moods or the particularities of personal circumstance. It is even beyond the selflessness and altruism of placing the happiness of our beloved above our own, because with genuine simcha there is no distinction between the two. This is alluded to in the chassidic maxim coined by the Rebbe Rashab,[223] Rabbi Shalom Dovber Schneersohn:

שִׂמְחַה פֹּרֶץ גֶּדֶר.

Simcha poretz geder.
Joy breaks all boundaries.
(Sefer HaMaamarim 5657, p. 223ff.)

The implication of this statement is not merely that joy can penetrate the barriers that separate two individuals from one another. Even more profoundly, it indicates that joy can eliminate the barriers completely so that there is no longer a sense of individuality at all. Rather the two previously individual beings become one. What is this profound experience that can elevate us to such unbounded levels, and how can we access it during Sukkos in order to bring it with us into the rest of the year?

The sages provide us insight into the ultimate nature of simcha through a statement made in the Talmud regarding one of the unique rituals performed on this holiday. Throughout the week of Sukkos, there was a special ceremony that was performed daily in the Temple in Jerusalem that was called "שִׂמְחַת בֵּית הַשֹּׁוֹאֵבָה/Simchas Beis Hashoevah." Regarding this ceremony, the sages taught the following:

---

[223] The fifth Rebbe of the Chabad dynasty. 1860-1920

מִי שֶׁלֹּא רָאָה שִׂמְחַת בֵּית הַשּׁוֹאֵבָה לֹא רָאָה שִׂמְחָה מִיָּמָיו.

Mi shelo raah Simchas beis hashoevah lo raah simcha miyamav.
One who did not see the "Simchas Beis Hashoevah"
never saw joy in his days.

(Talmud, Sukkah 51a)

This statement is surprising even before we know what the ceremony entailed. Regardless of what tremendous joy the "Simchas Beis Hashoevah" elicited, how is it possible to say that one has *never seen* joy if s/he has not experienced this particular event? Perhaps it would be reasonable to suggest that one has not encountered happiness *like* this particular happiness - in other words, that it reflects a qualitatively different type of joy than the joy that other experiences evoke. Or we might be able to understand if the sages asserted that one has never known such an intense level of happiness as the happiness that attends the "Simchas Beis Hashoevah" - in other words, that there is a quantitative difference here in the amount of joy experienced. But to claim that without this experience one has never seen joy at all, this is truly baffling. What could the sages possibly mean?

Knowing the details of the "Simchas Beis Hashoevah" ceremony will only add to our confusion. "שׁוֹאֵבָה/Shoevah" is from the verb "לִשְׁאוֹב/lishov," which means to "draw" or "pump," and it is commonly applied to the drawing of water from a well. "Simchas Beis Hashoevah" literally means the "celebration of the house of drawing," and it refers to the ritual in which water was drawn from the Shiloach spring next to the Temple Mount in Jerusalem and then poured as an offering on the altar in the Temple. What is it about this drawing of water and the subsequent pouring of it on the altar that generates joy at all, let alone the greatest joy of the year? Even more so, how does it create joy so unique that no other joy can be classified as joy at all if this particular type of joy has not been experienced?

Throughout each of the days of Sukkos, the drawing of the water and its offering on the altar was performed with tremendous celebration and revelry. The people would dance and sing as the priest drew the water, carried it to the Temple, and poured it on the altar. The festivities would last throughout the day and into the nights as thousands of people would gather at the Temple to rejoice and to bask in the bliss of the occasion. Even today, when the Temple no longer stands and the water drawing is no longer performed, it is a custom in many chassidic and orthodox communities to gather on the nights of Sukkos to dance and sing and express the intense joy that is evoked by the mere memory of this unique ritual. But why? Why does a water offering make us so happy?

<hr />

Lower And Higher Waters

Libations, or liquid offerings, were poured on the altar in the Temple every day. Oil was offered regularly, and every animal sacrifice was accompanied by a libation of wine. Wine was always a precious commodity in the ancient world, and it was commonly used for sacramental purposes. Holy rituals and occasions were blessed with the drinking or offering of wine in order to demonstrate their importance and distinctiveness. There was only one time a year, however, that water was offered on the altar. That is during Sukkos, and this is the offering of the "Simchas Beis Hashoevah." While we can understand the value and significance of offering precious liquids like wine and/or oil, it is difficult to comprehend the advantage of bringing water on the altar. Not only is water commonplace and inexpensive, but it is furthermore tasteless. It lacks both the flavor and the intoxicating qualities of wine, and it does not possess the rich and healthy benefits of oil. It makes sense that these other substances were frequently poured on the altar, but we must wonder not only why water was offered at all, but why this water offering engendered the greatest exultation of the year. To understand the profundity and the elation of this event, we must go all the way back to the second day of creation.

On the first day of creation, God created light and darkness. On the third day, He created the land and the sea and the vegetation. What was it that was created on the second day? The "expanse," or in Hebrew, "הָרָקִיעַ." What is this expanse? It is sky, or the "heavens" that would separate between the "higher waters" and the "lower waters."

וַיַּעַשׂ אֱ-לֹהִים אֶת־הָרָקִיעַ וַיַּבְדֵּל בֵּין הַמַּיִם אֲשֶׁר מִתַּחַת
לָרָקִיעַ וּבֵין הַמַּיִם אֲשֶׁר מֵעַל לָרָקִיעַ וַיְהִי־כֵן: וַיִּקְרָא
אֱ-לֹהִים לָרָקִיעַ שָׁמָיִם וַיְהִי־עֶרֶב וַיְהִי־בֹקֶר יוֹם שֵׁנִי:

*Vayaas E-lohim es-harakia vayavdeil bein hamayim asher
mitachas larakia u'vein hamayim asher me'al larakia vayehi
kein. Vayikra E-lohim larakia shamayim vayehi erev vayehi
boker yom sheini.*

And God made the expanse and it separated between
the water that was below the expanse and the water
that was above the expanse, and it was so. And God
called the expanse Heaven, and it was evening, and it
was morning, day two.

(Genesis 1:7-8)

On the first day, subsequent to the creation of light and darkness,
"God saw ... that it was good."[224] On the third day, having created the
land and sea and vegetation, "God saw that it was good."[225] But on the
second day, it was not good. The second day is the only one of the days
of creation that was not referred to as "good." What was it about this day
and its creation that was less positive than the others? Whereas the creations on the other days were productive and constructive, the creation
on the second day was intended not for the sake of that thing itself, but
rather in order to divide and separate between something else, as we can
see from the verse that explains the purpose of this day's creation:

וַיֹּאמֶר אֱ-לֹהִים יְהִי רָקִיעַ בְּתוֹךְ הַמָּיִם וִיהִי מַבְדִּיל בֵּין מַיִם
לָמָיִם:

*Vayomer E-lohim yehi rakia b'toch hamayim viyhi mavdil
bein mayim l'mayim.*

And God said, Let there be an expanse in the midst of
the water, and let it be a separation between water and
water.

(Genesis 1:6)

---

[224] Genesis 1:4

[225] ibid 1:12

It seems that the primary point and reason for the expanse was not the expanse itself, but rather for the stratification of the higher and lower waters. Division and separation, according to God Himself, is not "good," and that is why this term is not applied to this day. The water clearly concurred. In the Zohar, we find that the lower waters were devastated by their dissection and exile below. They called out to God in agony and protest:

מַיִם תַּתָּאִין אִינוּן בּוֹכִין וְאָמְרִין אֲנַן בַּעְיָין לְמֶהֱוֵי קֳדָם
מַלְכָּא עִלַּת הָעִלּוֹת:

Mayim tata'in inun bochin v'amrin anan ba'iyan l'mehevay kadam Malka ilas ha'ilos.

The lower waters cry and say, "We too want to stand before the King!"

(Tikkuni Zohar 5, 19:9)

Why must we be relegated to the physical world, the lower waters lamented, where we will be far from our Source? Why must we dwell in a realm of concealment and separation, where God is unrecognized and where the apparent distinction and individuality of various aspects of the creation engenders conflict and disunity? God understood their complaint and sympathized with their plight. But separation was a necessary condition for the creation. It was instituted on the second day because it was a prerequisite for all of the creations that would follow. Without separation, there could be no "otherness," and therefore no creation (as we have explained at length on several previous occasions). Nevertheless, God offered the lower waters comfort and consolation. First, He commanded that salt should be sprinkled on every sacrifice on the altar.

עַל כָּל־קָרְבָּנְךָ תַּקְרִיב מֶלַח:

Al kol karbancha takriv melach.

You shall offer salt on all your sacrifices.

(Leviticus 2:13)

Salt comes from the oceans, and by bringing salt on the altar, this component of the lower waters would be elevated above and reunited on a daily basis. Yet this was only a partial remedy, as salt is merely an element and representative of the water. The real reunion would come when water itself would be offered on the alter. This, as we have discussed, would happen once a year during Sukkos at the time of the "Simchas Beis Hashoevah."

The altar was the meeting place between heaven and earth. When the Temple stood, fire would descend from the heavens and join with the earthly fire that was kindled on the stone platform below. Whatever was sacrificed on the altar would be consumed by the intermingling earthly and heavenly flames, and as its corporeal form would be eradicated, its spiritual essence would be freed and enabled to reunite with its universal source. When water was drawn from the Shiloach spring on Sukkos, it was with tremendous celebration as it represented all of the lower waters which had been separated from above by the expanse on the second day of creation. Poured onto the altar, the water returned from its long and distant estrangement and embraced the higher waters to once again fuse with them completely. There is no greater joy than this. When an entity is torn apart - its two segments kept from one another for ages, pining for one another all this time - and then they are finally reunited, this is the true and ultimate definition of simcha. Compared to this consummate joy, all other joy is as nothing. This is why the sages declared that one who has never experienced the "Simchas Beis Hashoevah" has never seen joy at all. One may have experienced worldly pleasure and fleeting forms of enjoyment or happiness, but if s/he has not known true spiritual reunion, then s/he has no comprehension of what simcha really is.

But why is this ritual performed specifically on Sukkos? Why are the waters reunited on the altar then and not any other time during the year? It is because this is precisely what has occurred in the universe five days earlier on Yom Kippur. Like the waters on the second day of creation, everything that exists in this world had previously been torn away from its source when it was embodied in this physical realm. As long as the spark of Godliness, the "Pnei Hashem," which is the core reality of every being, is covered by a material crust, it is divided from its entirety and it pines every moment to be reunited. This is the existential angst that every one of us experiences at every moment of our lives. We may not recognize it as such. We may ignore it or try to distract ourselves from it. But when we are quiet and still, and exceedingly honest and attuned to our deepest core, we can sense this intense yearning to cast off the shell that confines and conceals us and to reunite with everything around us. On Yom Kippur, as we discussed above, when the "yechida" is revealed, for a glorious moment everything is reincorporated into its infinite oneness. This is the meaning of true and ultimate "teshuvah/return," and the joy of this reunion is unspeakable. It can hardly be put into words, and it can only be alluded to with the allegory of the lower waters reconvening with the higher. It is the absolute bliss and ecstasy of the reunification of every single disparate fragment of the universe. This simcha is so great that it is celebrated for an entire week which is referred to, uniquely, as "zman simchaseinu/the time of our joy."

We can now understand the deeper relevance of the literal "sukkah" or "booth" that we construct and dwell in during the holiday of Sukkos. The mystics teach that the structure represents the divine embrace in which we are enwrapped during this time. The "halacha/law" is that the sukkah must be composed of at least two and a half walls. These three parts - two longer, and one shorter - correspond to the three sections of the arm - the segment from the shoulder to the elbow, the segment from the elbow to the wrist, and then the shorter segment from the wrist to the end of the fingertips. After the days of awe and the culmination of Yom Kippur, we build the sukkah to symbolize the embracing arm of God. We step inside, and we are not only embraced by our Beloved, but we are re-included in His infinity. In His arms, we are no longer isolated or alienated, but we are complete. We are no longer "alone," but we are "All One." The sukkah, like all of the Torah's rituals, is a practice and a visual aid that enables us to materialize our deepest spiritual concepts and see them with our limited physical eyes.

With this, we will appreciate the profound mystic connotation of a verse from the Torah that seems, on its surface, to simply command us to dwell in booths during the holiday:

בַּסֻּכֹּת תֵּשְׁבוּ שִׁבְעַת יָמִים כָּל־הָאֶזְרָח בְּיִשְׂרָאֵל יֵשְׁבוּ בַּסֻּכֹּת:

Basukkos teshvu shivas yamim kol ha'ezrach b'Yisrael yeshvu basukkos.

For a seven day period you shall live in booths. Every resident among the Israelites shall live in booths.

(Leviticus 23:42)

On this seemingly straightforward verse, the Alter Rebbe asks[226] why the fairly unusual term "הָאֶזְרָח בְּיִשְׂרָאֵל/ha'ezrach b'Yisrael" is used to describe the people. The word "אֶזְרָח/ezrach" means "resident" or "citizen." But in cases of direction to the people as a whole, as in the quoted verse, the terms "bnei Yisrael/children of Israel" or "am Yisrael/nation of Israel" would more commonly be used. This peculiar term is employed here, the Alter Rebbe informs us, because the word "אֶזְרָח/ezrach" is from the root "זרח," which means "to shine." The inner meaning of the verse is therefore that "kol ha'ezrach b'Yisrael/all of *those who shine* from within Israel," will sit in the sukkah. In other words, this is not simply a command, but it is a guarantee. It informs us that we will experience the true unifying embrace that the sukkah represents when that which is deep inside of us will be illuminated and enabled to shine forth. This shining and radiating of the "Pnei Hashem" from within our "pnimyus" is what is accomplished on Yom Kippur. Subsequently, we dwell in the sukkah because we are manifesting in the outward physical plane the spiritual reality of the divine embrace and reunification that has been accomplished throughout these holy days.

Fire And Water

True joy, we have seen, is the reunion that follows separation and distance. This is alluded to by the sages with the "Simchas Beis Hashoevah" ceremony because the reuniting of the lower and higher waters perfectly expresses this theme. Yet there is another reason why the festival of water was chosen as a fitting imagery for this time. Water, the chassidic masters explain, represents the state of blissful completion, tranquility, and satiation that comes when one has attained and acquired what s/he has previously sought. Fire, on the other hand, signifies the intense and passionate pursuit of something that one lacks and craves.

Throughout our lives, we are, so to speak, playing with fire. We are constantly reaching, like flames of fire, toward something that is beyond us. Life is a constant yearning, tension, and striving to find and

---

[226] *Likkutei Torah*, B'yom Hashemini Atzeres, ch. 3

have what is missing. It is a feverish pursuit of union, and an agonizing thirst for consummation and completion. This is the fire within us that is always burning. We offer daily "karbonos/sacrifices" on the flames of the altar, trying to "draw close" (the literal meaning of the Hebrew "karbon") and to consume the animal that conceals us so that our spiritual essence can fuse with the infinite Godliness that surrounds us. Finally, on Yom Kippur, we achieve this reunification when we access our "yechida" which is one with everything. The "Neila" prayer on Yom Kippur is the consummation of our marriage - the doors close us in the bridal chamber, and we unite with our beloved.[227] Afterwards, on Sukkos, our offering is water, not fire. We have reached and merged with the One that we have desired, and finally there is no more lack, no more agony, no more scorching flame, because we have attained what we have always sought. We have become one with our lover. We are entangled, ecstatic, and at peace.

When there is distance, there is noise. We call out, we whistle, we cry. 'I'm here! Where are you? Come to me! Don't leave me behind! Don't flee from me!' We are like a blazing, raging fire that crackles and pops and hisses and roars. The closer we are, the louder we call. We see our lover in the distance, and we beckon, 'hey, over here, this way, can you hear me?!' This is the beauty of song, the passionate sounds we make when we yearn and reach.[228] When there is union, on the other hand, there is silence, like the quiet calm of being submerged or 'in utero.' With water, the fire is quenched. Simcha is the release of all tension and fever. We want and lack nothing, because we have become one with everything.

In chassidic discourse, these two states that we are comparing to fire and water are referred to as "hispaalus/arousal" and "dveikus/cleaving." To be clear, the fiery level of "hispaalus/arousal" is not lowly or negative. An intense desire and yearning which is caused by the sense of what one lacks is far superior to the coldness, indifference, or despondency that is experienced by those who don't believe that there is anything to aspire to and have therefore given up hope. "Hispaalus/arousal" is a very holy level of stretching and striving to elevate oneself

---

[227] As we discussed above in section "Neila"

[228] As we discussed in chapter two, in section "Singing in the Dark"

and transcend one's current limitations. However, this arousal itself is a sign that one has yet to achieve what s/he is reaching for. It may be passionate, and it may even be pleasurable. One may even come to peace with the fact that what s/he craves is always just beyond her/his fingertips. In such a case there is simultaneous yearning and contentment; there is calling out and aspiring without frustration or desperation. But when we reach and embrace the one we have desired, there is a silent and consummate bliss that is called "dveikus/cleaving." We are no longer trying to touch or grab or maintain, because we have joined and fused together. The distance between us has been gulfed, and all divisions have given way. "Hispaalus" is the passionate desire and arousal before we unite, and "dveikus" is the ecstatic release that follows when all desire is fulfilled and all tension resolves.

Yet this bliss is fleeting. "Dveikus" is an extremely tenuous and rarefied state. It is not an experience that one can hold on to indefinitely or enjoy constantly. The nature of this "olam/world" is "helam/concealment." We dwell in a realm of darkness, division, and multiplicity, and as we have discussed repeatedly, there are reasons for these dynamics that keep us from an open perception of our ultimate reality. It would be difficult, if not impossible, to function within the world if the artificiality of its boundaries were perceptible. We were placed here to function within the structure of this creation in order to purify it and perfect it, so our vision must be limited and our perception must be obscured. However, Torah provides us the opportunity to occasionally see through the walls and experience "dveikus" and bliss for brief moments in order to keep us conscious of our potential and focused on our goal. We pray/meditate three times a day to keep our consciousness beyond the world,[229] but prayer is mandated only three times a day, because we must remain within the world the rest of the time. We study Torah every day, but not all day. Each mitzvah provides us an opportunity to experience the bliss of "dveikus" with the divine for a split second, and then we resume our work and journey in the darkness.

This is the rhythm of "ratzo v'shov/running and returning" that we discussed previously in regards to our daily prayer,[230] our Torah

---

[229] As we discussed in chapter nine, section "Meditation"

[230] See chapter nine, section "Bringing It Down"

study,[231] and our weekly cycle.[232] We are constantly surging to reach beyond the limitations of the world in order to access our infinite source, and then we are stepping back into the confines of our material existence in recognition of the task of rectification and illumination that we are assigned here. This dynamic will enable us to answer the question that we posed at the beginning of our discussion of Sukkos regarding the end of the festival cycle: why it is that our journey must start over after it has been completed? Why do we once again find ourselves in the dark after we've seen the light? Why in the six months after Sukkos do we become lost and eventually enslaved anew so that we must once again begin with Passover in the coming spring?

Coming full circle, so to speak, these questions parallel the questions that we asked in the very first chapter at the beginning of our journey:[233] Why does God create us in Eden and then expel us? Why, if He oversees everything with "hashgacha protis/divine providence," does He give us the Torah and then allow us to create the golden calf? If He wants us to see Him and experience Him, then why does He permit us to cast Him away so quickly and easily? Why all of these moments of revelation and "dveikus" followed once again by concealment and alienation?

As we noted in the first chapter, when Moses asked God to explain Himself, God responded "You will not be able to see my face, for man shall not see Me and live."[234] By now, we can fully understand God's response. Water is offered on the altar only once a year, and the rest of the time we offer fire. The "dveikus/cleaving" and revelation that we seek is not the natural state of this hidden existence. This is a realm of concealment where we must constantly light a fire to illuminate the darkness. This fire is our "hispaalus/arousal," and if we light these fires assiduously, we will have moments of "dveikus," which are glimpses of the "Pnei Hashem" that is hidden within our "pnimyus." We will thereby experience the ecstasy of water, but we cannot live in water. We are not

---

[231] See chapter nine, section "Torah - From Prayer To Study"

[232] See chapter ten, section "Seven"

[233] See chapter one, section "The Face of Death"

[234] Exodus 33:20

aquatic creatures. If we stay too long in the water, we will drown. We can only enjoy the bliss of submersion for short bouts.[235] And then after the water comes fire again. After the water offerings of "Simchas Beis Hashoevah" on Sukkos, we return to the regular offerings of flesh and grain that are burnt on the flames of the altar throughout the rest of the year.

Regarding the messianic era, the prophet Isaiah assures us that we will be immersed in the perception of God's infinite oneness, and we will experience the bliss of water and "dveikus" constantly.

מָלְאָה הָאָרֶץ דֵּעָה אֶת־יְ-הוָה כַּמַּיִם לַיָּם מְכַסִּים:

Malah Haaretz deah es A-donai k'mayim layam michasim.
The land shall be full of knowledge of the Lord as waters cover the sea bed.
(Isaiah 11:9)

"דֵּעָה/Deah" is translated as "knowledge," but as we saw above in chapter nine,[236] it also means intimacy and fusion, as in the verse "וְהָאָדָם יָדַע אֶת־חַוָּה אִשְׁתּוֹ וַתַּהַר/And Adam **knew** Eve his wife and she became pregnant."[237] In the messianic era, we will be intimately fused with Godliness so completely that it will be as if we are immersed in it like water. Yet we are not yet ready for this ecstatic messianic reality. We are working toward it, and this is precisely what we were created to do. Our task is to precipitate this time of universal divine perception with individual acts of revelation amidst the darkness.

We are bound to get lost again along the way, for the journey is difficult and the darkness is thick. But we need not fear, because even as we inevitably descend once more into the depths of the Egyptian bondage in which we forget that we are not subject to the limitations of this world, Passover will come again in the spring, and we will be liberated and awakened anew. In the meantime, every mitzvah we perform, every aspect of the practice that the Torah provides us - the daily, weekly,

---

[235] This can help us understand the significance of the ritual of mikvah, which for women is practiced monthly, and which some men have the custom to practice daily. But this is not the place for a detailed exposition of this profound subject.

[236] Section "Torah - From Prayer to Study"

[237] Genesis 3:1

monthly, yearly and lifecycle rituals that we have discussed throughout the past three chapters - are sparks of Godly fire that we release from the shells that conceal them. As they multiply and aggregate, they will eventually create a glow so bright that it will eradicate the darkness completely. We will then be able see the "Pnei Hashem" in the "pnimyus" of all things. The cycle will be complete, as we will have followed the spiral of time to the heights of the highest heavens and to the ends of the most profound depths. Until then, we practice. Engaging in the practice that Torah provides us, we share the warmth and light of our fire with the world. We journey inward through the darkness, carrying the torch of Torah, breaking through the boundaries that impede our progress, and tearing away the many veils that cover our innermost essence and the face of God that is awaiting us there.

Dancing In Circles

At the very end of the holiday of Sukkos comes Shemini Atzeres and Simchas Torah, which are simultaneously distinct festivals in their own right, and concluding components of Sukkos itself. In the land of Israel, these are celebrated on the same day, the eighth day after Sukkos begins, while outside of Israel, Shemini Atzeres is celebrated on the eighth day, and then Simchas Torah is observed on the ninth. In both cases, they essentially represent a single theme, which is the ultimate culmination, celebration, and integration of everything that has come before. "Shemini" means "eight," and "Atzeres" means "to stop." On this eighth day, we stop and reflect on the entire process that we have just completed. The sages teach that the holiday of Sukkos has been like a celebration that the king throws for his entire kingdom. At the very end of the festival, all of the guests say their goodbyes and head home. But the king detains his beloved child and says 'stop, wait, spend one more day with me before you go back to your daily life.'[238]

The theme of Simchas Torah is likewise one of intense closeness and completion. The name means "the celebration of the Torah," and one

---

[238] Talmud, Sukkah 55b

might wonder why we would be celebrating the Torah now rather than on Shavuos when it was given. Yet the Torah that we celebrate on Simchas Torah is subtly different from the Torah that was celebrated on Shavuos. As we have discussed in the section entitled "Elul" above, Moses shattered the first set of tablets that he brought down from Mount Sinai when he descended forty days after Shavuos and found that the nation had built the golden calf. He then climbed the mountain and begged forgiveness for forty days. Then he spent a third period of forty days on the mountain carving a second set of tablets to replace the first set that he had shattered. It was on Yom Kippur that this third period of forty days ended and Moses descended with the second set of tablets, indicating that the sin of the golden calf had been forgiven. Simchas Torah, two weeks after Yom Kippur, is a celebration of these second tablets. Whereas the first tablets were more miraculous in that they were the handiwork of God Himself, the second set has an advantage in that they represent "teshuvah/return" and "kapara/atonement," the awareness that we can come back and reunite even after we have fallen and strayed. This reunification, as we have discussed in the previous sections, is the greatest joy. And this is why Simchas Torah is the last day of Sukkos, which is the time known uniquely as "zman simchaseinu/the time of our joy."

Shemini Atzeres and Simchas Torah are celebrated in a very particular fashion. The annual cycle of reading the Torah is completed with the final portion of Deuteronomy, and then it is immediately begun again with the reading of the opening portion of Genesis. But the primary practice of the holiday is dancing with the Torah in circles known as "hakafot," which means "to go around." On the first six days of Sukkos, the congregation makes a circuit around the Torah each day carrying four species of plants. On the seventh day (known as Hoshana Rabba), seven revolutions are made around the Torah. And then on Simchas Torah, the Torah itself is lifted as the congregation makes seven formal circuits around the synagogue. This is followed by dancing in circles for hours, similar to the traditional "horah" circle-dance that many are familiar with from Jewish weddings, bar/bat mitzvahs, and other celebratory events. Why is it that Jews are always dancing in circles, and what do these circles represent specifically on these last days of the festivals?

We have been discussing cycles throughout this entire chapter, and it is no coincidence that we end the cycle by going in circles. It is also significant that the way we make our circles at the end of the process is specifically by *dancing* around them. The annual cycle, as we have described, takes us into the light, and then back out to the darkness, and then around and around again. The traditional circle dance even includes this inward and outward motion, this "ratzo/running" and "shov/returning," as we converge toward the center and then retreat back to a wide circumference again, all the while continuing to progress in a circular motion. The significance here is that **the darkness does not make us despondent, but rather it makes us dance**. We are not frustrated by the cyclical nature of our reality. As passionately as we desire revelation and reunion, and as much as we delight in the ecstasy of water after fire, we recognize that we have a job to do and a responsibility to return to the darkness in order to alleviate it for those who continue to be lost within it.

Yet before we leave the palace and the king, we "stop/atzur" on the "eighth day/shemini" - Shemini Atzeres - to revel in the recognition of our true and inevitable closeness. We dance on Simchas Torah with the *second* set of tablets specifically, rejoicing in the knowledge of the infinite power of "teshuvah" and our ability to be one even as we seem to be distant and distinct. We dance back out of the light and back into the darkness with the awareness that we are simply fragments of Godliness concealed. We will lose this consciousness at times. Yet if we continue to dance with the Torah and embrace the practices that it provides us, we will not only return to the light once again, but we will eventually reveal our "pnimyus" and thereby make the darkness shine.

Chapter 11: END GAME

Yemot Hamashiach

We began a journey at the beginning of this book, and as the book draws toward its end, our journey continues. Though we now know precisely what we are searching for (the "Pnei Hashem/Face of God"), where it is awaiting us (in our "pnimyus/innermost core"), and how to get there (by following the intricate liberation practice that is established in Torah), the journey may not end in this life. Nor, for that matter, will it necessarily end when this life is over. It may continue into our next life, and perhaps multiple future lives. Though it is not widely known or understood, reincarnation is very much a Torah concept. It is referred to in Hebrew as "גִלְגּוּל/gilgul," which literally means "wheel." The soul's cycle keeps spinning even after one particular life-cycle is over.

It is said that a soul must return to this world repeatedly until its task is fulfilled. That may be a task that is specific to a particular soul, or it may be the task of fulfilling all of the mitzvos, which is common to all souls and takes longer for some than others. As we have discussed from the first chapter on, the ultimate task that is incumbent upon each of us individually, and all of us collectively, is "Breishis bara Elokim es hashamayim v'es haaretz," to make God revealed throughout His creation. As mentioned in chapter nine,[239] every mitzvah one performs is a contribution to this effort, another shell broken and another fragment of light revealed. Though the process may not be completed in a single lifetime, or even in a series of reincarnations, every life is contributing to the task.

There is, however, an "end" to the journey, so to speak. That is when the revelation that we have been working toward will be accomplished. It is when the "Pnei Hashem" is manifest throughout the creation. When the "pnimyus," or ultimate reality, of all things will be visible through the veil of physicality that had previously concealed it, all will be conscious of God's exclusive unity, even amidst the multiplicity of this lower realm. This time of revelation and fruition is referred to in Torah by a variety of names, among them "olam haba/the world to come" and "yemot hamashiach/the days of the messiah." It is one of the Torah's thirteen principles of faith that we expect this messianic revolution every single day. We long for it, and we therefore labor tirelessly to precipitate its occurrence. While the Torah's concept of the messiah is complex, and a thorough treatment of the subject is beyond the scope of this book, for the purposes of our subject it will suffice to understand that "Mashiach/the messiah" will come when God determines that the time of darkness and concealment is complete. His coming will usher in a new age of "enlightenment," in which the conduct of the world will be transformed completely because we will all be able to see what was hidden from us until now.

In one of the most renowned and idyllic descriptions of this future time, the prophet Isaiah proclaims:

וְגָר זְאֵב עִם־כֶּבֶשׂ וְנָמֵר עִם־גְּדִי יִרְבָּץ וְעֵגֶל וּכְפִיר וּמְרִיא יַחְדָּו
וְנַעַר קָטֹן נֹהֵג בָּם: וּפָרָה וָדֹב תִּרְעֶינָה יַחְדָּו יִרְבְּצוּ יַלְדֵיהֶן
וְאַרְיֵה כַּבָּקָר יֹאכַל־תֶּבֶן: וְשִׁעֲשַׁע יוֹנֵק עַל־חֻר פָּתֶן וְעַל
מְאוּרַת צִפְעוֹנִי גָּמוּל יָדוֹ הָדָה: לֹא־יָרֵעוּ וְלֹא־יַשְׁחִיתוּ בְּכָל־הַר
קָדְשִׁי כִּי־מָלְאָה הָאָרֶץ דֵּעָה אֶת־יְ-הֹוָה כַּמַּיִם לַיָּם מְכַסִּים:

---

[239] End of section "Mission Accomplished"

V'gar ze'ev im keves v'namer im g'di yirbatz v'egel u'chphir u'm'ri yachdav v'naar katon noheig bam. U'phara va'dov tirenah yachdav yirbitzu yaldeihen v'aryeh ka'bakar yochal teven. V'shiashah yoneik al chur pasen v'al m'uras tziphoni gamul yado hada. Lo yariu v'lo yashchisu b'chol har kadshi ki malah ha'aretz deah es A-donai ka'mayim la'yam michasim.

And a wolf shall live with a lamb, and a leopard shall lie with a kid; and a calf and a lion cub and a fatling [shall lie] together, and a small child shall lead them. And a cow and a bear shall graze together, their children shall lie; and a lion, like cattle, shall eat straw. And an infant shall play over the hole of an old snake and over the eyeball of an adder, a weaned child shall stretch forth his hand. They shall neither harm nor destroy on all My holy mount, for the land shall be full of knowledge of the Lord as water covers the sea bed.

(Isaiah 11:6-9)

Isaiah here describes the peace and camaraderie that will envelop all of the world's creations. In the final phrase, he explains what will cause this new state of affairs to arise. There will be no violence or conflict because "דֵעָה אֶת-יְ-הֹוָה/the knowledge of the Lord" will permeate the creation. This does not simply mean that because all of the beings of the world will come to *believe* in God, therefore they will resolve to live in peace. Indeed, throughout history there have been many who have waged violent wars precisely because of their belief in God. The mere awareness of a Creator and a divine ruler of the world has certainly not precluded conflict until now. Why, then, would we assume that it would do so in the future?

As we have explained previously, the word "דַעַת/daas/knowledge" (appearing in this verse in an alternate form, "דֵעָה/deah") also means "fusion" or "intimacy," as in the verse "Adam *knew* Eve his wife."[240] What Isaiah is informing us, therefore, is that with the advent of the messianic age, God will be "known" throughout His creation not simply in the sense of an intellectual cognition. Rather, His unity will be revealed throughout the creation, as everything will perceive its inherent oneness with Him. In other words, all of the various creatures of the

---

[240] Genesis 3:1

world will recognize that they are simply varying manifestations of God-ly expression. We will see through the materiality that distinguishes and individualizes us, and we will therefore perceive the common Godliness that pervades and unites us. With such awareness, conflict will cease because there will no longer be any "other" with whom to battle or contest. Even the animals will possess this inner vision, and the erstwhile predator will coexist peacefully with its former prey.

Eyes To See

As we have discussed many times, the nature of this "olam/world" is "helam/concealment." This is a realm of darkness and obfuscation. We have little ability to perceive the truth, and in fact it is so dark that most of us are not even aware that it is dark.[241] We have become so accustomed to blindness that we don't even realize that we are blind. Yet the Torah is our torch, and it sheds light in the darkness. It enables us to see - at least with our mind's eye, even if not with our fleshy eyes. We are therefore able to be aware of the truth even if we cannot clearly perceive it. We have described this state of affairs in chapter four,[242] explaining that we may "modeh/acknowledge" and admit the ultimate reality, even though it is not yet "baruch/brought down" and revealed. Yet it is our goal to make it "baruch," to manifest the truth so clearly that it is not only an inner awareness, but an outward perception. This palpable vision will be available to all of us in the time to come.

In his final days on earth, at the end of the forty years throughout which he led the nation in the desert, Moses alludes to, and distinguishes between, the vision that we have had and the vision that we will eventually gain.

אַתֶּם רְאִיתֶם אֵת כָּל־אֲשֶׁר עָשָׂה יְ-הֹוָה לְעֵינֵיכֶם בְּאֶרֶץ מִצְרַיִם לְפַרְעֹה וּלְכָל־עֲבָדָיו וּלְכָל־אַרְצוֹ: הַמַּסֹּת הַגְּדֹלֹת

---

[241] As we described in chapter two, section "Double Darkness"

[242] Section "From Knowing to Showing"

אֲשֶׁר רָאוּ עֵינֶיךָ הָאֹתֹת וְהַמֹּפְתִים הַגְּדֹלִים הָהֵם: וְלֹא־נָתַן
יְ-הֹוָה לָכֶם לֵב לָדַעַת וְעֵינַיִם לִרְאוֹת וְאָזְנַיִם לִשְׁמֹעַ עַד הַיּוֹם
הַזֶּה:

Atem r'isem es kol asher asah A-donai l'eineichem b'eretz
Mitzrayim l'Pharaoh u'l'chol avadav u'l'chol artzo. Hamasos
ha'gedolos asher ra'u einecha ha'osos v'hamophsim
ha'gedolim ha'heim. V'lo nassan A-donai lachem leiv la'daas
v'einayim liros v'aznayim lishmoa ad Hayom hazeh.

You have seen all that the Lord did before your very
eyes in the land of Egypt, to Pharaoh, to all his servants,
and to all his land; the great trials which your very eyes
beheld and those great signs and wonders. Yet until this
day, the Lord has not given you a heart to know, eyes to
see and ears to hear.

Deuteronomy 28:1-3)

You have seen miracles and wonders, Moses tells the people, but
"until this very day" you have still not been given "a heart to know, eyes
to see and ears to hear." In other words, there are varying degrees of clarity and perception. The Exodus from Egypt was the first redemption
from exile, and thus the beginning of the process of illumination. Prior to
that great liberation, our vision and understanding of ourselves and our
world was so limited that we believed in our ability to be enslaved by
the forces of concealment and constraint. God took us out of there with
signs and wonders, granting us the capacity to see beyond the natural
world. Our eyes were opened as the sea split open and as the heavens
opened over Mount Sinai when the Torah was delivered. This granted us
far greater perception than we previously had, but even this vision was
not yet true and permanent. The heavens closed after the Sinai experience, and we were once again subject to the myopia of physical sight
within the world of darkness that was created specifically to conceal the
truth of God's oneness.

Even as miracles followed us throughout the forty year journey
in the desert - manna raining down daily from heaven, Miriam's well
following the nation to provide water, the clouds of glory providing shelter and protection from the elements - still we did not have "eyes to see"
the ultimate truth. This condition persists until today. Therefore, we
might have moments of clarity, but they are fleeting and unsustained.

They do not infuse our being permanently and completely, and we are thus able to "see" and embrace God at one moment, and then revert to our brute egocentrism the next moment. This, as we explained in the very first chapter, is not our fault, because the very existence of a finite creation depends on our inability to perceive God's infinity.

"You have seen all that the Lord did before your very eyes in the land of Egypt," Moses says. God had granted us this glimpse and glimmer of the truth. But He had still not given us the capacity to fully see. He provided us the Torah, which would enable us to train our eyes and hone our vision throughout millennia of additional exiles ahead. But true vision will come only with the final redemption. This is alluded to by the prophet Michah, who augurs the following in God's name in regards to the onset of the messianic era when this final exile will end:

כִּימֵי צֵאתְךָ מֵאֶרֶץ מִצְרָיִם אַרְאֶנּוּ נִפְלָאוֹת:

Kimei tzeischa me'eretz Mitzrayim, arenu niflaos.
Like the days of your going out of the land of Egypt, I
will show them wonders.
(Michah 7:15)

The sages debate the meaning of this verse. Does it indicate that the miracles that will be performed at the time of the final redemption will be similar to the miracles that were performed at the exodus from Egypt - "like the days of your going out of the land of Egypt"? Or does it mean that just as the miracles in Egypt were totally unprecedented and beyond all experience, so too the future miracles will be so wondrous that in comparison, those previous miracles from the Exodus will no longer seem wondrous at all? After all, if the future redemption is only comparable to the former redemption, then what is its advantage? And if there is no advantage, then what is the reason for all of the hardship and suffering that we have had to endure in the interim?

The Lubavitcher Rebbe[243] proposes that one of the keys to understanding this verse is the word "אַרְאֶנּוּ/arenu/I will show." The prophet does not say that God will "perform" wonders, as He did previously, but rather that He will "show" wonders this time. What is the difference between "performing" miracles and "showing" miracles? The

---

[243] In his discourse "Kimei Tzeischa MeiEretz Mitzrayim."

Rebbe explains that there are miracles that God has performed throughout history which we have not recognized as miraculous, because He has
garbed and hidden them in the framework of the natural world. These
hidden miracles, the Rebbe says, are even loftier than the obvious miracles that have abrogated the laws of nature. This is because they come
from such a high level of Godliness that they cannot be perceived within
the confines of the world. Therefore, they go unnoticed, seeming to be
merely natural, though they are in fact so subtle and ethereal that they
are completely imperceptible to our dull and insensitive physical senses.
Miracles like the splitting of the sea are beyond the nature of the world,
but they are able to come down into the world and interrupt its regular
functioning. Yet miracles like the conception of new life and the constant
creation of matter from nothingness are so profound and sublime that
they are not even recognized as miraculous. With the ultimate redemption at the end of this current and final exile, "arenu niflaos" - God will
show us the wonders. He will enable us to see Him in everything and to
understand that everything is miraculous. The ultimate reality to which
we had previously been "modeh" will finally become "baruch."

Eye To Eye

Based on the above, we can say that the sum of human history
has been an "eye-opening experience." We begin with severe visual challenges, and throughout our spiritual evolution, we become increasingly
percipient. As we have explained, the redemption from Egypt was the
beginning of the process of eye opening, and the redemption from this
final exile will complete the process and grant us perfect vision.

Just prior to the Exodus from Egypt, God promises Moses "now
you will see." Moses had approached God in confusion after their first
interaction at the burning bush. In that first meeting, God had instructed
Moses to go down to Egypt and to command Pharaoh to "let my people
go." Moses did so, but the immediate result was not liberation. On the
contrary, his demand was met with further oppression. Pharaoh responded that the people were not working hard enough if they had time
to daydream about going to serve their God. He would therefore make

their work more difficult so that they would have no time for these types of idle thoughts. He ordered his taskmasters to stop supplying the slaves with straw with which they made their bricks. The quota of bricks would not be reduced, but now the slaves would have to go find and gather the straw themselves. The people were obviously upset by this outcome, and they railed against Moses for making their situation worse. Moses subsequently returns to God and asks Him to explain Himself:

וַיָּשָׁב מֹשֶׁה אֶל־יְ-הֹוָה וַיֹּאמַר אֲ-דֹנָי לָמָה הֲרֵעֹתָה לָעָם הַזֶּה:
לָמָה זֶּה שְׁלַחְתָּנִי וּמֵאָז בָּאתִי אֶל־פַּרְעֹה לְדַבֵּר בִּשְׁמֶךָ הֵרַע
לָעָם הַזֶּה וְהַצֵּל לֹא־הִצַּלְתָּ אֶת־עַמֶּךָ:

Vayashav Moshe el A-donai vayomer A-donai lamah hareiosa la'am hazeh lamah zeh shelachtani. U'meaz basi el Pharaoh ledaber b'shimcha heira la'am hazeh v'hatzeil lo hitzalta es amecha.

Moses returned to the Lord and said, "O Lord! Why have You harmed this people? Why have You sent me? Since I have come to Pharaoh to speak in Your name, he has harmed this people, and You have not saved Your people."
(Exodus 5:22-23)

God responds:

עַתָּה תִרְאֶה אֲשֶׁר אֶעֱשֶׂה לְפַרְעֹה:
Atta tireh asher e'eseh l'Pharaoh.
Now you will see what I will do to Pharaoh.
(Exodus 6:1)

A new vision would be introduced to Moses and the people as a result of the Exodus. What was this vision? On the surface, it was "what I will do to Pharaoh." They saw the miracles and wonders of the ten plagues and then the splitting of the sea. But the greater vision came just afterwards at the time of the giving of the Torah on Mount Sinai. Then, God informed the people of who and what they truly are:

פָּנִים בְּפָנִים דִּבֶּר יְ-הֹוָה עִמָּכֶם בָּהָר:
Panim b'panim dibber A-donai imachem bahar.

> Face to face God spoke to you at the mountain.
> (Deuteronomy 5:4)

As we have discussed previously,[244] the significance of the phrase "panim b'panim" - literally "face IN face" - is that God made us aware of the fact that His face - the "Pnei Hashem" - is embedded in our "pnimyus/innermost core." This was true from the time of our initial creation, but this essential truth had been hidden from us until the Torah was given on Sinai. It was with the Torah that we were granted the ability to "see" the face of God within us, at least with the power of our mental eye. This is expressed further by the verse "Reeh Anochi nosein lifneichem hayom/see I place before you today."[245] As we discussed in chapter four,[246] the "sod/deeper understanding" of this verse is that "Anochi," the level of God that is so lofty that it is beyond all names, is "nosein lifneichem," placed into our "pnimyus." This new vision is alluded to by God's promise to Moses "now you will see."

Yet there is a level of vision that is even greater than this concept of "panim b'panim/face to face," and that is the level of "ayin b'ayin/eye to eye." While the vision of "panim b'panim/face to face" was granted at the time of the Exodus and the giving of the Torah, the vision of "ayin b'ayin/eye to eye" will be granted at the time of the ultimate redemption, as the prophet Isaiah declares:

כִּי **עַיִן בְּעַיִן** יִרְאוּ בְּשׁוּב יְ-הֹוָה צִיּוֹן:

*Ki **ayin b'ayin** yiru b'shuv A-donai Tzion.*
Eye to eye they shall see when the Lord returns to Zion.
(Isaiah 52:8)

Quoting this verse, the Alter Rebbe comments that the quality of vision in the messianic age will be:

בְּיֶתֶר שְׂאֵת וְיֶתֶר עֹז מִבְּמַתַּן תּוֹרָה, שֶׁלֹּא רָאוּ עַיִן בְּעַיִן כִּי

אִם שׁוֹמְעִים הַנִּרְאֶה.

*B'yeser s'es v'yeser oz mi'b'matan Torah, shelo ra'u ayin
b'ayin ki im shomim ha'nireh.*

To a greater extent and with greater strength than at the
giving of the Torah, for then they did not see eye to eye,
but rather they heard what was visible.

(Torah Or, Vaeira, Vayidaber)

The perception at the time of the giving of the Torah, the Alter
Rebbe informs us, was like hearing as opposed to seeing. Sound is a less
powerful, clear, and definitive form of perception than sight. It provides
us a sense and impression, but it is not certain and unmistakable. The
level of "panim b'panim" that we acquired at the giving of the Torah was
like this type of 'hearing' vision. As the Alter Rebbe states, we then
"heard what was visible." We became aware of the fact that the "Pnei
Hashem" is lodged in our "pnimyus." However, we could still not see
this reality clearly. With the coming redemption, we will see "ayin
b'ayin/eye to eye" - the existence of the "Pnei Hashem" within us and
within all things will not simply be conceptual, but it will be plain for all
to observe.

This is expressed in another prophesy of Isaiah, when he claims:

וְנִגְלָה כְּבוֹד יְ-הֹוָה וְרָאוּ כָל-בָּשָׂר יַחְדָּו כִּי פִּי יְ-הֹוָה דִּבֵּר:

*V'nigleh k'vod A-donai v'rau kol basar yachdav ki pi A-donai
dibber.*

And the glory of the Lord shall be revealed, and all
flesh together shall see that the mouth of the Lord
spoke.

(Isaiah 40:5)

On this verse, the Alter Rebbe[247] comments on the specificity of
the wording "all *flesh* shall see." Not only will there be a spiritual or intellectual knowledge of God in the time to come, but His omnipresence will
be perceptible to the flesh itself. Furthermore, not only will this vision be
applicable to our physical, fleshy eyes, but "*all* flesh shall see." In other
words, this perception will not be limited to optics, but we will be able to
"observe" the face of God with every one of our senses and every aspect

---

[247] In *Torah Or*, maamar Vayoshet Hamelech

of our being. We will feel, smell, taste, hear, and see God constantly. This is because it will be revealed to us, finally, that there is nothing other than God, and therefore everything we experience with any and all of our senses, is simply and exclusively divine.

◄────►

Seers

While the vast majority of humanity is yet unable to see the "Pnei Hashem" "ayin b'ayin / eye to eye," there are those in every generation who already possess this capacity. The great Torah scholars in general are referred to as "עֵינֵי הָעֵדָה / einei ha'eida / the **eyes** of the congregation."[248] But the greatest visionaries, those who have immersed themselves in the Torah's deepest secrets, have been granted by God the perception that the rest of us will acquire only in the messianic age.

In this light, there is a story recorded in "Toras Shalom" about the Rebbe Rashab.[249] Once at a chassidic gathering, the Rebbe Rashab was explaining to his disciples the existence of God in everything. He said, "bring me a plate and I will show you the power of God within it." The precise phrase he used was "hislabshus koach hapoel b'nifal / the clothing of the power of the Creator within the creation." His followers eagerly brought him a plate, anxious to witness the promised wonder. But at the last minute, the Rebbe changed his mind. He explained that he was worried that if he revealed the Godliness within the plate, then the observers would begin to worship the plate. They would be so overwhelmed by the Godliness in the plate that they would forget that it is Godliness and think that it is the power of the plate itself. Such is the nature of the concealment of this world - even if we were to be shown the vitality that animates the material garments, we would attribute the power to the garments themselves and forget that they are merely the outer trappings of a more essential and underlying reality. It is therefore not only sight that we are lacking, but also the capacity to properly trans-

---

[248] A phrase borrowed from Numbers 15:24.

[249] Rabbi Shalom Dovber Schneersohn, fifth rebbe of the Lubavitch Chassidic dynasty. 1860-1920

late and integrate the wisdom that clear vision imparts. Through their tremendous devotion to plumbing the depths of the Torah's secrets, the great mystics and tzadikkim have acquired both sight and vision.

Another story is recorded about two of the Rebbe Rashab's predecessors, the Alter Rebbe and the Mitteler Rebbe.[250] One Rosh Hashana, after the morning prayers, the Alter Rebbe approached his son Dov Ber (who would later succeed his father and become the Mitteler Rebbe, the second Rebbe of the Lubavitch dynasty) and asked him "with what did you daven/pray today." His question, in other words, was what was his son's "kavana/concentration" focused on throughout the holiday prayers. The Mitteler Rebbe responded with a very deep and esoteric kabbalistic idea about the souls standing before their Creator. He then asked his father the same question - with what did you "daven/pray" today? The Alter Rebbe responded "I davened/prayed with the shtender." A "shtender" is the wooden lectern or stand that many are accustomed to rest their prayerbook on as they pray. Throughout his prayer, the Alter concentrated deeply on the idea that the wooden "shtender" that held his prayerbook was constantly being recreated by the word of God that comprises and vitalizes all matter. What everyone else saw merely as a structure of lifeless wood, the Alter Rebbe was able to perceive as a form of condensed divine energy. What he expressed to his son and future successor here is that Godliness is not to be found only in abstruse and esoteric dimensions, but it is here, in this lowest world, in even the most seemingly base and lifeless creations.

It is related that just before his death, as the Alter Rebbe lay on his deathbed, he stared up at the wooden ceiling and said that he no longer sees the wooden beams, but only the holy letters. As we mentioned previously in chapter ten[251] it is taught in Kabbala that all physical matter is ultimately composed of Hebrew letters which were spoken by God in order to effect the creation, as it says in Genesis "And God *said*, let there be...." In the final moments of his time on this earthly plane, the Alter Rebbe was not only able to see the Godliness that exists within all matter, but he was no longer able to see the matter at all. So refined and

---

[250] Rabbi Dovber Schneuri, second rebbe of the Lubavitch Chassidic dynasty. 1773-1827

[251] Section "Flow"

elevated was his vision at that point that he could detect only the "Pnei Hashem," and not the veils that concealed it.

It is true that few of us are on the level of such mystics, but we all have the potential deep within us to see what they have seen. It is therefore incumbent upon each of us to train ourselves, to the extent of our ability, to perceive the Godliness that underlies everything. But we need not travel this journey alone. There are guides who have been blazing trails through the darkness for generations. They may not transport us directly to our destination, for each of us must conduct her/his own search and must carry her/his own weight. But as we make our way and hone our vision, it behooves us to attach ourselves to those who can already see.

Helping Others See Themselves

In addition to seeking out and learning from those whose vision is sharper than our own, there is another way that we can precipitate the promised time of vision, peace and unity. And that is by helping those whose vision is duller than our own. Each of us is a guide, and each of us holds a torch. Wherever we may be along the journey through the darkness, it is certain that there are others who are behind us, or who haven't yet begun. Hopefully, through this book, we have now at least identified the fundamental human task and have taken, at least, the first few steps along the path. We understand that we are here to "lech lecha/go to yourself" and to "bara Elokim es hashamayim v'es haaretz/reveal God within the heavens and the earth." We know where the "lecha," our true self, is hidden - deep within our "pnimyus/core." We are aware that when we arrive there and find it, we will also find the "Pnei Hashem/the face of God," which is the innermost foundation of us and of everything else that exists. Unlike so many who are searching for meaning and fulfillment in external physical possessions or far-flung destinations, we are therefore aware that the direction we must travel is within. We can point to the scriptural sources that clearly lay out these ancient and eternal truths. We may feel like we have just begun the journey ourself, but equipped with all this, we are ready to share our light and help others delve inward through the darkness. This is why we are here, and this is the gift that we have been given in order to give it others.

What each of us must know is that everyone, no matter who they are or where they're from, wants nothing more than to see and reveal the "Pnei Hashem" within them. This desire itself may be hidden from them, but were they aware of the infinite goodness that is embedded in their core, they would stop at nothing to access and manifest it. Often, it is easier for others to recognize our inherent goodness than for us to identify it ourselves. This is especially the case with those of us who have stumbled in the past and have become convinced of our depravity or worthlessness. Our essence is so encrusted that we have come to identify ourselves with the crust rather than that which it conceals. Yet those who love us unconditionally can see through our veneer.

We find this in Torah with Abraham, whose first son, Ishmael, had become corrupted and began, at the age of fifteen, to worship idols like the Canaanites around him.[252] When his brother Isaac was born, Ishmael would shoot arrows at him, pretending to play, but putting the boy's life at grave risk. Sarah, Isaac's mother and Ishmael's step-mother, informed Abraham of Ishmael's degenerate behavior and urged her husband to send Ishmael away. "But the matter greatly displeased Abraham, concerning his son."[253] He was aware of his son's shortcomings, and he knew that Sarah was right that Ishmael would need to be sent away for the sake of Isaac's safety. Still he was pained, not only because he loved his son in spite of his shortcomings, but because he believed in Ishmael's potential to do and be better. Years earlier, when he had been informed that Sarah would give birth to Isaac, and that Isaac would be his spiritual heir, Abraham immediately prayed to God on his first son's behalf:

לוּ יִשְׁמָעֵאל יִחְיֶה לְפָנֶיךָ:
Lu Yishmael yichyeh lifanecha.
Would that Ishmael will live before you.
(Genesis 17:18)

---

252 Shemos Rabbah 1:1

253 Genesis 21:11

426

Why is it that upon hearing the news of Isaac's forthcoming birth, Abraham prays that Ishmael will live? Is there some reason to believe that Isaac's birth might be related to Ishmael's death? If we examine Abraham's request carefully, we see that it is not merely Ishmael's survival that Abraham is concerned with, but something deeper. He does not simply pray "Lu Yishmael yichyeh/would that Ishmael will live," but he adds the word "*lifanecha*." As we have seen repeatedly already, this term is plainly translated as "before you," but it literally means "in your face." As such, what Abraham prays for at this moment is that Ishmael should live at the level of God's face, the "Pnei Hashem" that dwells deep within him. He realizes that it will be his son Isaac who will carry his inheritance as the patriarch of the Hebrew nation, and he recognizes the failings of his son Ishmael that render him unfit for this responsibility. Yet he beseeches God to assist his first son in accessing the divine light that is hidden in his "pnimyus." Though Ishmael is unconscious of that light himself, his father perceives it clearly and wants nothing more for his child than that he should find it and reveal it from within him. Indeed, the sages teach that though he struggled with his corrupt tendencies throughout his life, "Ishmael did teshuvah in Abraham's lifetime."[254] His father's recognition of his essential goodness certainly aided him to manifest it.

Jacob And Esau

Similar to his father Abraham, we find that Isaac also had two sons with vastly divergent natures. While his son Jacob was an "אִישׁ תָּם יֹשֵׁב אֹהָלִים/ish tam yoshev ohalim/an innocent man dwelling in the tents" of Torah learning, his son Esau was "אִישׁ יֹדֵעַ צַיִד אִישׁ שָׂדֶה/ish yodea tzayid ish sadeh/a man of the field who knew how to hunt."[255] Rashi comments on this verse that "as soon as they became thirteen years old, this one (Jacob) parted to the houses of study, and that one (Esau) parted to idol worship." As he grew older, the sages teach, Esau indulged in

---

254 Bava Basra 16b

255 Genesis 25:27

every type of transgression, from murder to theft and adultery. Yet when Isaac neared his death and it came time for him to pass on the birthright that he had received from his father to one of his own sons, he chose Esau instead of Jacob. His wife Rebecca knew that it was Jacob who deserved the blessing - like her forebear Sarah, it is once again the mother who has clarity on such things - and she devised a plan whereby Jacob would dress in Esau's clothes and "trick" Isaac into blessing him. Yet the question remains, how is it possible that the wise and holy Isaac could make such an error?

The mystics teach that Isaac was able to perceive the root of Esau's soul, which derived from a heavenly realm so lofty that it was beyond this lowly "olam/world" of "helam/concealment" and limitation. He believed that if Esau were granted the additional power of the birthright "bracha/blessing," he would be able to harness his otherworldly potential and channel it into the world. After all, "bracha/blessing," as we have discussed in chapter four,[256] means to "bring down," and therefore Isaac believed that his "bracha" would enable Esau to bring his lofty essence down into manifestation. Rebecca also recognized her son Esau's hidden power, but she knew that some energies are too lofty for certain souls to bring down on their own. She understood that it would require a "partnership" of sorts between her two sons in order for this intense holiness to be accessed. She therefore instructed Jacob to dress himself in Esau's clothing. On the surface, the reason for this masquerade was so that Jacob could deceive his father Isaac, who was blind, and convince him that he was in fact blessing Esau as he originally intended. But the chassidic masters explain that when Jacob dressed in Esau's garments, it was as if the two brothers' energies were combined.

The Hebrew name for Jacob is "יעקב/Yaakov," the root of which is "עקב," which means "heel." According to the "pshat/simple understanding," Jacob was given this name because when he and his twin brother Esau were born, Esau emerged first, and Jacob came out second, clutching his brother's heel. But on a deeper level, the name "יעקב" is a combination of the letter "י/yud" and the word "עקב/heel." The letter "yud," as we have seen earlier,[257] is the first letter of God's name "י-ה-ו-ה"

---

[256] Section "Blessed Are You"

[257] Chapter six, section "Yudecha"

and represents "chochma," or the highest levels of wisdom. Jacob was named "יעקב" because he was able to transport the very highest levels, represented by the letter "י/yud," down to the very lowest levels, represented by the "עקב/heel." Esau's power was far beyond the world, and Rebecca knew that he required Jacob's power of combining the highest and lowest levels in order to channel it earthward.

What was the incredibly lofty Godly source of Esau which his parents and his brother were trying to access and manifest? It was, as the text explicitly records, the "Pnei Hashem":

הָבִיאָה לִּי צַיִד וַעֲשֵׂה־לִי מַטְעַמִּים וְאֹכֵלָה וַאֲבָרֶכְכָה לִפְנֵי
יְ-הֹוָה לִפְנֵי מוֹתִי:

Haviah li tzayid v'asei li mat'amim v'ocheila v'avarechecha
lifnei A-donai *lifnei mosi.*
Bring me game and make me tasty foods, and I will eat,
and I will bless you **before the Lord** before my death.
(Genesis 27:7)

The Alter Rebbe[258] addresses the significance of the words "לִפְנֵי יְ-הֹוָה/lifnei A-donai/before the Lord" in this verse. Could it not have said simply 'I will bless you before my death,' without adding the phrase "before the Lord"? The Alter Rebbe explains that the blessing needed to come from a level "lifnei/before,' or higher than, the name "יְ-הֹוָה/A-donai." This name of God represents the realm of worlds, and Esau's soul root was higher than all of the worlds. In order to reach it and bring it downward, Isaac would have to go "lifnei A-donai," beyond the worldly plane. And as we have explained multiple times already, in addition to "before" or beyond, "lifnei" literally means "to the face." Isaac could see the "Pnei A-donai/face of God" in his son Esau, though Esau could not see it himself. He wished to bless Esau "lifnei A-donai" - that he should be able to access this lofty level within himself. As his own father before him who prayed that Ishmael should be able to see God's face within him - "Lu Yishmael yichyeh *lifanecha*" - Isaac wished nothing more for his son Esau than that he could also find and reveal the "Pnei Hashem" at his core.

---

258 *Torah Or*, maamar Reeh Reiach Bni

Unfortunately, in spite of his father's efforts, Esau would be unable to do so. Unlike his uncle Ishmael, Esau did not return to the path of righteousness and "teshuvah." Nevertheless, though he was unable to allow his essence to fully manifest through the thick veils of his base animalistic nature, there were instances throughout Esau's life when his ultimate Godliness momentarily broke through. One of these moments occurred in the immediate aftermath of Isaac's bestowal of the blessing on Jacob. Unaware that Jacob had already secured the blessing by dressing in his clothing, Esau enters his father's tent and asks Isaac to bless him. At this moment, Isaac suddenly realizes that he has been deceived. Though Isaac quickly understands that Jacob did indeed deserve the blessing - for Esau admits that he had sold the birthright to Jacob previously - Esau is devastated with the recognition of what he has surrendered. Bless me too, he begs his father. But Isaac informs him that he has already given Jacob everything. Esau begins to weep, and in one of the most moving and heartrending episodes in all of Torah, he cries:

הַבְרָכָה אַחַת הִוא־לְךָ אָבִי בָּרֲכֵנִי גַם־אָנִי אָבִי:

Ha'bracha achas hi lecha avi, baracheini gam ani avi.
Have you [but] **one blessing**, my father? Bless me too, my father!

(Genesis 27:38)

The words "bracha achas" are simply translated as "one blessing," but they can also mean "the blessing of oneness." You have the blessing of oneness, Esau says to his father, cognizant in this moment of brokenhearted clarity that it is the recognition of God's absolute unity that has distinguished his grandfather Abraham and his family from all of the other people on earth. I, too, want this blessing, he admits as the tears begin to flow. He truly desired to experience the oneness that he sensed in his essence even if it seemed very far from him. Even the most egregious "sinner" has moments of clarity in which s/he glimpses her/his inner Godliness, though they may be infrequent and short-lived. We can - and must - feel for Esau here, like an addict who sobers up for a moment and perceives a glimmer of what his life could be if he were not controlled by his addiction. We can see his struggle and weep with him for his inability to be who he has the potential to become. All of us have these flashes of what we truly are and of how beautiful life could be if we

430

could simply reveal the truth that is within us. Like all of us who are imperfect, Esau had to deal with the painful tension of his fiercely competing internal drives. In a moment of complete honesty, he begged his father for the blessing of oneness. I want to be one, but it is so hard for me to control myself. Please help me!

Sadly, this introspection would not last long for Esau. As soon as he left his father's tent, a murderous rage burned within him. Rather than taking responsibility for losing the birthright through his own wanton actions, he blamed his brother Jacob and plotted his death. Jacob fled to the land of Charan where he lived for the next two decades in the home of his wicked uncle. There, he built a family, and allowed for time to pass in hopes that his brother's hatred would abate. On his return, the brothers meet again, and here we find another instance when Esau's essence momentarily transforms him.

Approaching his home after decades abroad, Jacob sent messengers ahead of him to inform his brother that he was coming and that he hoped that they could put their past conflicts behind them. The messengers carried lavish gifts to appease Esau in the event that any feelings of malice still remained. The night before their meeting, Jacob wrestled with Esau's guardian angel and was victorious. It was for this that his name was changed to "Yisrael/Israel," which indicates that "you have battled with God and won."[259] The following morning, Jacob's messengers returned to him and informed him that Esau was approaching with 400 men, clearly intent on doing battle. Yet when the two brothers finally come face to face, rather than attacking Jacob, Esau embraces him in reconciliation. What has happened to suddenly transform Esau from an angry man of war to a loving and forgiving brother? A careful reading of the text provides us a profound answer.

The word "panim/face," or some form of it, appears over a dozen times throughout the forty-five verses that tell the story of this interaction. The episode begins with the verse:

וַיִּשְׁלַח יַעֲקֹב מַלְאָכִים **לְפָנָיו** אֶל־עֵשָׂו אָחִיו:

*Vayishalach Yaacov malachim **lefanav** el Esav achiv.*
Jacob sent angels **ahead of him** to his brother Esau.
(Genesis 32:4)

---

[259] Genesis 32:29

Plainly rendered, this means that Jacob sent messengers before him to Esau. But on the deeper level of "לְפָנָיו/lefanav," we see that Jacob sent messengers to Esau's "panim/face." In order to make peace with his brother, he knew that he would have to reach beyond his exterior to access his innermost dimension. Jacob instructed the messengers to say to Esau:

אֲכַפְּרָה **פָנָיו** בַּמִּנְחָה הַהֹלֶכֶת **לְפָנָי** וְאַחֲרֵי־כֵן אֶרְאֶה **פָנָיו**
אוּלַי יִשָּׂא **פָנָי**:

*Achapra **panav** bamincha haholeches **lefanai** v'acharei kein ereh **panav** ulai yisa **panai**.*

I will appease his anger with the gift that is going before me, and afterwards I will see his face, perhaps he will favor me.

(Genesis 32:21)

The word face appears four times in this one verse. Twice it refers to "panav/his face" and twice to "panai/my face." The gift that Jacob sends to Esau's "face" is his own "face." In other words, Jacob wants to relate to his brother from one "pnimyus" to another. He is hoping that they will be able to communicate from the level at which they are both perfectly pure, completely Godly, and ultimately one. To that end, the night before their encounter, he stays alone in the wilderness and delves deep within himself to access his own essence. It is then that he encounters the angel, and in the morning, before setting out to meet his brother, he names the place to commemorate the deep mystical experience that occurred there:

וַיִּקְרָא יַעֲקֹב שֵׁם הַמָּקוֹם **פְּנִיאֵל** כִּי־רָאִיתִי אֱ-לֹהִים **פָּנִים**
אֶל־**פָּנִים** וַתִּנָּצֵל נַפְשִׁי:

*Vayikra Yaacov shem hamakom **Peniel** ki raisi E-lohim **panim** el **panim** v'tinatzel nafshi.*

And Jacob named the place **Peniel**, for [he said,] "I saw an angel **face** to **face**, and my soul was saved."

(Genesis 32:31)

The name he chose for that location was "Peniel," which means "The face of God." He chose this name because there he experienced God "panim el panim/face to face." Having reached this level of the "Pnei Hashem" deep within his own "pnimyus," he set out to encounter his brother. When they meet, he finds that his efforts have paid off. By accessing his own essence, he has likewise activated the essence of his twin brother. On meeting, he says to him:

רָאִיתִי פָנֶיךָ כִּרְאֹת פְּנֵי אֱ-לֹהִים וַתִּרְצֵנִי:

*Raisi **panecha** kiros **pnei** E-lohim vatirtzeini.*
I have seen your **face**, which is like seeing the **face of God**, and you have accepted me.
(Genesis 33:10)

In Esau's face, Jacob sees the face of God. This has enabled Esau, at least momentarily, to see the "Pnei Hashem" within himself as well. The conflict between them evaporates because they realize that they are one. They embrace one another and weep in this moment of true reunion. Jacob knows that it won't last long, and therefore though Esau invites him to come live with him, Jacob respectfully declines. They part ways in peace, and they will not meet again until their father Isaac's funeral at the cave of Machpelah in Hebron twenty-three years later.

It is at this same location, some three decades after Isaac's funeral, that Jacob and Esau will "meet" for the final time, and Esau's tremendous holiness and potential are finally revealed. The Midrash relates that on Jacob's death, his sons carried his body to Hebron to bury it in the cave where his grandparents, Abraham and Sarah, his parents, Isaac and Rebecca, and his wife Leah had been buried before him. But when they arrived, Esau and his soldiers blocked their entry. The final burial plot in the cave belonged to him, Esau claimed, denying the truth that he had sold his share to his brother decades earlier. Jacob's grandson Chushim drew his sword and decapitated Esau, whose head then rolled into the cave. Twins, Jacob and Esau were thus born on the same day and died on the same day. The Midrash relates that when Esau's head rolled into the cave, it landed in his father Isaac's resting place, as Targum Yonasan states: "Esau's head lies in the bosom of Isaac."[260]

---

[260] Targum Yonatan, Genesis 50:13

The chassidic masters teach that there is profound significance to the burial of Esau's head, and head only, in the cave of Machpelah with the three holy patriarchs and matriarchs. The head represents our highest root and potential. As mentioned above, Esau's soul-root was extremely lofty - even higher than the root of Jacob, which is why Isaac desired to give Esau the birthright blessing. But whereas Jacob was capable of bringing the highest levels down into the "עקב/heel," there was too great a gulf between Esau's head and his body. Throughout his life, therefore, the two aspects of his being - his Godly soul and his animal soul - battled incessantly. It was only at his death that his highest nature was freed from the anchor of his body. His head rolled into the cave and rested with his father who had always recognized his immense Godly potential and tried to bring it down to express itself in this world.

Like Abraham, Isaac, and Jacob, our job is to expose the face of God wherever it is hidden. All of those who act "ungodly" in this world are simply unable to access their Godly essence and potential. It is the lack of belief in, or awareness of, the "Pnei Hashem" within them that makes them act in ways that are contrary to their true and highest nature. To transform the world, and to hasten the arrival of the time of peace and perfect vision, we must work tirelessly to help those who are lost to find and reveal the Godliness within them.

As Water Mirrors The Face

What is the best and easiest way to help others to see the "Pnei Hashem" within them? It is to show them the "Pnei Hashem" that is within you. This will be effective for a number of reasons. First, it will provide an image of something beautiful and admirable that one will aspire to her/himself. The peace and presence that are exuded by one who has discovered her/his inherent Godliness is rare and alluring. It manifests in a confidence and a composure which suggest some understanding of life's mysteries and a mastery of one's faculties. We all desire to be more balanced and content. Encountering others who display this type of serenity motivates us to seek what s/he has found and to see if we too can learn to live this way.

On a somewhat deeper level, when we witness others acting in kind and altruistic ways, it inspires us to call forth the "better angels" of our own nature. Seeing someone acting contrary to her/his own self-interest complicates the notion, which is so prevalent in the modern conception of human nature, that we are merely animals evolved. As we have discussed earlier,[261] the Darwinian model of evolution allows us to rationalize and normalize our egoistic and animalistic impulses. This further shrouds our Godly nature. But on those wonderful occasions when someone transcends our expectations and provides evidence of something more generous and noble than what we would expect of an evolved ape, then our self-concept is freed from the restraints of our biology. We begin to believe, even if only for a moment, that we can be far more than we have been until now.

On a more subtle level still, because we all contain the face of God deep within us, when we see it revealed elsewhere, it reminds of us of something we have always known vaguely and indistinctly. It is like a memory that is deep and distant, but so potent that though it is just beyond our grasp, it is on the tip of our consciousness. It evokes more of a feeling than a clear remembrance - a sense of something so familiar, but so elusive. It is like recognizing someone you have never met, and knowing that you are related. You are relatives because you come from the same place, you are made of the same stuff, you are the same energy expressed through different packaging. Eventually, we recognize that there are no strangers, only new wrappers that we have not yet opened. As soon as we open them, and as soon as we open ourselves, we see that the contents are the same.

In this sense, we can understand the following verse from Proverbs:

כַּמַּיִם הַפָּנִים לַפָּנִים כֵּן לֵב־הָאָדָם לָאָדָם:

Kamayim hapanim l'panim kein leiv haadam l'adam.
As water mirrors a face to a face, so is the heart of man to man.

(Proverbs 27:19)

---

[261] Chapter three, section "In Me?"

On the simple level, what this proverb informs us is that just as the surface of water acts as a mirror, reflecting one's face back at her/him, so too does our heart mimic and match the emotions and energies that it perceives and receives. Our reactions are typically commensurate with the actions that come our way, and similarly, our words, deeds, and emotions will tend to elicit a reciprocal response from those with whom we interact. In other words, when one treats another with kindness, then that person is inclined to respond with positivity. And conversely, if one is rude, mean, or aggressive, then s/he is most likely going to receive negativity in kind. We experience this frequently in life in simple ways. Smiles and laughter are contagious, and likewise others' tears often make our own eyes well. Though we tend to downplay it in our modern and rational world, energy is infectious. We are influenced, either positively or negatively, by those around us. When we surround ourselves with cheerful and peaceful people, we experience greater joy and contentment. And when we mingle with those who are bitter and hostile, we take on their stress and agitation.

This truth is recognized in both neurological science and social science. Neuroscientists have identified "mirror neurons" in the brain which render a person likely to respond sympathetically to the stimuli that s/he encounters. This accounts for our capacity for compassion and empathy. It also explains why yawning is contagious. Social scientists have identified a similar dynamic which they refer to as emotional reciprocity. This is the unspoken social contract which generally assures us that people will treat us with respect and integrity if we grant them the same courtesy. Cultural anthropologists have suggested that this social-emotional reciprocity is one of the uniquely human traits which enabled humans to survive and thrive. While other species do not have the nature or tendency to repay kindness with kindness, this uniquely human trait enabled humankind to create groups of allies that worked together to protect one another and promote mutual success.

Yet with their proverb "as water mirrors a **face** to a **face**, so is the heart of man to man," the sages are teaching us something even more subtle and insightful here than what scientists have attributed to neurological processes and anthropological developments. Just as water mirrors a face, and just as one heart responds reciprocally to what it experiences from another, so too does one's innermost face, her/his hidden "pnimyus," respond to the "pnimyus" of another. In other words, when we experience the "Pnei Hashem" radiating from another, the "Pnei Hashem" within us will be activated. And when we allow the face of God to shine from within us, it will reciprocally elicit the face of God from within those around us.

We witnessed this in the story of Jacob returning to encounter his brother Esau. He knew that in order to reach and activate Esau's Godly core, he would have to access his own "pnimyus" and let it be manifest. The reason this was effective is because at that fundamental level, there is no difference or distance between one and another. When the infinite radiates, the finite can no longer interpose or exist. When Jacob allowed his core to shine outward, Esau's core responded, and the physical Esau that usually suppressed his essential being no longer had the power to keep it hidden. This being the case, imagine the radical change our world will experience as each of us allows our Godly essence to be manifest. As increasing numbers of people become aware of the Godliness within them, there are ever more mirrors for those who have not yet peered inward and seen their inner truth.

It is told that the Baal Shem Tov, the founder of the chassidic movement, once elevated his soul to the heavens and spoke to the soul of the Messiah. When will you come, the Baal Shem Tov asked, to which the Messiah responded "when your wellsprings are spread outward." It is the Baal Shem Tov's teachings, the wellsprings of Chassidus, that publicized to the masses the Torah's deepest secret: that the spark of God is embedded in each of us, and that we are ultimately nothing but Godliness hidden within physicality; furthermore, this concealing physicality is only Godliness that pretends it is something other than Godliness. It is not surprising that the soul of the Messiah referred to the Baal Shem Tov's teachings as "wellsprings." They are equated with water because "water mirrors a face to a face." The teachings of Chassidus reveal the "panim/face" within each of us. When these waters will be spread throughout the world, then "the earth will be filled with the knowledge of God like the oceans fill the sea-bed."[262] Peering into the waters, we will all recognize what we essentially are, and then the time of perfect vision and peace will arrive.

---

[262] Habbakuk 2:14

א-Ray Vision

Of course, in order to reveal our "Pnei Hashem" to others in order that they should use it as a mirror to see the "Pnei Hashem" within themselves, we must remain conscious of our own "pnimyus." This requires us to see what is hidden, which is no easy task. As we have discussed at length throughout this book, the "olam/world" is designed for "helam/concealment," and therefore our vision is weak and faulty. Though we will eventually be able to see clearly and perfectly (as we described in the previous sections of this chapter), this is not yet our reality. But we have now been granted a glimpse of the light, and though we cannot be expected to see lucidly, we cannot pretend that we are blind. Torah has provided us a map to our inner core, and Chassidus has provided a cipher to interpret and follow the map more clearly. Yet in order to maintain the proper path through the darkness, we must train our vision and hone our ability to see Godliness in everything.

How do we do so?

In chapters eight, nine, and ten, we detailed the intricate regimen that Torah provides us to help us liberate ourselves from the veils that shroud our Godly core. As we discussed, the daily engagement in prayer, Torah study, and mitzvah performance; the weekly observance of the sabbath along with the monthly and annual observance of the holy days; and the lifelong performance of the lifecycle rituals; all of these are facets of an integrated practice through which we train ourselves to penetrate the darkness. The detailed and disciplined answer then to the question of how we can habituate ourselves to seeing the Godliness that is hidden within everything is to take advantage of the tactics and exercises that Torah offers us.

Yet there is a shorter answer, which does not in any way contradict the previous answer, but which provides us something more elementary and immediate. And that is, that in order to train our eyes to detect the ubiquity of Godliness beneath the veneer of everything we encounter, we must actively and earnestly look for it. This may sound overly simplistic, but the plain truth is that if we are not seeking Godliness, then it will certainly be more difficult to find it. If we don't believe that it is there to be found, then we will have little impetus to look, and little ability to perceive it when it makes itself evident. It is true that there are those who stumble upon God's face even if they are not seeking Him. And it is true that God will often appear in people's field of vision precisely when they have concluded that He does not exist. Yet it is also the case that He provides everyone occasional opportunities to see Him that are frequently ignored because we are not interested in changing our life, even if that life that we are reluctant to change is not particularly pleasant or fulfilling.

As we quoted at the beginning of our search,[263] and as we recite in the opening verses of our prayers every morning, "Yismach leiv m'-vakshei Hashem/Happy of heart is the one who seeks God."[264] We questioned why one would be happy if s/he is seeking something, as the act of seeking necessarily means that the object of the search has not yet been found. The answer is that the one who is seeking believes that s/he can, and eventually will, find what s/he is after. This hope and joy will bring success. Without it, life is dark and cold. Even when light presents itself, it is not perceived because the person's eyes are closed.

The essential thing, then, is to open the eyes and to gaze constantly into the darkness. We must be alert, and patient, and sensitive to even the smallest sparkle or the faintest glow. We must be conscious with everything we see that this, too, is Godliness, even if we cannot yet see beyond its concealing outer layers. Our task is to develop x-ray vision, to see through all surfaces and penetrate to the core where the Godly spark resides. When we can do so, we will already be living in the messianic future, even as we simultaneously find ourselves in the exiled present. The Lubavitcher Rebbe points this out by comparing the words "גולה/golah/exile" and "גאולה/geulah/redemption." The Hebrew terms are nearly identical, except for the presence of the letter "א/aleph" in the word "גאולה/geulah/redemption." "א/aleph" is the first letter of the Hebrew alphabet, thus corresponding numerologically to the number one. What this informs us is that the only thing that distinguishes "גולה/exile" from "גאולה/redemption" is oneness. When we can see the "aleph" within the exile - when we recognize that all is one even as it seems to be separate and many - we are already experiencing the time of ultimate peace

---

263 Chapter two, section "The Joy of the Search"

264 Psalms 105:3

and joy because we have transformed the "גולה/exile" to "גאולה/redemption." This is not just x-ray vision, it is "א-ray (aleph-ray) vision," the ability to see the "*alupho* shel olam/master of the world"[265] within every aspect of His creation.

It is important to note that this penetrative vision does not preclude us from seeing the surface as well. Perceiving the underlying Godliness in creation does not mean that we are to abandon all of our worldly pursuits - our social, familial, and community engagements - and to focus exclusively on spiritual rituals. It means, rather, that within our daily lives - our jobs and our interpersonal interactions - everything is undertaken with the consciousness of our infinite potential and our divine purpose. It is not a retreat from the world, but an engagement with the world in which we are constantly seeking and revealing its covert and inherent unity. "א-ray vision" does not merely take us to the innermost depths of life, but it reveals to us that the surface is no less Godly than that which is beneath it. Unlike other spiritual systems which relegate "holiness" to specific places, times, or behaviors, Torah reveals the "Pnei Hashem" in everyone and everything at every moment. There is only "א/aleph/one," and, therefore, there is nothing other.

Facefulness

What we are proposing with this idea of "א-ray (aleph-ray) vision" is a certain type of focus or mindfulness. Mindfulness is a term that has become popular in a modern and mechanized world that is increasingly mindless and soulless. Mindfulness can be defined as intentional consciousness, as opposed to being merely conscious, or sentient but unaware of one's true circumstances and condition. When we are not mindful, we go about our lives under the thrall of our routine. We sleepwalk, existing without questioning or examining our existence. We are under the spell of those who profit on our passivity and exploit the ease with which we are manipulated, indoctrinated, and compelled. We play the

---

265 "Alupho" means both "master" and "oneness," from the letter aleph.

game and keep its rules without knowing why we play or how to win. We live without knowing and celebrating what it means to be alive.

Mindfulness sweeps away the haze that leaves us numb and reflexive. It pulls us from our predictable and mechanical lethargy. It is the awakening and the search for some more essential truth and reality. It forces us to see ourself and our context and to try to make some sense of all this. Why do I do the things I do? Why am I here? Where is here, and what is my place or function in this strange and uncertain existence. Who has been pulling my strings until now?

Mindfulness is an important start, but what Torah affords, and what we have described throughout this book, is a consciousness that is beyond mindfulness which we can refer to as "facefulness." "Facefulness" is the cognizance of our "pnimyus/innermost core" and the "Pnei Hashem/face of God" that is found there. It is the awareness of what we truly are, and the rejection of the illusion that we are small and temporal and individual. It is recognition of our inherent Godliness and our unity with everything.

In some systems, mindfulness will lead to the confession and acceptance of one's insignificance. Because being mindful opens us to the consciousness of everything around us and not just our parochial and particular concerns, we therefore begin to see the much larger scope in which we exist. In the vast scheme of the universe, we are liable to conclude that we are minuscule, and that in the endless expanse of time, we are merely an inconsequential blip. There is wisdom and value in this type of humility and relinquishment of egocentricity. It is certainly true that we have inflicted significant damage on our world, our fellows, and ourselves because we deem ourselves overly important or focal. Yet it is precisely "facefulness," the consciousness of the "Pnei Hashem" in our "pnimyus," that will rescue us from our self-consumed and self-destructive culture. We are egotistical and confrontational because we feel small and empty inside. We assert ourselves aggressively because we secretly suspect that we are nothing, and therefore we must prove otherwise. When we are aware of our divinity, we will not need to justify our worth or power. We will choose to behave with dignity and love. We will act Godly because we are Godly - not because of ego, or guilt, or desire for reward or fear of punishment, but simply because it is what and who we truly are.

The goal of this book, then, has been to enable us to recognize our ultimate divinity. There is an obvious risk involved in such an awareness - that we will misinterpret this as a justification for self-assertion and self-aggrandizement as opposed to self-transcendence and translucence. While it is true that our inherent Godliness renders each of us incredibly holy and significant, we must express our greatness not by self-promotion, but by removing our outer trappings, releasing our ego, and expressing our Godly essence.

"Facefulness," or recognizing the "Pnei Hashem" within us, does not make us God, but rather it makes us nothing but God. There is a subtle but tremendous difference between the assertion "I am God" and "I am nothing but God." In the former case, I deify myself and therefore value and impose *my* will. In the latter case, I identify completely with the One and Only God, and I strive solely to channel His will through the vessel that He has created me to be. The sages discuss this subtlety in regards to a renowned mishnah from the Talmud that discusses the purpose of humanity's creation.

אֲנִי נִבְרֵאתִי לְשַׁמֵּשׁ אֶת קוֹנִי.

Ani nivreisi l'shameis es koni.
I was created to serve my Creator.
(Kiddushin 82a)

This statement succinctly establishes my raison d'etre. I am here as a servant and vessel for the One who fashioned me and placed me here. Yet in such a dynamic, there are two separate beings: the Creator, and "I." I recognize my subservience to Him, but I still consider myself a distinct and independent entity. An alternate version of the mishnah changes the language slightly:

אֲנִי **לֹא** נִבְרֵאתִי **אֶלָּא** לְשַׁמֵּשׁ אֶת קוֹנִי.

*Ani **lo** nivreisi **ela** l'shameis es koni.*
I was **not** created **except** to serve my Creator.

On the surface, these changes do not seem to alter the meaning substantively. In both cases, I recognize that the purpose of my creation is to fulfill the assignments of the One who created me. Yet, on a deeper level, the difference is profound. In the first case, "אֲנִי נִבְרֵאתִי/Ani nivreisi/I was created" - I see myself as a creation. In the latter case, "אֲנִי לֹא נִבְרֵאתִי/Ani lo nivreisi/I was not created" - I recognize that I do not exist "אֶלָּא/ela/except" as an expression of His desire and an agent of His service. There is only God, and I am simply a way that He manifests in this realm of seeming multiplicity. In the first case, I may be a *faithful* servant. But we are created to be more than faithful - we are created to be "*faceful*," to peer deep inside of ourselves and see the "Pnei Hashem" staring back at us.

Faithfulness will enable us to live with hope and confidence. But "facefulness" will allow us to live completely without fear. We find this in the Torah in regards to the ultimate man of faith, Moses. So faithful was Moses that he was referred to as the "Raya Mehemna," which is Aramaic for "the faithful shepherd," or otherwise translated as "the shepherd of faith." On account of his great faith, Moses obeyed God's command to go to Egypt and stand up against Pharaoh, the most powerful man in the world. Yet we find that in spite of his tremendous faith, Moses was at one point afraid. After six of the ten plagues had already been brought on Egypt, God instructs Moses to go to Pharaoh again and to warn him of the final plagues that he and his people will suffer if he refuses to let the Hebrew people go. Though Moses had confidently confronted Pharaoh multiple times already, this time he hesitates. This hesitation is not written into the Torah's text explicitly, but the sages recognize it in the specific wording of God's instruction:

וַיֹּאמֶר יְ-הֹוָה אֶל־מֹשֶׁה בֹּא אֶל־פַּרְעֹה:
Vayomer A-donai el Moshe bo el Paro.
And God said to Moses, come to Pharaoh.
(Exodus 10:1)

The verse is typically translated as "go to Pharaoh," but the word "בֹּא/bo" means "to come," and the verse therefore literally means "come to Pharaoh." The Zohar[266] asks why God invites Moses here to "come" to Pharaoh, rather than commanding him to "go" to Pharaoh. It answers that Moses was afraid because unlike previous meetings with Pharaoh in which he encountered only his physical presence, God was instructing Moses here to penetrate to Pharaoh's core, which is referred

---

266 Zohar II, 34a

to as the "mighty snake." In order to defeat Pharaoh completely, Moses would have to get to his root and essence. Though he had confronted his imposing physical presence until now, Moses feared the deepest, darkest levels of the evil that Pharaoh represented. Therefore, God told him "come," I will go with you and you will have nothing to fear.

With the reassurance of God's accompaniment, Moses penetrates to Pharaoh's deepest levels. There he finds not the fearful serpent that he had expected, but, to his astonishment, only God. He discovers that God is at the source and center of all things, even the most apparently "evil" and "ungodly" aspects of creation. God instructs Moses to "come" not only because He will accompany him to Pharaoh's depths, but because He is already there, beckoning Moses to come find Him. This is the revelation that enables Moses to overcome Pharaoh - that Pharaoh too, in his essence, is only Godliness. This is "facefulness," which is even deeper than faithfulness! And this "facefulness" is what will enable each of us to overcome anything and everything that we 'face' in life. Regardless of what we encounter, we will be able to reveal its inherent divinity. We will be able to transform it into the pure unadulterated Godliness that it has always been, and that it has always been waiting to express.

Blessing

We have come to the end of this book, but only the beginning of this journey. From here, we will continue on our respective paths to finding ourself (lech lecha) and finding the "Pnei Hashem," both of which we know by now are awaiting us in our "pnimyus." It is said that "chassidim (those who study the inner depths of Torah) never say farewell, for they never depart from each other."[267] We cannot part from one another, because we know that we are wholly and completely one. Yet in this realm of seeming multiplicity, we can feel as though we are going our separate ways. Therefore, we offer one another blessings for the journey

---

[267] *Hayom Yom*, 10 Adar Sheini

ahead, as the Friederker Rebbe guides us, "Before embarking on a journey … receive a parting blessing from your good friends."[268]

So we will conclude with a blessing, and there is no more appropriate blessing for this circumstance than the "Bircas Kohanim/the
Priestly Blessing" which God instructed Aaron the high priest and his
descendants to bestow on the people throughout the ages.

יְבָרֶכְךָ יְ-הוָֹה וְיִשְׁמְרֶךָ: יָאֵר יְ-הוָֹה **פָּנָיו** אֵלֶיךָ וִיחֻנֶּךָּ: יִשָּׂא
יְ-הוָֹה **פָּנָיו** אֵלֶיךָ וְיָשֵׂם לְךָ שָׁלוֹם:

*Yivarechecha A-donai v'yishmerecha. Yaer A-donai **panav**
eilecha vichunecha. Yisa A-donai **panav** eilecha v'yaseim
lecha shalom.*

May God bless you and watch over you. May God
cause His **face** to shine to you and favor you. May God
raise His **face** toward you and grant you peace.
(Numbers 6:24-26)

We will notice immediately the multiple references in this blessing to God's face. What does it mean that God should turn or raise His
face to you, and why is this the ultimate blessing that He can bestow
upon us? On the simple level, the Priestly blessing requests God's favor,
protection, and peace for those who are being blessed. But if we analyze
the verses more closely, we will discover their far deeper implications.

יְבָרֶכְךָ יְ-הוָֹה וְיִשְׁמְרֶךָ:

Yivarechecha A-donai v'yishmerecha.

May God bless you and watch over you.

The first word of this first verse, "יְבָרֶכְךָ/Yivarechecha," means
"may He bless you." The root of this word, "ב-ר-ך/barech" is familiar to
us by now. As we discussed in chapter four[269] and several times since,
the word "bracha" means "blessing," but it also means "to draw down,"
as in the phrase "הַמַּבְרִיךְ אֶת הַגֶּפֶן/hama**vrich** es hagefen/to draw down a
vine" as well as the word "בְּרֵיכָה/breicha", which means a "pool" or a

268 ibid. The Friederker Rebbe, Rabbi Yoseph Yitzchak Schneersohn, was the
sixth rebbe of the Chabad Lubavitch dynasty. 1880-1950

269 Section "Blessed Are You"

445

place where water has descended and gathered. Reading the words "yi-varechecha A-donai" with this alternate connotation, they can be rendered "may God be drawn down to you," blessing one with the ability to have God revealed to her/him below just as He is above. As we have discussed at length, our goal is that the Godliness which is at the root of all things should not only be acknowledged intellectually or spiritually, but that it should be clear and visible within this realm of physicality and darkness. The final word of the verse, "וְיִשְׁמְרֶךָ/v'yishmerecha" is from the root "ש-מ-ר/shamor," which means "to guard." Once the Godliness is brought down and revealed within you, it should be guarded and kept in you. Otherwise, it may once again become lost, forgotten, or stolen by the forces of darkness that constantly work to deprive us of our vision in this "olam/world" of "helam/concealment."

The second verse of the blessing refers explicitly to God's face:

יָאֵר יְ-הֹוָה פָּנָיו אֵלֶיךָ וִיחֻנֶּךָ:

Yaer A-donai panav eilecha vichunecha.
May God cause His **face** to shine to you and favor you.

On the simple level, this phrase wishes one God's kindness and grace, which are represented by the imagery of His radiant countenance as opposed to a dark countenance, which would symbolize anger or displeasure. Yet on a deeper level, this appeal for the "shining" of God's "face" is a clear allusion to the "Pnei Hashem" that is buried within our deepest "pnimiyus." It is a request that the face should "yaer/shine" brightly so that one can see it and be aware of it. The blessing is not merely that God should be kind to you, but that He should lavish you with the greatest of all kindness, which is that He should be apparent to you and revealed within you.

The final word of the verse, "vichunecha" is from the root "ח-ן/chein," which means "favor" or "grace." The ultimate divine favor or grace that we request of God is this shining revelation of His face. But the Alter Rebbe[270] points out that the word "vichunecha" also shares a root with the word "חָנָה/chanah," which means "to encamp." As in the first verse, where God is not only momentarily revealed, but thereafter guarded so that His presence remains, so too here in this second verse

---

[270] *Likkutei Torah*, maamar "Koh Tuvarchu Bnei Yisrael"

446

we pray that the face not only shines brightly within us briefly or temporarily, but that it "encamps" within us permanently so that we are constantly aware of our true essence and reality.

The face is specifically mentioned in the third verse of the blessing as well:

יִשָּׂא יְ-הֹוָה **פָּנָיו** אֵלֶיךָ וְיָשֵׂם לְךָ שָׁלוֹם:

*Yisa A-donai **panav** eilecha v'yaseim lecha shalom.*

May God raise His **face** toward you and grant you peace.

In this final verse of the blessing, God "raises" His face toward us, as opposed to "shining" His face to us as in the previous verse. What is the difference between these two bestowals of His face? The Alter Rebbe[271] explains that the raising of God's face represents the removal of His visible presence from this lowest world. As such, it is the opposite of the "bringing it down" that was referenced in the first verse of the blessing. How, then, is this removal and elevation of God's face a blessing?

Here, the Alter Rebbe expounds, we find the secret of exile and darkness. God hides from us precisely in order that we should seek Him, and it is this very search that will enable us to rise ever higher. For by seeking His face, we come to find our own face, and we realize that we are far higher and loftier than we had believed ourselves to be. Indeed, the verse says "may God raise His face *toward* you," not away from you or above you. If He is raising His face, we would assume that it is becoming more distant, as we are ostensibly grounded and stuck here below. But in fact, as God raises His face, it approaches us, because the most hidden and precious truth is that we are not below at all. We are rooted in the highest of all heights.

This three-part blessing, then, is a three-stage progression. First, "yivarechecha A-donai," we should be able to bring God down so that He is manifest within us. Then "yaer panav," His face should shine so that it radiates from within us to illuminate the darkness for us and for all of those around us. And finally, "yisa A-donai panav," the face should be lifted to reveal to us our ultimate source and root which is far beyond this coarse and limited realm. And this progression will bring us the ul-

---

271 *Likkutei Torah*, maamar "Bayom Hashemini Atzeres"

timate reward of "shalom/peace," as the blessing concludes "וְיָשֵׂם לְךָ שָׁלוֹם/v'yaseim lecha shalom/and He will grant you peace." "Shalom/peace" is the ability to see the light within the darkness, and to know that there is nothing to fear because there is only, and always, One.

May you be blessed with this peace as you journey onward. And may you be a source of this peace and blessing for all of those that you encounter on your way.

CPSIA information can be obtained
at www.ICGtesting.com
Printed in the USA
LVHW102046200123
737600LV00003B/106